MODERN SALTWATER FISHING TACKLE

MODERN SALTWATER FISHING TACKLE

by Frank T. Moss

International Marine Publishing Company
Camden, Maine

Copyright © 1976
by International Marine Publishing Company
Library of Congress Catalog Card No. 76-8780
International Standard Book No. 0-87742-068-8
Printed in U.S.A.

All rights reserved. Except for use in a review, no part of this book may be reproduced or utilized in any form or by any means, electronic or mechanical, including photocopying, recording, or by any information storage and retrieval system, without written permission from the publisher.

Contents

List of Charts, Tables, and Diagrams   vii

1. The Origins of Modern Tackle   1
2. How Fishing Rods Work   15
3. Anatomy of Fishing Rods   27
4. Star-Drag Reels   37
5. Lever-Drag Reels   45
6. Line Capacity of Modern Star- and Lever-Drag Reels   55
7. Light-Tackle Reels   61
8. Monofilament Lines   73
9. Dacron Lines   81
10. Wire Fishing Lines   89
11. Saltwater Fly Lines   95
12. Practical Fishing Knots   98
13. Tackle for Beginners and for Bottom Fishing   105
14. Tackle for Small-Game Surface and Deep Trolling   115
15. Tackle for Big Game and Record Hunting   123
16. Tackle for Boat and Surf Casting   133
17. Special-Purpose Tackle   141
18. Hooks and Terminal Tackle   149

19	Leaders for Game Fishing	171
20	Outriggers, Kites, Downriggers	181
21	Specialized Boat Equipment	189
22	Tackle Box and Cockpit Equipment	205
23	Electronics for Fishing	213
24	Natural Baits for Game Fish	225
25	Artificial Lures and Baits	235
26	Boats as Fishing Tools	251
27	Repairing Tackle	261
28	Dynamics of Modern Tackle	275
29	Line Capacity of Pre-World War II Reels	289
30	Manufacturers' Index	297
	Glossary	308
	Picture Credits	313
	Index	314

Special Charts, Tables, and Diagrams
(in order of occurrence)

Early development of hooks   2
Salt Water Fly Rodders of America, tippet-test table   18
IGFA line classes   18
Cross section of natural bamboo joint   19
Schematic cross section of typical fiberglass rod shaft   20
Cross sections of bamboo, wooden, and fiberglass rods   21
Comparative rod-loading diagram   23
Comparative sizes of saltwater rods   25
Parts of a standard saltwater trolling rod   28
Four types of casting rod action   34
Four types of trolling rod action   34
Parts of a Penn Senator reel   38
Representative star-drag assembly   39
Friction curves of reel drags   40
Reel capacity by "O" size   43
Conversion factor for changing from one line class to another in a given reel   43
Everol reel clutch assembly   48
Common striking drag values by popular species of game fish and tackle classes   49
Penn International reels, internal parts   52
Penn International reels, parts list   53–54
Line capacity of modern saltwater reels: 55–59; Eagle Claw reels, 55; Everol reels, 55; Daiwa reels, 56; Garcia reels, 56; Heddon reels, 56; Penn reels, 57–58; Reel-King reels, 59; Shakespeare reels, 59; St. Croix reels, 59; True Temper reels, 59; Tycoon/Fin-Nor reels, 59
Quick reel parts   63
Garcia spinning reel parts   65
Martin spinning reel parts   66
Popular saltwater fly reels: gear ratios, types of drag, line capacity   69–70
Johnson spin-casting reel parts   70
Comparison by thread count and breaking strain of linen line with IGFA class synthetic lines   74
Extrusion of monofilament line   75
Relative stretch of monofilament, Dacron, and linen lines   76
Nylon monofilament diameter/strength table   78
Monofilament diameter versus pounds-test   79
Diameter/strength values for soft-drawn Monel wire line   89
Effective lure trolling depths, using wire line plus one-ounce sinker   90
Color code for marking lengths on wire line   92
AFTMA line/weight fly line table   95
Symbols used to distinguish different weights of fly lines   96
Types of fly lines   96
Fly line shooting head layout   97
Practical fishing knots: 98–103; Improved Clinch Knot, 98, 102; Blood Knot, 98, 102, 103; Albright Special, 98; Surgeon's Knot, 98; Improved End Loop Knot, 98; Spider Hitch, 99; Bimini Twist, 100–101

Comparative strength of fishing knots   104
Beginner's basic tackle box contents   109
Seven categories of deep trolling techniques   118
Light, medium, and heavy deep trolling tackle   118
Maximum effective depths achieved with different types of trolling tackle   118
Depth versus line length for deep trolling with wire line   121
IGFA line classes in terms of ultra-light tackle through medium to heavy tackle   127
Mustad hook terminology, illustrated   148
Representative Mustad hooks: 150-156; Mustad O'Shaughnessy hooks, 150-151; Mustad Sea Demon hooks, 152; Mustad knife-edge tarpon hooks, 152; Mustad Hollow-Point salmon hooks, 153; Mustad Hollow-Point Beak hooks, 153; Mustad Treble hooks, 154; Mustad Aberdeen hooks, 154; Mustad Hollow-Point Sproat hooks, 154; Mustad Hollow-Point Viking hooks, 155; Mustad Chestertown hooks, 155; Mustad Kirby hooks, 155; Mustad Snapper hooks, 156; Mustad Sheepshead hooks, 156; Mustad Cincinnati bass hooks, 156; Mustad Pacific bass hooks, 156; Mustad Virginia hooks, 156
Representative Eagle Claw hooks: 157-158; Eagle Claw worm hooks, 157; Eagle Claw shank hooks, 157; Eagle Claw baitholder hooks, 157; Eagle Claw Siwash hooks, 158; Eagle Claw plain shank ringed-eye offset hooks, 158; Eagle Claw plain shank down eye offset hooks, 158
Seven types of hook shank shapes   160
Snelling your own hooks   161
Assorted swivels and connectors   163, 165
Swivels, ring connectors   164
Bead Chain swivels and connectors   166
Trolling sinker weight/depth table   167
Five popular bottom-fishing rigs   169
Weight/depth/speed trolling sinker table   170
Leader wire sizes and breaking strains   171
Game fish trolling leaders (29 tables of assorted game fishing leaders, fully described)   174-176
Shock leader characteristics   177
Leaders for saltwater fly casting (8 selected leaders, fully described)   178-179
Fly line weight compared to monofilament butt section diameter   179
Les Davis diving planer for deep trolling   187
How elevation increases underwater viewing area   202
The complete tackle box contents   205
First-aid equipment for fishing   211
Natural game-fish bait materials   225
Tools and supplies for rigging baits   225
The Bait Rigger's Handy Guide   229
Game fish temperature preference table   230
The Plug Rigger's Handy Guide   241
The Trolling Rigger's Handy Guide   242-243
The Jig Caster's Handy Guide   245
The Deep Jigger's Handy Guide   247
The Spoon Rigger's Handy Guide   248
What to look for in selecting a fishing boat   256
Special tools and supplies for rod repairs   261
Millimeter/inch scales for rod guides and ferrules   264
Placement of guides on a spinning rod   269
Casting distance versus lure speed   276
Line water-friction test results   283
Striking drag for IGFA line classes   285
Line Capacity of Pre-World War II Saltwater Reels: 289-295; J.A. Coxe reels, 289; Edward Vom Hofe reels, 290; Ocean City reels, 291; Pflueger reels, 293; Abercrombie & Fitch reels, 295; Shakespeare reels, 295; William Mills reels, 295
Instant Fish Weight Chart   312

Acknowledgments

My experience in saltwater fishing goes back to 1938 when, as a young and impressionable mate on a Montauk charter boat, I first learned about hooks, lines, rods, reels, baits, and other nautical things, in what since has been called the Bamboo Age of sport fishing. Since then, many hundreds of fishermen from all over the world have contributed ideas, facts, gimmicks, opinions, photographs, and nuggets of insight to the great mass of material that eventually became this book.

It would be impossible to recall and name them all, and equally impossible to describe and credit all of their individual contributions. But certain friends in the realms of fishing literature, tackle manufacture, professional fishing, and science and conservation have made contributions that were especially helpful and should be acknowledged.

In the field of fishing literature and writing: Robert N. Bavier Jr., Publisher of *Yachting* and *Sportfishing* magazines, New York, N.Y.; Frank M. Borth, author and artist, Montauk, N.Y.; Dave Edwardes, photographer, East Hampton, N.Y., and Cotati, Calif.; the late Edmund Gilligan, former outdoor columnist of The New York *Times*; Charles Horne, author and angler, Capetown, South Africa; Henry Lyman, Publisher of *Salt Water Sportsman* magazine, Boston, Mass.; the late Harlan Major, author of *Salt Water Fishing Tackle*, New York, N.Y.; Charles R. Meyer, former Field Editor of *Sportfishing* magazine, now of Southold, N.Y.; the late Critchell Rimington, former Publisher of *Yachting* and *Sportfishing* magazines, New York, N.Y.; Dr. Ferdinando Schiavoni, Publisher of the magazine *Mondo Sommerso*, Milan, Italy; Roger C. Taylor, President, International Marine Publishing Co., Camden, Maine; Bill Wisner, former Associate Editor, *Sportfishing* magazine, Brightwaters, N.Y.; Frank Woolner, Editor of *Salt Water Sportsman* magazine, Shrewsbury, Mass.; Robert Zwirz, former Contributing Editor of *Sportfishing* magazine, Ridgefield, Conn.

Assistance with material, information, analyses of tackle, catalogs, etc., was given by scores of tackle and accessories manufacturers (a complete list of manufacturers appears at the end of this book). Assistance of considerable value was rendered by the following individuals and companies:

Ande, Inc., Riviera Beach, Fla.; Edward S. Benson, Mildrum Mfg. Co., East Berlin, Conn.; Jack E. Carlston, MacJac Mfg. Co. Inc., Muskegon, Mich.; J. Leon Chandler, Cortland Line Co., Cortland, N.Y.; Philip Clock, Fenwick Inc., Westminster, Calif.; E. I. du Pont de Nemours & Co., Wilmington, Del.; Everett R. Hames, Shakespeare Co., Kalamazoo, Mich., and Columbia, S.C.; Fred Hooven, Gudebrod Bros. Silk Co., Philadelphia, Pa.; Paul Johnson, Berkley & Co., Spirit Lake, Iowa; Leon J. Martuch, Scientific Anglers Inc., Midland, Mich.; Bingham McClellan, President, American Fishing Tackle Manufacturers Association (AFTMA), and Burke Tackle Co., Traverse City, Mich.; William I. Miller, Riviera Tool & Die Inc., Grand Rapids, Mich.; O. Mustad Inc., Auburn, N.Y., and

Oslo, Norway; Penn Fishing Tackle Mfg. Co., Philadelphia, Pa.; Leigh H. Perkins, The Orvis Company, Manchester, Vt.; John Rybovich, Rybovich Bros. Boat Yard, West Palm Beach, Fla.; Tycoon/Fin-Nor Tackle Corp., Miami, Fla.; J. J. Vander Mause, Uncle Josh Bait Co., Fort Atkinson, Wis.; Vlchek Plastic Co., Middlefield, Ohio; Woodstream Corp., Lititz, Pa.; The Worth Co., Stevens Point, Wis.; Wright & McGill Company, Denver, Colo.; Zebco Div., Brunswick Corp., Tulsa, Okla.

The following tackle builders, boat captains, and other professionals in saltwater sport fishing especially influenced my understanding of tackle and its uses: Mickey Altenkirch, Hampton Bays, N.Y.; Capt. Stu Apte, Miami, Fla.; Rys Davis, Vancouver Island, British Columbia; Baron Victor de Strasser, Rio de Janeiro, Brazil; Michael Falla, Island of Malta; Peter Fithian, Honolulu, Hawaii; the late Capt. Tom Gifford, Montauk, N.Y.; Peter Goadby, Australia; Larry Green, San Francisco, Calif.; Johnny Kronuch, Montauk, N.Y.; Capt. Bob Marvin, Key West, Fla.; Don McCarthy, Nassau, Bahamas; Vic McCrystal, Australia; Capt. Cliff North, Cozumel, Mex.; S. L. Perinchief, Bermuda; H. F. Rice Jr., Kona, Hawaii; Capt. Linwood I. Simmons, Montauk, N.Y.; Elgin White, Tallahassee, Fla.

Marine science has an increasing impact on the understanding of fish, fishing and the use of tackle. These leaders in science and conservation have been especially helpful: Dr. Frank E. Carlton, President, National Coalition for Marine Conservation (NCMC), Savannah, Ga.; William K. Carpenter, Chairman, International Game Fish Association (IGFA), Fort Lauderdale, Fla.; John Casey, biologist, Narragansett Marine Laboratory, Narragansett, R.I.; Elwood K. Harry, President, IGFA, Fort Lauderdale, Fla.; Frank J. Mather III, biologist, Woods Hole Oceanographic Institution (WHOI), Woods Hole, Mass.; Dr. Luis Rivas, biologist, National Marine Fisheries Service Laboratory, Miami, Fla.; Dr. F. G. Walton Smith, President, International Oceanographic Foundation (IOF), Miami, Fla.; Richard Stroud, Executive Vice President, Sport Fishing Institute (SFI), Washington, D.C.; Dr. Wayne Tody, Michigan Department of Natural Resources, Lansing, Mich.; Dr. Lionel A. Walford, Director (retired), Sandy Hook Marine Laboratory, Sandy Hook, N.J.

To these late and living friends and associates, and to all those whose names were not mentioned, but whose understanding of tackle helped to make mine more complete, this book is dedicated.

FRANK T. MOSS

Foreword

Back in 1875, Genio C. Scott, in his classic book, *Fishing in American Waters*, wrote that the art of angling "requires as much enthusiasm as poetry, as much patience as mathematics, and as much caution as housebreaking." If the good Genio were alive today, he might have added that a complete analysis of tackle and methods for saltwater sport fishing requires almost as much research as that needed to land on Mars.

Few realize the amount of poring over references, winnowing out basic facts from tackle catalogs, tabulating results of tests of all kinds, and interviewing specialists required to produce a book such as *Modern Saltwater Fishing Tackle*. The task is immense and might best be done by some sort of computer programming, except for one factor—experience in fishing itself. No machine is capable of translating into print years of time spent on the water, lessons learned from literally tons of fish caught or lost, handling of boats and tackle for more than four decades, and observing life in and on the oceans.

Frank T. Moss has had such experience. Not only did he serve as a charter boat skipper out of one of the great sportfishing ports of this country — Montauk, New York — for more than 20 years, but also he has taken a more than casual interest in all aspects of marine angling from conservation of saltwater species to the development of fishing boat hulls, from photography to advising governmental agencies. Fortunately Frank can also write well and clearly. As former editor of *Sportfishing* magazine and present Associate Editor of *Yachting*, he has learned what the fishing public wants to know. He also has an inquiring and analytical mind, undoubtedly due in part to his training in mechanical engineering.

The results of all these talents are combined between the covers of this book. It is not a volume for light bedtime reading: it is a compendium of hard facts that will be of inestimable value to both the neophyte and the experienced ocean angler. Those looking for escapist fishing literature must turn elsewhere, but those who want a basic reference book covering all facets of tackle and methods used can find it here.

Marine angling is a comparatively young sport. The literature in this country reflects this. Near the turn of the century, Genio Scott and others wrote primarily about the pleasures of angling in the general style set by Izaak Walton. Zane Grey's accounts of fishing in faraway places brought a new dimension to writing on the subject in the 1920s. This was followed by a spate of articles and books, with more and more emphasis on particular species and areas, plus additional detail on both tackle and methods. With the exception of *Salt Water Fishing Tackle* by Harlan Major, first published in 1939, no one volume attempted to give technical details on all tackle for all types of ocean fishing. Major's work is now dated, for he wrote prior to the wide acceptance of synthetic materials for almost every component of a modern saltwater outfit.

Frank's work has brought such information up to date. Some may quarrel over details or may disagree with the author's personal preferences when selecting tackle. If all anglers agreed, it would be a dull world indeed! However, the details are here, ranging from kirbed hooks to star-drag reels, from lure acceleration on a cast to deep jigging. Even though saltwater sport fishing and writing about it is my business, I am amazed at the mass of material the author has been able to compile. Frankly, I did not realize that so much technical information was available. When someone else does the job of digging it out and presenting it concisely, he deserves the thanks of all who turn to the sea for their sport.

Without question, there will be further developments in fishing tackle as this space age produces new materials that may be adapted for use in the angling world. However, I am convinced that *Modern Saltwater Fishing Tackle* will stand as a reference work — and a practical one — for many years to come. The basic facts are here and, as a result, future products have standards against which they may be judged.

In book reviews, one of the clichés most often used is: "It should be in every angler's library." In this case, I disagree. There is a host of fishermen, technically anglers, content to struggle along with shoddy equipment and inefficient methods. This group never will join the ranks of experts — a word that may best be defined as "those who want to learn more." Frank's work is for those who take their fishing comparatively seriously, who enjoy getting the best out of good equipment, and who are seeking to improve their skills. To them, I recommend what follows. As a fellow author, I can only say that I wish I had written the book myself. My temperament is wrong, and I would have been climbing the technical wall after the first chapter if I had even attempted such a task.

I have only one worry: what book is Frank going to write next? He is too young to retire, yet anything else may well be an anticlimax!

Henry Lyman
Publisher
SALT WATER SPORTSMAN
Boston, Massachusetts

In pre-Castro days, author-fisherman Ernest Hemingway fished out of Cuba in his boat the Pilar for Atlantic blue marlin like this tremendous specimen. His experiences were reflected in the classic angling adventure The Old Man and the Sea.

1   The Origins of Modern Tackle

There is no reason to suppose that ancient men were any different from the modern variety when it came to enjoying the catching of fish. Fishing as a food-gathering occupation is as old as mankind, and fishing for pleasure is equally ancient.

In the valley of the Somme River in France, a fishing gorge, predecessor of the hook, has been retrieved from a peat bog. Scientists estimate it may be 30,000 years old. Murals discovered in Egypt show fishermen of 3,000 years ago fishing in the Nile with spear, net, and hook and line. Hooks and other fishing artifacts found in the ruins of Pompeii and Herculaneum, cities destroyed by the eruption of Mount Vesuvius in 79 A.D., indicate that a fishing industry flourished in the Bay of Naples at the time of Christ.

Mosaics unearthed at Trapani in Sicily show boats of the fifth century A.D. grouped around a vast net full of huge fish, unmistakably tuna. The trap-net system of fishing for tuna has persisted without interruption in the Mediterranean almost to the present day.

A catastrophic decline of bluefin tuna populations in the early 1970s caused most if not all of the ancient trap-net sites to be abandoned. While this form of fishing was essentially commercial, certainly it contained elements of danger and drama that excited fishermen and landlubbers alike for a span of possibly 2,000 years.

Probably the earliest reference to fishing as sport, as we know it, appears in *De Natura Animalium* by the Roman historian Claudius Aelianus. In the second century A.D., he accurately described dry fly fishing for troutlike fish in the river Astracus in Macedonia.

Aelianus told how the Macedonians tied and used an artificial fly to entice and take these fish when the fish refused to rise to dead natural insects used as bait. The fly was probably the direct ancestor of the present-day Red Hackle.

The Macedonian incident occurred on fresh water, but that does not change the fact that artificial lures date far back into ancient times. The original Polynesians, in their migrations that populated the vast reaches of the Pacific, sustained themselves at sea by catching bonito and small tunalike fishes with artificial trolling lures fashioned of bone, feathers, and mother-of-pearl. In fact, a Tuamotu Pearl is still a trolling lure much prized by twentieth-century fishermen in the South Pacific.

Indians and Eskimos of Canada and the Pacific Northwest used to fashion artificial jigs with barbs of thorn, bone, stone, or native copper for taking such active fish as salmon and halibut, fish that usually could not be caught except by deep-jigging or deep-fishing with natural bait.

Even the modern fishing kite has a historical ancestor in the fishing kite used by Malay and Melanesian fishermen at the time of European exploration. It was made of broad leaves fastened to a framework of stiff palm-frond fibers. The

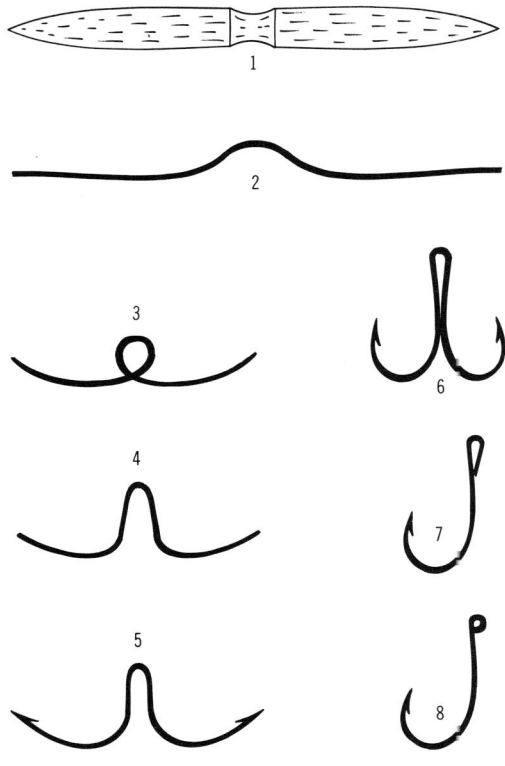

Development of the modern fishhook:
1. The primitive gorge was carved of bone or wood with the line tied at the middle.
2. The bricole, made of tempered bronze wire, was an outgrowth of the gorge.
3. An advanced form of the bricole had an eye twisted into the center of the wire before it was tempered.
4. An improved version of the bricole had a hump in the middle rather than an eye
5. Barbing the points of the humped bricole gave them better holding power.
6. The next step was to create a double hook by tightening the mid-wire bend.
7. Cutting or breaking off one half of the double hook produced a single hook.
8. Single hook with a rolled eye is not very different from modern hook styles.

who perfected many sport-fishing techniques in California waters during the first two decades of the present century. Farnsworth evidently "invented" his kite because of a need to present baits to wary fish without frightening them by the nearby presence of the boat. It is said that he did not know about the earlier South Pacific handline fishing kites.

Kites used as bait-presenting devices were eclipsed in the 1920s with the perfection of the trolling outrigger, generally credited to Captains Bill Hatch and Tom Gifford of Florida and the East Coast. In the 1950s the kite made a comeback, and currently it enjoys popularity in south Florida and the Florida Keys for light-tackle sailfishing.

HOOKS

Together with the fishing line, the hook is the most basic tool of the sport fisherman. The ancestor of the hook was the gorge, a straight shaft of bone or artfully worked stone that tapered to a point at each end and was equipped with a shallow ring or depression at the middle, around which the line was tied.

In use, the gorge was turned parallel to the line, and some bait was placed or tied over it in such a way that, after a fish had swallowed the bait, a sharp yank on the line would rip the gorge out of the bait and turn it sideways in the fish's mouth or gullet, making it impossible for the fish to eject the gorge.

In the fifth century B.C., Herodotus recorded that the Lacustrine fishermen of the Swiss lake region were using the bricole, a hooklike instrument developed from the original gorge. The bricole was a tempered bronze wire gorge with a slight hump in the center and upturned ends (see illustrations).

Gradually, more bend was put into the wire and the wire itself was twisted once at the center, before tempering, to form a true eye. In time, the upturned wire ends were given barbs and the double hook was invented. The double hook was finally divided at the eye into

kite line was sennit-braided vegetable fiber. A line hanging from the kite carried the bait or lure.

The earliest modern version of the fishing kite is credited to Captain George Farnsworth, a noted West Coast guide two hooks, and the hook as we know it was born.

Mention of a bent, barbless hook is made in ancient writings from Egypt's First Dynasty, 5700-2700 B.C. Early fishhooks were made individually, and no two were exactly alike. Production-line manufacture of hooks did not begin until about 1560, when needle-makers at Redditch, England, worked out a system for making iron hooks by the batch, using the following method.

(1) Raw iron wire was chopped to a standard length by placing the end of the wire against a stop and clipping it to the desired length with a cutter.

(2) Barbs were cut in one end of the wire by putting the wire end into a special grooved stop and making the barb by striking with a knifelike hardened-steel chisel.

(3) The wire lengths were then annealed to make them extra-soft for pointing and bending. This was done by heating them and allowing them to cool slowly.

(4) The point was shaped by hitting it with a drop hammer, then dressing it with a file.

(5) The hook bend was formed by bending the shank around a peg in a special form.

(6) The finished hooks were hardened by heating them red-hot and dunking them in oil. This hardened the iron, but it made it brittle.

(7) The brittle iron hooks were spring-tempered by an annealing process using hot sand.

(8) Each hook had to be tested for correct spring-temper by being pulled by hand against a prepared stop. A hook that was too hard would break without springing against the pull. If the iron had not achieved the correct spring-temper, it would not spring back into shape after testing.

Essentially the same techniques are used to make hooks today. Over the years, improvements in machinery and working techniques were developed, but it was 1800 before volume production really boomed in Great Britain. In the period that followed, British manufacturers hired many Scandinavian workers to man their needle and hook factories. Some of these workers later returned home, taking their hookmaking skills with them.

The famous O. Mustad Company of Oslo, Norway, was founded in 1832; through mechanization and constant improvement of methods and products, it became a world leader, a position it still enjoys today.

In the United States, the Enterprise Manufacturing Company of Akron, Ohio, was one of the first to develop a machine that could take in raw wire at one end and spew out completed hooks, ready for tempering, at the other. In the late 1920s, the Wright and McGill Company of Denver, Colorado, began production of a new style of hook that combined two major innovations. One was a mechanically ground hollow point. The other was a new style of bend called the Eagle Claw. The hollow point and the Eagle Claw bend were combined to align the angle of penetration of the point exactly with the line of traction of the fishing line. This produced a hook with quick penetration that could be struck home into a fish with less line tension.

Selection of hooks for different types of fishing, and samples of various hook styles, are discussed and shown in detail later in this chapter and elsewhere in the book.

LINE

The ancients were quite skilled at making cords and line. Polynesians laboriously stripped, dried, and plaited the long, supple fibers of palms, pandanus, and certain other plants. Cotton was easy to work, but not always available. It was apt to rot unless it was well tarred.

Horsehair was widely used in Great Britain and Central Europe during the early days of sport fishing for trout and similar fish. When horsehair was unavailable, long human hair was sometimes knotted and twisted together for

4 MODERN SALTWATER FISHING TACKLE

TV personality Curt Gowdy (left) and editor Frank Woolner use modern monofilament and braided Dacron lines, respectively, with their spinning and "conventional" surf outfits.

fine lines. Wool was sometimes used, but its shortness of fiber caused woolen line to lack durability. Flax, or linen, made excellent strong, durable lines and was, one day, to become the standard by which all fishing lines would be judged.

Specialized lines have a very ancient history. The late fishing historian Harlan Major has credited the Chinese Emperor Wu of the Han dynasty with using silk fishing line in the first century A. D. The use of silk line is said to have spread from China to Rome.

Dame Juliana Berners, Prioress of Sopwell Nunnery in England, described in detail the method of making horsehair lines in her famous *Book of St. Albans* (1486). Two centuries later, Izaak Walton echoed Dame Juliana's sentiment that while a three-hair line was standard for trout, a single-hair line would get more strikes.

The need among freshwater anglers for special, weighted lines for fly casting resulted in considerable experimentation and development. Saltwater sport fishermen, on the other hand, had to content themselves mainly with lines of sea-island cotton or flax. It was not until Captain Lester Crandall of Rhode Island perfected a special hard-laid linen line, which eventually became known as Cuttyhunk line, that saltwater anglers had a line that could be cast or trolled indefinitely, and one that had uniform quality. In 1838, Captain Crandall built a dam across the Ashaway River near his home to power a mill for manufacturing quality linen fishing lines. Today, the Ashaway Line and Twine Company, in Ashaway, Rhode Island, continues to manufacture quality textile threads, although linen line has been supplanted by braided and monofilament lines of artificial fiber.

Cuttyhunk line was the standard of comparison when the International Game Fish Association (IGFA) first set up its

Tight-lipped Captain Lester Crandall was the originator of the famous Cuttyhunk linen line.

line-class system for recognizing saltwater game-fish records. The present IGFA line classes of 12-pound, 20-pound, 30-pound, 50-pound, 80-pound, and 130-pound breaking strain originally represented the ultimate breaking strains expected for lines of 3, 6, 9, 15, 24, and 39 threads layup. Linen line was tested wet, when it was strongest, and line of 50-leas composition was considered to test about three pounds per thread.

Two unavoidable troubles plagued even the best linen lines. They were subject to rot if they were not carefully washed and dried after use before storing, and they were damaged if a revolving bait or lure untwisted the strands.

It wasn't until the 1950s that modern synthetic lines of Dacron, nylon, and similar materials became generally available. Since then, the new synthetic braided and monofilament lines have completely replaced linen. Under close chemical and engineering control, synthetic lines are now available in a tremendous variety of types, sizes, tests, and working characteristics. They will be dealt with in the chapters on lines.

LEADERS

Early anglers attached the hook directly to the line, but observant fishermen soon discovered that when a fine section of special line (called a trace in Britain) was placed between line and hook, more strikes were had from wary fish. Likewise, a short piece of flexible wire or heavier line spliced between hook and main line would often prevent loss of bait, hook, and fish to sharp teeth.

We have few examples of early lines and leaders. These highly perishable objects seldom survived organic rot or chemical corrosion. But there are still a few hooks and lures that carry what are obviously vestiges of leaders made of twisted or braided copper, bronze, or wrought-iron wires. Antique Norse cod-fishing jigs, for example, were often bound with copper or bronze wire, and

Tarpon expert Captain Johnny Brantner of Marathon, Fla., uses a hair-fine stainless-steel wire leader with live mullet bait for trophy tarpon under Florida's Seven Mile Bridge.

the wire was sometimes extended a few inches from the lure body in the form of a short tooth-leader.

The development of the natural silk industry in Europe in the seventeenth and eighteenth centuries gave anglers one kind of raw leader material they needed. The "gut" leader material that came into vogue was actually silkworm gut, not catgut. The worms were fed on mulberry leaves, and just before they were ready to weave their cocoons, they were placed in vinegar and pickled. At this stage the fluid in the worms' silk sacs was still liquid and ready to spin. When judged ready, the worms were removed from the vinegar, seized by head and tail, and pulled apart. The viscous fluid in the sacs was stretched into a single filament that hardened immediately upon contact with air. The speed or slowness of the stretching determined the fineness or coarseness of the strand. Heavier gut was the result of slower pulling.

One English writer described young girls and old women drawing silk gut this way, cleaning the filaments between their teeth. "Rather gaggy business," he called it.

American sericulturists, seeking a substitute for the delicate Chinese silkworms, experimented with the larvae of various New World moths, including worms of the cecropia. Gut lengths of eight or nine feet eventually were obtained from hybrid cecropia-moth worms, but a market never developed for the product.

Gut leaders had their drawbacks. Their thickness was seldom uniform, and the outer layers of the gut were stronger than the inner portion, so drawing gut through a die to create a leader of uniform thickness produced a leader of variable tensile strength.

Strong, reliable leader material for saltwater use, especially for sharp-toothed fish, was not available until metallurgical developments of the Industrial Revolution began to produce iron and steel wires of uniform quality. Early ferrous wires were enameled to retard rust. Tinning gave iron-bearing wires longer life in salt water, and some big-game specialists still prefer tinned piano wire over other materials for billfish and giant tuna leaders.

But anglers had to await the development of noncorrosive alloys, such as Monel metal and stainless steel, before leaders could be made that would withstand repeated use in salt water.

The second great modern improvement in leader material, of course, was the invention of nylon monofilament. Weight for weight, nylon has the tensile strength of mild steel wire. Its specific gravity is only slightly greater than that of water. It is much less visible in water, and its suppleness helps to deceive the fish. Nylon's faults are: low knot strength unless special knots are used, a tendency to lose strength by exposure to sunlight and the absorption of water, and a greater tendency to be cut or abraded by sharp objects than metal wire.

RODS

Rods for saltwater sport fishing were a late development. More advances have occurred in the design, construction, and use of rods in the last half-century than took place during the thousands of years of man's early enchantment with fish.

Ancient pleasure fishing was largely freshwater oriented, and while fishing rods or poles are depicted in Egyptian papyrus paintings from 3,000 B.C., saltwater pleasure fishing was mainly a handline affair until a comparatively short time ago. Early British trout and salmon rods were cumbersome poles up to 18 feet long that often were used as much for beating off vicious dogs or vaulting a brook in flood as for fishing.

Early saltwater rods followed freshwater models. Salmon-style rods of hickory and greenheart were used by the Victorian gentlemen who originated the striped bass angling cults of New England. Bamboo started to invade the rod market in the mid-1800s. By 1880, the bamboo/hardwood controversy was in full storm. At the turn of the present century, split bamboo ranked first in freshwater rod production, and it was a serious contender on salt water.

Hardwood rods for big game, however, persisted until well after World War II. My own first swordfish rod, for example, was a solid hickory war club purchased from a Montauk, New York, tackle builder in 1949.

Tubular metal rods enjoyed some popularity among freshwater fishermen as early as the Victorian era, following introduction of a solid steel "fencing foil" rod in Britain in 1842. This rod had little success in salt water, however, largely because of the constant problem of rust.

In 1936, the American True Temper firm brought out a series of tubular metal rods. Those that were made of beryllium-copper alloy withstood salt corrosion much better, but it was not until the Shakespeare Company introduced the first resin-bonded glass-fiber rods in the late 1940s that rod builders had a truly first-rate material.

Since then, fiberglass has completely dominated the manufacture of saltwater rods and has taken over a large part of the freshwater market. But even fiberglass is not without a serious competitor. High-modulus graphite fibers, a product of the space age, are now being used in lieu of glass fibers to produce resin-bonded rods of very light weight and remarkable flexibility.

Characteristics of modern rods, and recommendations of specific types and styles for various kinds of fishing, are discussed in detail later.

REELS

Before reels were invented, early rod anglers kept a number of coils of "running line" in one hand. They were thus able to cast a bait or lure much farther than the normal reach of a line tied directly to the rod tip. They also could drop weighted lines to the bottom in much deeper water.

A reputedly authentic Chinese print, dating from before the start of the Christian era, shows an angler in a small rowing sampan using a fishing rod with an open-frame type of reel attached to the rod.

Use of rod-mounted fishing reels did not receive serious literary attention until Thomas Barker, in his *Art of Angling*, and Izaak Walton, in his second edition of *The Compleat Angler*, mentioned "wheeles" in the 1650s.

Saltwater game-fishing reels are primarily an American development that got its start in the late nineteenth century. Three problems confronted the early designers of these reels. The first was to eliminate salt corrosion by using noncorrosive materials. The second was to design a reel large enough to hold the great length of heavy line deemed necessary for large game fish. The third was to invent some sort of adjustable slip-brake or clutch that would force the fish to work hard for the line it took out.

Chrome-plated brass, "German silver," Bakelite, bronze, and similar materials solved the first problem. The second was easily overcome by scaling up existing reel designs. The third took quite a bit of ingenuity.

The earliest reel-attached line drag was a leather thumb pad mounted on the reel frame. This was better than a bare thumb, which tended to overheat and

Author and fisherman-explorer Zane Grey used a hardwood rod and "cargo winch" reel when he caught this shark-chewed 14½-ft. marlin in Tahitian waters in 1930.

blister, but the pad left much to be desired. The free-spool feature had not yet been perfected, and the reel handle was direct-connected or directly geared to the spool shaft. Busted knuckles were a hazard of the game.

With such primitive equipment, Charles Frederick Holder, one of the founders of the famed Catalina (California) Tuna Club, in 1898 took a 183-pound tuna, a catch that Harlan Major later called, "one of the most remarkable ever made."

William Boschen, a Catalina Tuna Club colleague of Holder's, is credited with developing the idea for a big-game reel with an internal clutch-type drag. Julius vom Hofe, a Brooklyn, New York, reel manufacturer, turned out a prototype that Boschen used to capture the first broadbill swordfish ever taken by rod and reel. Boschen accomplished this feat off Catalina Island in 1913, fishing with the legendary Captain George Farnsworth, and soon afterward he caught a 358-pound striped marlin with the same equipment.

Joseph Coxe also worked with Boschen to develop game-fish reels with an internal drag system. The earliest reels of this type required much skilled hand labor, and they were expensive. But organizations like the Penn Fishing Tackle Manufacturing Company of Philadelphia found ways to mass-produce star-drag reels in many sizes and with uniformity of performance and quality. Penn's Senator series of reels is still a good seller in today's sophisticated tackle market.

While the star-drag reel and its modern counterpart, the lever-drag reel, have dominated the big-game trolling field and some phases of saltwater small-game casting, the advent of the spinning reel for casting probably turned more potential fishermen toward the path to fun and fresh seafood than any other reel design. The basic idea of a fixed-spool reel is not new.

Early New Englanders cast handlines into the surf to catch striped bass, squeteague (weakfish), bluefish, and cod long before the surf rod was invented. They frequently used an open, circular wheel with a concave rim, around which the extra line was wound. This handline "reel" was turned from hardwood or shaped from heat-softened steer horn.

When the caster whirled his weighted bait around his head and let fly toward the water, the line stored on the circular, stationary hand wheel spun off in exactly the same manner that line spins off the spool of a modern spinning reel.

Hand-held handline casting spool inspired the modern spinning reel. Sandeel bait is rigged on a heavy silk-gut leader with small lead sinker clamped on to provide weight.

Years later, the stationary spool concept was adapted to reel construction. Line was wound onto the reel spool by a revolving metal arm or bail, which, in turn, was rotated by a gear system in the reel body, driven by the handle. For casting, the bail was folded back out of the way. The beauty of the modern spinning reel is that one does not have to spend months or years m tering a casing technique. Instant success is the order of the day.

LURES

Think of the frustration of those early Macedonians, confronted with fish that took live flies hovering over the water, but refused dead natural flies presented on a hook. Did the original idea for an artificial fly leap full-fledged from some sudden flash of insight? Or did those ancient anglers of Asia Minor know of an even earlier type of artificial fly-lure that they were able to adapt to solve their local fishing problems?

We know from experience that many species of fish will take artificial lures that resemble nothing, as far as we can tell, that the fish should be able to recognize as food. But we also now know that fish respond to tactile as well as visual stimuli, receiving impressions via their sound-perceiving organs and, presumably, integrating these with impressions received through the eyes.

The simulation of baitlike action,

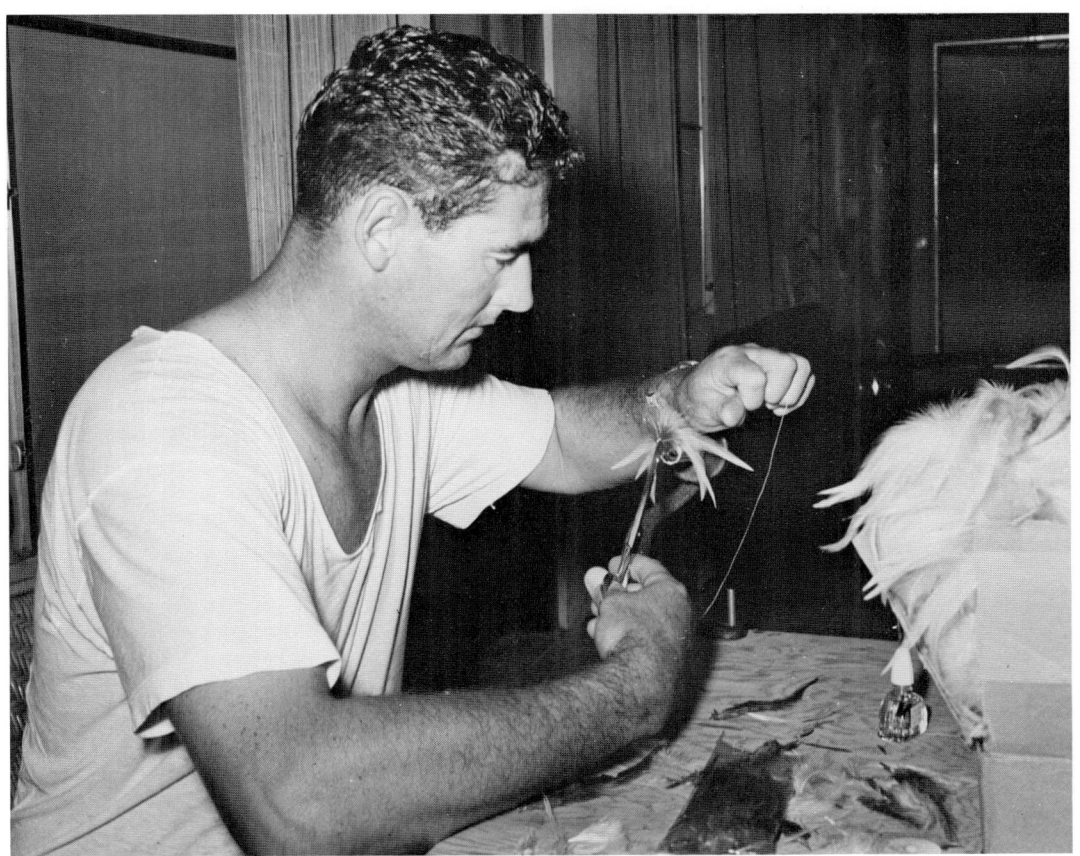

Former baseball star Ted Williams is also an ardent fisherman. In tying a tarpon streamer he is following a precedent established in Asia Minor more than 2,000 years ago.

rather than mirrorlike imitation of the bait itself, often appears to trigger feeding behavior. Ancient Norse seafarers knew that — next to the herring itself — the best cod bait was a lead-weighted, white bone jig shaped vaguely like a small herring. The classic double-hooked bone jig has remained virtually unchanged for more than 1,000 years.

The top-water, angler-activated lure is a relatively modern invention, however. In 1896 James Heddon was sitting on the bank of Dowagiac Creek in Michigan, whittling on a piece of soft wood as he waited for a fishing companion. He idly tossed a scrap of wood onto the water. Suddenly, a big black bass made a pass at it, flipping the wood into the air. Later, at home, Heddon whittled fish-shaped floating lures and attached hooks to them. Soon he was catching huge bass on his lures in a new and extremely exciting mode of fishing. Heddon went into the lure business and was highly successful. Many of our most popular and effective saltwater surface, subsurface, and diving casting lures can be traced back to the plugs originated by James Heddon.

Many saltwater artificial lures, on the other hand, owe their origin to commercial fishing. The well-known "Japanese" feather jig, for example, is so named because Japanese tuna and salmon trollers were among the earliest to discover the value of chicken feathers attached to a lead-lure head with a mother-of-pearl eye.

The popular and effective East Coast diamond jig is a direct descendant of lead handline jigs used for centuries for jigging cod on the Grand Banks. In California waters, the gaudy, weighted, lead-and-plastic jigs used for yellowtail, white sea bass, and similar species have an equally commercial origin.

The discovery of the metal fishing spoon appears to have been one of those fortunate accidents in which an observant angler saw a fish respond with obvious feeding action to an unexpected stimulus. Julio T. Buell, a Vermonter, was fishing on Lake Bomoseen when he happened to drop overboard a tablespoon from his lunchbox. As he watched, a large pike rushed forward and struck at the spoon as it wobbled down through the clear water.

Back at home, Buell experimented with cutting the handles from old spoons and wiring hooks to the bowls. They proved to be superior lures for catching pike and large bass. Now we have spoons ranging from tiny willow-leaf models, hardly larger than a dragonfly's wing, to huge bunker spoons as long as a man's forearm.

In recent years, the development of soft, tough plastics has stimulated lure designers to produce remarkably lifelike imitations of natural baits, such as squid, balao, mullet, herring, shiners, eel, shrimp, and the like. Those who have mastered the use of the new, natural-looking artificials swear that the imitations catch as many fish as fresh natural bait, and they don't stink when you run out of ice.

WHAT IS "BALANCED TACKLE"?

We hear and read a lot about something called "balanced tackle." Nonfishermen often equate the term with the act of balancing a rod on a finger to find its

Modern surface-action plugs owe their genesis to the whittling of James Heddon, who found the secret of artificial lure attraction back when natural bait was king in 1896.

The Origins of Modern Tackle 11

Two early exponents of fishing with light balanced tackle were author-angler Harlan W. Major (left) and Captain Tom Gifford, shown with a white marlin taken by fishing kite.

center of gravity. This is a meaningless exercise.

The term *balanced tackle* refers to a combination of rod, reel, line, and lure or bait, in which all of the components are in dynamic balance. For example, a rod built to match 30-pound-test line would normally carry a 3/0 or 4/0 reel filled with 30-pound line. This would be "balanced tackle" in the 30-pound-line class.

An unbalanced outfit would be the same rod carrying a huge, 9/0 reel filled with 12-pound-test line. Here, rod, line, and reel are out of dynamic balance with each other.

In every type of fishing there is a combination of tackle that is balanced for that type of fishing. Usually the balance range of a given type of tackle is fairly broad, and it permits considerable personal choice or variation in selecting components. Tackle sometimes may be unbalanced deliberately to achieve special characteristics, but in general, the tackle selected for most saltwater fishing (not including fly fishing) falls quite close to the values in the accompanying table.

AUXILIARY EQUIPMENT

It is in the field of auxiliary equipment that some of the most startling advances in fishing gear have been made in recent years. Outriggers give lift and spread to trolling lines, permitting anglers to troll surface baits for predatory species of game fish. Fishing kites present live baits to wary fish under the most natural conditions possible.

Downriggers, which are underwater outriggers, allow trolling of lures or baits to depths in excess of 100 feet without heavy weights on the fishing line. The modern fighting chair, with its footrest, lets an angler bring the power of his legs against the pull of the strongest fish and heaviest tackle. Other aids, like the socket belt and the light shoulder harness, make light-tackle, stand-up fishing possible.

The electronics industry has given anglers means of probing the depths for fish and likely fishing habitats, an art that has vastly increased the availability of fish. Modern fishing boats are now

Fish weight	Tackle rating	IGFA line class	Reel size
Up to 100 lb.	Ultra-light	6 lb.	1/0
	Very light	12 lb.	2/0
	Light	20 lb.	3/0
	Medium	30 lb.	4/0
	Heavy	50 lb.	6/0
100-250 lb.	Ultra-light	6-12 lb.	2/0
	Very light	20 lb.	3/0
	Light	30 lb.	4/0
	Medium	50 lb.	6/0
	Heavy	80 lb.	9/0
250-500 lb.	Ultra-light	12-20 lb.	3/0
	Very light	30 lb.	4/0
	Light	50 lb.	6/0
	Medium	80 lb.	9/0
	Heavy	130 lb.	12/0
Over 500 lb.	Ultra-light	12-20 lb.	3/0
	Very light	30 lb.	4/0
	Light	50 lb.	6/0
	Medium	80-130 lb.	10/0-12/0
	Heavy	130 lb.	14/0

Working overboard with a gaff in each hand, Florida Keys guide Stu Apte saves a large tarpon for a client whose specialty is fighting these great fish on the fly rod.

designed to be real fishing tools, rather than mere transportation over the water.

A few critics complain that the modern trend in tackle and equipment is robbing the sport of some of its intrinsic appeal. I disagree strongly. Present-day fishermen catch their share of fish with less waste of time than did their forebears, but not because tackle and equipment have taken sport out of the fishing. Instead, efficient equipment and tackle have vastly increased the angler's understanding and appreciation of fish and fishing, "enriching his experience," as the sociologists like to say.

Sport fishermen still catch fish to eat and for fun, but they also recognize that the ocean is the last great frontier for individual exploration and adventure, and they work tirelessly to preserve this heritage for the future.

Rods designed for modern fishing combine fish-fighting and casting ability to a remarkable degree. Foster Bam of New York puts a heavy bend into his spinning rod after hooking a Pacific sailfish off Baja California, Mexico.

2 How Fishing Rods Work

A good deal of misunderstanding has developed over the role of the rod in fishing. Part of this is due to the fact that most efforts to analyze and describe the dynamics of fishing rods have concentrated on the rod as a casting tool. Casting is extremely important to many types of fishing, but after the cast has been made and the fish hooked, the rod enters into a new phase of work, that of a flexible lever or crowbar with which the angler lifts the weight of the fish and counters its attempts to gain freedom by swimming.

Practically all casting rods are designed primarily for casting and only secondarily for fish-fighting. This is not a "fault" of modern tackle. In fact, the general success that anglers display with their tackle shows how well rod designers and builders have managed to reach a workable compromise between the sometimes contradictory requirements of a rod as a casting tool and the same rod as a fish-fighting lever.

To bring the problem into perspective, fishing rods can be divided into three main classes, depending on the work they are required to do. These can be likened to an old-fashioned buggy whip, a slingshot, and a crowbar.

The fly rod is a perfect example of a buggy-whip rod. It is designed to cast the fly line and the almost weightless fly, and because of this, it is not a very good rod for lifting or fighting large fish. The fly rod's limberness and flexibility are a function of line-casting, so you buy it for this quality and hope for the best when you hook a big one.

A spinning or conventional-reel casting rod, on the other hand, is designed to work like a slingshot, hurling a weighted lure or a bait-and-sinker combination. Here the lure or sinker is a ballistic projectile that drags the fishing line along with it after being cast. The lure-casting rod must have considerable flexibility in the tip, in order to store energy that is quickly transmitted to the lure in the form of motion. It must also have stiffness in the lower shaft section to give the fisherman leverage against the weight of the lure. With its stiffer lower shaft section, the lure-casting rod is a better fish-fighting rod than the fly rod, but it is not as good on very heavy fish as a properly designed trolling rod.

The phrases, "better than. . ." and "not as good as. . .," in this discussion, are not meant to put down anglers who use and prefer one type of tackle over another. These phrases are used only for comparing the various types of rods with the ability of each type to act as a fish-fighting lever.

The true trolling rod is a poor casting rod. Because casting ability has little bearing on the success of a trolling rod, the rod can be designed with enough overall shaft stiffness for lifting heavy fish in deep water, for striking home heavy hooks, and for stopping and turning the run of a powerful fish. The trolling rod is not a buggy whip for casting a fly line, nor a slingshot for throw-

16 MODERN SALTWATER FISHING TACKLE

THE BUGGY-WHIP FLY ROD. Designed specifically for casting the fly line, which has little weight, the fly rod is not a particularly good rod for fighting large fish, but it does its designed job well.

ing a weighted lure. It is a flexible lever or crowbar designed to enable the angler to use the strength of the line to the greatest lifting advantage.

In practice, rods designed for modern fishing combine casting and fish-fighting ability to various degrees in order to fulfill specific fishing requirements. But before we go into the wide field of specialized rods, let us take a look at examples of the three major types of rods just discussed.

THE BUGGY-WHIP FLY ROD

Purpose: To cast the specially designed fly line. The weightless fly goes along for the ride, so to speak.

Construction: Tubular fiberglass, resin-impregnated bamboo, or graphite or boron fiber.

Design: The shaft is long and slender, with a slow rate of taper. Rate of shaft flexure or vibration is quite slow, compared to that of other rod types. When the rod is held vertically overhead and line tension is applied horizontally to the tip, the shaft forms a quarter-section of a circle, or an almost circular section of a parabola. The shaft is very quickly overloaded when line tension is applied in excess of that required to bend the rod.

Use: On salt water, the fly rod generally is used on those species of fish that take artificial flies or streamers resembling shrimp or small bait fish. These species include striped bass, bluefish, bonito and small tunas, weakfish (sea trout), salmon, and the like. The saltwater fly rod has been used successfully on tarpon, bonefish, permit, sailfish, and even small marlin, but admittedly it is more difficult to use on these species than casting, trolling, or live-bait tackle specifically designed for the species.

THE SLINGSHOT CASTING ROD

Purpose: To cast a weighted lure or sinker-and-bait combination. The lure or bait, acting as a projectile, pulls the line from the reel when cast.

Construction: Tubular or solid fiberglass, laminated or resin-impregnated bamboo, graphite or boron fibers. Split bamboo and tubular metal, in vogue for many years, now are seldom used.

Design: The rod may be fairly short (as in freshwater bait-casting gear adapted to salt water) or very long (as in the Hatteras Heaver type of surf-casting rod). Rate of shaft flexure or vibration is much faster than that of the fly rod; varies from slow, for light rods designed for use with very light line, to quite fast, for long, powerful rods designed to cast lures weighing several ounces. When the rod is held vertically, and line tension is applied horizontally to the tip, the fully loaded shaft assumes a parabolic shape,

THE SLINGSHOT SURF CASTING ROD. Surf and other weighted-lure casting rods, on the other hand, are designed to work as mechanical power transformers, converting the slow-moving power of the arms into the faster motion of the sinker or lure.

with the tip at the apex of the parabola. The rod tip tends to flatten, and the maximum bend of shaft tends to migrate down the shaft to the mid-section as the rod is overloaded.

Use: A very wide variety of casting situations, plus some light trolling and bait fishing on the bottom. There are many variations of casting rods. They range from those that can be used as substitute fly rods to those that have most of the characteristics of trolling rods, but are used in special casting applications, such as live-bait fishing on West Coast party boats.

THE CROWBAR TROLLING OR BOTTOM-FISHING ROD

Purpose: To act as a fairly stiff but flexible lever between the angler and the fish. Emphasis is on permitting the angler to put maximum line tension on the fish without excessive bending of the rod shaft.

Construction: Almost universally tubular fiberglass.

Design: The shaft is shorter in proportion to diameter than in most casting rods, with a higher coefficient of stiffness, and has a very high flexure or vibration rate. When the rod is held vertically overhead and horizontal line tension is applied, the rod's bend is that of a segment of the limb of a parabola. The line comes off the tip of the rod at a fairly sharp angle. In casting rods designed for the same class of line and stressed to the same maximum load line tension, the rod tip usually is tangent (i.e., parallel) to the direction of line pull.

Use: For trolling, bait, or bottom fishing where a flexible lever-action rod is needed.

Incidentally, when the term *heavy fish* is mentioned here, it is used in relative, not actual, terms. Remember that much modern saltwater fishing tackle is now designed to conform to the balanced-tackle limits of the line-test classifications of the International Game Fish Association (IGFA). These line classes, by maximum line-breaking strain, are:

6-pound test
12-pound test
20-pound test
30-pound test
50-pound test
80-pound test
130-pound test

An important exception to the IGFA line-test tackle-classification system is that of saltwater fly casting. IGFA does not maintain a separate list of fish taken by the fly rod, so the Salt Water Fly Rodders of America, an independent nonprofit organization, has established leader-tippet breaking strain as the line-test criterion, and it recognizes the following tippet-test record classes:

6-pound test
8-pound test
10-pound test
12-pound test
15-pound test

THE CROWBAR TROLLING ROD. *Conventional medium- and big-game trolling rods are designed to be flexible levers for lifting large fish in deep water. These short, heavy shafts are poor casting rods.*

Tippet-test is *not* a function of fly-rod design, although it is definitely a function of fly-rod technique. You can use any weight of tippet you want, with any weight of fly line, provided the overall leader design is correct for the fly line itself, and for the weight and air resistance of the fly, streamer, or bug. The tippet is the weakest link in the line-leader combination, so it is the logical choice for a standard by which records and fly-fishing skill may be measured.

The wonderful paradox of modern fishing tackle is that while you can go the the nth degree of extracting efficiency from tackle designed for specific fishing tasks, you can also find broad-banded tackle (to borrow a radio term) that will deliver consistently high scores in diversified fishing, provided you observe the normal limits of properly balanced tackle.

THE FIBERGLASS ROD

When fiberglass rods first appeared shortly after World War II, they were greeted with reservation by many experienced fishermen. After all, split bamboo and tubular metal rods had been brought to a fairly high state of development. Whole-cane Calcutta bamboo rods were popular with many anglers, because they were inexpensive and easy to build at home. Most big-game rods were built of hickory, archery-quality lemonwood, or laminated hardwoods. It didn't matter much that they tended to take a set (a permanent curvature) after strenuous use.

But Calcutta bamboo and Tonkin cane became expensive and hard to import in the late 1940s. Manufacturers who had gained experience in bonding glass fibers with synthetic resins to form war-related molded products began to experiment with these materials to form fishing rods. By the mid-1950s, they had developed a fast-growing line of fiberglass rods that possessed excellent action and were almost indestructible.

One characteristic of the new rods that appealed to many anglers was the fact that no matter how you overload a fiberglass rod, up to the breaking point, it refuses to develop a set. Bamboo and wooden rods were notorious for taking on a swaybacked look after fighting a few heavy fish.

How does fiberglass avoid this condition? The walls of a hollow fiberglass rod, or the shaft of a solid fiberglass rod, are composed of a dense mixture of glass fibers bonded together by a heat-cured synthetic resin. There are no bubbles or air spaces trapped inside the fiberglass material. The only natural wood that comes close to having this circumstance of elastic fibers (cellulose) bonded together by a natural resin (lignin) is the outer, enamel-bearing layer of high-quality Tonkin cane or similar members of the bamboo family.

Before the advent of fiberglass, the best casting and big-game rods were built up of splints or layers of this outer bamboo material. They were expensive, but among rods built of natural materials, they were, and still are, the least susceptible to taking a set under heavy stress.

Less expensive rods built of ordinary bamboo contain more of the porous inner

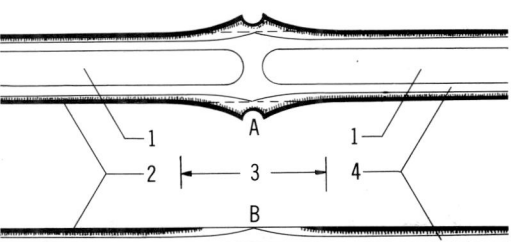

What happens when a joint of bamboo is cut and trimmed for rod-making.
A Untrimmed joint section of bamboo
B Trimmed splint, ready for rod-making
  1 Hollow bamboo interior of stem
  2 Hard enamel and dense outer wood
  3 Joint section
  4 Soft inner wood of bamboo stem
Cutting and trimming to make an even splint removes the hard enamel and dense outer wood, leaving a weak spot in the splint at every joint location. Rod-makers overcome this weakness by staggering the weak joint areas when they make up a bundle of splints to be glued into a rod blank. The rod will be strong as long as two weak joint spots do not come together in the made-up shaft.

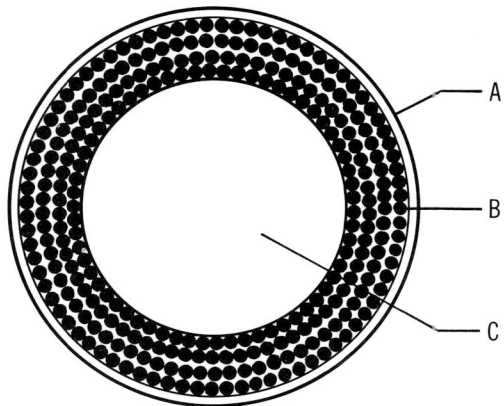

Schematic cross section of a typical fiberglass rod of modern construction.
A Outer resin finish coating
B Fiberglass wall
C Hollow inner space
The fiberglass cloth, or roving, is wrapped around a tapered steel mandrel that occupies the hollow interior. After rolling and heat-curing, final coat (A) is applied and the mandrel is removed.

wood. Woods like hickory, oak, ash, lemonwood, and even greenheart contain thousands of tiny air spaces and empty sap passages running through the lignin, between the fibers of cellulose. When a rod built of these woods is heavily bent, the air spaces in the compression side of the rod's cross section tend to collapse as lignin is squeezed into them. The corresponding air spaces in the tension side of the rod cross section are stretched and elongated.

In addition, under very heavy stress, the walls of the cells of the wood, composed largely of cellulose, are compressed and collapse. Many of these cells are filled with natural material, but many more cells contain nothing more substantial than air. It is no wonder that when the wood fibers and the lignin that bonds them together are stressed beyond the point of elastic recovery, the rod shaft develops a curvature.

Certain manufacturers of quality bamboo casting rods, especially fly rods, have overcome the air-space problem of natural cane by soaking their rod splints in liquid resin before joining the splints together in the form of a rod blank and solidifying the resin by heat treatment. Properly done, the resin soaking fills the air spaces between the fibers and even in the wood cells. When cured, the resin-impregnated rod has practically the same modulus of elasticity as quality top-layer Tonkin cane.

Impregnated bamboo rods are practically impervious to moisture, do not require an external finish, are self-glued, and hardly ever take a set. They are also quite expensive, and present-day builders may be forced to use fiberglass or graphite fibers when their small hoards of quality cane are exhausted.

Two major types of construction are used for fiberglass rods. Solid rods are made up of closely packed parallel glass fibers that are bonded together with resin and usually wrapped with a thin, continuous strand of glass fiber, before final bonding, to give the shaft good hoop strength. Solid rods are used primarily for certain types of plug and bait casting where a short, stiff rod is required.

Manufacturers of hollow fiberglass rods (or blanks, as the raw rod shafts are called) start off with special fiberglass cloth woven to their specifications. This fabric usually contains many more fibers running the length of the shaft than the width. Lengthwise fibers give a rod its strength and flexibility. Crosswise fibers merely hold the other fibers together. The exact design of the cloth has a strong influence on the characteristics of the finished blank.

In one method of blank manufacture, bolts of the selected cloth are dipped in a bath of liquid resin of the proper color and chemical properties. The cloth is rolled through special rollers to remove excess resin, then it is dried and partially cured. It is then rerolled with a layer of special plastic sheeting between the layers of slightly tacky cloth. This pre-

How Fishing Rods Work 21

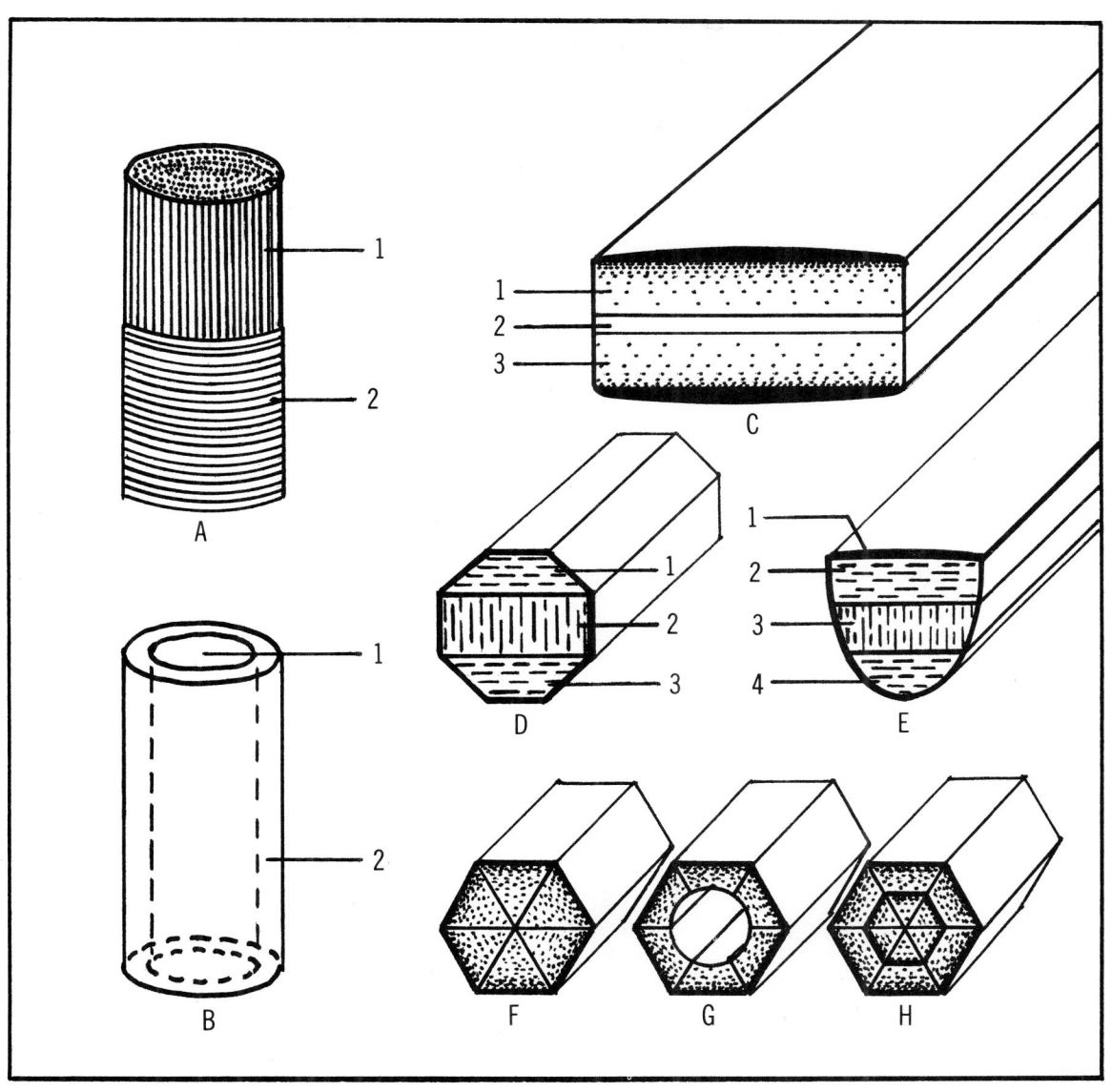

Typical fiberglass and wooden rods

A Solid fiberglass rod shaft
   1 Parallel bonded glass fibers
   2 Glass-fiber wrapping
B Tubular fiberglass rod shaft
   1 Hollow interior
   2 Fiberglass wall
C Double laminated bamboo rod
   1 Upper bamboo layer
   2 Rawhide shear layer
   3 Lower bamboo layer (inverted)
D Octagonal laminated wooden rod
   1 Flat-grain hardwood
   2 Edge-grain hardwood
   3 Flat-grain hardwood
E Longbow laminated wooden rod
   1 Rawhide or plastic backing
   2 Flat-grain hardwood
   3 Edge-grain hardwood
   4 Flat-grain hardwood
F Solid single-built bamboo rod
G Hollow single-built bamboo rod
H Solid double-built bamboo rod

vents the layers of impregnated cloth from sticking together and becoming a solid mass. The prepared cloth is stored under strict temperature and humidity controls to prevent premature curing.

Manufacturers have worked out systems for obtaining uniform qualities and action in blanks of any particular design. The thickness and amount of glass fiber, the quantity and quality of resin, and the diameter and rate of taper of the mandrel (male mold) are carefully controlled. The resin-impregnated glass-fiber cloth is laid flat and carefully cut to the exact shape of a stainless-steel pattern. The pattern is perfectly straight along one edge. The other edge is tapered from the wide butt end to the narrow tip end. The taper may be straight, curved, or stepped, depending on the desired rod characteristics.

The straight edge of the cut cloth is then heat-tacked to the mandrel, which is slightly longer than the finished rod blank. Mandrel and cloth are next rolled between high-pressure rollers that wind the cloth tightly and evenly around the mandrel. Careful control of rolling pressure ensures uniform density of the shaft walls. The mandrel, with its jacket of fused glass fiber and resin, is then placed in a machine that encircles it with a continuous strip of cellophane under regulated tension.

The cellophane-wrapped shaft is then hung in a curing oven, where a carefully controlled heat-curing cycle completes the curing of the resin, while driving out any last remnants of air or volatile portions of the resin. After curing, the mandrel is extracted and the blank is polished and trimmed to the prescribed length.

THE ROLE OF TECHNOLOGY

For hundreds of years, builders of top-quality fishing rods were a rather rarefied group. They were very highly skilled craftsmen who, by trial and error, intuition, and plain native knack, created rods that qualified anglers considered superior to the great mass of fishing tackle. This superiority in casting and fish-fighting ability, in appearance and "feel," was something that for many years defied reduction to a mathematical formula.

In recent years, however, trained engineers have invaded the fields of tackle design and manufacture. Many of them are understandably reluctant to discuss the fine points of their rod making. This reluctance stems from the twin-barreled urge to build a better product than the competition for the same retail dollar, and to reduce manufacturing expenses without sacrificing a standard of quality.

Fiberglass gave the engineers a wide-open field for the development of rods that could match the performance of the old handmade beauties and also were within the budgets of millions of anglers. Paul Johnson, chief engineer for design and development for Berkley and Company, tackle manufacturers of Spirit Lake, Iowa, expressed the typical engineer's viewpoint of fishing rods this way:

"A casting rod is nothing more than a special type of energy-transformer that takes the muscular energy of the angler, stores it momentarily as the cast is being made, then applies this energy to the fly line or casting lure in the form of aimed motion."

In one way, the rod could be likened to an alternating-current transformer. Suppose, for instance, you want to step down household current (120 volts) to 12 volts to operate a door bell. You purchase a door-bell transformer that has a primary-to-secondary coil turns ratio of about 10 to 1. This accomplishes the desired voltage reduction.

Or suppose you want to step up the 120 volts of household current to 600 volts for a special electrical purpose. You obtain a transformer of the proper power rating that has a primary-to-secondary coil turns ratio of about 1 to 5. This gives the increased voltage needed.

The fishing rod does mechanically what the step-up transformer does electrically. It converts the rather slow but powerful energy of the body muscles to the high speed required to pitch the fly line or the fishing lure toward its distant target, something the unaided human arm and hand could never do.

In order to work, any transformer has to have a "load" and a source of primary power. The "load" of the door-bell transformer is the door bell when the button is pressed, which completes the circuit. The "load" of the fishing rod is the weight of the lure on the end of the line. In casting, as the cast is made, the lure "loads" the rod, which, in turn, "loads" the fisherman's casting arms and hands. The success of the cast depends on how well the fisherman has selected an energy-transformer, or rod, to match the weight and air resistance of the lure and the distance to be cast to the muscle power of his body.

In simple words, this means that there is an optimum type and weight of rod for every type and weight of lure, and also for every build and strength of fisherman. Fortunately, you don't need to know involved mathematical formulas to select the proper rod for a given casting

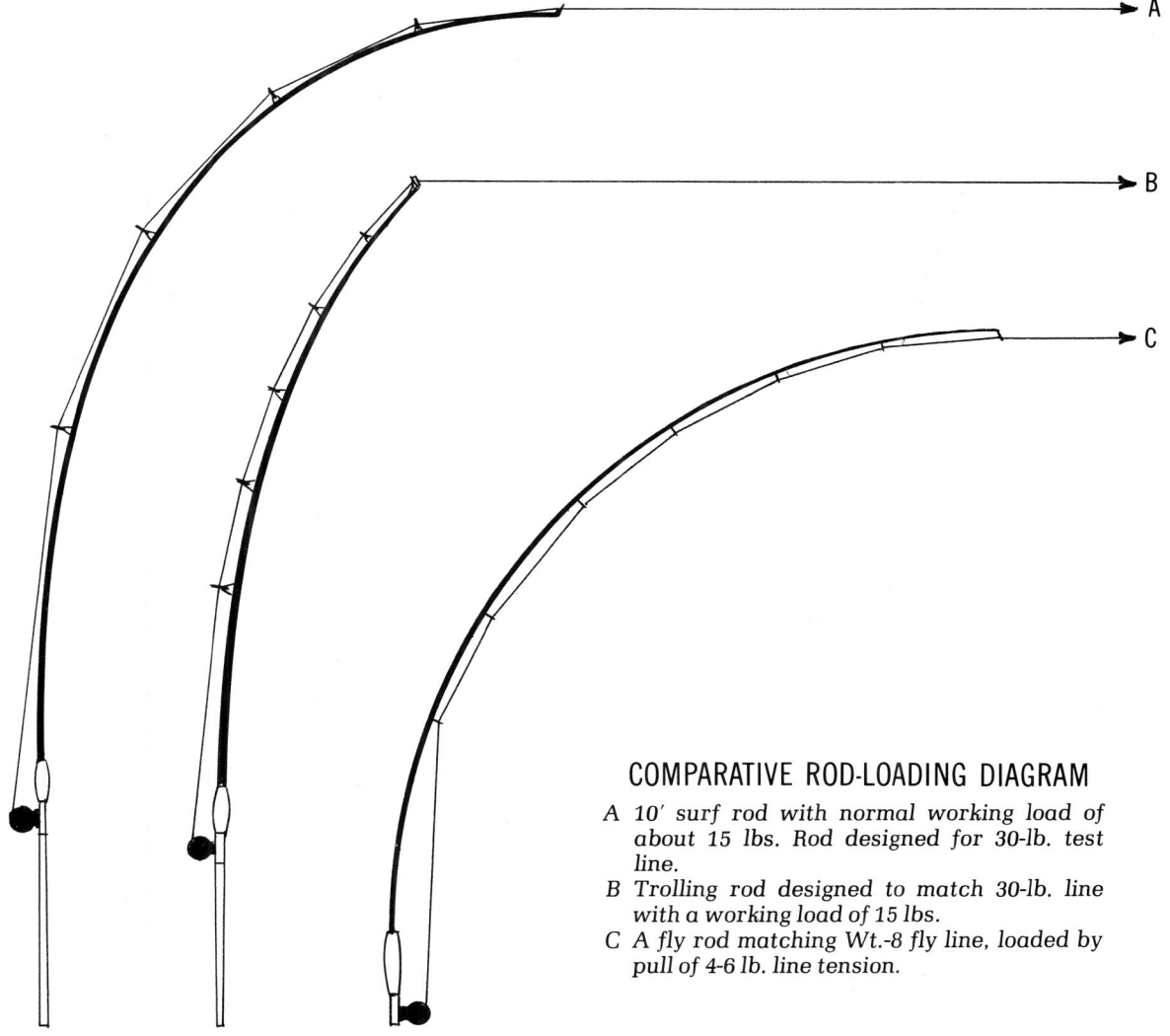

COMPARATIVE ROD-LOADING DIAGRAM

A 10′ surf rod with normal working load of about 15 lbs. Rod designed for 30-lb. test line.
B Trolling rod designed to match 30-lb. line with a working load of 15 lbs.
C A fly rod matching Wt.-8 fly line, loaded by pull of 4-6 lb. line tension.

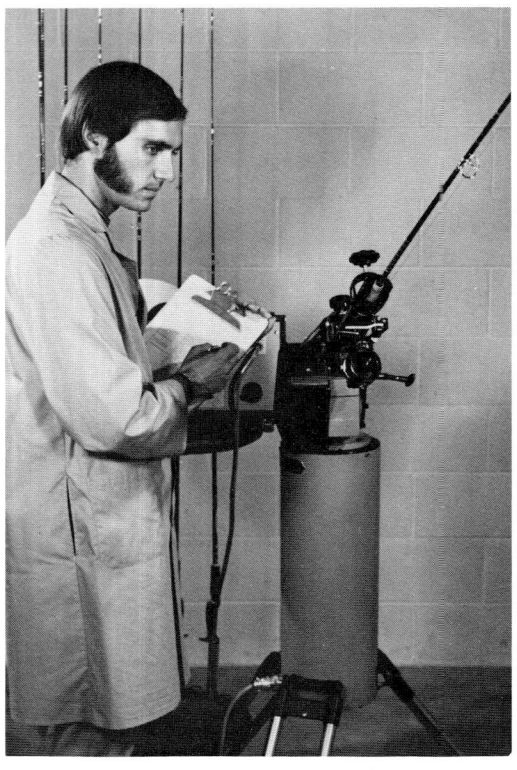

This casting analysis machine was developed by the Berkley Tackle Company to reduce the casting characteristics of any rod to input form for computer analysis, permitting a close check on quality control.

job. All you need is your own sense of "feel" to find a rod that does the best job for you.

Formulas, however, do mean a great deal to engineers. Paul Johnson, for example, has a testing machine that will take any rod, make test casts with it, and deliver a mathematical readout by means of which the sample rod can be duplicated as to casting quality and action in either fiberglass or graphite-fiber construction.

"This doesn't mean," Johnson says, "that we go around buying up other manufacturers' rods to steal their secrets. We don't have to do that. The machine gives us a means of testing our own rods under scientifically controlled conditions, thereby greatly reducing the time we used to spend in human field testing, while vastly increasing the reliability of the tests."

What does all this mean for the average fisherman? For one thing, it means that if he is not inclined to try to build his own tackle for specific types of fishing, he can obtain manufacturers' catalogs, or go to a good local tackle store, and come up with a rod or rods that will be close approximations of the ideal energy-transformer for the job at hand. And these expertly engineered, well-built rods will not, in most cases, cost more than he can afford to pay.

Engineering technology has revolutionized the design and manufacture of fishing tackle. We now have lighter, stronger, better-handling, more durable tackle than ever before. Engineering alone cannot take the place of experienced anglers out on the water, testing and using tackle under the conditions that cannot be duplicated in a factory, but field-testing usually makes fishermen out of engineers, and it's hard to beat a good engineer who is also a dedicated fisherman.

How Fishing Rods Work 25

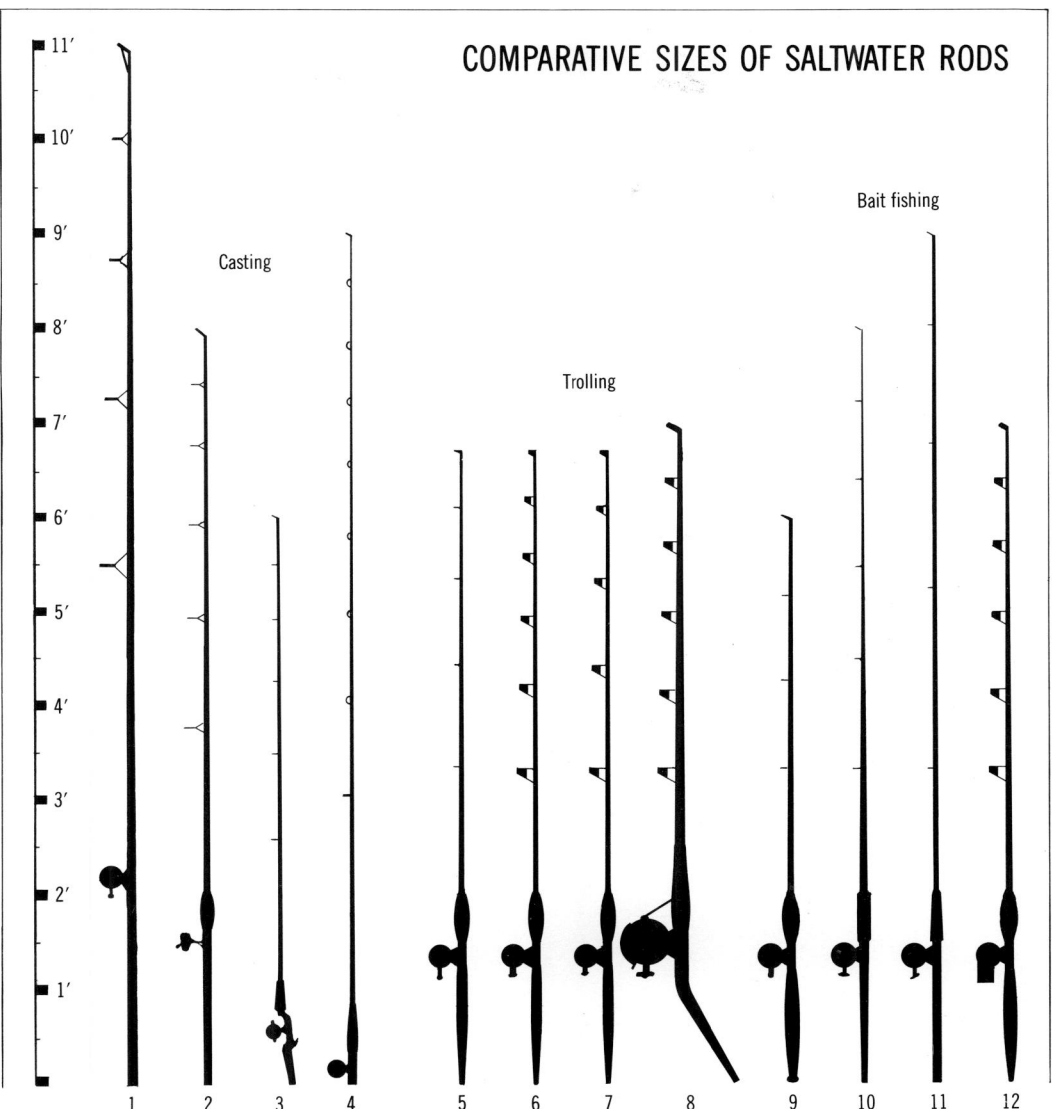

1 Surf casting, conventional and spinning
2 Spinning, on boats or ashore
3 Bait casting, adapted from fresh water
4 Salt water fly casting
5 Light surface trolling
6 Light tournament trolling
7 Deep trolling with wire line
8 Heavy duty big game trolling
9 Common boat rod for bottom fishing
10 West Coast live bait fishing
11 East Coast live bait fishing
12 Gulf Coast deep reef snapper fishing

Gunnard Bergman's heavy-duty Fenwick surf rod has a midsection fiberglass ferrule above the first guide, cork grips, fiberglass extension butt, stainless hardware.

3 Anatomy of Fishing Rods

In order to understand completely how fishing rods work, it is necessary to know the names of the parts of different kinds of rods, and how these parts interact. In saltwater fishing, there are three major classes of rods.

Casting:
    surf casting
    general spinning
    bait-casting (from fresh water)
    saltwater fly casting

Trolling:
    general light surface trolling
    light tournament trolling
    heavy tournament trolling
    deep trolling, wire line

Bottom and live-bait fishing:
    general bottom fishing with bait
    West Coast live-bait fishing
    East Coast live-bait fishing
    Gulf Coast deep reef fishing

These rods vary tremendously in appearance and action, but they all have important parts in common. The parts, in turn, have variations in material and construction, even though they are designed to do parallel or identical jobs. The following list helps sort them out in terms of the work they are designed to do.

Rod shaft or tip

Fiberglass is by far the most commonly used material, although graphite fibers are starting to show excellent characteristics when made up into lightweight, high-quality casting rods. Graphite fibers have a very high modulus of elasticity and are quite light. This permits the building of rod shafts that, for the same power and action, are at least 30 percent lighter in weight than the average weight of fiberglass rods.

Impregnated bamboo rods are still being built by a few relatively small manufacturers of high-quality fly and light spinning rods. Lack of raw materials and the high cost of manufacture, however, severely limit the production of these rods. Laminated wood and bamboo rods are obsolete; they are manufactured only by special custom order. A good, laminated bamboo big-game rod (one in which the glue is still good) is the equal of almost any fiberglass rod for responsive power and action.

Tip-top fittings

The tip-top fitting of a rod is vital to the rod's functions, and there are a number of tip-top designs for special fishing purposes. The simplest tip-top is a loop of chromed-brass or stainless-steel wire set into a suitable metal sleeve that is cemented onto the tip of the rod. This style is popular for fly rods, because they have relatively low line pressure and friction on the tip-top.

For light casting and inexpensive trolling and bottom-fishing rods, the chromed-brass, ring-eye tip-top is very popular. It is inexpensive and performs well, as long as the hard outer chrome surface is intact. Brass ring-eye tip-tops,

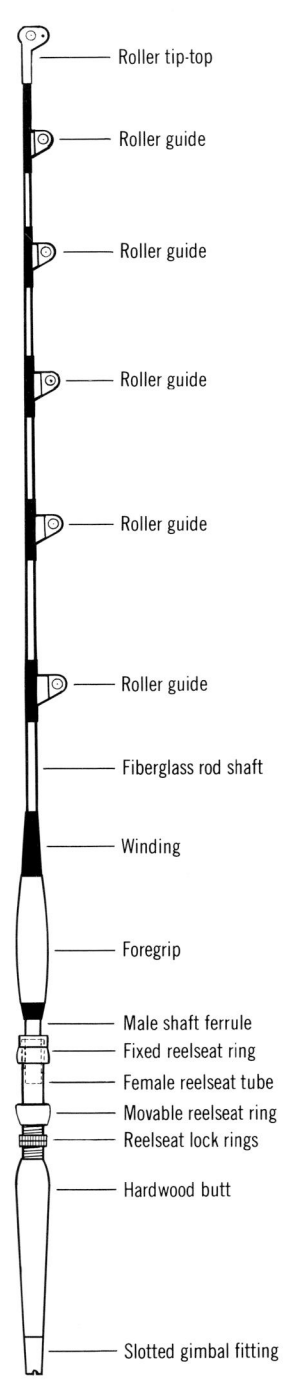

PARTS OF A STANDARD SALTWATER TROLLING ROD

with or without chrome, are prone to grooving after prolonged heavy use. A grooved tip-top or rod guide is worse than useless, for it wears and abrades fishing line like sandpaper or a knife edge.

One solution to the problem of ring grooving has been the Carboloy ring-eye. Carboloy is a trade name for this form of tungsten carbide, one of the hardest man-made substances. The best Carboloy rings are diamond-polished, because nothing of lesser hardness will cut the material. While Carboloy strongly resists grooving, even by wire line, it does have one problem. One manufacturing process made use of sintered (finely powdered) tungsten-carbide particles that are bonded together by a special matrix material and polished after bonding. Under some conditions of saltwater use, the matrix dissolves away from the surface of the ring, leaving exposed microscopic, sharp-pointed bits of carbide. Electron-microscope photographs of monofilament line drawn through such a carbide ring show severe abrasion of the surface of the monofilament.

The new ceramic guide and tip-top rings promise to overcome this problem. The material is a space-age one, developed for the nose cones of ICBM weapons. Ceramic rings also must be diamond-polished. They are mounted in special shock-resistant metal shaft-mounts. Their coefficient of line friction is extremely low, and it is claimed that good ceramic guides will not wear fishing line any more than good roller guides. This may depend on whether the line is wet or dry.

A wet line is water-lubricated and cooled, and it can withstand friction pressures that will abrade dry line. The problem is that both nylon monofilament and Dacron braided lines are made of synthetic polymer fibers that are susceptible to quick damage by heat. The mere friction of rubbing over a dry ring of metal or ceramic may be enough to induce surface-damaging heat in the outer layers of the line. Once this vulnerable outer surface of the line is broken, further friction damage soon follows.

Friction, especially under heavy line tension, is what kills fishing line. Roller tip-tops, when they roll, practically eliminate this damaging source of friction. The best roller guides are built of stainless steel or molded nylon, with stainless or bronze shaft bushings to hold oil. Roller tip-tops are not much good for casting, but they are an absolute must for any type of trolling with soft or wire lines where the lines are worked to a high percentage of their normal breaking strain, as they are in tournament fishing.

Old-fashioned agate-eye tip-tops are no longer used. Their friction coefficient is low, but they are prone to fracture on impact, a condition that has cut many lines in the past.

Rod shaft guides

The remarks made about tip-tops pertain equally to line guides wrapped onto the shaft of the rod. Fly rods frequently are equipped with the simplest of "snake" guides, mere elongated loops of wire that keep the line from running wild during the cast.

The commonest rod shaft guides are chrome-plated brass ring-eyes held in a chrome-plated brass frame. These are all right for light fishing with inexpensive tackle, but friction on even soft monofilament line soon wears grooves in any brass-based guide, once the chrome starts to let go. Salt is the big enemy of chrome on salt water. Too few people wash their rods after use.

The observations about Carboloy and ceramic ring-eye tip-tops apply also to rod shaft guides. Roller guides are not suitable for casting, but they are the choice of many hard-fishing anglers for all forms of trolling. The wrapping of guides to a rod shaft is described in Chapter 27.

Foregrip

The grips of any rod are merely enlargements of the shaft that make it easier to hold and manipulate the rod. Specie cork rings are easily applied and shaped, and they give a soft, nonskid "feel" to the rod. Varnished hardwood foregrips and butts are used on some rods, although a varnished wooden surface sometimes tends to slip in the grasp of a wet hand.

Rod builders sometimes cover a foregrip with felt or similar nonslip material.

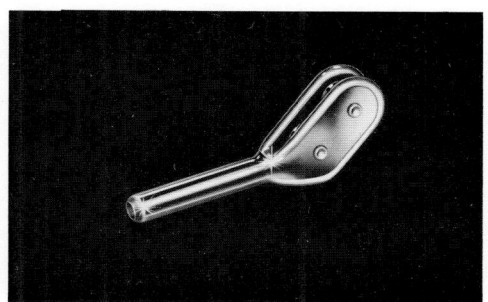

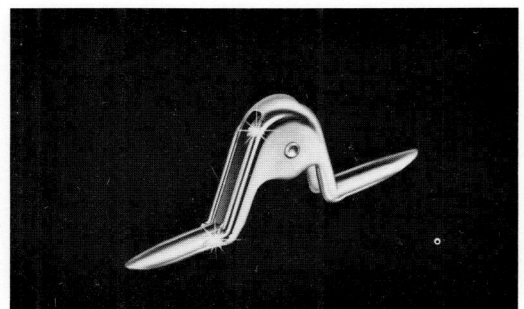

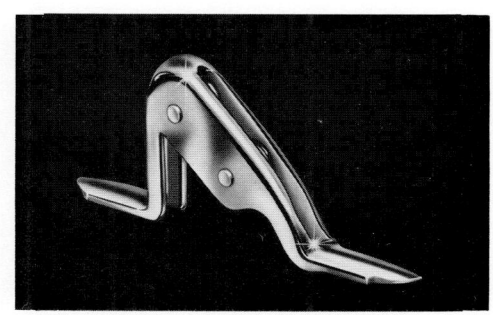

A—*AFTCO double roller tip-top.*
B—*AFTCO single roller rod guide.*
C—*AFTCO double roller stripping guide.*

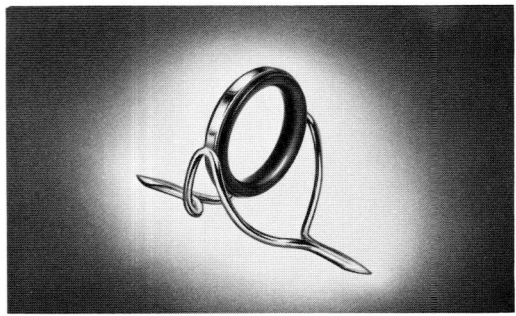

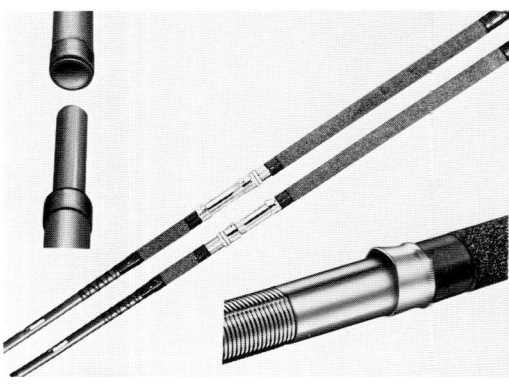

Top: *New development in line guides is the almost frictionless ceramic ring guide. The CerAllan ceramic guide ring is set in a polished stainless-steel frame with tapered feet.*
Bottom: *Garcia's Conlon custom deluxe casting rods feature slim-line, cork-tape-wrapped grips, patented fiberglass ferrule between sections, brass reelseats, and carbide tip-tops.*

This is especially useful in tournament and big-game tackle, where a good grip on the rod may make the difference between utilizing the power of the tackle to its fullest capability, or learning a lesson in frustration as a slippery rod turns and skids in one's grasp.

Rod shaft mid-section ferrules

There is a growing tendency to build long casting rods in two sections of equal length. This certainly facilitates packing and transportation, but some anglers feel that the ferrule in the rod tip's middle does not improve the rod's casting or fish-fighting qualities. Rods built for light-to-medium casting tend to work well in two-piece construction if modern ferrules are employed.

For heavy-duty, saltwater surf casting, one-piece rods (without a removable butt) are the choice of most dedicated surf anglers. For tournament fishing and all big-game fishing, the conventional two-piece rod, consisting of a single-piece tip and a separate heavy wooden or metal butt, joined at the reelseat, is standard equipment.

In recent years, there has been an invasion of saltwater fishing precincts by the fly rod and the freshwater bait-casting rod. Most saltwater fly rods are two-piece ones, with the upper and lower sections joined by a metal, plastic, or fiberglass ferrule. Some bait-casting rods come with the rod shaft jointed at the middle of the overall length. Others utilize a one-piece tip section that mates with the lower butt section at the reelseat.

Fly rods and light spinning rods often are built with "German silver" shaft ferrules. The best such ferrules are manufactured with a diameter increase of about .005 inch between the female and male sections. This assures a smooth fit that will hold under working stress, but one that can be pulled apart by hand tension without injuring the rod shaft.

Manufacturers of fiberglass casting rods have invented several different types of so-called fiberglass ferrules. One simple variety employs a female fiberglass shaft section, which is made up with close tolerance to fit over the slightly tapered upper male rod section of the next section below, in the shaft. Usually the female portion of this ferrule is also the location of a rod guide, so the wrapping thread of the rod guide serves the double purpose of adding hoop strength to the female portion of the joint.

Another type utilizes a solid fiberglass or plastic plug that is inserted into the lower part of the rod shaft. This slides up into the hollow portion of the shaft just above, both parts having been made with a slight taper. The outside of the female or upper portion of the joint is usually enlarged with an extra fiberglass or external wrapping to provide hoop strength and prevent splitting of the upper section.

Reelseat ferrules

The traditional saltwater boat rod, trolling rod, or heavy-duty casting rod has a one-piece tip section that mates into a heavier butt section at the reelseat. This is true of rods ranging in work capability from the lightest IGFA 6-pound-line class up to the 130-pound-line class big-game equipment. In light-duty tackle, the male ferrule at the lower end of the tip section and the female reelseat are very often made of chrome-plated brass. Stainless steel is favored for heavy-duty equipment. Measurement tolerances are held to very small limits.

Ferrules are cemented to wooden or fiberglass rod shafts with a variety of cements. The most popular is old-fashioned "ferrule cement," a waxy substance that comes in finger-size sticks. It is applied hot to the portion to be cemented. Then the ferrule is also heated and pressed on over the shaft, melting and sealing the cement at the joint. The ferrule is then cooled with water or fresh air, forming a shrink-fit over the cemented joint. Ferrule cement has the advantage of a fairly low melting point, permitting easy repairs with a cigarette lighter in the field or on a boat.

Reelseats and their male ferrules vary greatly in quality and cost. Anodized aluminum reelseats are popular for some light casting rods where the rod tip does not enter the reelseat in the manner of a ferrule. In selecting a rod, it pays to buy one with quality ferrules and reelseat.

Single reelseat lock rings often work loose during strenuous fishing. Quality reelseats of the saltwater type always have two lock rings with knurled outer

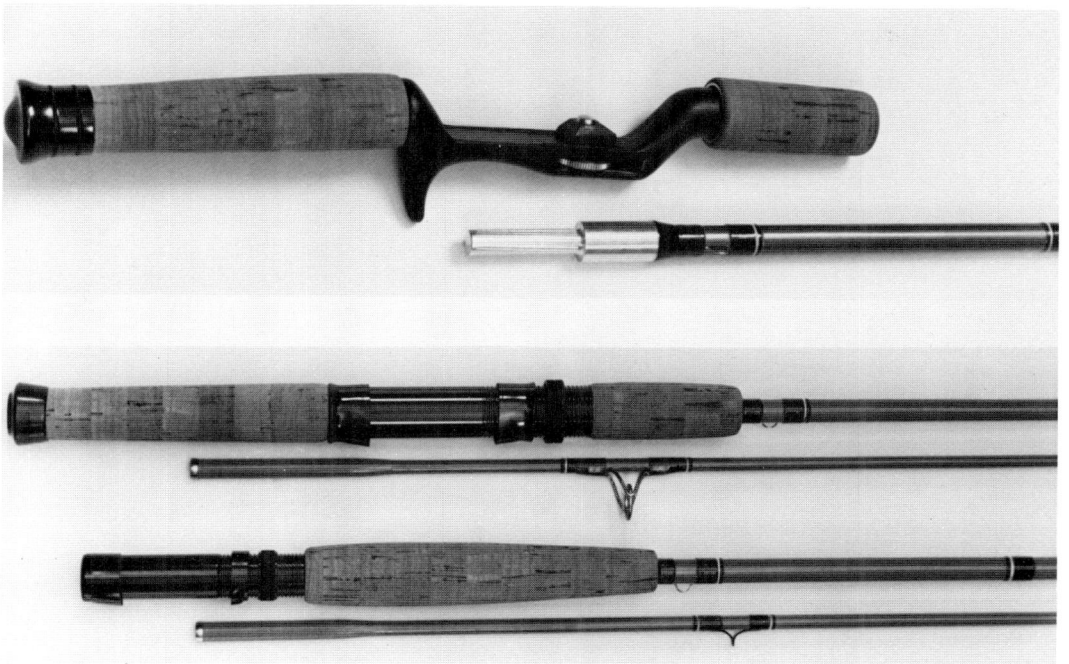

Top: *Phillipson-3M Bass Tamer casting rod has positive-locking tip-to-butt ferrule.*
Bottom: *Phillipson-3M spinning rod (upper) and fly rod (lower) have all-fiberglass midsection ferrules.*

surfaces. These sometimes take a beating when anglers tighten the lock rings with a pair of pliers.

Butt or lower end

Saltwater trolling and boat rods, and some casting rods, usually have a separate lower butt section of turned hardwood. Hickory, oak, and ash are favored. (Ash is lighter than other hardwoods.) The upper end of the butt is cemented into the reelseat, and the lower end is provided with either a plastic, rubber, or metal cap, or a slotted gimbal fitting if the rod is to be used with a fishing chair or a gimbal-equipped stand-up fishing belt.

Some big-game rods come with the so-called boomerang or curved butt. This specialized equipment is discussed in detail in the chapters on tackle for specific fishing purposes and the dynamics of modern tackle.

Exterior protective finishes

Fiberglass dating from the early days of manufacture usually requires a coat of quality rod varnish. Nowadays, most fiberglass rod blank makers apply a special hard outer layer of resin to the cured fiberglass blank. This outer layer is pigmented to the desired color, takes a high polish, and is surprisingly impervious to sun, salt, and moisture. Only the guide wrappings of such rods require color-preserver and rod varnish.

Anodized aluminum rod fittings withstand salt corrosion quite well, provided they are cleaned with fresh water and dried after use. The same precaution applies to chrome-plated brass and stainless steel. Cork grips do not need protective coatings of any kind, but they should be protected from abrasion during transportation and storage.

Rods built of resin-impregnated bamboo are said to be self-finished, and they only need to be rinsed and rubbed dry after use in salt water. Rods built of natural wood laminations should be carefully rubbed and varnished each season to prevent moisture from entering the wood fibers, and to keep the bonding glues from oxidizing. Rods that require varnish should be stripped down to the bare shafts after every six or eight years of normal use, revarnished, and rewrapped.

POWER VERSUS ACTION

Two entirely different qualities are at work in every fishing rod — power and action. Power can be defined as the ability of a rod to transfer human muscle energy into lure motion or line tension. Earlier, we considered the rod as an energy transformer. All transformers have a power rating beyond which they are overloaded.

An electrical transformer's power rating is expressed in watts or kilowatts, and it usually has a normal load factor, plus a short permissible overload factor. If the transformer is operated at power levels higher than the normal load factor for any appreciable time, it is subject to overheating and probable failure.

An internal combustion engine's

Matched pair of fiberglass 50-lb.-line class trolling rods was built for competitive fishing by a Florida tackle specialist. It has cork foregrips, stainless reelseats, and aluminum curved butts, roller guides, and tip-tops

gearbox is an energy transformer. Like the electrical transformer, it has both a normal working load and a temporary overload rating, which usually is expressed in horsepower but sometimes is defined in kilowatts. Here again, consistent overloading will cause gear and bearing damage and eventual failure.

All fishing rods have a power rating, although this may not always be expressed in the same terms. In the days of linen line, the power rating of a rod was defined as the particular thread-count of linen line that the rod worked best against. For example, a rod designed to work with 15-thread linen line was actually designed to work against a line of about 45-pound breaking strain.

When monofilament and Dacron lines supplanted linen, IGFA switched to a pounds-test rather than a thread-count system for rating classes of tackle. Thus, the rod that was once rated for 15-thread linen line is now rated to match line of a maximum 50-pound breaking strain. Of course, nothing prevents you from using heavier line if you want to. The line itself does not overpower the rod. But if you were to fill the reel of a 50-pound-test rated rod with 80-pound-test line, the rod would be overloaded as soon as you let the line tension exceed 50 pounds. The result would be loss of the best action of the rod up to its rated power, and possibly a broken rod.

Action, while related to power, is a different concept. In wheeled vehicles, for example, we might consider three that start with a rating of 100 horsepower. One is a tractor, designed for slow, powerful pulling, or slow action. The second is a family sedan, built for medium speeds, comfort, and what might be called medium action. The third is a class-type racing car, built for fast acceleration, high speed, a delicate degree of control, and fast action.

The same idea can be applied to fishing rods. The figure on page 34 defines the four basic types of action found in popular casting rods: slow, medium, fast, very fast. Action is a relative quality: the degree of action of a rod often depends on its use. For example, what might be fast action in a fly rod might be considered slow-to-medium action in a bait-casting rod. Therefore, in judging the action rating of any rod, we must consider how the rod is being used.

In the rod-action diagram, the progress of the start of the bend of a casting rod from slow to very fast is exaggerated. No rod shaft is perfectly stiff for 79 percent of its length and then suddenly breaks into a power curve, as is shown in the very-fast-action rod. But many very-fast-action rods do have a tendency to develop very little curvature in the lower portion of the shaft and quickly go into a fast power curve at the upper tip end.

The action ratings of slow, medium, fast, and very fast apply primarily to casting rods. In trolling rods, the corresponding terms for defining action are soft, medium, stiff or heavy, and very stiff or heavy. The way action affects the rod shaft is different in trolling rods. In casting rods, the start of the power curve or bend progresses toward the tip of the rod from the lower end as the rating gets faster.

In trolling rods, on the other hand, the position of the overall curve remains the same, a portion of the limb of a parabola. But the curve itself becomes flatter as the action rating progresses from soft to very stiff or heavy.

There are good reasons for this basic difference in rod design. The migrating curve of the casting rod is a function of the rod's casting ability. Some types of casting require a slow type of action. Others require medium or fast action. This range of casting action is best achieved by designing a rod shaft with a very exact position and degree of curvature along the shaft.

The trolling rod, on the other hand, is not designed for casting. Its most important use of power is to act as a flexible lever for applying strong line tension, up to the maximum for which the rod is rated, for stopping the run of a fish or lifting a heavy fish in deep water. Therefore there is no need to design a series of rods with a migrating curve. Instead, the

34 MODERN SALTWATER FISHING TACKLE

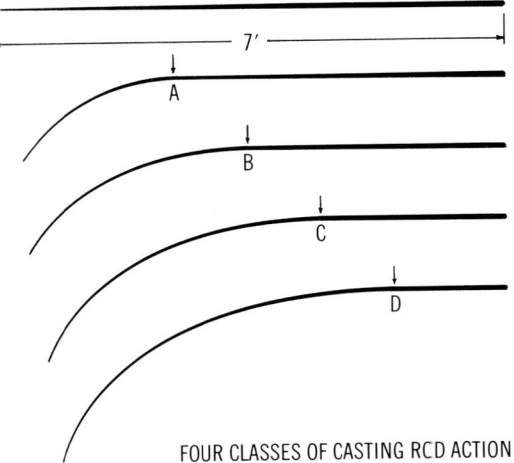

FOUR CLASSES OF CASTING ROD ACTION

A Very fast action: bend starts 64 percent from lower end of shaft.
B Fast action: bend starts 50 percent from lower end of shaft.
C Medium action: bend commences 36 percent from lower end of shaft.
D Slow action: bend starts 21 percent from lower end of shaft.

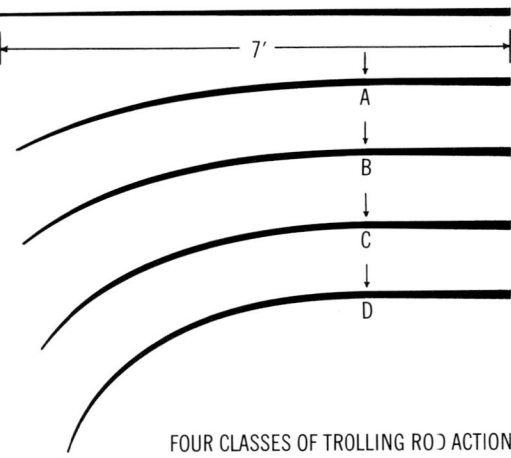

FOUR CLASSES OF TROLLING ROD ACTION

A Very heavy action: rod designed for maximum leverage, minimum flexibility.
B Heavy action: the normal big-game degree of stiffness and backbone.
C Medium action: probably the most popular of all trolling rod types of action.
D Soft action: for special applications such as weakfishing.

rod is designed to maintain an approximate parabolic curve throughout its working length. The degree of stiffness or flatness of curve is a function of selecting the proper amount of flexibility for the job at hand.

For example, you would select a soft-action rod to use on weakfish with 12-pound-test line, because of the softness of the weakfish's mouth. But you would choose a medium-to-stiff-action rod for use with the same line for bottom fishing for tautog, fish that have a strong yen to bore down into the rocks when hooked.

What happens when a trolling rod is overloaded? When the rod shaft is bent beyond its power rating, the upper end tends to straighten out in a line tangent to the pull of the fishing line, and a strong bend starts to develop at the lower end of the shaft. This is most pronounced in soft-action rods. When this happens, the rod rapidly loses relative lifting power. The more the angler lifts, the more he puts an overload bend into the lower end of the rod shaft without moving the fish.

Stiff-action trolling and bottom-fishing rods usually have a considerably higher overload factor than soft-action rods. But a stiff rod may rip the hook out of a soft-mouthed fish, whereas a soft rod has the delicate flexibility to cushion the

This light trolling rod, designed for 20-to-30-lb. line, shows proper shaft loading with the drag set to slip at about 10-lb. line tension and boat speed of 3 to 4 knots.

sudden yanks of the fish in its effort to escape the hook.

How do power and action relate to each other? Here again, there are excellent examples outside the realm of fishing. Take the tractor, family sedan, and racing car, each powered by the same 100-horsepower motor. In the tractor, a gearbox with a large reduction ratio enables the small, high-speed motor to turn big driving wheels very slowly, producing enormous pulling power but very little speed.

The fishing equivalent might be a short, stiff, bait-casting rod designed to hook a game fish on 30-pound-test line and stop the fish dead before it can make the cover of a lily pad.

In the family sedan, a lighter but not so heavily geared-down gearbox provides the car with a selection of gear ratios that allow hill climbing, traffic speed control, and highway cruising speeds up to perhaps 100 miles an hour. The fishing equivalent would be a good, light trolling rod designed for 30-pound-test line. This will work well on fish from a two-pound porgy up to a 100-pound white marlin.

In the racing car, the gearbox features a series of gear ratios designed to combine maximum acceleration with a top speed 50 to 100 percent faster than that of the family car. The fishing equivalent could be the Hatteras Heaver 11-foot surf rod, which is designed to cast a four-ounce lure more than 100 yards out into the surf, using 30-pound-test line.

Fishing rods do not create or amplify power. Some energy is always lost to internal friction and bending stress in overcoming rod weight and inertia, and to friction of the line running through the guides. The measure of a successful fishing rod is how efficiently it transforms the angler's muscle power into the velocity and range of a cast lure, and the control and recovery of a hooked fish.

To achieve peak success, the angler must choose his rod or rods with an eye to finding the best overall compromise between a number of sometimes conflicting requirements. The chapters on selecting saltwater tackle for specific fishing purposes contain many examples of tackle that have been developed over the years to meet these requirements — the equipment is light, good looking, and a real joy to own and use in fishing.

Increasing the drag tension to about 30 lb., while fishing with 50-lb.-test line, overloads the shaft heavily. Curve migrates down the shaft toward the foregrip.

In 1970 Glen Gibson of Cape Breton Island, Canada, took this 1065-lb. bluefin tuna with a Penn Senator 14/0 star-drag reel and 130-lb. line, setting a new world record for the species.

4 Star-Drag Reels

As was mentioned in Chapter 1, credit for developing the concept of a game-fish reel with multiplying gears and a non-reversing slip-clutch drive is given to William Boschen, who used the original prototype to take the first rod and reel swordfish, back in 1913. Julius vom Hofe built Boschen's first drag-equipped reel, which is reported to have held 500 yards of 24-thread linen line.

By the 1920s, the ranks of manufacturers of saltwater game-fishing reels had swelled to include such names as Bronson, Pflueger, Edward vom Hofe, Ocean City, J. A. Coxe, Perez, and Kovalovsky. Some concentrated on big-game reels. Others majored in surf casting and inshore fishing models. A few handled both.

In 1932, Otto Henze, a workman at the Ocean City reel plant, quit that company to form the Penn Tackle Company of Philadelphia, a concern that one fishing writer later called the Ford Motor Company of saltwater reel production. At about the same time, a group of Florida fishermen and machinists were tinkering with early versions of the famous Fin-Nor reels, machines that one day would be called the Rolls-Royces of fishing winches.

At the time of this writing, the following companies manufactured or distributed revolving-spool saltwater game-fishing reels in the United States.

Eagle Claw Reels. Four star-drag models rating from 1/0 to 4/0 in size.

Everol Reels. Seven lever-drag models, built in Italy, ranging from 2½/0 to 14/0 in capacity.

Daiwa Reels. Three lever-drag models, built in Japan, rated at 2½/0, 4/0, and 6/0 capacity.

Garcia Reels. Three lever-drag models of the Mitchell 1000 series, built in France, rated at 4/0, 6/0, and 9/0 capacity. Also a number of smaller Mitchell and Ambassadeur series star-drag reels rating from about 2/0 to 3/0 in capacity, although not so designated by Garcia. Ambassadeur reels are made in Sweden.

Heddon Reels. Six star-drag models, two with level-wind feature, in nominal 15-, 20-, and 30-pound-line-test classes, rating 200-300 yards line capacity.

Penn Reels. Five lever-drag reels of the International series, rating from 2½/0 to 12/0 in capacity. Ten star-drag reels of the standard Senator series, rating from 1/0 to 16/0 in capacity. Three models of the high-speed Senator series rating 3/0, 4/0, and 6/0. A large number of other, smaller star-drag, level-wind, and free-spool models not "O"-rated, but designed for saltwater use.

Reel-King Reels. Three lever-drag models, rating 4/0, 6/0, and 9/0 in capacity.

Shakespeare Reels. Two star-drag models, one with level wind, of the 1960 series, not "O"-rated.

St. Croix Reels. Six models of star-drag reels in the Compac series, rating 1/0 to 3/0 in capacity, although not "O"-rated by the maker.

True Temper Reels. Six models of the Ocean City series of star-drag reels, rating 3/0 to 12/0. Also four smaller star-drag models not "O"-rated.

Tycoon/Fin-Nor Reels. Seven models of lever-drag reels in the Fin-Nor series, ranging in capacity from 2½/0 to 12/0. Also, three models of lever-drag reels in the Golden Regal series, rating 2/0, 4/0, and 6/0.

Star-drag reels are so named because the slip clutch mechanism is activated by a radial-arm star wheel that usually is mounted coaxially on the main drive cylinder. The star wheel increases or decreases the amount of drag-plate friction by squeezing or releasing pressure on the drag plates and discs when rotated clockwise or counterclockwise on the main drive cylinder. The drag wheel turns on a threaded portion of the drive cylinder and also rotates at the same speed as the reel handle, since both are mounted on the same cylinder.

While the number and composition of star-drag plates and friction discs vary from model to model, the principle of operation remains the same. Some of the clutch plates are keyed to the main drive cylinder. Alternating plates are keyed to the outer rim of the drag assembly, which is also part of the main drive gear. Between the keyed brass plates are friction rings of felt, leather, brake lining, Teflon, or other heat-resistant brake material.

As long as the drag-slip friction is greater than the tension on the line, the reel handle will turn the main gear and the reel spool, and line can be taken in. But when line tension becomes greater than drag friction, the reel spool will revolve against handle pressure, and whatever is pulling on the line can pull line off the reel spool. A small metal dog and ratchet prevent the reel handle from turning backward.

The star-wheel enables the angler to adjust the amount of drag friction from a theoretical zero to locked-tight, or to any desired value in between. The drag and handle assembly (the drive train) can be disengaged from the reel spool with the well-known free-spool lever, which disengages the secondary spool driving gear from the main drive gear containing the drag assembly.

The main drive cylinder is hollow and revolves around a fixed main shaft that is riveted or welded at its lower end to the metal drag bridge. The latter, in turn, is screwed to the body of the reel's drive plate. Needless to say, all sources of friction, gears, bearings, etc., require careful lubrication. Internal lubrication is achieved with a number of small external grease or oil injection fittings. Most reel manufacturers provide a tube of the preferred lubricant with each reel, plus a combination wrench/screwdriver for disassembling the reel.

The star-drag reel, when it first appeared, was popular immediately. Here was a reel that combined the desired characteristics of an adjustable friction clutch, a free-spool device, light weight, and moderate cost. The famous Penn Senator big-game reels soon were chal-

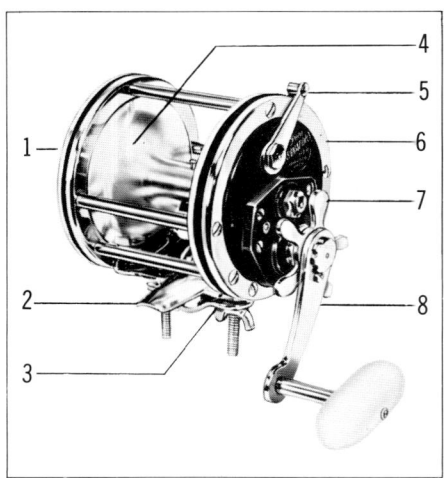

MAJOR PARTS OF PENN SENATOR
STAR-DRAG REEL

1 Left-side plate
2 Reel stand
3 Rod clamp
4 Line spool
5 Free-spool lever
6 Right-side plate
7 Star-drag adjustment wheel
8 Handle assembly

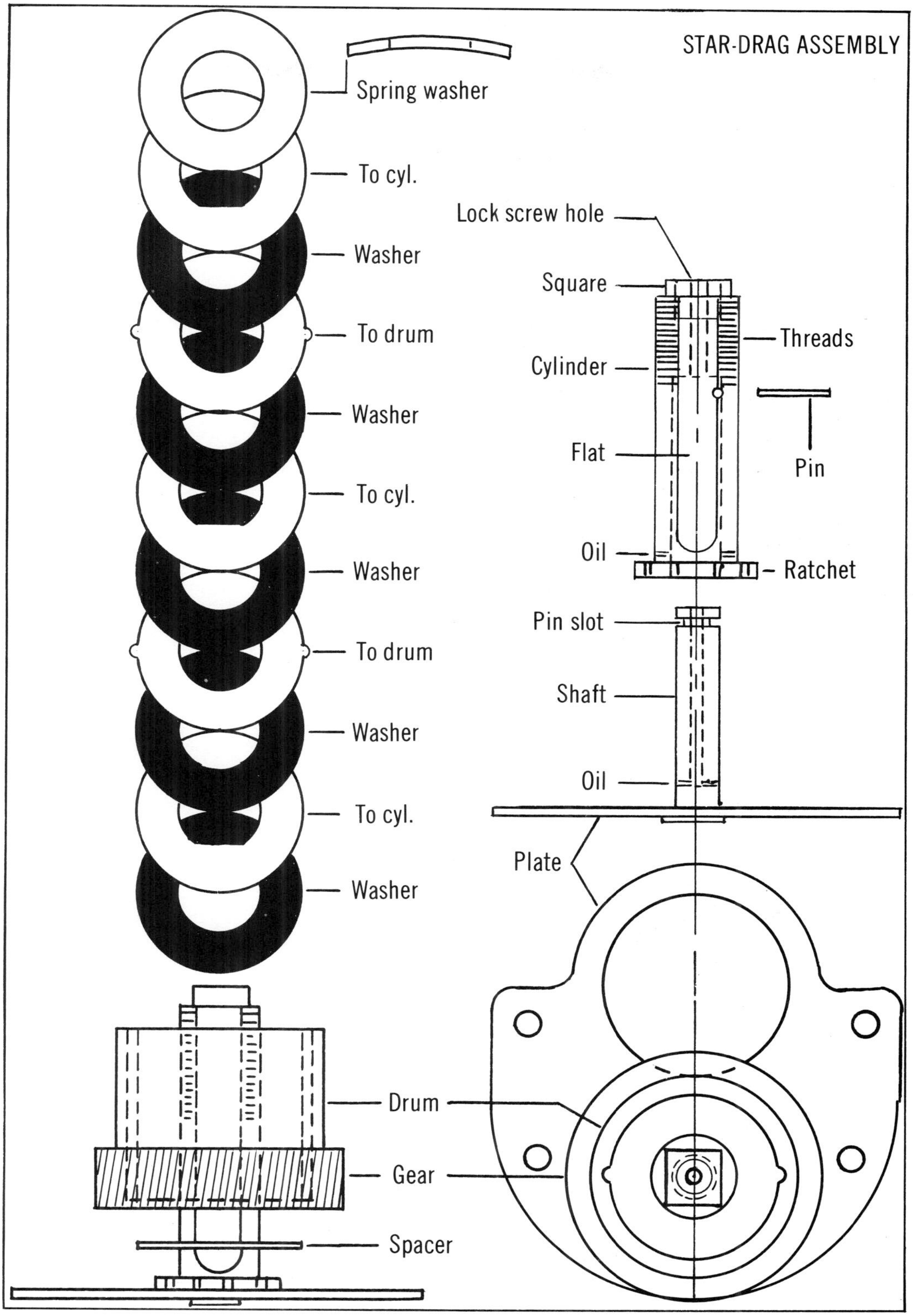
STAR-DRAG ASSEMBLY
Spring washer
To cyl.
Washer
To drum
Washer
To cyl.
Washer
To drum
Washer
To cyl.
Washer
Lock screw hole
Square
Threads
Cylinder
Pin
Flat
Oil
Ratchet
Pin slot
Shaft
Oil
Plate
Drum
Gear
Spacer

lenging the most expensive big-game reels, and proving their reliability. The Senator series of game-fishing reels probably did as much to popularize both heavy-duty and light tackle ocean-game fishing as any other single factor.

But star-drag reels also have certain built-in restrictions. One problem is the star-wheel drag system itself. The number of turns required to achieve a desired degree of drag friction varies from model to model, and even from reel to reel, within the same model series. It is usually difficult to change the drag of a star-drag reel and then reset it to a previously used drag value without using a spring balance to calibrate the drag.

Some anglers become adroit enough to reset their own personal star drags by hand, and they can come within 5 20 percent of the desired drag friction value most of the time. But for the average fisherman, who has only a hazy idea of what, say, seven pounds of drag friction feels like when the line is pulled, the degree of error may approach 5 60 percent with hand calibration. Such a large margin of error may be disastrous with active, unpredictable fish.

Another problem is the relatively small friction surface provided in most star-drag assemblies. A 100-pound tuna can bring a 4/0 reel loaded with 50-pound class line to the smoking point in just the first run. Once the brass washers become heated to the point of wiping metal onto the intervening friction washers, the reel becomes grabby and unreliable. Enjoyable fishing requires a reel with smooth, steady action of the drag. If the drag is grabby, the drag friction must be set to a dangerously high figure to ensure that the drag will maintain a reasonable friction value once it has stabilized after the initial friction-lock has been broken.

The accompanying diagram shows how a smooth-acting reel drag differs from a moderately grabby and a very grabby reel drag. A smooth reel drag releases the reel spool when the preset degree of drag friction is reached. This release is smooth, and the drag quickly

FRICTION CURVES OF REEL DRAGS

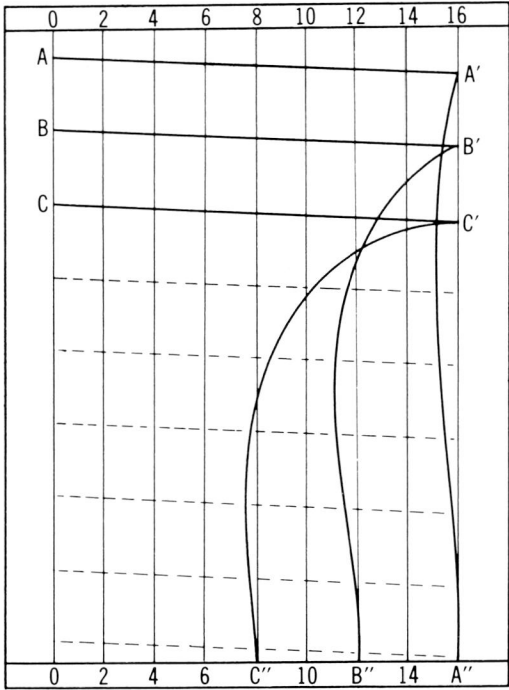

What happens when a reel drag is grabby? Take three identical reels, one with an almost perfectly smooth drag (A), one with a moderately grabby drag (B), and one with a very grabby drag (C). Exactly the same amount of line is on each reel. Preset the drag of each to slip at just 16 lb., as you would for striking drag. Drag A starts to slip smoothly at point A' and experiences a slight reduction to 15-lb. slip tension before stabilizing at 16 lb., 100% of original setting, at A". Drag B starts to slip suddenly at 16 lb. and experiences reduction of slip tension to 11 lb. before stabilizing at 12 lb. at B", 75% of original presetting tension. Drag C starts to slip with a jerk at C', 16 lb., and experiences a serious drop of slip tension to 7 lb. before stabilizing at 8 lb., 50% of original setting, at C". The slanted dashed lines in the diagram represent the passage of time as action progresses from start of tension through reaching the preset drag slip point, and terminating in stabilized drag friction. A smooth-working reel drag is a pleasure to operate. It soothes frustration and saves many valuable fish.

stabilizes at a friction rate very close to the preset value.

But a grabby reel drag releases the spool with a jerk, and once the initial lock of the drag is broken, the friction that the drag maintains against line tension falls to a value that may be one-half or less of the original preset value. The cure for a grabby reel is replacement of the full set of metal and soft-material plates and washers. "Wiped" drag plates will continue to grab with fresh washers. New metal plates will continue to grab with old washers.

Two kinds of abuse make a star drag become grabby. The first is well understood: overheating and wear from long-continued heavy fishing pressure. The second is more obscure. This is a result of the fact that when a reel is stored for any length of time with the drag screwed up tight, the soft braking washers and the metal drag plates tend to weld together. This produces a grabby reel.

You can't do much to save a reel from becoming grabby under conditions of heavy fishing, but you can form the habit of backing the drag wheel back to zero pressure before storing the reel, even just for overnight. If a reel becomes grabby from overwork, only fresh washers and possibly new drag plates will effect a cure. But a drag made grabby by having been stored in a tight-drag condition can sometimes be salvaged by disassembling the drag, gently prying apart the soft and metal washers and plates, steel-wooling them, and working the drag under moderate tension after reassembling it.

Water absorbed during wet fishing conditions often forms a gummy, waxlike emulsion inside the reel. This is destructive to smooth drag operation. The cure is to overhaul the reel often enough to prevent gummy deposits from forming inside. Kerosene is a good cleaning agent.

Drag washers and plates are inexpensive and usually easy to obtain. When ordering them from the manufacturer or a supplier, be sure to specify the correct parts numbers. A number of Penn reel models, and reels of some other manufacturers, have a thin, hard, red-fiber washer under the main drive gear drum, between the drum and the bottom plate or ratchet wheel. Never try to use red-fiber washers of this kind as friction washers in the drag itself. The result will be a horrendously grabby drag.

In recent years, Teflon drag washers have proved quite effective with many models of star-drag reels. There are a few small companies that specialize in producing and marketing Teflon washers for many popular models of reels. A few manfacturers also provide Teflon washers either as standard equipment on some models, or as optional equipment at a slight extra cost.

A few years ago, when Penn Tackle Company introduced its famous International series of lever-drag reels, and several other companies developed lever-drag reels in the popular 2/0 to 6/0 size range, many anglers felt that the last word in light-tackle reel design had finally been heard. But experience showed that, fine as they were, the new, small, lever-drag reels did have two major drawbacks. One was much greater

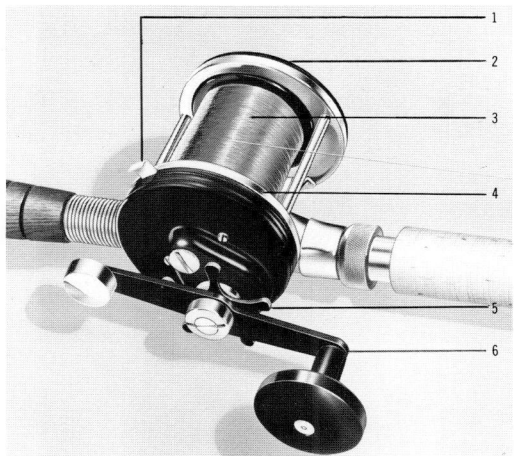

MAJOR PARTS OF GARCIA AMBASSADEUR STAR-DRAG REEL
1   Free-spool button
2   Left-side plate
3   Spool
4   Right-side plate
5   Star-drag adjustment wheel
6   Handle assembly

weight than a star-drag reel of equal capacity. The other was the tendency of some models not to go completely into a zero-drag condition if critical adjustments were made with insufficient care.

In light-tackle tournament fishing, especially, many anglers now feel that advanced star-drag reels like the Penn Senator high-speed series, with gear ratios of 3.7:1 for the 3/0 model, 3 5:1 for the 4/0, and 2.8:1 for the 6/0, are the equal of most small lever-drag reels.

When IGFA created the new six-pound-test line class for saltwater fish records, ocean light-tackle fishing became a whole new ball game. Anglers quickly discovered that freshwater fishing tackle shops offered a galaxy of jewel-like bait-casting reels designed to use light lines. The result has been a noticeable swing toward new ultra-light saltwater tackle with a distinctly freshwater flavor.

Unfortunately, there isn't space here to catalog every freshwater reel that conceivably could be used on salt water. But a number of manufacturers recently have developed new, larger versions of their most popular freshwater star-drag bait-casting, level-wind, and even drag-equipped fly-casting reels, specifically for light tackle use on salt water. Where information on these reels is available, it has been included in the book. Recommendations of tackle using these reels are made in the chapters on selecting tackle for particular types of saltwater fishing.

Yale University Outdoor Recreation Director Edward Migdalski, author of books on sport fishing and game fish identification, carries a half-dozen medium-duty star-drag outfits to be used for jigging Nova Scotia pollock.

REEL CAPACITY BY "O" SIZE

While reels of different manufacturers vary in line capacity for the same "O" size, the average line capacity for accepted "O" sizes works out as follows:

"O" size	Capacity (in yds./lb. test)	Reel capacity (in cubic in.)
1/0	1000/6	2.3
2/0	660/12	2.9
3/0	500/20	3.6
4/0	550/30	6.2
6/0	550/50	10.1
9/0	550/80	16.0
10/0	750/80	21.8
10/0	460/130	21.8
12/0	1050/80	30.5
12/0	640/130	30.5
14/0	1000/130	47.5

If you have a reel filled with a known yardage of line closely approximating one of the IGFA line classes in size, and you wish to refill the reel with line that is one class lighter or heavier, you can determine the amount of line needed by using one of the following factors.

Going from 6 to 12 .. factor = 2
Going from 12 to 20 .. factor = 1.67
Going from 20 to 30 .. factor = 1.5
Going from 30 to 50 .. factor = 1.67
Going from 50 to 80 .. factor = 1.6
Going from 80 to 130 .. factor = 1.625

When shifting *down* in pounds test from one IGFA line class to another, *multiply* your known reel capacity by the factor between the two classes. For example: Your reel holds 475 yards of 20-pound-test IGFA class line. You wish to refill it with 12-pound-test line of the same type and manufacture. Multiply 475 by 1.67 (the factor between 12-pound and 20-pound-test lines). Your reel should hold 793 yards of 12-pound-test line. It would be safe to buy an 800-yard spool.

When shifting *up* in pounds test from one IGFA line class to another, *divide* your known reel capacity by the factor between the two classes of line. For example: You decide to fill another reel with 30-pound-test line. You know it holds 550 yards of 20-pound class line. Divide 550 by 1.5 (the factor between 20- and 30-pound lines). The reel should take 367 yards of 30-pound class line. If you buy a 400-yard spool, you'll have a few yards left over for making up light casting or trolling leaders.

This system works accurately when the lines are close to IGFA standards in breaking strain, or of the same type and manufacture. It works for monofilament or Dacron line, if you stick to the same type when switching. It's not accurate if you try to switch from mono to Dacron, or vice versa. The relationship between various types and sizes of lines is analyzed in greater detail in the chapters on lines.

Tournament angler Clyde Woeber puts pressure on a blue marlin off Cozumel, Mexico, with a 9/0 Penn International lever-action reel filled with 80-lb.-test Dacron line.

5 Lever-Drag Reels

One advantage of the lever drag over the star drag is that the lever-drag mechanism is separate from the reel's drive handle. The lever does not turn with the handle as the star drag's adjustment wheel does, and its position is constantly visible to the angler. Another advantage is that most lever-drag reels have some sort of striking-drag stop device that temporarily limits the lever's throw.

The Fin-Nor reel, for example, has a small striking drag stop dog halfway up the lever arc. This can be turned out of the way when maximum drag is needed. Penn International reels, and some similar makes, utilize a spring-loaded metal button on which the lever momentarily catches when pushed forward. Depressing the button permits the lever to be pushed to full drag. Everol reels use a circular wire stop ring that locks at any desired position to act as a stop, but the ring is easily pushed ahead when not needed.

Like the star drag, the lever drag operates by squeezing shaft-keyed and drum-keyed friction plates to produce varying degrees of drag friction. The big difference between the two is that the star drag's clutch is built coaxial with the handle drive cylinder, whereas the lever-drag assembly is located coaxial with the reel spool shaft.

Another difference is that the star-drag clutch has only one means of adjustment, the star wheel working against a strong coil spring or spring washer, but the majority of lever-drag reels have two drag adjustments. The main adjustment is the lever. The secondary adjustment is a knurled nut or knob, with which the drag can be fine-tuned to provide any desired degree of striking drag when the lever is at the striking-drag position.

Fin-Nor reels have the auxiliary drag adjustment nut located at the upper end of the drag lever. Penn International reels, and some similar models, have a large knurled knob located on the right-hand reel face plate. Everol reels do not have a secondary means of drag adjustment, but they do have the adjustable striking-drag stop ring previously mentioned.

The compression range of the Everol reel can be changed by increasing or decreasing the number of small compression springs in the drag assembly. This requires disassembling the reel, so it cannot be done while the reel is in operation. However, the range of drag tension across the full throw of the Everol drag lever is sufficient for any fishing situation, provided the reel is loaded with the class of line for which it is designed.

Lever-drag reels have a reputation for being able to take more abuse from big fish than star-drag reels. There is reason for this feeling. A typical 12/0 Penn Senator star-drag reel, for instance, has five metal clutch plates — three keyed to the drive cylinder and two to the drag drum. Four brake-lining washers are placed between the five metal plates, and a fifth washer is located between the bottom plate and the

46 MODERN SALTWATER FISHING TACKLE

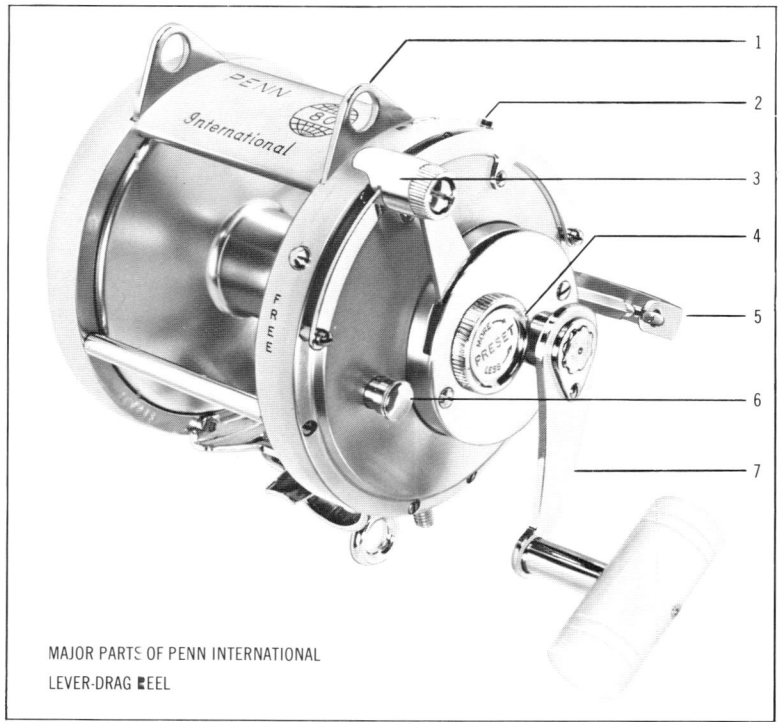

1   Harness ring
2   Striking-drag stop button
3   Drag adjustment lever
4   Preset adjustment drum
5   Rod yoke
6   Alarm (click) button
7   Handle assembly

MAJOR PARTS OF PENN INTERNATIONAL LEVER-DRAG REEL

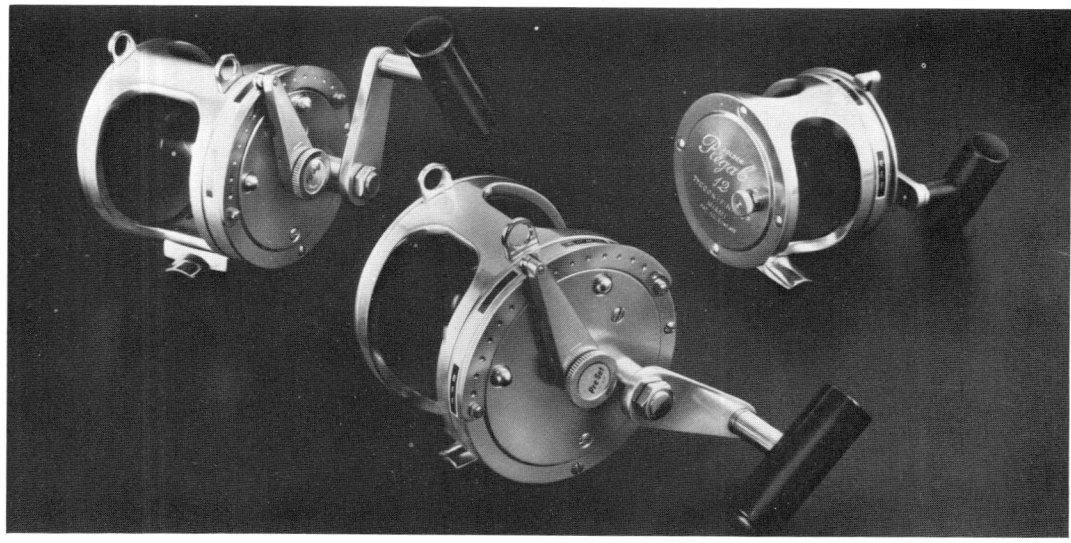

Tycoon Fin-Nor Golden Regal lever-drag reels in sizes (left to right) for 20-, 30-, and 12-lb. test line.

Lever-Drag Reels 47

Garcia Mitchell lever-drag game fishing reels in sizes (left to right) 9/0, 4/0, and 6/0.

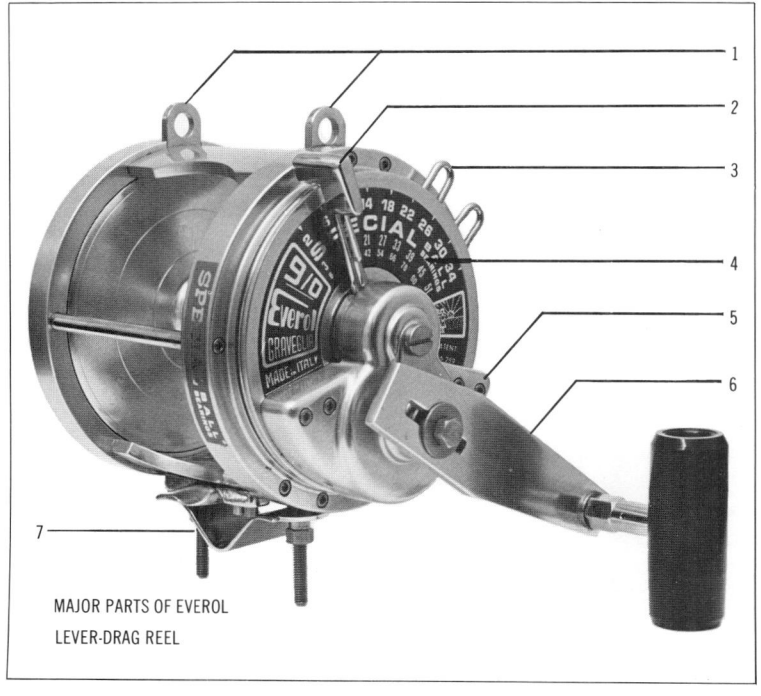

MAJOR PARTS OF EVEROL
LEVER-DRAG REEL

1 Harness rings
2 Drag adjustment lever
3 Striking-drag adjustment ring
4 Right end plate
5 Drive gear cover
6 Handle assembly
7 Rod clamp

48 MODERN SALTWATER FISHING TACKLE

lower end of the drag drum (see illustration of star-drag assembly).

Because the brake-lining washers are not keyed to the drive cylinder or the drum, they are free floating. Theoretically, they should provide drag friction with both of their surfaces. Actually, one side of a washer frequently binds itself to an adjacent plate, thereby reducing the washer surface area available for friction.

The total surface area of the five washers of a Penn Senator 12/0, counting both sides, is 9.2 square inches. This is the maximum available friction surface if all of the washers are working in the free-floating condition, not bound to any plates. But if each of the five washers has one side bound to a plate, then the effective available drag-friction surface is cut in half, to only 4.6 square inches.

A typical 12/0 Everol reel also has five metal drag plates, three of which are keyed to the drum of the right-hand end of the reel spool, and two to the spool transaxle. Power to rotate the spool is transferred from the transaxle to the spool via these plates.

Each drum-keyed plate at the end of the assembly has a friction band of brake lining cemented to its inward-facing surface. The center drum-keyed plate has similar friction bands on each side, making four friction bands in all. The two stainless-steel, shaft-keyed plates are placed between the facing friction bands of the drum-keyed plates. Total friction area of the four brake-lining bands is 23.56 square inches.

The star-drag reel has an effective drag friction area of anywhere between 4.6 and 9.2 square inches, depending on how many washers are free-floating and how many are bound to metal plates by accumulated dirt and grease under pressure. There is no way to determine this, short of taking the drag apart. This means that the lever-drag reel has an effective drag-surface friction of at least 2.56 times, and at most 5.12 times, that of the star-drag reel. (23.56/9.2 = 2.56; 23.56/4.6 = 5.12)

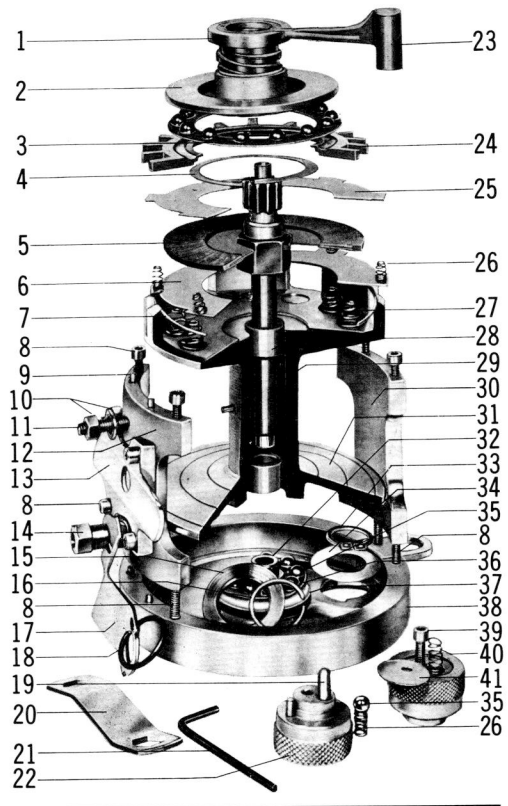

CLUTCH ASSEMBLY, EVEROL REELS SIZES 4/0, 6/0, 7½/0, 9/0

What does this prove? It certainly doesn't prove that the star-drag reel is "inferior" to the lever-drag reel. The star-drag reel may chew up plates and washers at a faster rate than the lever-drag reel, but replacements are inexpensive and easy to install. With new plates and washers, drag action is like new.

But the lever-drag reel definitely runs more coolly on a long, hard fight with a big, powerful fish. Its big drag plates produce the same amount of line tension at anywhere from 39 percent to only 19½ percent of the pounds-per-square-inch of drag pressure required by the star-drag reel. The larger lever-drag plates also are better situated to dissipate the heat of friction that, in a star drag, sometimes builds up to the smoking point.

Lever drags show less tendency to

1 Male clutch adjusting screw
2 Female clutch adjusting screw
3 Clutch thrust bearing ring
4 Thrust bearing lock ring
5 Shaft-keyed clutch plate, lined
6 Drum-keyed spring plate, unlined
7 Internal lock spring ring
8 Allen screws, 6/32" dia.
9 Centering pins
10 Nut and washer
11 Clamp screw
12 Frame post, lower
13 Reel stand
14 Clamp collar nut
15 Bearing retainer
16 Spring lock ring
17 Right-side plate
18 Rod clamp ring
19 Alarm (click) striker
20 Double-ended wrench
21 Allen wrench, 7/64" size
22 Alarm (click) selector
23 Clutch adjusting handle
24 Clutch ball-race plate
25 Drum-keyed plate, unlined
26 Separation springs
27 Clutch compression springs
28 Spool bearing
29 Pinion shaft (transaxle)
30 Frame post, upper
31 Spool
32 Side plate shaft bearing
33 Alarm spring lock ring
34 Alarm selector washer
35 Bearing balls, 5/32" dia.
36 Spacer ring
37 Bearing race
38 Left-side plate
39 Alarm (click) cover screw
40 Striker springs
41 Alarm (click) selector cover

require readjustment or recalibration after long, hard use than do star drags. Some lever-drag reels can be repaired by the owner if he has the necessary parts. Others can be repaired only by the manufacturer or a properly equipped reel repair shop. The care of reels of all types is discussed in detail in the chapter on tackle maintenance and repairs.

Before investing in an expensive reel, it's good to learn the manufacturer's policy on parts and service. Many anglers schedule a period during the off-season when their essential reels can be sent to the repair shop for cleaning, testing, and recalibration.

It is important that both star- and lever-drag reels be operated within the limits of their work capacity. You'll never hurt a 4/0 reel, for example, by fishing nothing but 12- or 20-pound-test line, but the same reel should not be filled with 80-pound-test line and be expected to do the work of a 9/0 model. Reels should be filled with line of a class normal for their size rating (see Reel Capacity by "O" Size, Chapter 4).

CALIBRATING STRIKING DRAG

For star- and lever-drag reels, the calibration procedure is generally the same, but it may vary slightly, depending on reel type and model. Striking drag is usually between 20 and 30 percent of the line's nominal breaking strain. It also varies according to the species of fish. The table below gives an idea of striking drags commonly used.

Species	Line class	Striking drag
White marlin	30 lb.	8 lb.
Sailfish	20 lb.	5 lb.
Blue marlin	130 lb.	20-24 lb.
Swordfish	80 lb.	14-18 lb.
Mako shark	50 lb.	15 lb.
Bluefish	12 lb.	3 lb.
Striped bass	20 lb.	8 lb.
Giant tuna	130 lb.	30-40 lb.
Tarpon	20 lb.	7 lb.
Bonefish	6 lb.	1½ lb.

50 MODERN SALTWATER FISHING TACKLE

To calibrate your own reel for a desired striking drag, obtain a strong spring balance with a weight range at least as great as the maximum striking drag needed. Set up the rod and reel in a rod holder in the normal fishing position, and run the double line out through the rod guides.

For a double-adjustment lever-drag reel, start with a low degree of drag adjustment and with the drag lever at the striking-drag stop position. Pull on the fishing line with the spring balance, gradually adjusting the secondary (knurled knob) drag adjustment until the drag just starts to slip at the desired pounds of line pull, with the lever at the striking-drag position. Some reels require that the drag

Ethel Philips, one of the few women licensed as a fishing guide, works out on a striped marlin with a 12/0 Fin-Nor lever-drag reel and 130-lb. line.

lever be returned to the zero position when the adjustment knob is turned. With others, the knob can be turned with the lever in the striking-drag position, if line tension is relaxed momentarily.

With a single-adjustment lever drag like the Everol, drag calibration is very easy. Set up the rod and reel in a rod holder and attach the spring balance to the end of the line. Push the striking-drag lock ring far forward so it won't interfere. Starting with the lever near the zero point, gradually push the lever forward until the exact proper striking drag is obtained, as measured by the spring balance. Then bring the lock ring back until it is stopped by the drag-lever handle.

In both cases, it's a good idea to test the drag tension at maximum or near-maximum lever position, to make sure that you can apply all the drag tension the line can stand if you have to hold a very strong fish. This may take a spring balance testing as much as 150 pounds, and may require the help of a couple of strong assistants.

My own 12/0 Everol reel is filled with 130-pound line and has the numbers 10, 20, 30, and 40 applied in self-adhesive tape to the upper rim of the right-hand reel face plate. The numerals correspond to the drag lever positions for that many pounds of drag tension.

A star drag is calibrated for striking drag in almost exactly the same way, but one big problem with these reels is the fact that unless you mark one or more wheel prongs, it's almost impossible to reset the reel to the desired striking drag without resorting to the spring balance.

Here's how to reset the reel the easy way. Set up the rod and reel in a rod holder as before, and attach the spring balance to the end of the line. Starting with a fairly low drag setting, gradually increase drag tension by turning the drag wheel until the desired striking drag has been achieved. Star-drag reels have no striking-drag stop, but if you look at the wheel, you may note that one wheel prong is just under the bar of the handle, or in close proximity to the handle.

Mark this prong with a daub of paint, a twist of wire, or a bit of friction tape. Now, when you wish to return the drag to striking-drag tension, just bring the marked prong back to this position with respect to the reel handle. It is easy to learn how to return to striking drag, even during fishing.

After you have calibrated the star drag for the desired striking drag, advance the wheel setting until the next prong is in the same relative position with the handle. Now measure the drag tension with the spring balance. If, for example, it has increased from 20 to 24 pounds, you will quickly see that an advance of one prong beyond 20-pound striking drag increases the drag tension by four pounds to 24 pounds. Continue to advance the drag wheel, one prong at a time, measuring the drag tension with the spring balance each time. Doing this, you can find out exactly how many extra pounds of drag there are for each succeeding extra prong of increased drag.

You can even make up a small card with a schedule of prong-by-prong drag settings, starting with a marked prong in line with the reel handle at any nominal fairly low striking-drag value. This card can be taped or glued to the reel's left end plate for future reference. Once calibrated this way, a reel should be free of the need for further striking-drag calibration, unless the amount of line on the spool is changed or the reel has had a workout with a very powerful fish.

All reels, whether star or lever drag, should be recalibrated for striking drag after fighting a big, bad fish. They should also be tested for holding the striking-drag setting after being stored for any length of time. You may not have to recalibrate for small changes in striking drag when shifting from one species to another, but large changes of striking drag, such as switching from a swordfish striking drag of 15 pounds to a giant tuna striking drag of 35 pounds, should be made with the spring balance, unless your reel is of the type where the striking-drag stop can be adjusted, as in the Everols.

52 MODERN SALTWATER FISHING TACKLE

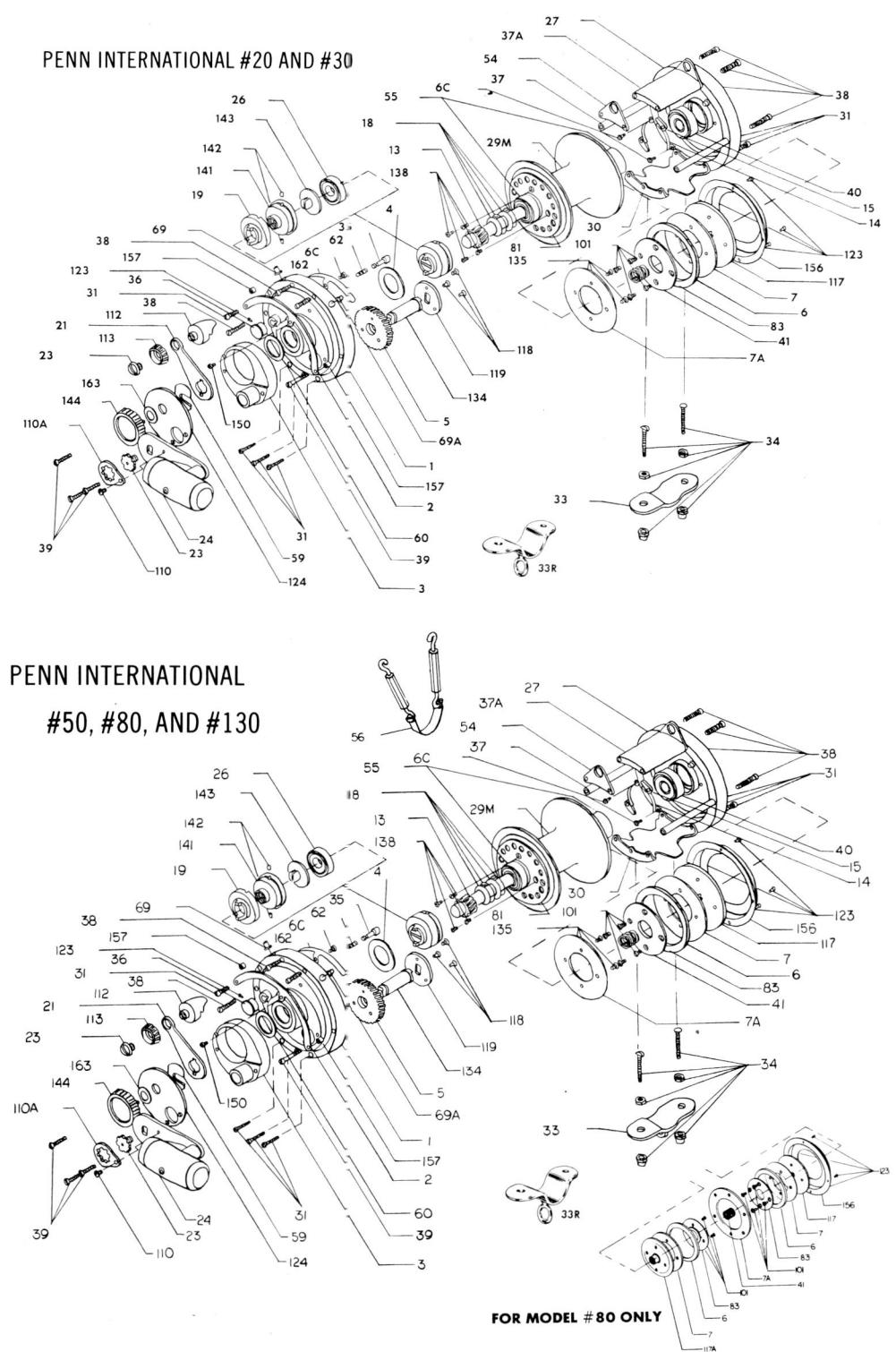

PARTS LIST FOR PENN INTERNATIONAL REELS #20, #30, #50, #80, #130

*Designate parts also for #20. Example: Pinion 13-20.

Part No.	Description	#20-#30	#50	#80	#130
1	Right side plate assm.	*1-30	1-50	1-80	1-130
2	Quadrant ring	2-30	2-50	2-80	2-130
3	Bridge assm. w/bushing	3-30	3-50	3-80	3-130
3A	Outer bridge	—	—	—	3A-130
4	Thrust washer	4-30	4-50	4-80	4-130
5	Main gear	5-50	5-50	5-80	5-130
6	Drag washer brk. ln.	6-30	6-50	6-50	6-130
6C	Stop pin spring screw	6C-700	6C-700	6C-700	—
7	Drag washer mtl.	7-30	7-50	7-50	7-130
7A	Floating drag washer	7A-30	7A-50	7A-80	7A-130
13	Pinion gear	*13-30	13-50	13-80	13-130
14	Flat dog spring	14-50	14-50	14-50	14-130
15	Dog	15-50	15-50	15-50	15-130
16	Bridge screw	—	—	—	16-130
16H	Bridge screw hidden	—	—	—	16H-130
18	Disc clutch spring	18-30	18-50	18-80	18-130
19	Eccentric cam	19-30	19-50	19-80	19-130
21	Eccentric cam lever	21-30	21-50	21-80	21-130
22	Lever knob screw	22-50	22-50	22-50	22-130
23	Handle screw	23-114	23-114	23-116	23-116
24	Handle, complete	24-30	24-50	24-80	24-130
26	Right side bearing	26-30	26-50	26-80	26-130
27	Left side plate	*27-30	27-50	27-80	27-130
29M	Spool	*29M-30	29M-50	29M-80	29M-130
30	Reel stand	*30-30	30-50	30-80	30-130
31	Stand screw	31-30	31-50	31-80	31-130
33	Rod clamp	*33R-30	33R-50	33R-80	33R-130
34	Rod clamp screw	*34-30	34-50	34-80	34-130
35	Click tongue	35-50	35-50	35-80	35-130
36	Click button	36-50	36-50	36-50	36-130
37	Frame post	*37-30	37-50	37-80	37-130
37A	Spacing post	*37A-30	37A-50	37A-80	37A-130
38	Post screw	38-50	38-50	38-80	38-130
39	Bridge assm. screw	39-12	39-12	39-12	—
39	Special post screw	39-50	39-50	39-50	39-130
40	Left side bearing	40-50	40-50	40-50	40-130
41	Left side bearing spr.	41-50	41-50	41-50	41-130
51	Handle knob	—	—	—	51-130
54	Harness lug	54-50	54-50	54-80	54-130
54A	Rod brace lug	—	—	—	54A-130
54B	Dowel pin	—	—	—	54B-130
55	Spool bearing	55-30	55-50	55-80	55-130
56	Rod brace	—	—	—	56-130
59	Slotted washer	59-50	59-50	59-50	59-130
60	Backing washer	60-50	60-50	60-50	60-130
60A	Backing washer, outer	—	—	—	60A-130

Part No.	Description	#20-#30	#50	#80	#130
62	Click spring	62-50	62-50	62-50	62-130
69	Free spool stop	69-50	69-50	69-50	69-130
69A	Strike stop	69A-50	69A-50	69A-50	69A-130
69B	Snap ring	—	—	—	69B-130
81	Ratchet	81-50	81-50	81-80	81-130
83	Spacing collar	83-50	83-50	83-50	—
91	Handle screw	—	—	—	91-130
95	Click bushing	—	—	—	95-130
95A	Click bushing washer	—	—	—	95A-130
95B	Click bushing nut	—	—	—	95B-130
101	Drive plate screw	101-30	101-50	101-30	101-130
110	Handle lock screw	110-50	110-50	110-50	—
110A	Handle locking plate	110A-50	110A-50	110A-50	—
112	Eccentric knob	112-50	112-50	112-50	112-130
113	Eccentric knob cap	113-50	113-50	113-50	113-130
117	Drive plate, outer	117-30	117-50	117-80	117-130
117A	Drive plate, inner	—	—	—	117A-130
118	Main gear plate screw	118-50	118-50	118-50	—
119	Main gear plate	119-50	119-50	119-80	—
123	Drag cover screw	123-50	123-50	123-50	123-50
124	Bridge assm. cover	124-30	124-50	124-80	124-130
124A	Bridge cover, inner	—	—	—	124A-130
134	Gear shaft	134-50	134-50	134-80	—
134A	Spacing sleeve	—	—	—	134A-130
134B	Handle spacer	—	—	—	134B-130
135	Drag washer screw	135-30	135-50	—	—
138	Ratchet screw	138-30	138-50	138-80	138-50
141	Cam follower	141-30	141-50	141-80	141-130
142	Cam follower pin	142-50	142-50	142-50	142-130
143	Adjustable screw	143-30	143-50	143-80	143-130
144	Preset knob	144-50	144-50	144-50	144-130
144C	Preset pinion	—	—	—	144C-130
144D	Adjusting screw gear	—	—	—	144D-130
150	Quadrant center screw	150-50	150-50	150-80	150-80
156	Drag cover	156-30	156-50	156-80	156-130
157	Quadrant spacer bush.	157-50	157-50	157-50	157-130
161	Stop pin bushing	—	—	—	161-130
162	Stop pin spring	162-30	162-50	162-80	162-130
163	Leather spacer washer	163-50	163-50	163-50	163-50
187	Bridge dowel	—	—	—	187-130

For prices of parts, consult manufacturer.

6 Line Capacity of Modern Star- and Lever-Drag Reels

The following table gives type of drag, rated size, gear ratio, recommended line class, and line capacity in average Du Pont monofilament and standard Dacron line, for contemporary saltwater star- and lever-drag game-fishing reels manufactured by the companies previously mentioned. The increase of capacity of Dacron line over monofilament is conservatively rated at seven percent from industrial estimates.

Reels lacking "O" size ratings are not so designated by their manufacturers. In a few instances, missing "O" size ratings have been supplied for size comparison of popular models of smaller reels. (Note: A similar table of characteristics and line capacity — calculated in terms of modern synthetic lines — of early star- and lever-drag game-fishing reels appears in Chapter 29.)

Name/Model	Drag (star or lever)	Rated size	Gear ratio	Line class	Capacity (in yards and type of line)
EAGLE CLAW REELS					
544 HD	S	4/0	2.4:1	30#	400 mono
540 HD	S	3/0	2.4:1	30#	300 mono
524 HD	S	2/0	3:1	20#	400 mono
522 HD	S	1/0	3:1	20#	300 mono
EVEROL REELS					
Everol	L	2½/0	3.7:1	6#	2000 mono, 2150 Dacron
				12#	1000 mono, 1070 Dacron
				20#	600 mono, 640 Dacron
				30#	350 mono, 375 Dacron
Everol	L	4/0	3.7:1	12#	1600 mono, 1700 Dacron
				20#	1000 mono, 1070 Dacron
				30#	550 mono, 600 Dacron
				50#	300 mono, 325 Dacron
Everol	L	6/0	2.9:1	30#	1000 mono, 1070 Dacron
				50#	550 mono, 600 Dacron
				80#	300 mono, 325 Dacron

Name/Model	Drag (star or lever)	Rated size	Gear ratio	Line class	Capacity (in yards and type of line)
Everol	L	7½/0	2.9:1	50#	800 mono, 850 Dacron
				80#	450 mono, 480 Dacron
Everol	L	9/0	2.9:1	50#	1200 mono, 1300 Dacron
				80#	600 mono, 640 Dacron
				130#	450 mono, 480 Dacron
Everol	L	12/0	2.9:1	80#	1000 mono, 1070 Dacron
				130#	600 mono, 640 Dacron
Everol	L	14/0	2.9:0	130#	1000 mono, 1070 Dacron
DAIWA REELS					
Ventura 25	L	2½/0	3½:1	12#	1100 mono, 1200 Dacron
				20#	650 mono, 700 Dacron
				30#	400 mono, 425 Dacron
Ventura 40	L	4/0	3½:1	20#	750 mono, 800 Dacron
				30#	530 mono, 500 Dacron
				50#	300 mono, 315 Dacron
Ventura 60	L	6/0	3:1	30#	900 mono, 950 Dacron
				50#	575 mono, 600 Dacron
				80#	380 mono, 400 Dacron
GARCIA MITCHELL REELS					
Mitchell 1040	L	4/0	4:1	20#	900 mono, 1000 Dacron
				30#	560 mono, 600 Dacron
Mitchell 1060	L	6/0	4:1	30#	1070 mono, 1150 Dacron
				50#	670 mono, 720 Dacron
Mitchell 1090	L	9/0	3:1	50#	1280 mono, 1370 Dacron
				80#	800 mono, 850 Dacron
				130#	480 mono, 500 Dacron
Mitchell 624	S			30#	*425 Royal Bonnyl mono
Mitchell 622	S			30#	*300 Royal Bonnyl mono
Mitchell 600A	S			30#	*400 Royal Bonnyl mono
Ambassadeur 10000C	S		4¼:1 2½:1	30#	*475 Royal Bonnyl mono
Ambassadeur 9000	S		4¼:1 2½:1	30#	*374 Royal Bonnyl mono
Ambassadeur 7000	S		4:1	25#	*350 Royal Bonnyl mono

*Manufacturer's catalog rating and line description.

HEDDON REELS					
Model 409 level wind	S		3:1	20#	300 mono
Model 499 level wind	S		3:1	15#	250 mono
Model 445	S		3:1	20#	300 mono
Model 450	S		3:1	30#	200
Model 422	S		2.5:1	30#	300 mono
Model 421	S		3:1	30#	240 mono

Capacity of Modern Reels 57

Name/Model	Drag (star or lever)	Rated size	Gear ratio	Line class	Capacity (in yards and type of line)
PENN REELS					
International 20	L	2½/0	3½:1	12#	1200 IGFA class Dacron
				20#	700 IGFA class Dacron
International 30	L	4/0	3½:1	20#	800 IGFA class Dacron
				30#	600 IGFA class Dacron
International 50	L	6/0	3:1	50#	600 IGFA class Dacron
				80#	400 IGFA class Dacron
International 80	L	10/0	2.1:1	80#	750 IGFA class Dacron
				130#	550 IGFA class Dacron
International 130	L	12/0	1.6:1	130#	850 IGFA class Dacron
Senator 110	S	1/0		6#	900 mono (est.)
				12#	450 mono (est.)
				20#	275 mono, 300 Dacron
				30#	240 mono, 255 Dacron
Senator 111	S	2/0		12#	640 mono (est.)
				20#	400 mono, 430 Dacron
				30#	250 mono, 275 Dacron
Senator 112	S	3/0		20#	650 mono, 700 Dacron
				30#	400 mono, 430 Dacron
				50#	260 mono, 280 Dacron
Senator 113	S	4/0	2:1	20#	800 mono, 855 Dacron
				30#	500 mono, 535 Dacron
				50#	320 mono, 340 Dacron
				80#	140 mono, 150 Dacron
Senator 114	S	6/0	2.1:1	20#	1050 mono, 1225 Dacron
				30#	650 mono, 700 Dacron
				50#	415 mono, 445 Dacron
				80#	230 mono, 250 Dacron
Senator 115	S	9/0	2½:1	30#	1075 mono, 1150 Dacron
				50#	675 mono, 725 Dacron
				80#	380 mono, 400 Dacron
				130#	235 mono, 300 Dacron
Senator 116A	S	10/0	2:1	80#	675 mono, 725 Dacron
				130#	420 mono, 450 Dacron
Senator 116	S	12/0	2:1	80#	780 mono, 800 Dacron
				130#	480 mono, 550 Dacron
Senator 117	S	14/0	1.6:1	80#	1100 mono, 1175 Dacron
				130#	750 mono, 850 Dacron
Senator 118	S	16/0	1.6:1	130#	950 mono, 1000 Dacron
Senator 112H (high speed)	S	3/0	3.7:1	20#	650 mono, 700 Dacron
				30#	400 mono, 430 Dacron
				50#	260 mono, 300 Dacron
Senator 113H (high speed)	S	4/0	3¼:1	20#	800 mono, 855 Dacron
				30#	500 mono, 550 Dacron
				50#	320 mono, 350 Dacron
Senator 114H (high speed)	S	6/0	2.8:1	20#	1050 mono, 1225 Dacron
				30#	650 mono, 700 Dacron
				50#	415 mono, 500 Dacron
				80#	230 mono, 250 Dacron
Long Beach 66	S	3/0	2¼:1	20#	575 mono, 620 Dacron
				30#	360 mono, 385 Dacron
				50#	225 mono, 250 Dacron

58 MODERN SALTWATER FISHING TACKLE

Name/Model	Drag (star or lever)	Rated size	Gear ratio	Line class	Capacity (in yards and type of line)
Long Beach 67	S	4/0	2½:1	20#	770 mono, 800 Dacron
				30#	480 mono, 500 Dacron
				50#	300 mono, 325 Dacron
Long Beach 68	S	6/0	2½:1	20#	1000 mono, 1100 Dacron
				30#	640 mono, 680 Dacron
				50#	400 mono, 430 Dacron
Jigmaster 500	S		4:1	20#	350 mono, 375 Dacron
				30#	220 mono, 240 Dacron
Jigmaster 500M	S		4:1	20#	400 mono, 425 Dacron
				30#	240 mono, 250 Dacron
Master Mariner 349, 349H, 349HC	S		3¼:1	30#	325 mono, 350 Dacron
Super Mariner	S		3½:1	30#	235 mono, 250 Dacron
Super Mariner 49M, 149M, 349 349H, 349HC	S		3½:1	30#	325 mono, 350 Dacron
				50#	175 mono, 200 Dacron
Leveline 350	S		3:1	36#	175 casting nylon
Leveline 350M	S		3:1	36#	225 casting nylon
Super Peer 309M	S		3:1	30#	275 mono, 300 Dacron
Peerless 9 level wind	S		3:1	15#	225 mono, plastic spool
				15#	275 mono, metal spool
Peer 109 level wind	S		3¾:1	15#	225 mono, plastic spool
				15#	275 mono, metal spool
Peer Sr. Monofil 209S, F, MS, MF	S		3:1	20#	300 mono, plastic spool
				20#	350 mono, metal spool
Squidder 140 140M	S		3⅓:1	20#	325 mono, plastic spool
				20#	400 mono, metal spool
Squidder 145 145M	S		3⅓:1	20#	275 mono, plastic spool
				20#	325 mono, metal spool
Squidder 146 146M	S		3⅓:1	12#	250 mono, plastic spool
				12#	325 mono, metal spool
Surfmaster 100 100M	S		3:1	30#	125 Dacron, plastic spool
				30#	150 Dacron, metal spool
Surfmaster 150 150M	S		3:1	30#	150 Dacron, plastic spool
				30#	200 Dacron, metal spool
Surfmaster 200 200M	S		3:1	30#	175 Dacron, plastic spool
				30#	225 Dacron, metal spool
Surfmaster 250 250M	S		3:1	30#	250 Dacron, plastic spool
				30#	300 Dacron, metal spool
Silver Beach 99	S		3:1	30#	275 mono, 300 Dacron
Baymaster 180S 180MS	S		2.3:1	20#	200 nylon, plastic spool
				20#	250 nylon, metal spool
Beachmaster 155 155M	S		2.3:1	30#	175 Dacron, plastic spool
				30#	225 Dacron, metal spool
Beachmaster 160 160M	S		2.3:1	30#	150 Dacron, plastic spool
				30#	200 Dacron, metal spool
Delmar 285 285M	S		2.3:1	36#	200 nylon, plastic spool
				36#	250 nylon, metal spool
Sea Boy 85	S		2.3:1	36#	200 nylon
Sea Mate 79				36#	200 nylon
Sea Scamp 78				36#	150 nylon
Sea Hawk 77				36#	125 nylon

Capacity of Modern Reels

Name/Model	Drag (star or lever)	Rated size	Gear ratio	Line class	Capacity (in yards and type of line)
REEL-KING REELS					
Reel-King 20/30	L	4/0	3:1	20#	750 mono, 800 Dacron
				30#	560 mono, 600 Dacron
Reel-King 50	L	6/0	3:1	30#	1000 mono, 1070 Dacron
				50#	650 mono, 700 Dacron
				80#	400 mono, 430 Dacron
Reel-King 80	L	12/0	2.8:1	80#	1070 mono, 1000 Dacron
				130#	660 mono, 700 Dacron
SHAKESPEARE REELS					
1961	S		4:1	6#	1200 mono, 1300 Dacron
				12#	600 mono, 640 Dacron
				20#	375 mono, 400 Dacron
				30#	200 mono, 215 Dacron
1960 Levelwind	S		4:1	6#	1200 mono, 1300 Dacron
				12#	600 mono, 640 Dacron
				20#	375 mono, 400 Dacron
				30#	200 mono, 215 Dacron
ST. CROIX REELS					
Compac 7000	S		2.4:1	36#	300 nylon
Compac 6000	S		2.4:1	30#	350 mono, 375 Dacron
Compac 5000	S		2.3:1	30#	250 mono, 270 Dacron
Compac 3000	S		3:1	30#	300 mono, 325 Dacron
Compac 2000	S		3:1	25#	250 mono, 270 Dacron
Compac 1000	S		3:1	12#	300 mono, 325 Dacron
TRUE TEMPER REELS					
Ocean City 603	S	3/0	3¼:1	20#	600 mono, 640 Dacron
				30#	400 mono, 430 Dacron
				50#	275 mono, 300 Dacron
Ocean City 604	S	4/0	2:1	20#	850 mono, 900 Dacron
				30#	600 mono, 640 Dacron
				50#	400 mono, 430 Dacron
Ocean City 651	S	5/0	3.2:1	20#	900 mono, 960 Dacron
				30#	650 mono, 700 Dacron
				50#	450 mono, 430 Dacron
Ocean City 6061	S	6/0	2.75:1	30#	925 mono, 1000 Dacron
				50#	625 mono, 670 Dacron
				80#	350 mono, 375 Dacron
Ocean City 609	S	9/0	2:1	50#	950 mono, 900 Dacron
				80#	525 mono, 560 Dacron
				130#	315 mono, 325 Dacron
Ocean City 612	S	12/0	2:1	80#	975 mono, 1040 Dacron
				130#	550 mono, 590 Dacron
True Temper 112	S		2¼:1	20#	400 mono, 430 Dacron
True Temper 113	S		2¼:1	20#	450 mono, 480 Dacron
True Temper 981	S		3:1	20#	250 mono, 270 Dacron
True Temper 905M	S		4:1	20#	300 mono, 320 Dacron

TYCOON/FIN-NOR REELS

Name/Model	Drag (star or lever)	Rated size	Gear ratio	Line class	Capacity (in yards and type of line)
Fin-Nor	L	2½/0	4:1	6#	4460 mono, 4800 Dacron
				12#	2230 mono, 2400 Dacron
				20#	790 mono, 850 Dacron
Fin-Nor	L	4/0	4:1	20#	1100 mono, 1280 Dacron
				30#	750 mono, 800 Dacron
				50#	460 mono, 500 Dacron
Fin-Nor	L	6/0	3:1	30#	930 mono, 1000 Dacron
				50#	600 mono, 650 Dacron
				80#	375 mono, 400 Dacron
Fin-Nor	L	7½/0	3:1	50#	1070 mono, 1000 Dacron
				80#	560 mono, 600 Dacron
Fin-Nor	L	9/0	2.75:1	80#	745 mono, 800 Dacron
				130#	450 mono, 480 Dacron
Fin-Nor Standard (two-speed)	L	12/0	2:1 / 1:1	130#	790 mono, 850 Dacron
Fin-Nor Special (two-speed)	L	12/0	3:1 / 2:1	130#	790 mono, 850 Dacron
Golden Regal 20	L	2/0		6#	1850 mono, 2000 Dacron
				12#	930 mono, 1000 Dacron
				20#	560 mono, 600 Dacron
Golden Regal 30	L	4/0		20#	1200 mono, 1280 Dacron
				30#	745 mono, 800 Dacron
Golden Regal 50	L	6/0		30#	890 mono, 960 Dacron
				50#	560 mono, 600 Dacron
				80#	335 mono, 360 Dacron

7 Light-Tackle Reels

BAIT-CASTING REELS

To many anglers, the bait-casting reel is primarily a freshwater item, but in recent years the versatility and light weight of this excellent small star-drag reel has recommended it to saltwater fishermen who need a reel with the bait-casting reel's special qualities.

The original freshwater bait-casting reels were perfected for casting small live baits like minnows and, later, small wooden plugs. They were among the earliest reels to have a multiplying gear drive, and therefore they can be considered direct ancestors of the modern saltwater game-fishing reel. The star drag was added during the first and second decades of the present century.

Two more refinements brought the bait-casting reel up to its present state of perfection. One was the addition of a level-wind mechanism that spreads the line evenly across the face of the reel spool as it is wound in. The other was some sort of antibacklash device to prevent overrun of the spool in casting. Both are incorporated in one form or another in most bait-casting reels designed for or adaptable to saltwater use.

As with a number of other types of reels, the bait-casting reel usually is used with a rod specially designed for this type of casting. The bait-casting rod is fairly short, sometimes rather stiff, and is usually a one-handed rod with a characteristic offset handle and reelseat. Rod and reel combinations are divided into four major classes by their ability to handle baits or lures of varying weights.

Extra light: Rod, reel, and line matched to lures of less than 3/8 ounce. Rods range between six and 6½ feet in length, with a taper designed to handle such light lures. The level-wind reel may be a simple free-spool model or have a star drag; it is filled with line in the four- to eight-pound-test range. One analyst defines the extra-light bait-casting outfit as one engineered to achieve full rod deflection with casting lures weighing between 60 grains (1/8 ounce) and 140 grains (a little more than ¼ ounce).

Light: This class of bait-casting outfit is designed to cast lures weighing between 120 grains (¼ ounce) and 240 grains (½ ounce), while employing lines in the six- to 12-pound-test range. Both the extra-light and light classes are primarily freshwater equipment, although the light class is sometimes used for small-to-medium snook, baby tarpon, and small bonefish, wherever these fish are found.

Medium: Designed to handle lures ranging from 300 grains (5/8 ounce) to 360 grains (3/4 ounce), with lines of 10- to 20-pound test. Rod length may vary from four to 6½ feet, depending on the type of casting action and holding power desired. Used on fresh water for pike, big bass, muskies, and lake trout, and on salt water for school stripers, bluefish,

Vic Dunaway is understandably pleased with a fat redfish (channel bass) taken on a popping plug cast with a saltwater bait-casting reel.

medium-to-large snook, medium tarpon, large bonefish, and similar species.

Heavy: Designed for saltwater use and for the largest freshwater game fish, this class handles lures ranging from 360 grains (3/4 ounce) up to 600 grains (1¼ ounces). Rod lengths vary from 4½ to 7½ feet, with the generally preferred length about 5½ feet. Reels are designed to hold 200 to 300 yards of 20- to 30-pound-test line, and they are equipped with a star drag and a level-wind mechanism. Bait-casting tackle can be used for light trolling when necessary.

The varying lengths of bait-casting rods reflect the need to provide tackle that can deliver lures under very different casting conditions. A short, stiff rod, for example, is preferred where a flat lure trajectory is required for placing the lure under low-hanging branches. A longer rod gives a higher trajectory and is more accurate for pinpointing lures to small targets at greater casting distances.

The bait-casting tackle approach to saltwater fishing is quite popular with anglers who are used to freshwater tackle and who want to try saltwater fishing without having to switch to unfamiliar tackle. While this book is not organized to deal with casting techniques, it should be said that bait casting is no mystery, and it is easily mastered by any dextrous angler. The tackle is especially useful for fishing from small boats in relatively tight quarters for game fish that respond to artificial casting lures.

Recommendations covering bait-casting tackle for specific types of saltwater fishing will be found in the chapters on selecting tackle for various types of fishing.

SPINNING REELS

While reels employing the fixed-spool casting system were in use in Great Britain and Europe in the nineteenth century, the spinning reel in its modern form did not become popular in the United States until after World War II. The spinning reel is essentially a casting reel, and only secondarily a trolling or bottom-fishing instrument. In recent years, some saltwater tournament fishermen have used spinning tackle for bait and lure trolling with outriggers, but the majority of light-tackle competitive anglers prefer properly designed trolling tackle for this kind of work.

Spinning tackle's great popularity came when anglers discovered that it allowed a casting technique that did not require years of concentrated effort to perfect. Now we have spinning rod and reel combinations capable of handling the most delicate of lures and lines, and other combinations that can cast a half-pound plug or jig a country mile. For the sake of convenience, spinning tackle in general can be divided into three major categories.

Light: Reels (with rods to match) that are designed to work with lines of eight-pound test or less. Weight of the reel is usually 10 to 12 ounces. Line capacity averages 175 to 200 yards of eight-pound monofilament line. Gear ratios of 3.7:1 to 4.5:1 are common, with special high-speed models offering ratios as high as

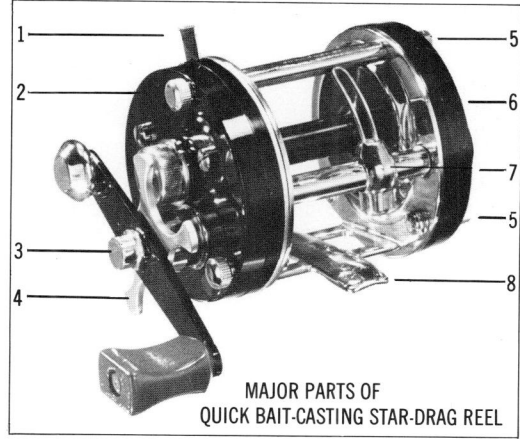

MAJOR PARTS OF
QUICK BAIT-CASTING STAR-DRAG REEL

1 *Free-spool button*
2 *Right-side plate*
3 *Handle assembly*
4 *Star-drag adjustment wheel*
5 *Takedown screws (both sides)*
6 *Left-side plate*
7 *Level-wind mechanism*
8 *Reel stand*

6.6:1 for very fast retrieve. Often used with one-handed rods.

Medium: Reels with a weight of 12 to 18 ounces and line capacity of around 400 yards of 15-pound-test monofilament. Available in standard retrieve (3.5:1 to 4.5:1 gear ratio) and fast retrieve (over 4.5:1 gear ratio). Used with light, two-handed boat and surf spinning rods.

Heavy: Reels with a weight range of 18 to 24 ounces and line capacity of 450 to 500 yards of 20-pound-test monofilament. Available in multidisc drag and various gear ratios, although very high gear ratios are not usually used with spinning reels of this caliber. Designed primarily for use with the heaviest surf spinning rods and special competition game-fish spinning-trolling rods. The latter usually are custom-built to the angler's specifications.

Very early spinning reels had a revolving, roller-equipped arm that guided the incoming line onto the spool. This was known as a manual-pickup arm, because, after casting, the angler had to pick up the loose line with one finger and guide it onto the roller of the revolving arm. Interestingly, some surf experts are reverting to the manual pickup with modern reels, citing special casting advantages. With no pickup bail, for instance, there is no metal hoop to snap down accidentally during a cast and spoil the cast.

Later on in the evolution of the spinning reel, the open or cowhorn bail became popular. I still have a Luxor spinning reel, made in France in the 1940s, that gives excellent service with an open cowhorn bail. The modern closed bail, however, is generally more satisfactory,

On a shallow Bahamian flat, Don McCarthy uses a light spinning outfit to cast shrimp to a small school of bonefish.

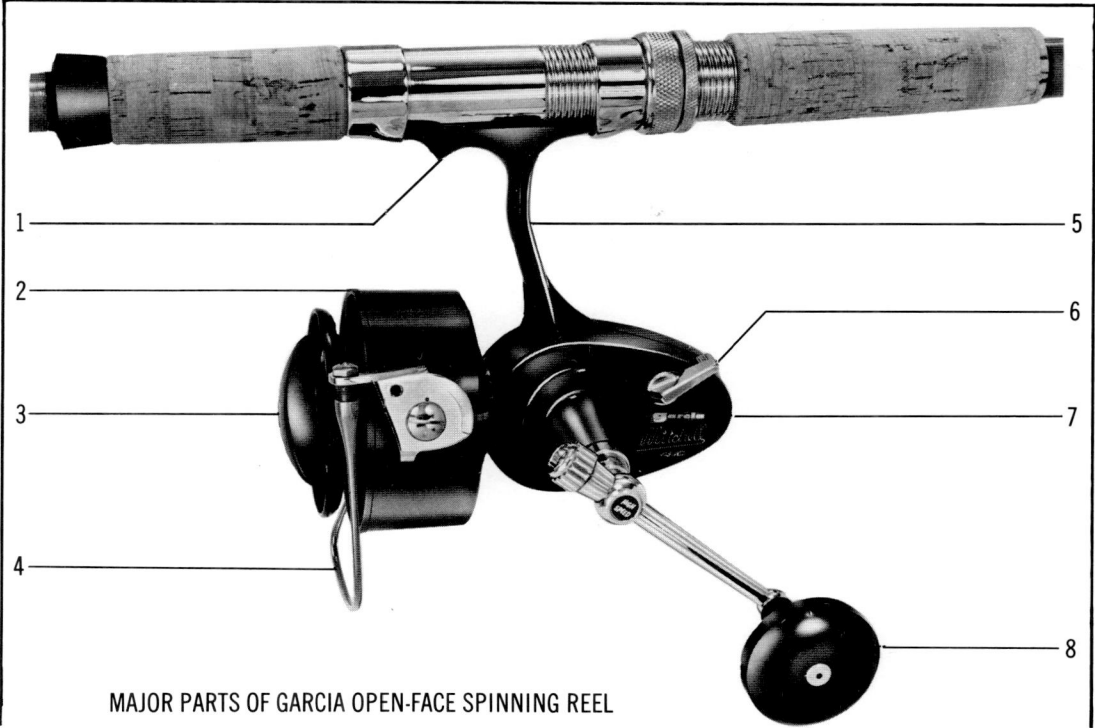

MAJOR PARTS OF GARCIA OPEN-FACE SPINNING REEL

1 Finger grip
2 Reel skirt
3 Drag-adjustment knob
4 Line-pickup bail
5 Reel stem
6 Free-spool lever
7 Gear housing
8 Handle assembly

especially with anglers who do not consider themselves to be casting experts.

All modern spinning reels are equipped with a friction clutch or drag that enables the fish to take out line under adjustable tension. The drag usually is a fairly simple arrangement of a spring-loaded clutch mounted coaxially with the front end of the spool. The spool is fixed when it comes to casting, but it can rotate about the central shaft, and it does so whenever the external pull on the line becomes greater than the friction setting of the drag. Drag adjustment is made by means of a winged or knurled knob at the front end of the spool.

In light models, the friction washer is often a disc of oiled felt. In heavy-duty models, however, other disc materials are employed to deal with the friction heat that develops naturally. Teflon washers are available for some models, and they generally have given smooth, satisfactory service under continued heavy fishing pressure.

The drive handle is mounted on the left side of most spinning reels, although left-right drive models are available. The handle turns a main gear that, in turn, turns a worm gear that gives rotary motion to the bail. At the same time, an eccentric arm on the main gear imparts a reciprocating action to the spool body, which, in combination with the revolving bail, lays the line evenly onto the spool.

At least one manufacturer mounts the drag and its control knob at the rear of the reel, rather than toward the front. This means the angler does not have to reach in front of the reel to adjust the drag and possibly sustain a line cut on his hand or fingers if a hooked fish makes a sudden, hard run.

All spinning reels are adaptable to

salt water, but some are more suitable than others. Suitability is not so much a function of design as it is of materials that resist salt corrosion, and of line capacity. Because of the great overlap of salt- and freshwater suitability, and the great and constantly changing number of models available, it is not practical to try to list here all models designed for or adaptable to saltwater use.

Specific recommendations are made, however, where they fit into combinations of tackle mentioned in the chapters on selecting tackle for saltwater fishing. Of all reels used by saltwater fishermen for casting, spinning reels are probably the most generally versatile and the most capable of absorbing abuse. Skilled anglers agree, however, that while spinning tackle has a multitude of general uses, and a number of specific uses for which it is best, it does not replace other forms of tackle that are designed to do special jobs.

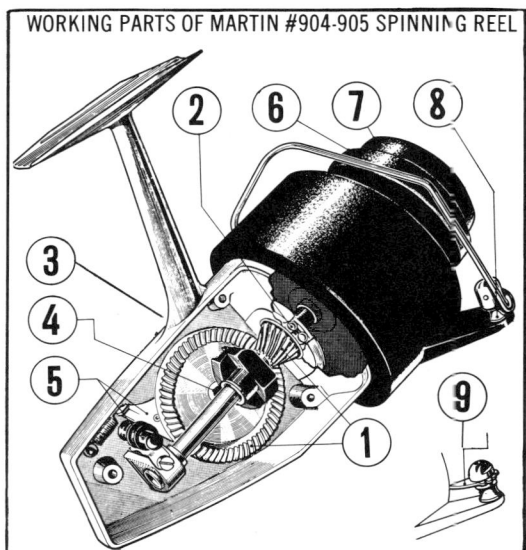

WORKING PARTS OF MARTIN #904-905 SPINNING REEL

1 Machine-cut hypoid gears
2 Precision ball bearings
3 Folding handle (behind)
4 Stainless-steel main shaft
5 On-off antireverse
6 One-piece metal insert spool
7 Multiple-disc drag
8 Carbide line roller
9 Manual pickup (#905)

SALTWATER FLY REELS

Not long ago, the idea of using a fly-fishing outfit on salt water appeared to be about as contradictory as trying to use snowshoes to go water skiing, but now saltwater fly fishing is one of the most exciting and fastest growing phases of the sport-fishing picture.

What is the appeal of this sometimes difficult, often unproductive method of fishing? It can probably be explained as offering to the really experienced saltwater angler a fresh and very demanding test of his perception and personal fishing skill. To the confirmed freshwater fisherman, it seems to offer a way for him to wet his feet in the salt while adhering to a style of fishing with which he is familiar.

Snob appeal definitely does have some influence here, but the growing success of saltwater fly fishing is not built on snob appeal alone. One large factor is the fact that modern teaching methods have taken much of the mystery and hocus-pocus out of learning to cast with the long rod. Another is the fact that modern fly-casting equipment, designed for saltwater conditions, gives both neophyte and expert a much better chance of success with the fish.

As some writers about freshwater fishing are apt to explain, the fly reel in many freshwater contexts is nothing more than a device in which to store extra line. Most light freshwater fly reels do not have a drag, in the clutch-brake sense. A button-click is sufficient. Very often the angler hooks, plays, and takes his trout or bass without ever resorting to using the reel to take in line.

In saltwater fishing, things usually are different. The fish, generally speaking, are much larger and more powerful than those usually sought in fresh water, and they are found in much broader, deeper waters. This is not stated as a put-down of freshwater fly fishing. Rather, it is intended merely to spell out the facts.

The late, great Joe Brooks focused attention on saltwater fly fishing when he captured, in 1947, a 29-pound, 6-ounce, striped bass at Coos Bay, Oregon, using a 12-pound-test tippet. Since then, scores of heavier game fish have been added to the list of fly-rod-caught saltwater game, including several species of billfish, tuna, shark, and even a mighty 356-pound Florida Keys jewfish.

Captures of large, powerful fish like these with the fly rod have been made possible by reels that combine the appearance and basic function of the original fly reel with the line-holding capacity and drag-applying ability of small saltwater game-fishing reels. Because saltwater records are recognized within tippet-test breaking strains not exceeding 15 pounds, the drag of a good saltwater fly reel does not have to cope with the heavy line tensions that some small trolling and casting reels must overcome. This simplifies design and construction to some degree.

Most saltwater fly reels are single-action, meaning that they are not geared. A few have gear ratios of about 2:1. A higher gear ratio hardly seems worthwhile, because line retrieve usually is accomplished by stripping in the line by hand, and because the amount of line tension that can be applied is limited by the tippet class being used.

As was explained earlier, there is a direct relationship between the weight class of the fly line and the designed power of the rod. Reel size has little to do with rod or line size, except that the reel must be large enough to store 90 to 120 feet of fly line of the proper weight class, plus at least 200 yards of suitable backing line. In most cases, backing is standardized at 20-pound-test Dacron line.

The most vital consideration in a saltwater fly reel, aside from proper size, is a silk-smooth drag, one that will retain both smooth action and holding power during what may be a prolonged battle with a large fish. Many large freshwater fly reels have a drag device of some sort, plus good line capacity. Not all of these have an antibackup device that prevents the reel handle from revolving as the fish takes out line against drag tension. Most

Two sizes of Seamaster saltwater fly reels equipped with powerful drags and specially built for the abuse of saltwater fly fishing.

Arthur Jansik was 17 when he caught this 91½-lb. tarpon on a Fenwick fly rod with Fin-Nor fly reel and Air-Cel line at Flamingo in the Everglades National Park.

Stu Apte fights a 154¼-lb. tarpon on 12-lb. tippet off Loggerhead Key. This is the kind of tension a big tarpon can put on fly tackle.

saltwater fly reels do have the antibackup dog or pall, a great knuckle saver when you hook a big tarpon or a leaping sailfish.

The accompanying table lists the important characteristics of a number of popular saltwater fly reels. The term *lever drag* does not refer to the type of lever drag found on larger game-fishing reels; it designates an internal drag operated by an external lever. *Screw drag* indicates an internal drag operated by an external screw. *Manual drag* indicates an external manual pressure drag. Capacities are approximate and may vary somewhat from those quoted here, depending on type and manufacture of fly line, type of backing, etc. NR means nonreversing control; reels without NR in the drag column are those in which the line spool is not equipped with an antireverse feature. Backing-line yardages are in terms of 20-pound quality Dacron trolling line.

POPULAR SALTWATER FLY REELS

Name/Model	Gear	Drag	Weight class and backing line
BOGDAN REELS			
Small	2:1	lever, NR	W9 + 200 yds.
Medium	2:1	lever, NR	W10 + 200 yds.
Large	2:1	lever, NR	W11 + 200 yds.
EAGLE CLAW REELS			
EC3B	direct	star	W9 + 200 yds.
FIN-NOR REELS			
#2	direct	star, NR	W9 + 150 yds.
#3	direct	star, NR	W10 + 250 yds.
GARCIA REELS			
Mitchell 754	direct	star	W9 + 50 yds.
Mitchell 758	direct	star	W9 + 150 yds.
HARDY REELS			
St. Aidan	direct	lever	W9 + 200 yds.
St. Aidan	1.67:1	lever	W9 + 200 yds.
Zenith	direct	lever	W10 + 200 yds.
Zenith	1.67:1	lever	W10 + 200 yds.
Husky	direct	lever	W10 + 200 yds.
Husky	1.67:1	lever	W10 + 200 yds.
LEONARD REELS			
TBS 312	direct	star, NR	W11 + 250 yds.
MARTIN REELS	3:1	disc, NR	W9 + 125 yds.
McCHRISTIAN REELS			
SeaMaster	direct	star, NR	W11 + 300 yds.
Marlin	direct	star, NR	W12 + 300 yds.
ORVIS REELS			
C.F.O. IV	direct	lever	W8 + 50 yds.
C.F.O. V	direct	lever	W10 + 150 yds.
Magnalite	2:1	lever	W8 + 50 yds.
Magnalite Wide	2:1	lever	W9 + 175 yds.
Orvis Salt Water	direct	star, NR	W9 + 250 yds.
PFLUEGER REELS			
Medalist 1498	direct	screw	W10 + 250 yds.
Supreme 577	direct	star, NR	W9 + 275 yds.
Supreme 578	direct	star, NR	W11 + 300 yds.
SCIENTIFIC ANGLERS REELS			
System 9	direct	manual	W9 + 200 yds.
System 10	direct	manual	W10 + 200 yds.
System 11	direct	manual	W11 + 200 yds.

70 MODERN SALTWATER FISHING TACKLE

Name/Model	Gear	Drag	Weight class and backing line
SHAKESPEARE REELS			
Purist 7594	direct	screw	W7 + 50 yds.
Purist 7595	direct	screw	W8 + 75 yds.
Purist 7596	direct	screw	W10 + 100 yds.
Purist 7597	direct	screw	W12 + 200 yds.
Purist 1898 HD	direct	lever, NR	W11 + 200 yds.
ST. CROIX REELS			
Salmon Reel #47	direct	screw	W11 + 200 yds.
VALENTINE REELS			
Model 375	direct	star, NR	W10 + 250 yds.

OTHER TYPES OF REELS

Closed-face, spin-casting reels

These small, fixed-spool reels look and act like spinning reels with the spool enclosed by a round metal can or shroud. Actually, they are quite different from what we normally call spinning reels, in that the line pickup is an internal disc or spider, and the drag often is a star-drag mechanism coaxial with the drive shaft, which is usually right-handed rather than left-handed. Furthermore, the spin-casting reel sits on top of the shaft, like a conventional revolving-spool reel, not under the shaft, as does a true spinning reel.

Spin-casting reels are a sort of cross between spinning and bait-casting reels, hence their peculiar name. Line release is accomplished by means of a thumb pad, and the reels are used almost exclusively with bait-casting rods. They sometimes are seen in use on salt water, but they are prone to corrosion inside the reel shroud. They are not normally considered adaptable to serious saltwater fishing.

Scarborough and Alvey reels

While these large reels are really a throwback to the very early days of spinning-reel design, they continue to be quite popular in Australia, South Africa, and among some American West Coast surf fishermen. Basically, the Scarborough and Alvey reels are movable-spool spinning reels. They are used direct drive, without any sort of internal gear mechanism. The large spool is held by a strong metal yoke in such a way that the reel can be swiveled broadside to the casting direction, so the line will spin off when cast. Then the reel is turned back

MAJOR PARTS OF JOHNSON MODEL 160 SPIN-CASTING REEL

1 *Fixed-spool housing*
2 *Handle assembly*
3 *Star-drag adjustment*
4 *Casting line-release thumb button*
5 *Gear case*
6 *Reel stand*

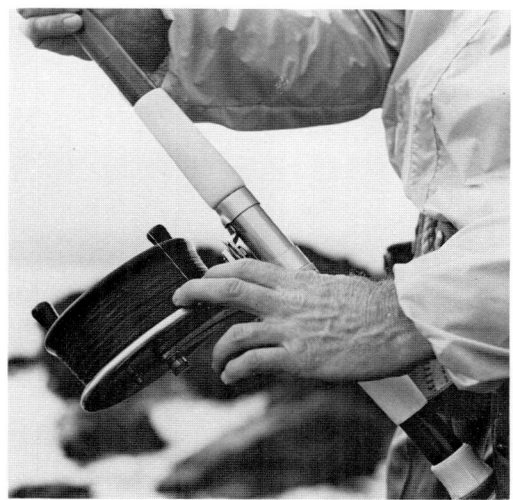

with the reel axis at 90° to the rod shaft, so the line can be brought in by turning the reel.

Because they are heavy, these reels normally are under the rod shaft. Surprisingly heavy line can be cast to great distances with these reels. Some are drag-equipped. Others are innocent of any brake or drag, other than the angler's horny palm pressed against the reel's rim to slow the run of a powerful fish. To be used effectively, they all require strength and skill, but fishermen who have learned how to handle them swear by them for long-range surf casting, inshore fishing for rays and sharks, and general indestructibility under difficult fishing conditions.

Left: *The Alvey reel, like the Scarborough, is turned with its axis parallel to the rod for casting. Some of these reels have drags.* **Right:** *South Africans favor the simple, rugged Scarborough reel for fishing for everything from small snook and tailors to giant sharks.* **Bottom:** *New Zealand anglers fish the surf with small versions of Scarborough, Alvey, and similar reels. Americans on the West Coast are discovering the effectiveness of these reels.*

Tense and alert, Canadian Jean Beliveau waits out the first wild run of a freshly hooked bluefin tuna as the line connecting him to the fish streams from the spool of the 12/0 Everol reel.

8 Monofilament Lines

Even though linen line no longer is used by the majority of sport fishermen, it did have three distinct advantages over the many types of cotton line with which it competed for many years. First, linen fibers are much longer than cotton fibers. This means that linen thread under tension resists pulling apart better than cotton. Long fibers do not separate as readily as short fibers.

The second advantage is that when both are wet, linen increases its strength at a faster rate than cotton. The "wet test" for breaking strain was the standard test for linen line for many years. Third, linen generally is more durable than cotton, more able to withstand friction under heavy strain, especially when it is wet.

Looking back, we can also say that linen lines had certain advantages over modern synthetic lines. Linen's stretch is negligible, it has high knot strength, it can be spliced as easily as rope, and, unlike some synthetics, it becomes stronger rather than weaker when it is wet. Its low degree of stretch gives linen a type of sensitivity that is not surpassed by the best modern Dacron lines. You can tie a loop in the end of a linen line using a plain overhand knot and expect it to hold nearly 80 percent of the line's unknotted strength.

It is easy to splice a loop or double line in linen. You unlay the three strands for a few inches, thread each strand into the eye of a small darning needle, and then short-splice the loop or double line just as you would rope. A four-tuck splice, waxed and whipped with dental floss, is as strong as the unknotted line.

But linen has a number of important disadvantages. Its penchant for rotting when stored wet, and the ease with which it can be damaged by under- or over-twisting, were mentioned earlier. Another disadvantage is its larger diameter for the same pounds-test. Still another is its greater water friction. The last two disadvantages combine to the detriment of deep trolling. A four-ounce sinker will carry a Dacron or nylon monofilament line considerably deeper than a linen line of the same test.

Linen line was, and occasionally still is, manufactured by twisting together or "laying up" three strands of twisted linen thread. The strands, in turn, are twisted from individual threads of 50-leas standard composition. Each thread has a nominal wet-test breaking strain of three pounds. Thus, a nine-thread line is composed of three strands of three threads each and has a rated breaking wet test of about 27 pounds.

The table on the next page gives the ratings of previously manufactured linen lines and their present IGFA weight test counterparts in synthetic lines.

The big switch from natural to synthetic lines was bound to happen. World demand for fibers for fabrics and thread was increasing at an exponential rate shortly after World War II, while acreage for growing flax was diminishing.

Linen line was produced by a number of small firms with the experience and equipment to handle this rather special natural fiber.

Nylon, the first of the synthetics, was originally manufactured by just a few huge concerns with the capability for handling vast volumes of petrochemicals. As time went on, the synthetic-fiber manufacturing technique was licensed to scores of smaller companies throughout the world. Now synthetic fibers are produced by manufacturers in a broad spectrum of industry.

Linen line disappeared rapidly from use and manufacture between 1950 and 1960. Once they became adjusted to the switch to synthetic lines, most fishermen breathed a sigh of relief.

Threads	Linen test	IGFA line class
		6 lb.
*3	9 lb.	12 lb.
*6	18 lb.	20 lb.
*9	27 lb.	30 lb.
*12	36 lb.	
*15	45 lb.	50 lb.
18	54 lb.	
21	63 lb.	
*24	72 lb.	80 lb.
27	81 lb.	
30	90 lb.	
33	99 lb.	
36	108 lb.	
*39	117 lb.	130 lb.
*54	162 lb.	**180 lb.
72	216 lb.	

*These formerly were commonly used linen lines.
**Early IGFA records included 180-pound class line. Present records recognize, but do not post, records taken on lines of more than 130 pounds, but under 180 pounds.

NYLON MONOFILAMENT

The word *nylon*, originally a trade name of the Du Pont Corporation, was used to describe a long-chain synthetic polymeric amide, with recurring amide groups as a part of the main polymer chain. Common usage has reduced *nylon* as a word to the level of a household term. This class of polymers exhibits the ability to be drawn into filaments with the molecular structural elements oriented in the direction of the filament's axis.

There are many different types of nylon, each with its own characteristics. One universal advantage of this synthetic is that the characteristics of a given type or style of nylon remain very similar. This means that a fisherman can select a type of line that meets his requirements and rest assured that performance will remain practically the same when he has to buy new line in the future. But it also means that any attempt to classify nylon in specific terms is limited by many qualifications. The size-strength tables and graphs in this chapter, for example, were prepared from published data describing a mythical "average" nylon monofilament, and differences between these tables and actual tests of specific types of monofilament may be as much as 20 percent in some cases. The tables serve as a guide that shows the overall relationship of monofilament size to strength. Readers should consult manufacturers' data on the diameter and strength test of specific lines.

Monofilament is manufactured by placing a batch of granules of the basic raw petrochemical resin in a closed, heated container, from which it is extruded as fine filaments that solidify on contact with a bath of water. Each filament is then drawn over a series of rollers and through a series of heat-tempering ovens. Each set of rollers revolves faster than the set behind it, stretching the monofilament and reducing its thickness. This combination of stretching and heat tempering, plus the basic chemical makeup of the original resin batch, governs the characteristics of the finished product.

Nylon averages between 70,000 and 100,000 pounds per square inch tensile strength and has a specific gravity of 1.08 to 1.15. Monofilament will stretch 15 to 30 percent when dry before breaking, and 20 to 35 percent when wet. It is described as

Monofilament Lines 75

HOW MONOFILAMENT IS EXTRUDED, STRETCHED, AND TEMPERED

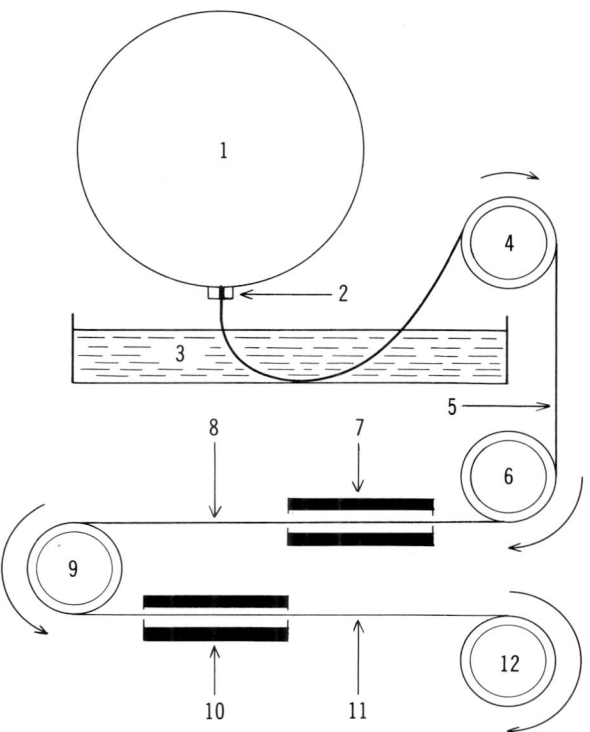

1 Heat liquid resin
2 Extrusion die
3 Cooling water bath
4 Pickup drum
5 First stretch region
6 First tension drum
7 Heater
8 Second stretch region
9 Second tension drum
10 Heater
11 Final stretch, cooling, and tempering region
12 Storage drum

Each drum rotates faster than the one before, stretching the monofilament by a carefully calculated amount. The arrows around the drums indicate the direction of rotation and the relative increase of rotational speed. Sensitive temperature and heat sensors monitor every phase of the operation.

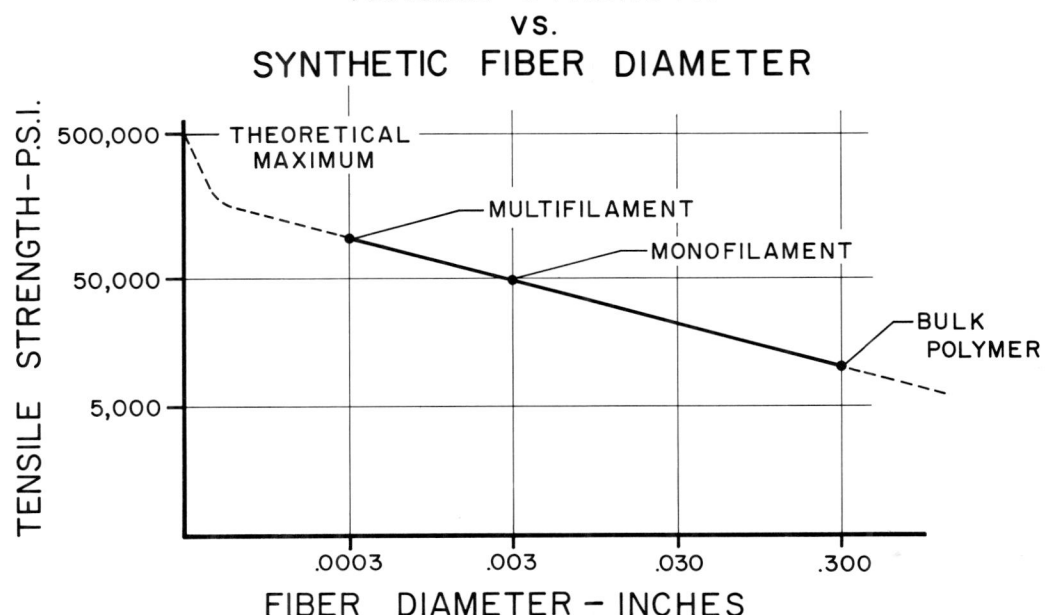

Developed by Berkley & Co., this diagram illustrates how the tensile strength of synthetic fibers increases with reduction of diameter. Horizontal and vertical scales are logarithmic rather than linear.

waterproof, but it will absorb three to 12 percent of its weight of water, depending on type. It shows a tendency to lose up to 10 percent of its strength when wet.

One odd characteristic of nylon monofilament is that thinner filaments are stronger than thicker ones, even those from the same original batch of resin. Engineers explain that when the hot liquid nylon is extruded, stretched, and heat-tempered, the molecules of polymer close to the surface tend to orient themselves along the axis of the line. This is more evident just under the surface than in the interior of the line. Thus, a thin filament contains more "aligned" molecules than a thick one, in comparison to the cross-sectional area of the filament. (Increase of surface is at the square of increased diameter, while increase of volume is at the cube.)

This explains why some larger monofilaments of the same batch or type of nylon do not test quite as strong as one might expect if one were to apply the logical rule that a monofilament with twice the diameter (and therefore four times the cross-sectional area) would test four times as strong as the original filament. Fortunately, manufacturers know this, and, in preparing batches of line to test no lower than a given rating, or no higher than a recognized line-class test, they select extrusion dies with diameters that produce lines of predictable test ratings.

Monofilament was quickly recognized as superior to linen and other twisted or braided lines for use with spinning reels. Advances in quality of monofilament and spinning reels seem to have progressed hand in hand. Mono is highly popular for bait and bottom fishing, and for trolling and casting in tackle classes up to about 30-pound-line test. Over 30-pound test, however, lines of braided Dacron are favored.

Nylon monofilament comes in many degrees of stretch and stiffness. Limp mono is usually considered to be more stretchy than stiff mono, but this is not always true. Monofilament displays two types of stretch, short term and long term. In an interesting experiment, the Gudebrod Bros. Silk Company, Inc., of Philadelphia, tested the stretch qualities of its own Dacron line against that of a competing monofilament of equal test, and a braided nylon.

Three-foot sections of all three lines were attached to a frame. Each line was rated at 25-pound breaking strain. Then

RELATIVE STRETCH OF MONOFILAMENT, DACRON, AND LINEN LINES

O Original unstressed line length.
A Monofilament: 30% maximum elongation with stretch fairly evenly spaced on the stress curve.
B Dacron: 10% maximum elongation with stretch concentrated in last 25% of the stress curve.
C Linen: 5% maximum elongation, stretch evenly spaced along the stress curve.
Vertical scale: percentage of elongation before breaking.
Horizontal scale: percentage of tension from zero to breaking point of line.

Monofilament Lines 77

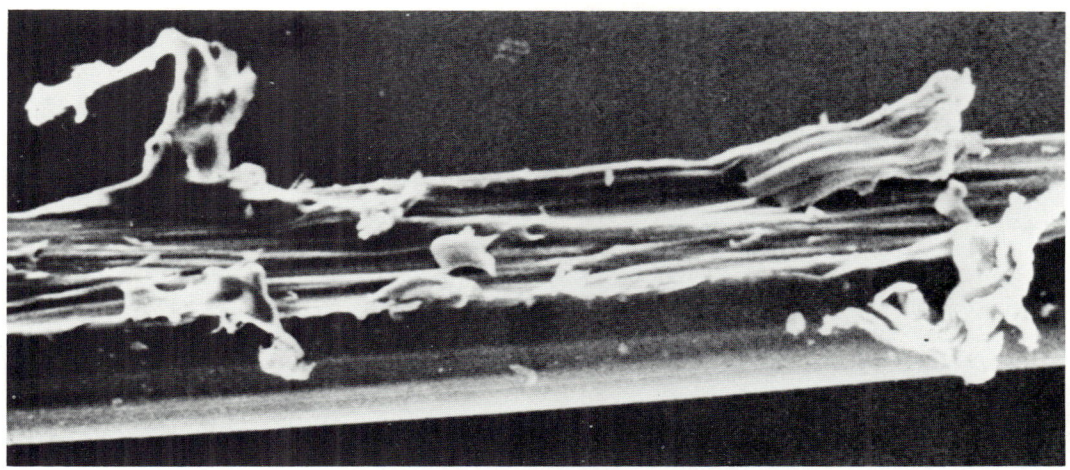

This is what happens to monofilament when it is pulled over a sharp edge, like a grooved rod guide. Electron-microscope photo was made by the Du Pont Company during line tests.

a 20-pound weight was attached to each line, stressing the line to 80 percent of its breaking point. After 15 seconds, the 36 inches of Dacron had extended to 38 inches, an elongation of 5.55 percent; the braided nylon lengthened to 39 inches, a gain of 8.3 percent; the nylon monofilament stretched to 39½ inches, an elongation of 9.7 percent.

After 30 minutes, the Dacron had extended to 39½ inches, or 9.7 percent; the braided nylon to 40½ inches, for 12.5 percent elongation; and the monofilament to 41½ inches, or 15.3 percent. Some monofilaments have been tested at as much as 30 percent elongation before breaking. Monofilament tends to stretch throughout its range of tension at a fairly steady rate, whereas Dacron tends to accumulate most of its stretch in the top 25 percent of tension before breaking.

Some manufacturers and fishermen tend to point out these differences as "proof" of the superiority of Dacron over monofilament, or vice versa. I prefer to refrain from such comment, except when the superiority of one type over the other for a particular purpose is directly related to angling success.

Two weaknesses of monofilament line cannot be overlooked. One is mono's rather low knot strength when certain knots are used. Fortunately, over the years a number of knots have been developed for special purposes, and they retain a high degree of knot strength when tied properly.

The other weakness is monofilament's vulnerability to surface damage if the guides and tip-top of the rod are not perfectly smooth. Photos made by the Du Pont Company with an electron microscope show how the surfaces of monofilament are scarred and abraded when the line is pulled under tension over roughened metal guides.

Which rod guides are best? This depends largely on how the rod is to be used. Roller guides, for example, are excellent for trolling rods, but they interfere with line action in casting. Metal guides with a good plating of hard chrome are good when perfectly smooth and new, as are carbide and the new ceramic ring guides. The business of rod guides is discussed in detail in Chapter 27.

There are two systems for rating lines in pounds-test. One is the manufacturers' gambit of guaranteeing that the line will not break *under* its stated rating. The other is the newer method of guaranteeing that it will not break *over* a stated maximum breaking strain. Unless otherwise noted, the tables and graphs in this and other chapters that relate to monofilament line were prepared from published data describing an "average Du Pont nylon monofilament" having the following characteristics:

Breaking strain for .020-inch-diameter line = 30 pounds.

Cross-sectional area that breaks at one-pound strain = .0000105 square inch; diameter = .00364 inch.

Tensile strength = approximately 95,000 pounds-per-square-inch.

Specific gravity = 1.12.

Volume = approximately 107 percent of "average" Dacron.

In the Nylon Monofilament Diameter/Strength Table, nominal breaking strains are listed for each .002 inch of line diameter, starting with .004 inch, except where an intermediate diameter has been selected because it gives a line with breaking strain just under one of the IGFA line class requirements. For example, to correspond with IGFA 12-pound line, a diameter of .0125 inch was selected. This gives a nominal breaking strain of 11.7 pounds.

In the table Reel Capacity by "O" Size (in Chapter 4), the capacities in yards for the various line classes are averages of existing reels. The reel capacity in cubic inches is calculated as the minimum for tightly packed monofilament or Dacron. Actual reel capacity may be 15 to 20 percent larger. This column of figures is included in the table to give another view of the relationship between average reels of the various "O" sizes. A recheck of Chapter 4 may be valuable.

The graph Monofilament Diameter versus Pounds Test illustrates the relationship between line diameter and pounds of breaking strain. Line A reads directly in pounds from the bottom scale at a 1:1 ratio. Line B gives pounds from the bottom scale at a 10:1 ratio.

For example, a line with a measured diameter of .006 inch would read 2.7 pounds on the A scale. A line measuring .040 inch in diameter would read about 120 pounds on the B scale. Sharp-eyed readers may detect slight differences between the values given in the Strength/Diameter table and those obtained from the graph. The graph was prepared from calculations made to construct the table, and the slight differences are the result of creating a fair line with a French curve during layout of the graph.

NYLON MONOFILAMENT DIAMETER/STRENGTH TABLE

Diameter	Nominal lb. test	IGFA class
.004"	1.2	
.006"	2.7	
.008"	4.8	
.009"	6.0	6 lb.
.010"	7.5	
.012"	10.8	
.0125"	11.7	12 lb.
.014"	14.7	
.016"	19.0	20 lb.
.018"	24.2	
.020"	30.0	30 lb.
.022"	35.9	
.024"	43.1	
.025"	46.7	50 lb.
.026"	50.6	
.028"	58.6	
.030"	67.3	
.032"	76.5	80 lb.
.034"	86.5	
.036"	96.9	
.038"	108.6	
.040"	119.7	
.041"	125.7	130 lb.
.042"	131.9	
.044"	144.8	
.046"	158.2	
.048"	172.8	*180 lb.
.050"	187.0	
.052"	200.	
.058"	250.	
.063"	300.	
.068"	350.	
.072"	400.	
.084"	500.	

*The IGFA recognizes, but does not post, records made on line testing over 130 pounds but under 180 pounds.

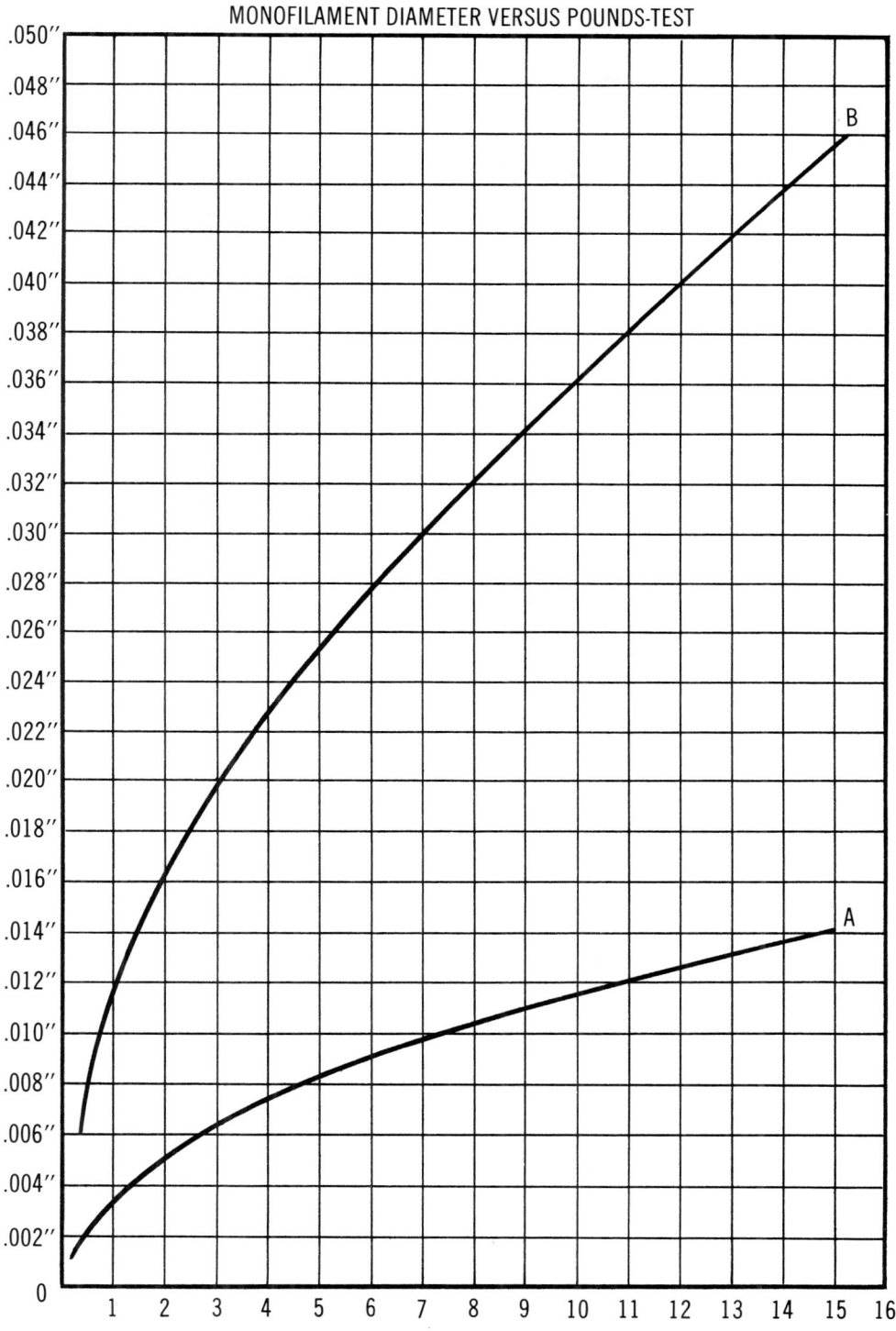

Line A — Read lb. ×1 from bottom scale   Line B — Read lb. ×10 from bottom scale

Remember that variations in strength for the same diameter may be as large as 20 to 25 percent between some types of monofilament. But in dealing with lines of the same or very similar diameter/strength ratios, it is possible to predict the capacity of a reel with an accuracy of plus or minus five percent, provided its capacity in yards (or meters) is known accurately in terms of line of known diameter.

One characteristic of both monofilament and Dacron lines caused considerable consternation when it first became evident. This is the tendency of compressed synthetic plastics to exhibit what may be termed "plastic flow." Natural cellulose fibers, including most woods, do not exhibit any great degree of plastic flow. Instead, they manifest what may be called "elastic compressibility."

A perfect example of elastic compressibility is a sponge: you can crush the dry (or wet) sponge in your hands, greatly reducing its volume, and the sponge will spring back to its original shape when the pressure is released. The same is true to a lesser degree of most woods. As an example, cut a short piece of almost any wood into a small cube about one inch square, and place it in a vise. You can compress the wood a fair amount before it is crushed so completely that it does not spring back into its original shape when the pressure is released. You will note that when the wood is compressed, it does not bulge out sideways to compensate for compression. This is crushability, or elastic compressibility.

Linen, cotton, and other natural fibers have elastic compressibility to a marked degree, since they are composed of natural cellulose fibers. Linen line wound onto a reel under heavy line tension crushes down into the layers of line underneath, with very little tendency to expand sideways against the reel end plates. But plastic lines, being composed of uncrushable solid-plastic fibers, act differently.

Take a nylon cube the same size as your wooden test cube and compress it in the vise. Since it is solid nylon, it bulges out on the sides as the ends are squeezed together. This is plastic flow, the result of nylon's condition of almost total incompressibility. The same thing happens when you wind any synthetic line onto a reel spool under heavy tension. The upper layers of the line bite down into the lower layers, but the lower layers cannot be crushed into a smaller volume. Responding with plastic flow, they expand sideways against the end plates of the reel spool, driving them against the reel frame and ruining the reel if the spool is not strong enough to withstand the pressure.

Reel spools made up of separate end plates soldered or force-fitted onto a shaft are especially vulnerable to plastic-flow failure of synthetic lines. Some plastic reel spools have been completely shattered by the great pressure built up by monofilament wound onto the spools at tension close to the line's breaking strain.

The cure is to select a reel with a spool machined from solid metal, or injection-molded of super-strong plastic. Most reel manufacturers are aware of this problem, so they specify specially constructed spools for service with synthetic lines under heavy tension.

BRAIDED NYLON LINE

When nylon first came out, before Dacron cornered a large portion of the saltwater braided-line market, braided nylon enjoyed a spell of popularity. It is still popular in some foreign countries, and it is used in the United States for special purposes. For example, it forms the outer cover of lead-core lines used for deep trolling. But the high stretch factor of braided nylon line has combined with relatively low knot strength to relegate it to a back seat in the estimation of most North American saltwater anglers.

9 Dacron Lines

Braided fishing line is not exactly new. Anglers have been using braided cotton, linen, and silk lines for many years. Braiding works best with lines of continuous or relatively long fibers, so braided cotton never gained much popularity with fishermen. When synthetic Dacron fibers became available at about the time that nylon monofilament became popular, a very superior braiding fiber for fishing lines was discovered.

Dacron is actually a Du Pont trademark for a polyester fiber made from ethylene glycol and dimethyl terephthalate. Dacron fibers are produced by extrusion of a liquid in exactly the same manner as nylon fibers are made. Dacron exhibits markedly different characteristics from nylon, however. Its strength is close to that of nylon, but, as was stated earlier, its average elongation under tension is about 10 percent, as against nylon's 15 to 30 percent.

Practically all Dacron fishing lines are braided from very thin extruded fibers. Dacron is affected little by water, with practically no change in strength between wet and dry conditions. It is more highly resistant to sunlight than nylon, and little affected by mildew. It feels relatively slick when drawn between the fingers and has surprisingly little water friction. It does have the common weakness of most synthetic lines of being relatively easily abraded by friction and lacking the knot strength of linen.

But what Dacron lacks in knot strength, it makes up in its splicing potential. Braided Dacron lines come in two forms: one is hollow and the other has a central fiber core around which the braided walls are formed. Of the two, the hollow form is by far the most popular with saltwater anglers. Splicing is accomplished by drawing the end of one line inside the other, or by drawing the line end into the standing part to form a loop or double line. A special splicing needle is used, but in a pinch, one can make a splicing needle from a piece of thin, stainless-steel leader wire. The splicing of Dacron line will be described later.

Because of its braided construction and hollow form, Dacron line does not assume a true cylindrical shape, so any attempts to relate strength to diameter are meaningless. Oddly enough, even though Dacron is usually regarded as just about equal to nylon monofilament in average tensile strength, Dacron is regarded as occupying seven to 10 percent less space on a reel than monofilament of the same length and breaking strain. This is probably caused by the great pliability of Dacron line and the fact that outer layers of line wound onto a reel spool have a tendency to crush the inner layers together, eliminating the small spaces between individual turns of line. Being plastic, Dacron has some of the plastic-flow characteristics of monofilament when it is wound on a spool under tension, but not to the same degree.

Dacron is the trolling fisherman's

Braided Dacron line is now standard for most trolling in tackle classes of 30-lb.-line test and heavier. This Penn Senator 6/0 carries 50-lb. Dacron line for school tuna.

favorite line, especially in ratings over 30-pound test. It is more forgiving of thumb carelessness than monofilament when it comes to casting or dropping back a bait to a fish. Its low stretch factor definitely increases the sensitivity of tackle when it comes to detecting nibbles or touches at the bait. Low stretch certainly is also helpful when it comes to setting the hook in a fish's mouth.

The matter of sensitivity has been reduced to mathematics by a Gudebrod Bros. Silk Company analyst in the following words: "The more a line stretches, the more the transmitted tension from one end of the line is softened and/or diluted before it reaches the other end. Using a factor of 12 percent stretch for Dacron and 20 percent for monofilament, we can say that Dacron is 60 percent more sensitive (12/20 = 60 percent) than monofilament when it comes to transmitting a strike."

Some anglers may argue over this percentage, but most will agree that when you hold the rod in your hand, expecting feedback from the fish via the line, a sensitive line is preferable to an insensitive one. Sensitivity of tackle, of course, is a highly subjective quality, and it is extremely difficult to pin down in exact terms. How do you describe the tiny thrill of vibration that comes up a six-pound monofilament when a bonefish picks up the shrimp? Or how do you compare this reaction to the sudden thud-thud that telegraphs to a big-game angler that his hooked marlin is banging at the leader with its tail?

The Gudebrod analyst also described an experiment in hook-setting with Dacron and monofilament lines:

"A line was tied to a popular deep-diving plug and tension was applied until one hook of a treble was pulled to the depth of its barb into the end grain of a block of balsa wood. The average tension required was five pounds, measured by an accurate hand scale. This five pounds was used in the succeeding comparisons.

"Twelve-inch lengths of 20-pound mono and 20-pound Dacron were used to pull the plug hook into the wood, each with exactly five pounds of tension. The 12 inches of mono stretched to 13 inches before five pounds tension was reached. The 12 inches of Dacron elongated to 12½ inches under five pounds of pull.

"This brings out the conclusion that the average 20-pound-test mono stretches some 8.3 percent (13/12 = 1.083) of its length in order to apply 25 percent of its breaking strain in setting the hook, whereas the 20-pound-test Dacron used showed a stretch factor of only four percent (12.5/12 = 1.04) when 25 percent of its ultimate breaking strain was applied to set the hook."

From this experiment, one could ask, "What difference does a mere half-inch

Jay De Mott of the Long Island Beach Buggy Association demonstrates how far back he must strike with a surf rod in order to set the hook with a "stretchy" type of casting line.

make in setting the hook?" The answer is "mighty little," until you start multiplying that half-inch-per-foot by the number of feet of line you may have out. For example, if you're striking the hook into a big striper at the end of 120 feet of line that you've just flung out into the surf with your Hatteras Heaver surf rod, you have to rear back a full 60 inches — five feet — with the tip of the rod after taking the slack up, just to achieve a five-pound striking tension with the type of monofilament just described. You'd achieve the same striking tension with a 30-inch — or 2½-foot — pull with Dacron.

This discussion is not intended to suggest that Dacron is "better" than monofilament. Rather, it is intended to point out the basic differences between these two popular types of synthetic lines, so the reader may make intelligent choices when it comes to selecting lines for specific types of fishing.

Naturally, not all Dacron lines are identical in quality and performance. Generally speaking, you get what you pay for. The characteristics of Dacron are closely governed by the manufacturing process, and each manufacturer claims to have line-making tricks that enhance those features of his lines that anglers consider admirable. Line engineering is a continuing process these days. Engineers and chemists are constantly looking for ways to reduce water friction, reduce excessive stretch, improve abrasion resistance and knot strength, and improve the "fishability" of their products.

SPLICING 2 DACRON LINES TOGETHER

Most Dacron lines used by anglers are hollow. A splice in Dacron calls for inserting the end of one line into the body of the other, and then repeating the process with the end of the second line into the body of the first. This results in a sort of "Chinese finger trap" grip of one line on the other. When properly made, it is as strong as the unspliced line. Use either the special splicing needle provided by the line manufacturer or, lacking such a needle, make your own by doubling a 12-inch piece of #5 stainless wire leader, as illustrated.

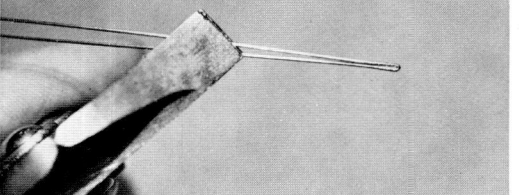

To join the ends of two Dacron lines . . .

Insert the loop or hook end of the splicer into the line about 4 in. from the end. Let it emerge 2 in. from the end. Pick up end of the other line in loop or hook of splicer.

Dacron Lines 85

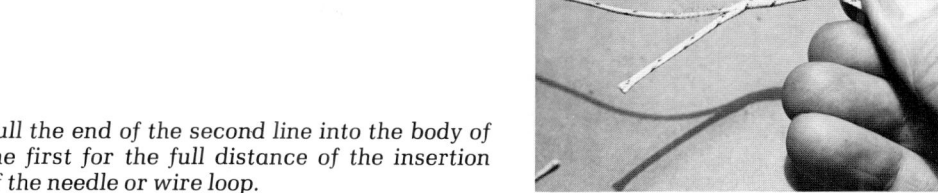

Pull the end of the second line into the body of the first for the full distance of the insertion of the needle or wire loop.

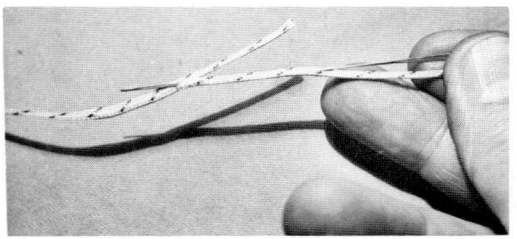

Leaving the line end buried inside the first line, reverse the positions of the lines and insert the splicer into the body of the second line 4 in. from its end, letting the splicer emerge close to where the end of the second line enters the first.

Pick up the end of the first line with the loop or hook of the splicer.

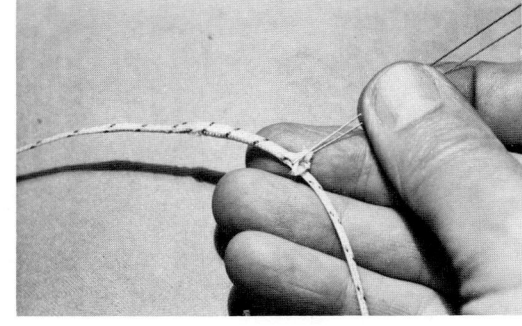

Pull the end of the first line into the body of the second. Remove the splicer from the end of line, and trim the line end flush with the emergence hole so the line end disappears into the body of the main line.

A slight bulge in the Dacron betrays the finished splice. It looks the way a snake would look after swallowing a smaller snake.

86 MODERN SALTWATER FISHING TACKLE

SPLICING A LOOP OR DOUBLE LINE IN DACRON

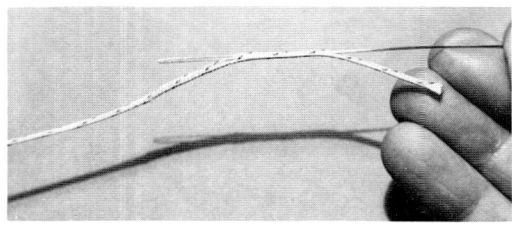

To splice a loop or double line in Dacron, insert the splicing tool into the end of the line 2 in. from the end, pointed away from the end. Let it penetrate the body of the line for 2 in. before emerging.

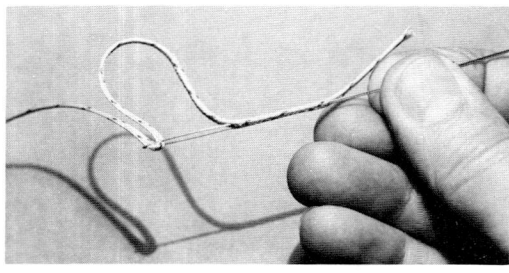

With the splicer, pick up a bight of the main part of the line a few inches beyond the point where the tool emerges.

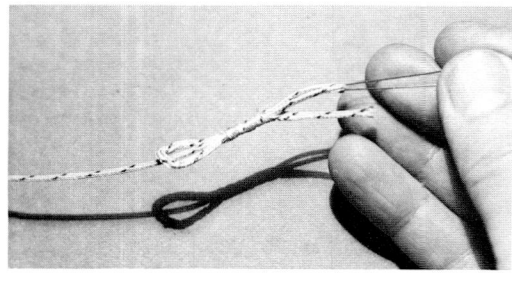

Carefully pull the bight of the line through the body of the line. Be careful not to break any strands.

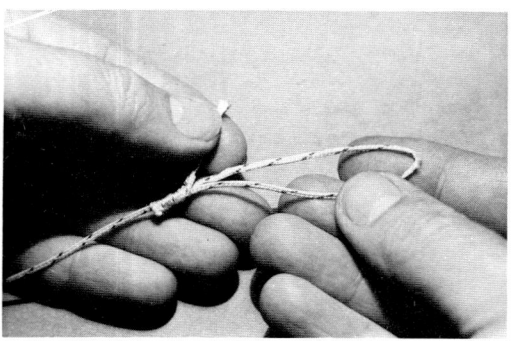

When all of the doubled line is pulled through, it will look like this. The tag end will appear to be turned inside-out and will point toward the loop. Grasp the tag end and pull it down.

Pulling down the tag end will turn it right-side-out, pointing away from the loop. This is the time to adjust the length of the loop or double line to the desired length by pulling the main part of the line through the 2-in. section where it lies inside the end. When loop is long enough, enter the splicer into the main line for about 2 in. just below the tag end. Pick up the end with the splicer.

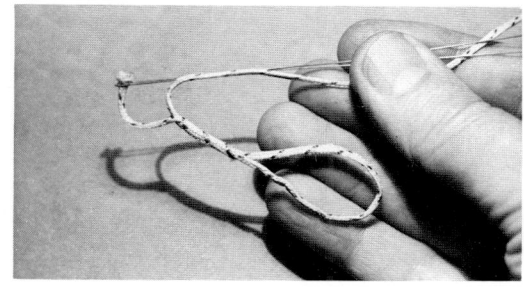

Pull the tag end through the main part of the line. Cut off any excess that comes out so the end will be buried inside the line.

The finished loop or double line splice is neat, thin, and will hold nearly 100 percent of the test of the unspliced line.

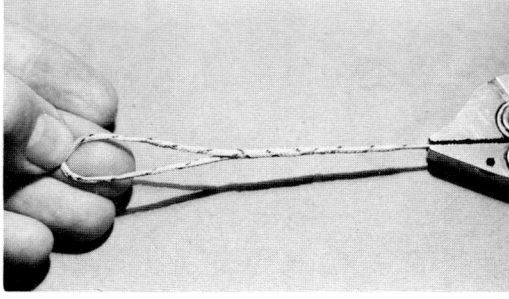

Expert wire-line angler Ted Sigler of Montauk, New York, places a wire-line rod in the rod holder with click engaged and reel drag set to light tension. He pulls wire line from the rod tip with a smooth hand-over-hand motion, maintaining constant line speed to avoid a backlash on the spool.

10   Wire Fishing Lines

Wire lines for fishing are used mainly for deep trolling and for certain kinds of very deep bottom fishing. The two types of wire line generally used are lead-core and solid Monel wire. Lead-core line is available in ratings from under 20-pound test to over 60-pound test, and it usually comes in a package of two or more connected 100-yard spools. Manufacturers usually color-code the outer nylon covering of the lead-core line so that an angler can see how many feet of line he has put out.

Lead-core line is easy to handle, packs easily onto a reel spool, and does not have a tendency to spring up and backlash when line tension is released from the reel. When stressed heavily, it is inclined to stretch without returning to its original length. It resists breaking when accidentally kinked, largely because the outer braid is the line's major weight-carrier. The interior core of lead supports little tension, but it provides the weight needed to make the line a linear sinker.

If the reel is to be stored after use in salt water, the lead-core line should be removed, wound on a line dryer, and washed thoroughly with fresh water before being dried and stored away. Some anglers prefer to fill the reel full of lead-core line. Others tie a suitable length of sinking line on top of Dacron or monofilament backing, which fills the reel at least half-full.

At normal trolling speeds, lead-core line has a length-depth ratio of about 8:1, about equal to that of solid wire. Thus, a 100-foot length of lead-core wire carrying a one-ounce leadhead lure can be expected to troll the lure at a depth of about 12½ feet at a speed of about three knots.

Solid Monel wire requires special care. Its popularity is the result of its durability and fish-catching ability. A number of years ago, stranded Monel wire was popular in many areas. Stranded wire is more flexible than solid, but it has one bad drawback: when one strand of the wire breaks, that strand has a tendency to hang up in a rod guide, causing a great fuzzy ball of fine wire loops, which is almost impossible to disentangle.

Solid, soft-drawn Monel wire comes in 100-yard or bulk spools in a number of diameters and pounds-test. Contrary to much popular opinion, Monel wire lines are not super-strong. A typical wire of .024-inch diameter, for example, tests only about 45-pound breaking strain. Average monofilament line of .024-inch diameter tests about 43 pounds, or just a shade under the test of Monel wire of the same diameter.

The following table gives typical diameter/strength values for average soft-drawn Monel wire.

Diameter	Test
.015 in.	18 lb.
.018 in.	25 lb.
.021 in.	35 lb.
.024 in.	45 lb.
.027 in.	57 lb.
.030 in.	70 lb.

Solid Monel wire line usually is measured to the exact length required, then spliced on top of a reel partly filled with Dacron or monofilament backing. The backing should be at least as strong as the wire, and preferably 20 to 30 percent stronger. Specific recommendations for tackle for deep trolling with wire line are included in Chapter 14.

Solid wire has the fastest sink rate and least water drag of any deep-trolling line. It is prone to metal fatigue after prolonged stress, however. When soft-drawn, solid Monel wire starts to feel unusually stiff between the fingers, this is a sure sign of fatigue and eventual failure. Fatigued wire crystallizes and breaks unexpectedly, usually under little or no strain.

Wire has no elastic-rebound feature after it is stretched under heavy strain. It stretches until it breaks, sometimes gaining as much as 20 percent over its original length. Rods for wire-line fishing, therefore, usually are extra-soft in action to make up for the wire's lack of elasticity.

Kinks in solid wire are always a problem. They are best avoided by careful handling, especially when letting wire out from the reel. A kink that has not been drawn tight can be bent out the way it was made, but a tight kink must be cut out and the cut ends of the wire have to be spliced together. (Splicing wire to backing line and wire to wire is described and illustrated in detail in the pages that follow.)

The safest way to put out wire is to engage the reel's click, put one thumb on the spool, and pull out the wire a bit at a time against a combination of thumb pressure, click, and very light drag. One method used by experts is illustrated here. The rod is put into a side rod holder, the click is engaged, and a very light drag is used. The line is then hauled out from the tip of the rod with a smooth, steady, hand-over-hand pulling motion.

The following table indicates the depths at which a one-ounce lure can be trolled, and the workable depths of water with various standard lengths of solid Monel wire, at a standard trolling speed of about three knots.

Line length	Lure depth	Water depth
100 ft.	12½ ft.	15 ft. +
150 ft.	19 ft.	22-27 ft.
200 ft.	25 ft.	30 ft. +
250 ft.	32 ft.	35-40 ft.
300 ft.	38 ft.	45 ft. +
350 ft.	44 ft.	50 ft. +
400 ft.	50 ft.	60 ft. +

SPLICING AND MARKING WIRE LINES

Before you start to put wire lines on your reels, consider carefully how you intend to use the wire. For example, will you be trolling deep in waters of from 10 to 30 or more feet in depth? If so, you may be wise to spool a full 100 yards of wire onto each reel. On the other hand, if you expect to work primarily in shallower water, seldom having to attain a lure depth of much more than 20 feet, 150 or 200 feet of wire may be quite sufficient.

If the wire is not color-coded, plan at the same time to mark your wire at various spots along its length so you can tell exactly how much wire you have out on any given rig.

The most popular wire line in salt water is soft-drawn, solid Monel; the best reel is one with a wide, open face. The metal gadget on this rod is a handmade line-layer that eases the task of level-winding the wire across the face of the reel.

Once you have decided how much wire you need on each reel, and have a supply of wire at hand, find yourself an open ground area at least as long as the longest wires you plan to rig. If there is a wooden wall or fence at one end, fine. Drive a stout nail into the wall or fence, leaving the top inch of the nailhead exposed. Otherwise, pound a strong two-by-four stake into the ground and drive the nail into the top of the stake in the same manner.

Carefully measure off on the ground the exact full length of wire that you need. Standing at the end of the measured distance from the stake or nail, lead the backing line out through the guides of the rod and splice the end of the wire on the storage spool to the end of the backing line. The easiest splice for joining the wire to the backing is done as follows:

Tie a four- to six-inch loop in the end of the backing line, using the Surgeon's Knot. Next, using the end of the wire line, tie a Becket Bend with the wire into the end of the backing loop, leaving a tag end of wire at least four inches long. Pull the Becket Bend of wire tight with your pliers, marry the tag end and the main part of the wire for a few twists, then finish off with close turns as you would finish off a leader eye. This splice will hold at least 80 percent of the original wire test, but it may cut the backing after prolonged use.

To put the wire on the reel spool, run a dowel or screwdriver shaft through the wire-line storage spool, lay the rod on the ground at the exact distance spot, then walk toward the nail-stake, unspooling wire as you go. Let the wire-storage spool rotate on its axle to prevent putting twists into the wire.

When you have the exact length of wire unspooled, cut it a few inches long, apply a stainless-steel snap swivel to the end, and hang the snap swivel on the nail in the stake. Leave the wire stretched out on the ground and rig the other wire line rods with wire cut to exactly the same overall length.

Finally, starting at the stake end of

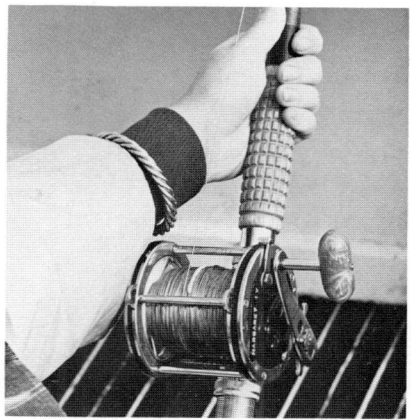

A measured shot of wire line is spooled on top of a reel one-half to two-thirds full of good-quality soft-line backing.

the wires, measure off the various distances at which you want to mark the wires. Place a marker on the ground at each distance spot. I mark my 300-foot wires every 75 feet with marks at the 75-, 150-, and 225-foot locations between the stake and the rods. One of the easiest ways to mark wire is with spools of colored plastic striping tape. Get the narrowest you can find, about 1/8 inch wide.

Cut strips about six inches long from the various tape colors, and wind the

The simplest wire-to-backing splice is to make a loop in the backing, then tie the wire into the loop using a Becket Bend.

strips around the wires at the proper spot, marking each spot with the same color, naturally. A useful color code goes like this:

>   Black   — at 75 ft.
>   Red   — at 100 ft.
>   Green   — at 125 ft.
>   Yellow — at 150 ft.
>   Blue   — at 200 ft.
>   White   — at 225 ft.

A strong, reliable splice is the so-called Basket Weave splice, illustrated in this chapter. The Basket Weave backing-to-wire splice is flexible enough to store easily on the reel, renders easily through roller or ring guides, and will hold 90 to 95 percent of the test of the wire or backing, whichever is the lighter.

Backing line usually does not take much of a beating, but you should cut off the last few feet of backing each time you splice on fresh wire. Take care of your wires and they will give you many days of excellent fishing.

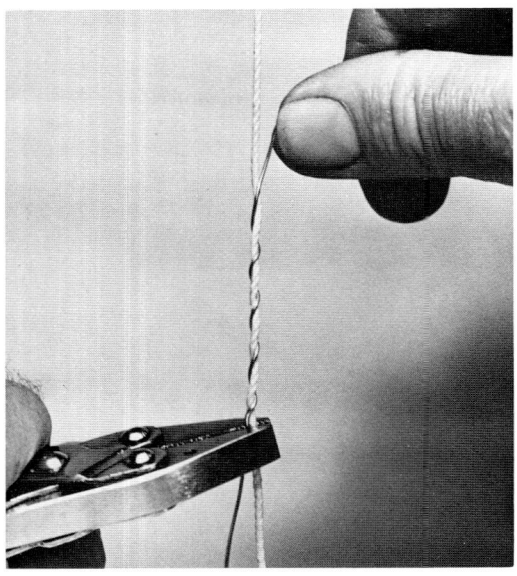

(1) To start the Basket Weave Splice, tie the end of the backing line to a firm object like a heavy desk, and tie the main part of the line to your belt buckle so you can lean back and put a strain on the line. Take the tag end of the wire, at least six inches long, grasp wire and line together, and wrap the wire tightly around the line, working away from you.

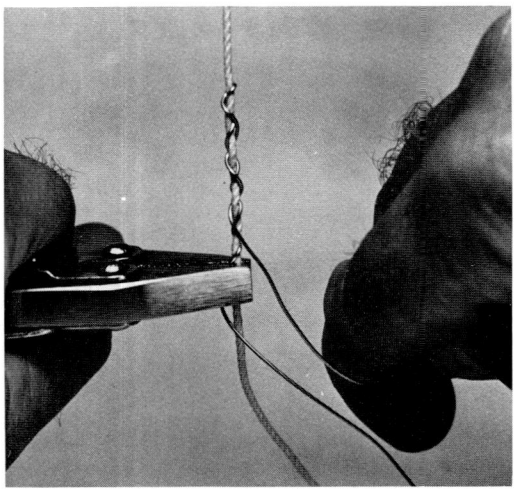

(2) Next, keeping strong tension on the line with pliers, wrap the wire down over its own original turns, laying the turns on as strongly as possible. The wire should bite into the backing line and form a nonslip grip.

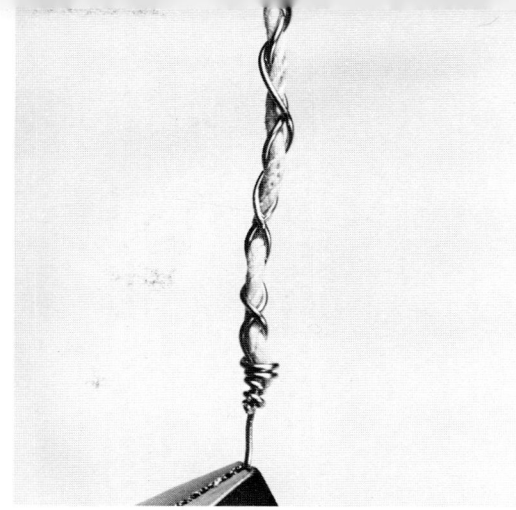

(3) Shift the pliers to the body of the turns and apply several close finishing turns.

(4) Cut the tag end of the wire off close and bend the burr end in onto the main wire so it is smooth to the touch. The Basket Weave Splice is not easy to make, but will hold 95 percent of the wire's rating.

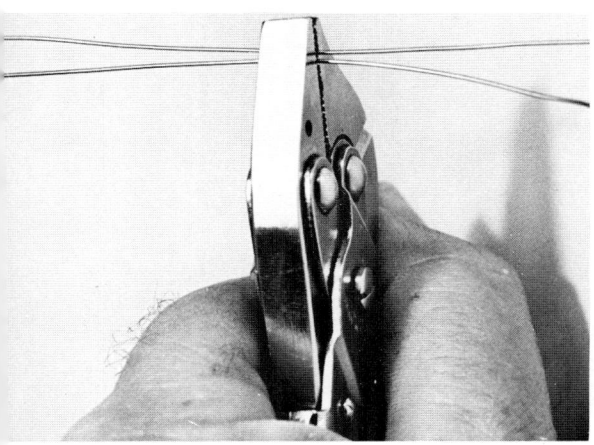

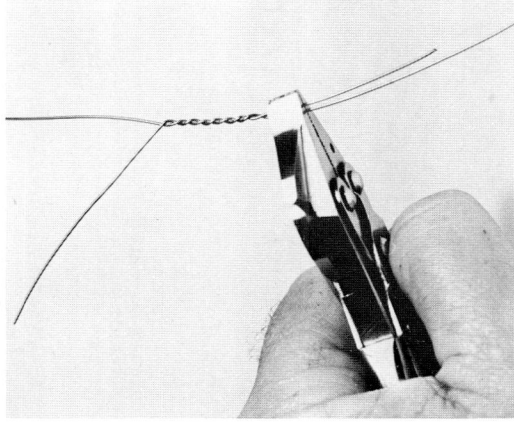

(1) Above: To splice two ends of wire line together, overlap the two ends by six to eight inches, then grasp the overlapped wires a little to the left of center, using pliers.

(2) Above: Holding the pliers firmly in the left hand, marry the two parts of wire together carefully, taking at least eight half-turns and forming a true, even twisted-pair.

(3) Below: Finish off the twisted-pair by taking several close finishing turns with the tag end of the wire over the main part. Cut close in and bend down the end.

(4) Below: Finish off the other end of the splice the same way. The twisted-pair or "hay-wire" splice will hold up to 90 percent of the rated strength of the wire line.

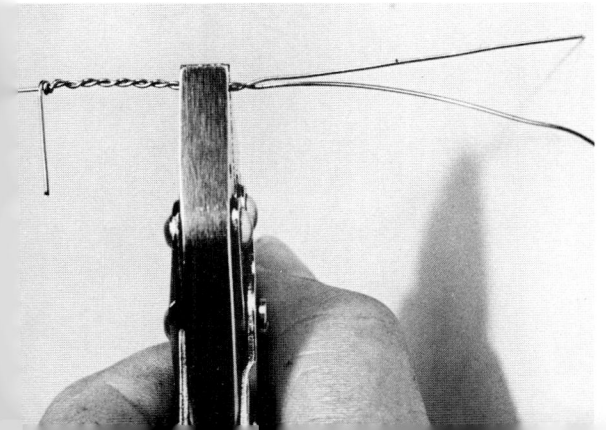

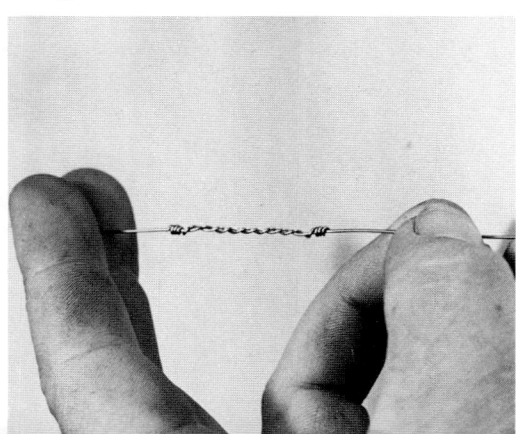

In fly casting you cast the line rather than the lure, as Larry Green is demonstrating to his wife, Mary, in California.

11 Saltwater Fly Lines

Saltwater fly fishing is a fairly recent addition to the piscatorial sport. Actually, it is only slightly different from the freshwater variety, and the difference is one of degree rather than kind. Rods, reels, and lines used for fly fishing on salt water are generally heavier and more robust than the average of similar freshwater tackle. But for those anglers who have never done it before, the whole idea of fly casting is basically different from conventional lure casting.

In spinning- or revolving-spool reel casting, the lure or bait has weight, and it is cast in the manner of a projectile, dragging the line along behind it from the reel. The casting fly, on the other hand, has negligible weight. To cast it toward a distant target, therefore, one has to cast the line and let the fly go along for the ride. Fly lines look remarkably thick and heavy to the uninitiated, but this thickness and heaviness is a function of making the fly line a sort of linear casting projectile.

Casting the fly line first involves working out enough line to give the rod something to move through the air. The rod, in turn, is carefully engineered to work against lines of a particular weight range. Ordinary fly lines have been classified by the American Fishing Tackle Manufacturers Association into 12 specific weight categories, ranging from what might be termed ultra-light to extra-heavy. These terms are not used to describe fly lines, except in a general sort of way.

Instead, the AFTMA line classification system assigns a specific weight in grains to the first 30 feet of each class of line in 12 increasingly heavy line classes. The first 30 feet was chosen as the measuring criterion, because this is the length of line normally used by an angler in making a distance cast. Fly lines average 90 to 115 feet long. They are spooled onto the reel on top of enough light, soft line backing to take up the extra space. The following table gives the 12 AFTMA fly-line weight classes in terms of class number, weight in grains of the first 30 feet of line, and permissible margin of weight error.

Class	Weight of first 30 ft.	Permissible error
No. 1	60 gr.	± 6 gr.
No. 2	80 gr.	± 6 gr.
No. 3	100 gr.	± 6 gr.
No. 4	120 gr.	± 6 gr.
No. 5	140 gr.	± 6 gr.
No. 6	160 gr.	± 8 gr.
No. 7	185 gr.	± 8 gr.
No. 8	210 gr.	± 8 gr.
No. 9	240 gr.	± 10 gr.
No. 10	280 gr.	± 10 gr.
No. 11	330 gr.	± 12 gr.
No. 12	380 gr.	± 12 gr.

Fly lines are not built like conventional fishing lines. Originally, they were made of braided silk, linen, or other natural fibers. Their bulk and weight have no direct bearing on the size or power of the fish. A special tapered leader is used between the line and the fly. The leader will be discussed further in Chapter 18.

Modern fly lines are made in a number of ways to achieve the end result of a line that incorporates a weighted linear casting section. Some are formed of nylon and other synthetic solids, in the form of a specially shaped monofilament. Others are formed of a braided core surrounded by a flexible plastic cover Two things are important: first, that weight be concentrated in the forward 30 feet of the line to facilitate casting; and second, that the line have a low-friction exterior finish to reduce casting friction.

Early fly lines were built "level," meaning that they were of the same thickness and weight throughout their length. It quickly became apparent that distance casting is easier if some of the weight of the fly line is concentrated or built into the forward 30-foot casting section. Thus, the weight-forward line was invented. In recent years, several types of weight-forward lines have been developed. Names and special symbols have been arranged to identify the various types of fly lines, as follows.

L = level line: uniform weight and diameter throughout; most economical. Fair to moderate casting ability.

ST (placed to the *left* of the line number, as ST6) = single taper: the front end of the line is tapered to form a power-transition zone between the main body of the line and the leader to facilitate casting. Moderate casting ability.

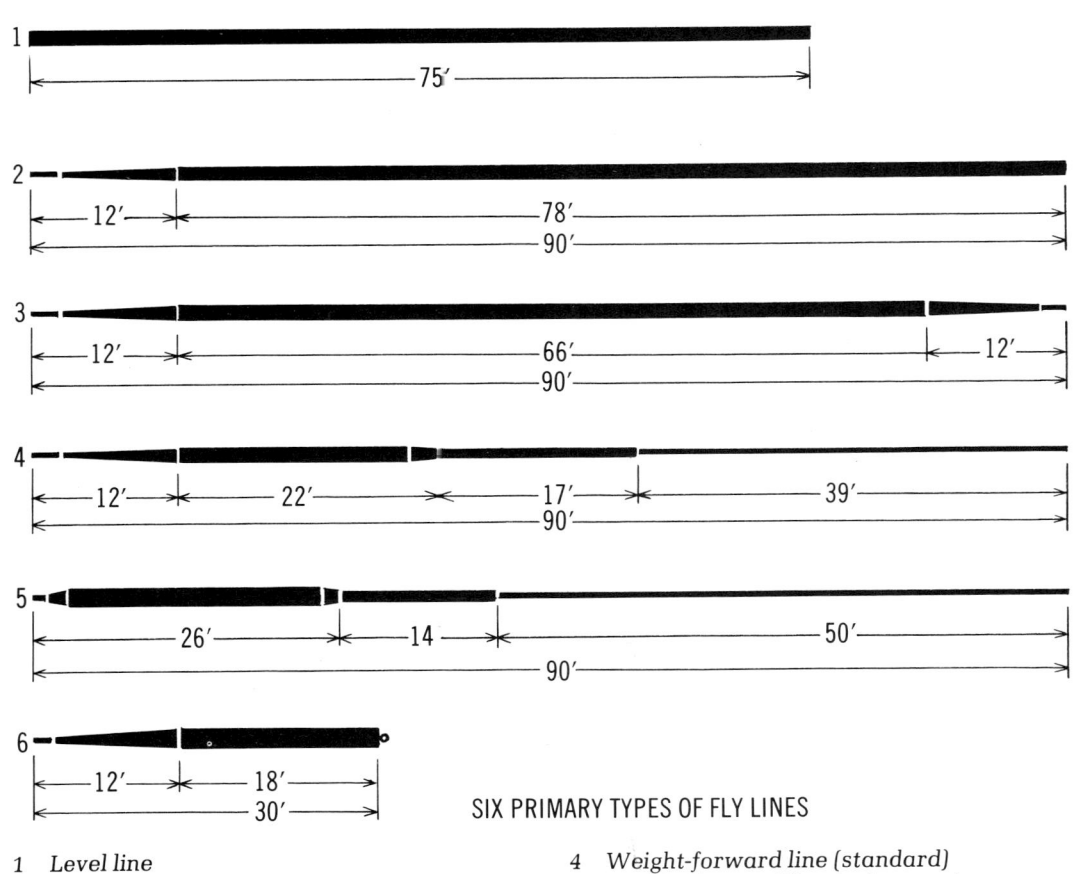

SIX PRIMARY TYPES OF FLY LINES

1 Level line
2 Single-taper line
3 Double-taper line
4 Weight-forward line (standard)
5 Weight-forward line (salt water)
6 Shooting head

ST (placed to the *right* of the line number, as WF8ST) = sinking tip: a special type of floating line with a sinking-tip section for specialized fishing.

DT = double taper: both ends of the line are built with a taper, so the line can be reversed on the reel if one end becomes worn from casting. Moderate distance-casting ability.

WF = weight-forward: a good part of the line's weight is concentrated in the forward 30 feet, which also has a tapered power-transition section forward of the weight-forward portion. Excellent distance-casting ability.

SWT = saltwater taper: modification of weight-forward construction with even more weight in the first 30 feet, and a shorter forward tapered section. Excellent distance-casting ability.

SH = shooting head: concentrates all of the line's casting weight in the first 30 feet. Special light monofilament line takes the place of the usual body trailing section. Superior distance-casting ability.

F = floating: a line with surface-floating characteristics. No effect on casting ability, other than the fact that a floating line is always easier to pick up for recasting.

S = sinking: a line designed to sink. It may require a quick roll cast to bring it back to the surface before recasting.

F/S = floating/sinking: main body of the line floats, but the forward section sinks. Special uses.

SHOOTING-HEAD FLY-LINE MAKEUP

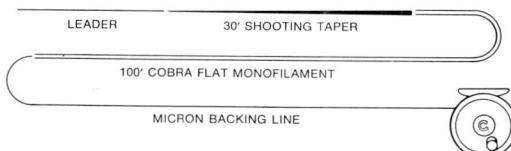

As suggested by the Cortland Line Company, a typical West Coast steelhead shooting-head fly-line combination consists of the normal tapered leader, a 30' shooting head, 100' of special flat monofilament (about 20-lb. test), and 20-lb. test backing line.

I = intermediate: line floats when dressed with flotation dressing, but sinks when not dressed.

The various symbols are combined with the weight number of the line to indicate its full characteristics. For instance, WF8-S indicates a weight-forward, Weight-8, sinking line. The lines most frequently used in saltwater fly fishing range from Weight-7 through Weight-12, and usually they have at least a weight-forward configuration. Rods to match the line weights must be selected for best overall performance, plus reels must have adequate storage capacity and smooth, powerful drags.

Complete selections for various types of saltwater fly fishing are given in the chapters on selecting saltwater tackle.

12 Practical Fishing Knots

The advent of synthetic lines has reduced the number of practical knots that fishermen use. Knots now have to have good holding power without damaging the line or causing the knot to lose line strength. The five basic knots on this page, plus those that follow, preserve a high percentage of the original line strength when tied properly, and hold without rendering.

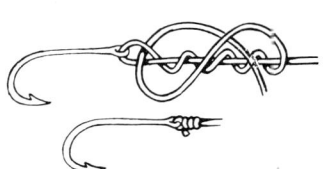

IMPROVED CLINCH KNOT: for tying line or leader to a hook eye or swivel eye. Tests 90-95% of line test.

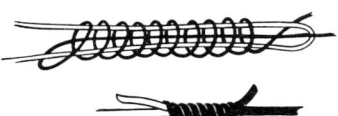

ALBRIGHT SPECIAL: for tying Dacron to mono, or two mono lines of unequal diameter. Tests 90-95% of line test.

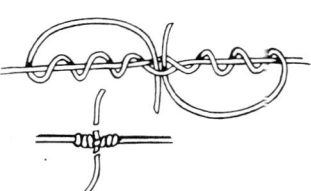

BLOOD KNOT: for tying two pieces of mono of equal or unequal diameter. Tests 90-95% of line test.

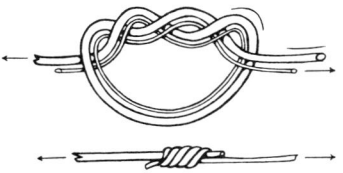

SURGEON'S KNOT: for tying lines of unequal diameter or making an end loop. Tests 90-95% of line test.

IMPROVED END LOOP KNOT: an easy knot for tying a loop into the end of a line. Tests 70-80% of line test.

Practical Fishing Knots

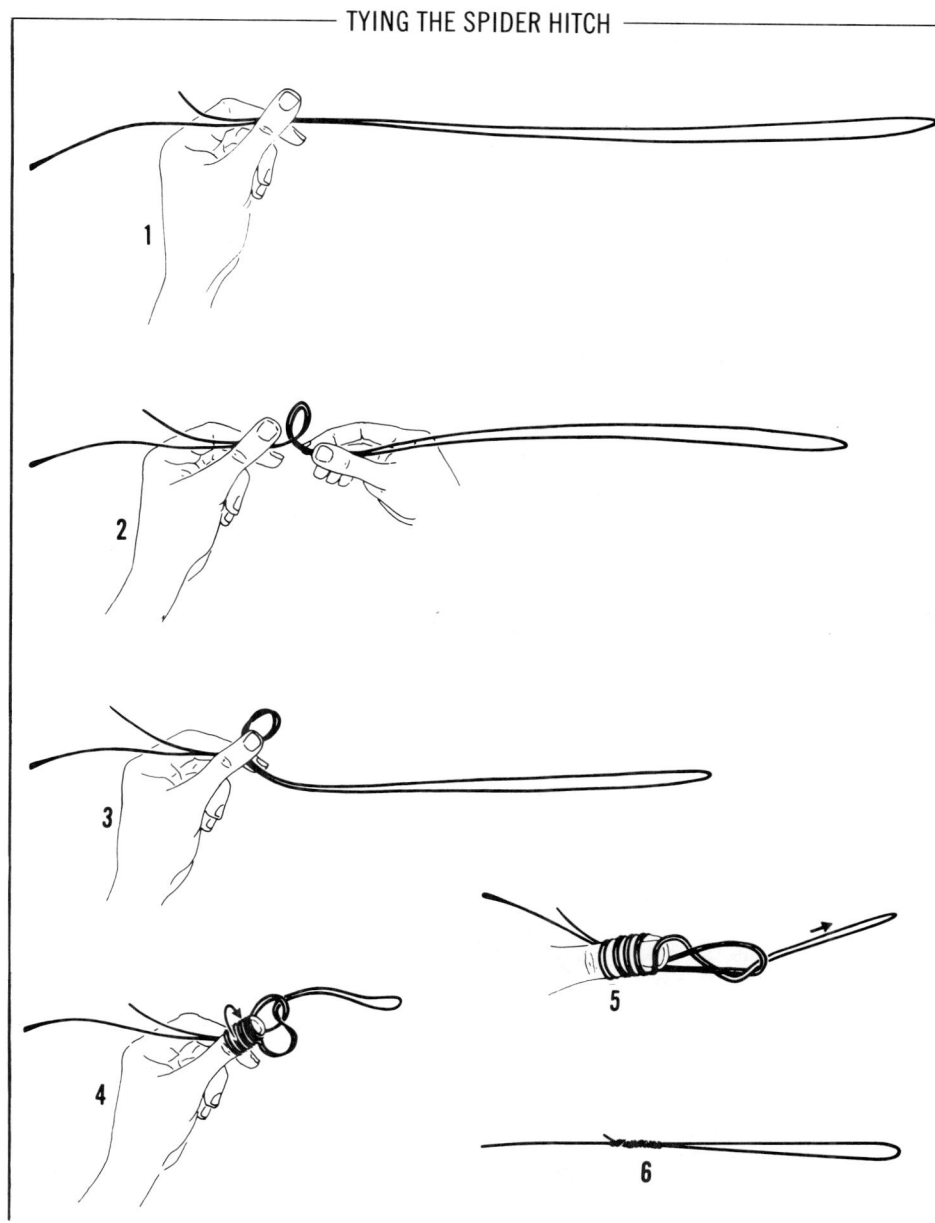

TYING THE SPIDER HITCH

(1) Measure loop to proper length, hold the loop between thumb and forefinger of left hand, as shown.
(2) Throw a half-hitch into the loop near thumb.
(3) Grasp half-hitch with thumb and forefinger.
(4) Make about 8 turns of loop around thumb and the half-hitch. Pass loop end through the half-hitch.
(5) Draw the loop through the bight of the half-hitch, letting turns come off thumb.
(6) Draw the hitch tight. Turns will bind firmly around loop, forming a knot or hitch with high knot strength.

Making the Bimini Twist

(1) With someone to help you, carefully measure the double line to be made, allowing up to 30 feet of double line for lines of 80 and 130-lb. test, or 15 feet of double line for lines of 50-lb. test and under. Plan to make the double line a few inches shorter than the legal maximum.

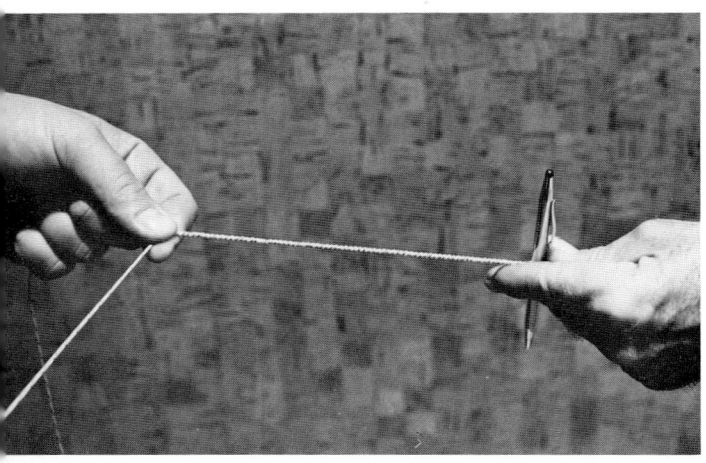

(2) Having selected the spot where the double line knot is to go, have your assistant grasp both parts of the double line at this spot with the thumb and forefinger of his right hand, the loop of the line facing away from him. There should be at least 16 inches of tag end of line projecting from between his fingers, pointed to his left where he can grasp it with his left hand.

(3) Now straighten out the loop of double line and slip the end of the loop up over your wrist. Maintaining light tension against your helper's grasp, throw at least 40 twists into the loop by rotating your wrist.

(4) Take the end of the loop and hook it over some solid object such as the top of a handy dock spile. Let your helper maintain his pull against this object while you take a pencil or some other smooth object and place it between the two parts of the twisted loop where the parts come open at the far end of the loop.

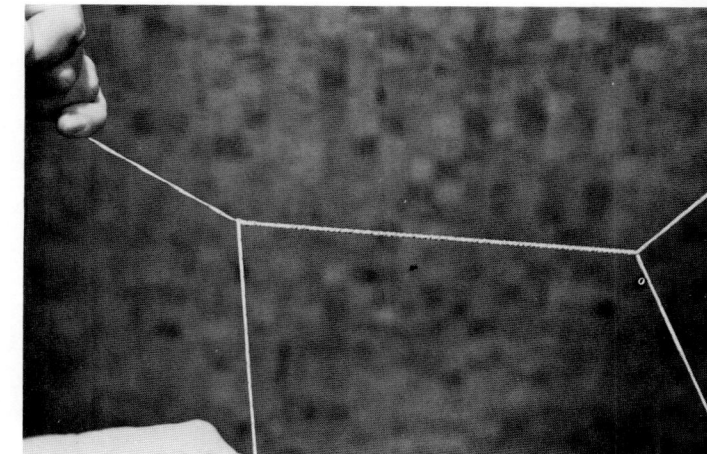

(5) Walk toward your helper, pushing the pencil between the two parts of the twisted loop, forcing the twists down the line toward your helper. Eventually you will have forced the twists into a very tight, compact twisted section only a few inches long.

(6) Instruct your helper to grasp the tag end of the line with his left hand and exert fairly strong tension on this end. While you continue to force the twists toward him, he now slips the grip of his fingers up onto the single part of the line, away from the twisted section.

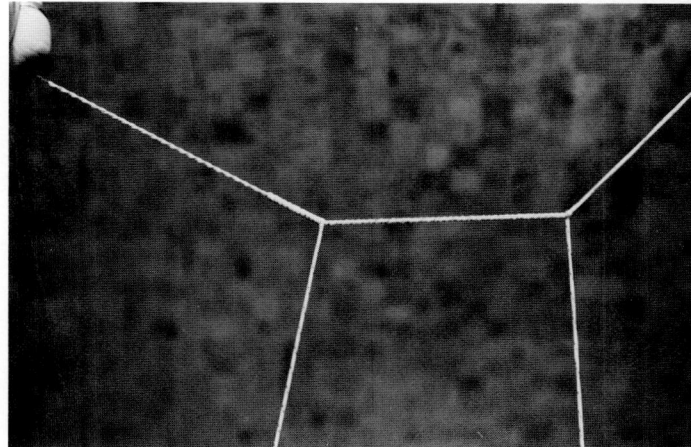

(7) At this point the twisted section will start to untwist and the tag end of line will spin onto the twisted section in the manner of a rope whipping. The helper carefully guides the end of the line as it rolls onto the twisted part, working toward the loop end. You continue to apply twist pressure by pushing the pencil forward.

(8) About half of the twists will be lost in the whipping process, but the final Bimini Twist will be a couple of inches long, flexible, but very tightly twisted and whipped. Clinch the tag end by taking a couple of half hitches through the open parts of the double line loop. Cut the end short and apply a safety whipping over the half hitches and tag end, using waxed dental floss. The double line should be tied together every two feet with a little dental floss.

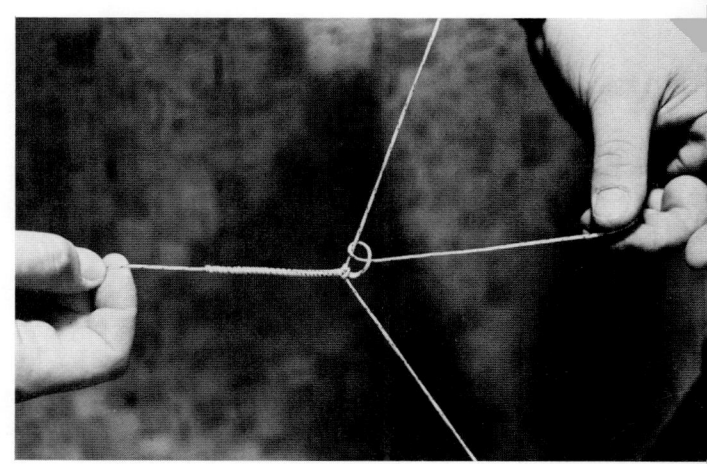

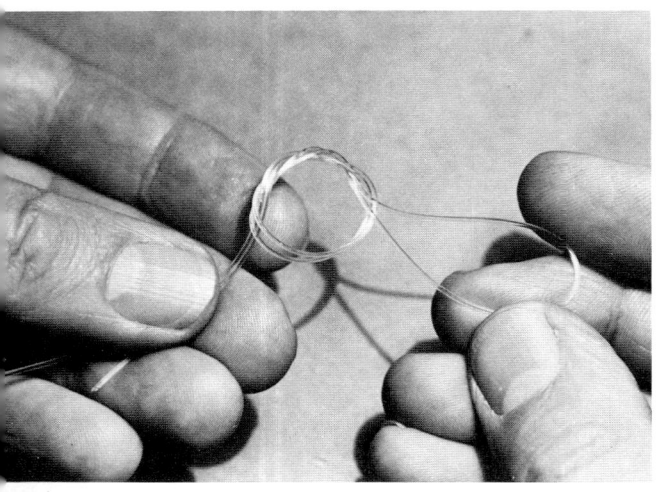

The Surgeon's Knot is a standard knot for making a quick loop in monofilament line. Double the line to make a loop of the proper length. Tie an ordinary overhand knot with the loop, taking one extra turn of the loop through the eye of the knot.

Moisten the knot with saliva before drawing the knot tight. This reduces friction and produces a better knot. Draw tight by pulling equally hard on both sides of the knot, grasping both strands on each side. Provides 85 to 90% of original line strength.

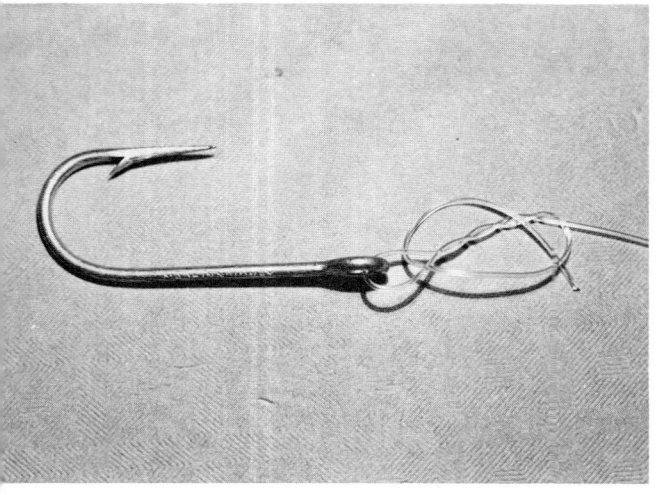

The Improved Clinch Knot is a good knot for attaching monofilament to any hook eye or metal ring. Pass the line end through the eye and take at least four turns around the main part. Pass the end back through the eye loop and its own loop, as shown.

Practical Fishing Knots   103

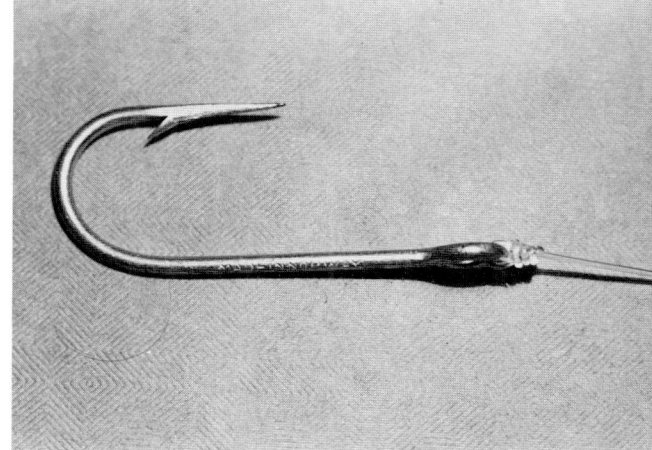

Moisten the knot with saliva before drawing it tight by pulling on the hook with one hand or a pair of pliers, and the main part of the line with the other hand. Don't try to untie mono knots from hooks or lures. Cut them away. Gives 90 to 95% of line test.

The Blood Knot is used to join two pieces of monofilament. Hold the two ends parallel, pointed in opposite directions. Wrap one end four turns around the other line, bringing the end back through the place between the two lines where the turns were started.

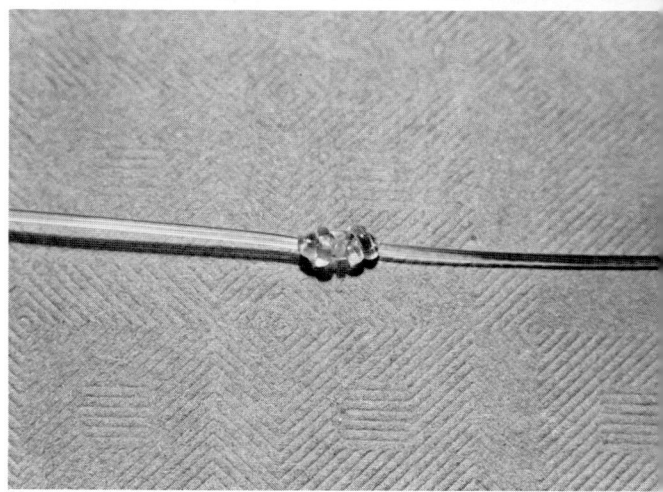

Wrap the other end the same number of turns around the first line, going in the opposite direction. Bring the end back through the starting point, from the opposite direction. Moisten with saliva and draw tight by pulling on both lines. Equals 85 to 90% of line test.

STRENGTH OF FISHING-LINE KNOTS

As measured in the research laboratory of the Du Pont Company, using Stren monofilament line, a Du Pont product. Knot strength equals the indicated percentage of unknotted line strength and is almost always under 100 percent.

Name of knot	Size of line	Knot strength
Improved Clinch	6 lb.	95-100%
	10 lb.	90-95%
	20 lb.	90-95%
Improved Clinch, Double Strand	6 lb.	90-95%
Improved Clinch, Double Loop/Eye	6 lb.	90-95%
Blood Knot	6 to 6 lb.	90-95%
	8 to 6 lb.	85-90%
	20 to 20 lb.	80-85%
	6 to 30 lb.	80-85%
Stu Apte, or Double-Strand Blood Knot	6 to 6 lb.	95-100%
	6 to 30 lb.	95-100%
	12 to 50 lb.	90-95%
Double Surgeon	6 to 30 lb.	95-100%
Improved End Loop	6 lb.	70-75%
Perfection Loop	6 lb.	60-65%
Double Turle	#6 to #8 hook	55-60%
Lark's Head Knot	6 lb.	75-80%
Tucked Sheet Bend	6 lb.	50-55%
Dropper Loop	6 lb.	65-70%
Overhand Knot	6 lb.	45-50%
	10 lb.	45-50%
	20 lb.	40-45%

13 Tackle for Beginners and for Bottom Fishing

How do anglers get started in fishing? Very often they become infected with the fishing virus by exposure to other fishermen. Their early attempts at collecting useful tackle often are haphazard. As beginners become more experienced, they also become more discriminating in their choice of equipment, and they tend to specialize on one wavelength or another of the great fishing spectrum.

Browsing through a well-stocked tackle shop can be great fun, but it often is confusing, even to fairly experienced anglers. The recommendations in this and the following chapters are intended to clear up this confusion, suggesting versatile tackle that time and use have proved effective. Some duplications are listed among the recommendations; this is because some items of tackle have broad practical applications.

Regarding costs, the price of tackle varies so much from shop to shop, area to area, and with the passage of time, that any attempt to suggest prices here would be ineffective and often misleading. Costs can be obtained from dealers' catalogs and brochures. Recommended tackle will be described in terms of rod, reels, and line. Terminal tackle is dealt with in detail in Chapter 18.

TACKLE FOR BEGINNERS

If the interest of beginning anglers is to be captured and held, they must catch fish. These can be small fish, but they should be easy to catch, and there should be enough of them to give the beginner a real sense of achievement in his early experiences. Porgies, small sea bass, weakfish, flounders, blowfish, surf perch, snappers, mackerel, fluke, and even bergalls are good for beginners. The tackle needed is simple and inexpensive.

If you are planning to buy tackle for a beginner, or to advise a beginning angler on what to purchase, the place to start planning is at the location where the neophyte will begin to fish. Will this be a party fishing boat? Then a versatile, inexpensive bottom-fishing boat rod and a light star-drag reel with 20- to 30-pound-test line, plus the necessary terminal tackle, will be the best bet.

Will he or she begin by fishing from a small outboard or inboard pleasure boat in an area where bottom fishing may be mixed with equal doses of casting and light trolling? Then the first outfit should be one that can perform these three functions reasonably well. Or is shore and surf fishing with natural and artificial baits and lures the most likely first step? Then, slightly more specialized casting tackle will be the best choice.

Beginner's party-boat outfit
Rod: Any light solid or hollow fiberglass rod designed for boat bottom fishing. Chrome-plated brass guides will do,

Expert anglers like Stu Apte, preparing to release a Florida Keys bonefish, only use tackle designed to cope with the fish and conditions they will encounter.

Tackle for Beginners and Bottom Fishing

June and Bobby Rosko use simple star-drag reels and light boat rods for rowboat fishing with sinkers, hooks, and bait for panfish, like this plump winter flounder.

as will a chrome-plated reelseat. A roller tip-top is nice, but not a real necessity. Hardwood butt with rubber cap.

Reel: Light star-drag or free-spool saltwater model capable of loading 100 to 200 yards of 20- to 30-pound-test monofilament line. Penn #155 or its equivalent is a good choice.

Line: 20- to 30-pound-test soft monofilament or Dacron line. Fill the reel to normal capacity. Line of this caliber is light enough for most small bottom fish, but it also will hold fish up to 20 or 30 pounds with a good star-drag reel.

Beginner's trolling, casting, bottom fishing outfit

Rod: Light- to medium-duty hollow fiberglass general-service spinning rod, 6½ to 7½ feet overall. Light two-handed butt and reelseat section. May be one- or two-piece. Chromed stainless-steel guides. Rod to match 12- to 18-pound line.

Veteran angler Jerry Dominy shows a young friend how to handle a small bluefish he hooked on a popping plug fished on typical light fiberglass spinning tackle.

Dick Gutwein of Toms River, N.J., used a light surf spinning outfit to capture a fine mess of weakfish from the Atlantic surf not far from Cape Hatteras Light.

Reel #1 (primary choice): Light- to medium-duty spinning model of 12- to 16-ounce weight with capacity of 250 to 350 yards of 15-pound-test monofilament. Corrosion-proof, drag, and antireverse features.

Reel #2 (optional): Light saltwater star-drag reel for trolling and bottom fishing. Penn Peer 109 level-wind, Garcia Ambassadeur 7000, or Pflueger Bond level-wind models are excellent.

Line: Sufficient 15-pound-test spinning-quality monofilament to fill the spinning reel. Fill the star-drag reel with good-quality 15- to 20-pound-test general-service monofilament.

Beginner's shore and surf casting outfit

Rod: Fiberglass light surf spinning unit 7½ to 8½ feet long, matching 15- to 25-pound line. Chromed stainless-steel or ceramic guides and tip-top. Chromed brass reelseat. One- or two-piece construction.

Reel #1 (primary choice): Medium- to heavy-duty spinning reel weighing 15 to 20 ounces, with a capacity of 300 to 400 yards of 20-pound-test monofilament. Drag, antireverse, corrosion-proof, surf quality.

Reel #2 (optional): Light surf-quality star-drag casting reel. Penn Squidder 140, Penn Surfmaster 100, or equivalent is good. To be selected only if the beginner shows definite aptitude toward and preference for a revolving-spool reel for certain casting tasks.

Line: Surf-quality low-stretch 15- to 20-pound-test monofilament for the spinning reel. Extra spool with line slightly heavier or lighter than that usually used. Surf-quality braided nylon or Dacron squidding line, 20- to 25-pound-test, for the star-drag casting reel.

Beginner's basic tackle box

All mechanics need a toolbox, and fishermen are mechanics of a very special sort. Serious beginners should be

encouraged to equip themselves with a tackle box containing the following basic tools and supplies.
- Bernard parallel-jaw fisherman's pliers
- Bait and dressing knife (filet style)
- Oilstone for knives
- Reel wrench
- Reel lubricant
- Screwdriver set
- Spool, spare fishing line
- Small spools, leader material
- Snap swivels and connectors
- Assorted sinkers, as needed
- Assorted hooks, as needed
- Assorted lures, as needed
- Fish-scaling tool
- Fishhook remover
- Antiseptic and Band-Aids

Finally, there are a few personal items that help to make the fishing life more enjoyable, if not more productive.
- Sunburn lotion
- Polarized sun glasses
- Light foul-weather jacket and pants
- Light rubber boots or surf waders
- Fishing belt with rod-butt cup
- Light canvas gloves
- Insulated fish/beverage icebox
- Short-handled gaff for shore fishing
- Notebook and pencil
- Small camera and film
- Shoulder bag for personal gear

HOW MUCH SHOULD YOU BE PREPARED TO SPEND?

Another way of asking this question is, how far up the quality ladder should you be prepared to climb?

It's foolish to buy expensive tackle for a beginner who may discover that he hates fishing the first time he becomes seasick. On the other hand, there's a lot of junk tackle being offered that may look adequate to the uninitiated, but which later proves to be a waste of time and money.

In fishing, as in so many other walks of life, you get what you shop for. Tackle does not have to be expensive to be good. Cheap tackle, however, seldom stands up to the job at hand, and it marks its owner as a "tourist" in the eyes of knowledgeable fishermen.

Two emotions animate anglers and

This light-tackle fisherman's tackle box is well organized, contains tools, reels, lures, line, terminal equipment, everything he needs for fishing with spinning, bait-casting, or salt-water fly-fishing tackle.

Ten-year-old Robert Morris of New York, N.Y., had little trouble taking a 43-lb. white marlin off Bermuda, fishing with a 4/0 Penn Senator reel and 30-lb. line.

keep them going. The first and most important is the heady glow of excitement that comes with making a good catch. The second and often longer-lasting emotion is the feeling of satisfaction and anticipation that owning and caring for good tackle gives any serious angler.

Nothing beats the performance of a tackle combination that is selected to perform the fishing task at hand. You never go wrong by buying as far up the quality ladder as your budget and pocketbook will allow. Good tackle gets a beginner started off on the right foot, but poor tackle may make him disgusted before he learns the difference, and a potential angler may be lost to fishing forever.

TACKLE FOR BOTTOM FISHING

Bottom fishing used to be considered pretty mundane stuff, but in recent years, it has developed into rather specialized types of fishing in a number of different areas. It's still the business of lowering baited hooks or special lures to or near the bottom to attract bottom-dwelling species, but what passes as good bottom-fishing tackle off Long Island, for example, would be totally inadequate at a Gulf of Mexico deep reef for red snappers, or off a Baja California island for giant black sea bass.

Below are the types of bottom fishing for which tackle will be suggested, together with the fish the tackle is intended to take.

- Atlantic inshore party-boat fishing (also practiced by many private and charter fishing boats): sea bass, porgies, blackfish (tautog), ling, whiting, flatfish.
- Atlantic offshore wreck fishing: cod, pollock, tilefish; groupers in the southern region.
- Inshore Atlantic bay and inlet fishing: weakfish (sea trout), redfish, flatfish, croakers, spot, other small inshore species.
- Gulf of Mexico deep reef fishing: red and other snappers, scad, groupers, cobia.
- Southern inshore boat and bridge fishing: grunts, snappers, small groupers, sea bass, flatfish.
- Southern offshore reef deep jigging: large groupers, snappers, amberjack, other good-size reef fish.
- Pacific inshore kelp-bed party-boat fishing: kelp bass, flatfish, related species.
- Pacific big-game bottom fishing: giant black sea bass.
- Pacific party-boat live-bait fishing: yellowtail, bonito, albacore, tuna, related species.

Atlantic inshore party-boat fishing

Rod: Hollow fiberglass standard boat rod with chromed-brass or stainless-steel guides, roller tip-top, hardwood butt, chromed-brass reelseat, rubber butt cap. Built to match 20- to 30-pound-test line. Medium action.

Reel: Any star-drag saltwater unit

Bottom fishing from party boats calls for strong but inexpensive tackle capable of handling pan and food fish weighing anywhere from a pound or so up to the size of these fat Florida groupers.

with capacity of 200 to 300 yards of 30-pound-test line.

Line: Monofilament or Dacron line in the 20- to 30-pound-test range.

Atlantic offshore wreck fishing

Rod: Heavy-action hollow fiberglass boat rod or cut-down surf rod tip with boat-rod butt, matching 30- to 50-pound-test line. Chromed stainless-steel or ceramic guides, ceramic or roller tip-top. Hardwood butt, chromed-brass reelseat, rubber butt cap. Generally longer and heavier than a standard boat rod.

Reel: Star-drag 2½/0 to 4/0 unit.

Line: Low-stretch, 50-pound-test monofilament or Dacron.

Inshore Atlantic bay and inlet fishing

Rod: Light-action fiberglass boat rod, longer than standard boat rod, greater flexibility in upper tip. Chromed stainless-steel or ceramic guides and tip-top. Wooden butt, rubber cap, chromed-brass reelseat. Rod built to match 20- to 30-pound-test line.

Reel: Light star-drag or saltwater level-wind reel with capacity of 200 yards of 20- to 30-pound-test line.

Line: Top-quality, low-stretch 20- to 30-pound-test monofilament, or equal quality Dacron in same tests.

Alternate rig #1: Light-action fiberglass spinning rod and reel combination designed for use with 10- to 15-pound line.

Alternate rig #2: Medium-action saltwater bait-casting outfit designed to handle 15- to 20-pound-test line.

Gulf of Mexico deep reef fishing

Rod: Heavy-action hollow fiberglass boat rod or cut-down surf rod, similar to that used for Atlantic wreck fishing. Chromed stainless-steel, ceramic, or roller guides, roller tip-top. Hardwood butt, chromed-brass or stainless-steel reelseat, rubber butt cap. Butt gimbal fitting where intended for use with fishing

A long, light boat rod or cut-down surf rod with a light star-drag reel is ideal for bait fishing or casting for bluefish from a northeastern party boat.

Bait or jig fishing for Atlantic deep-water fish like this 40-lb. pollock is a job for a quality fiberglass boat rod and a star-drag reel with 30 to 50-lb.-test line.

112 MODERN SALTWATER FISHING TACKLE

Angler-writer Mark Sosin used a short, stiff-action jigging rod, a star-drag reel with level-wind, and 30-lb. monofilament to nail this big Walker's Cay kingfish.

Southern inshore boat and bridge fishing

Rod: Medium-duty fiberglass spinning rod adaptable to star-drag reel use, designed to match 15- to 20-pound line. Chromed stainless-steel or ceramic guides and tip-top. Chromed-brass, anodized-aluminum, or Delrin reelseat. Cork grips and butt section. Rod length 6½ to 7½ feet.

Reel #1: Medium-duty spinning reel weighing 12 to 16 ounces.

Reel #2: Light star-drag or level-wind reel, or medium bait-casting reel with star drag.

Line: Standard-quality 15- to 20-pound-test monofilament.

chair or gimbal-equipped rod belt. Rod to match 50- to 60-pound-test line.

Reel: Star- or light lever-drag 3/0 or 4/0 unit.

Line: Low-stretch monofilament or quality Dacron line in 50- to 60-pound-test class.

Alternate reel: 4/0 electric-drive, star-drag reel.

Southern offshore reef deep jigging

Rod: Stiff-action, saltwater jigging rod, progressive-taper tip, designed to match 20-, 30-, or 50-pound-class line. Ceramic or roller guides, roller tip-top. Stainless-steel or chromed-brass reelseat, hardwood or fiberglass butt, gimbal fitting if intended for use with fishing chair or gimbal-equipped fishing belt.

Reel, 20-pound-class line: Quality

Pacific expert Harry Bonner recommends a selection of four separate rigs for the demanding work of fishing the kelp beds from southern California party boats.

A 9/0 Penn Senator filled with 80-lb.-test Dacron line, mounted on a heavy fiberglass rod, plus belt gimbal and shoulder harness, is used for 300 to 500-lb. giant black sea bass.

large star-drag, level-wind reel, like Penn Peer 109M, Garcia Ambassadeur 8000, or Pflueger Bond level-wind.

Reel, 30-pound-class line: Quality 3/0 high-speed, star-drag reel, like Penn Jigmaster 500M, Penn Senator 3/0 113H, Garcia Ambassadeur 10000.

Reel, 50-pound-class line: Quality 4/0 high-speed, star-drag reel, like Penn Senator 4/0 113H.

Line: Low-stretch monofilament or quality Dacron in line class desired.

Pacific inshore kelp-bed party-boat fishing

Rod: Progressive-taper, hollow fiberglass, western-style boat rod designed for 20- to 30-pound-class line. Chromed stainless-steel, ceramic, or roller guides and tip-top. Hardwood butt, rubber cap or gimbal fitting.

Reel: Light star-drag or level-wind saltwater reel with capacity of 300 yards of designated line.

Line: Quality low-stretch, 20- to 30-pound monofilament.

Pacific big-game bottom fishing

Rod: Standard big-game fiberglass trolling rod to match 50- or 80-pound-test line. Roller guides and tip-top, stainless-steel or heavy chromed-brass reelseat with lock rings, hardwood butt.

Reel, 50-pound line: Star- or light lever-drag 6/0 reel, lowest available gear ratio. Harness rings.

Reel, 80-pound line: Star- or light lever-drag 9/0 reel, lowest available gear ratio. Harness rings.

Line: High-quality Dacron to match desired line class.

Pacific party-boat live-bait fishing

Rod: Progressive-taper, hollow fiberglass, western-style boat rod designed for 30- to 50-pound-test line. Chromed stainless-steel, ceramic, or roller guides and tip-top. Hardwood butt, rubber cap or gimbal fitting.

Reel: Star-drag reel in 2½/0 to 4/0 size to hold 300 to 400 yards of designated class line. Harness rings.

Line: Low-stretch quality monofilament line in 30-pound class, same monofilament or quality Dacron line in 50-pound class.

Californian Carl Newell favors a long, light, fast-taper rod and 30-lb. mono line with a 3/0 star-drag reel for Mexican yellowtails and yellowfin tuna.

The author's former mate, Harry Clemenz, Sr., gaffs a 45-lb. striper taken at Montauk on light trolling tackle including a Penn Long Beach #68 reel and 30-lb.-class line.

14 Tackle for Small-Game Surface and Deep Trolling

Surface small-game trolling is the most widely practiced form of trolling and encompasses a broad range of inshore and offshore small-to-medium-sized fish. It would be entirely possible to troll for any of the fish named here with just one rod-and-reel combination. Such an outfit would be ideal for only a few species, however. It would be seriously underpowered for some species, and it would heavily overpower others.

The variations of tackle described in this chapter have been developed to render top performance with the species and in the geographical regions concerned.

SMALL-GAME SURFACE TROLLING TACKLE

Tackle for bluefish, school stripers, pollock, school dolphin

Rod: Light-to-medium-action fiberglass trolling rod built to match 20- to 30-pound-test line. Ceramic or roller guides and tip-top, chromed-brass reelseat, hardwood butt, gimbal fitting for chair or belt gimbal.

Reel: Star-drag reel in 2/0 to 3/0 size, lightest lever-drag reel in same size, large star-drag level-wind or bait-casting reel with same capacity.

Line: Quality 20- to 30-pound-test monofilament to match rod action and power.

Tackle for trophy stripers, channel bass, black drum

Rod: Medium-action fiberglass trolling rod matching 30- or 50-pound class line. Lighter tournament-quality rod if light-tackle catches are desired. Ceramic or roller guides and tip-top. Hardwood butt, chromed-brass reelseat, gimbal fitting for chair or belt.

Reel: Star- or level-drag reel in 3/0 or 4/0 size. Harness rings.

Line: Quality monofilament or Dacron line in the class desired, selected to match rod action and power.

Tackle for mackerel, weakfish, redfish, kelp bass, small Pacific salmon, small tarpon

Rod: Light-action fiberglass trolling rod built to match 15- to 20-pound-test line. Ceramic guides and tip-top; hardwood butt; chromed-brass, anodized aluminum, or Delrin reelseat; rubber cap or light gimbal fitting.

Reel: Any good light star-drag, level-wind, or large bait-casting reel in the capacity range of 300 to 400 yards of 15- to 20-pound-test line.

Line: Low-stretch 15- to 20-pound-test monofilament.

Above: Author-fisherman Milt Rosko used a light fiberglass trolling rod, 4/0 Fin-Nor reel, and 20-lb. monofilament to catch this big African pompano in the Bahamas. **Below:** A light fiberglass rod, 3/0 star-drag reel, and 30-lb. line accounted for this school tarpon caught during the great spring run at Boca Grande on Florida's Gulf Coast.

Tackle for king and other large salmon

Rod: Medium-action, progressive-taper, western-style trolling rod built to match 30-pound class line. Fiberglass construction, hardwood or cork finished butt, chromed-brass reelseat, rubber cap or light gimbal fitting, ceramic or roller guides and tip-top.

Reel: Star-drag 2/0 to 3/0 reel, or very large level-wind star-drag unit of similar capacity.

Line: Quality low-stretch 30-pound monofilament.

Tackle for bonito, barracuda, large jacks, small tuna, medium dolphin, medium tarpon

Rod: Medium- to stiff-action fiberglass trolling rod built to match 30-pound-test line. Roller guides and tip-top, hardwood butt, chromed-brass or stainless-steel reelseat, standard gimbal fitting for chair or gimbal belt.

Reel: 3/0 to 4/0 star- or lever-drag reel.

Line: Quality low-stretch 30-pound monofilament or equal quality 30-pound Dacron line.

Tackle for large tarpon, cobia, king mackerel, wahoo, trophy dolphin

Rod: Medium- to stiff-action fiberglass trolling rod built to match 50-pound-test line. Roller guides and tip-top, hardwood or aluminum butt, chromed-brass or stainless-steel reelseat, standard gimbal fitting for chair or gimbal belt.

Reel: 4/0 to 6/0 star- or lever-drag reel.

Line: Quality 50-pound-class Dacron line.

Spinning tackle substitutions

Although spinning tackle is better for casting than for trolling, there is no reason why spinning gear can't be used for trolling when suitable trolling tackle is not available, or when an angler feels more at home with spinning gear. Spinning rods generally are quite a bit softer in power and action than trolling rods. Following is a list of classes of trolling tackle and the equivalent classes of spinning tackle that can be substituted for them in trolling for small-to-medium ocean game fish.

IGFA 6-pound line class: Light one- or two-handed spinning rod with 10- to 12-ounce reel, line of 6-pound test.

IGFA 12-pound line class: Light two-handed spinning rod with 12- to 15-ounce spinning reel, 20-pound-test monofilament.

IGFA 20-pound line class: Medium two-handed spinning rod with reel of 16- to 20-ounce, 20-pound-test monofilament.

IGFA 30-pound line class: Cut-down surf spinning rod with largest possible reel filled with 30-pound monofilament.

IGFA 50-pound line class: No comparable spinning tackle is available, except on special custom order.

Spinning tackle works well for some types of trolling, as Florida taxidermist Al Pflueger demonstrates with a 20-lb., 14-oz., blackfin tuna taken off Key West.

Warning on line substitutions

If you are record-conscious, make sure you buy *tournament-quality* line that tests *not over* the line's rated class weight. Standard line always tests *not under* its advertised breaking strain, and it may cost you a hard-earned record by testing *more than* the record class's stated maximum breaking strain.

TACKLE FOR DEEP TROLLING

Deep trolling used to involve nothing more than hanging a heavy sinker on the line, putting the sinker and the lure or rigged bait overboard, and hoping for the best. The fisherman usually had only a vague idea of how deep the water was under the boat, and he found the shallow spots only when his equipment hung up on the bottom.

Modern deep trolling is fishing with an engineering approach. The electronic sounding machine has removed forever any doubt about how deep the water may be. People also have a much better understanding about what kind of bottom cover or formations attract and hold fish, how the change of temperature with depth affects fish, and what kinds of lures and baits work best at what depth and speed.

To complicate matters, deep trolling is now divided into at least seven major categories of fishing techniques, some of which are further subdivided by the nature of the equipment used. These categories are:
- Sinkers fixed to the fishing line to achieve depth.
- Use of droppable sinkers and a sinker-dropping device.
- Use of planers or paravanes attached to lines.
- Use of downriggers (underwater outriggers) with weights.
- Downriggers using planers rather than weights.
- Use of wire trolling line.
  (a) Lead-core line.
  (b) Braided wire line.
  (c) Single-strand solid wire line.
- Use of self-diving lures on soft or wire line.

There would be a lot of duplication and waste of space if I were to list every possible combination of tackle that could be used under these categories. Therefore, let us look at deep-trolling tackle from the two really big viewpoints, soft line and wire line. The usual suggestions will be made concerning rods, reels, and line. Wire fishing lines were discussed in detail in Chapter 10. I have added notations on the maximum practical depth to which each category of tackle can troll, using a standard one-ounce leadhead lure.

Because wire lines have absolutely no stretch, there must be maximum flexibility in the rod. This means using a soft-action rod of the line class suggested, or a medium-action rod designed for soft line one class lighter than the wire being employed. Rods used with fixed sinkers, planers, or droppable sinkers on soft line, on the other hand, must be medium-stiff to stiff-action models of the line class suggested.

The majority of fish taken by deep trolling in salt water weigh under 70 or 80 pounds, and they can be caught on tackle of 50-pound line class or lighter. For the sake of convenience, the tackle in each category is listed under three sub-headings.
- Light: tackle with lines testing under 20 pounds.
- Medium: tackle with lines testing 20 to 35 pounds.
- Heavy: tackle with lines testing 35 to 50 pounds.

Tackle for deep trolling with soft lines

Maximum effective depths:

With trolling sinkers	40 feet
With self-diving lures	40 feet
With droppable sinkers	60 feet
With attached planers	80 feet
With downriggers	120 feet

With very light tackle, sometimes all you need for deep trolling is a barrel or cigar sinker attached to the line, as is used here for stripers in northern Florida.

Downriggers (underwater outriggers) let you troll baits or lures at almost any depth while using soft line, and without weight on the fishing line itself.

Spinning tackle, light duty: Bluefish, small stripers, small salmon, mackerel, weakfish, sea trout, fish under 15 pounds.

Rod: Medium- to stiff-action fiberglass rod with cork grips, one- or two-piece construction, seven to eight feet long. Chromed-brass or anodized-aluminum reelseat, chromed stainless-steel or ceramic guides and tip-top, light metal gimbal cap. Designed to work with lines of eight- to 15-pound class.

Reel: Medium-light saltwater spinning model in 12- to 14-ounce weight class, 3:1 to 3.5:1 gear ratio, heavy-duty drag, 300 yards of 15-pound class line capacity.

Line: Top-quality low-stretch monofilament, eight- to 15-pound test.

Spinning tackle, medium duty: Big bluefish, medium stripers, pollock, medium salmon, fish 15 to 40 pounds.

Rod: Medium- to stiff-action saltwater spinning model, cork grips, gimbaled butt, fiberglass one- or two-piece construction 7½ to 8½ feet long. Chromed-brass reelseat, chromed stainless-steel or ceramic guides and tip-top, designed to work with lines of 15- to 25-pound-test range.

Reel: Medium heavy duty saltwater spinning model in 15- to 20-ounce weight class, multidisc drag, 3:1 gear ratio, capacity 300 to 400 yards of 25-pound-test line.

Line: Low-stretch 15- to 25-pound-test monofilament.

Spinning tackle, heavy duty: Trophy stripers and salmon, king mackerel, school tuna, amberjack, yellowtail, fish to 80 pounds.

Rod: Medium- to stiff-action fiberglass spinning rod in one- or two-piece construction, designed to work with lines of 25- to 35-pound-test range. Hardwood boat-style butt with gimbal fitting, chromed-brass or stainless-steel reelseat, chromed stainless-steel or ceramic guides, roller tip-top if rod is not used for casting. Length 8½ to 9½ feet.

Reel: Heavy-duty, large-capacity saltwater spinning reel with multidisc clutch, 3:1 to 3.5:1 gear ratio.

Line: Low-stretch 25- to 35-pound-test monofilament.

Auxiliary equipment: Terminal tackle for deep trolling, downriggers, etc., are discussed in detail in the chapters on baits, lures, terminal tackle, and outriggers and downriggers.

Star-drag reel tackle, light duty: Bluefish, small stripers, small salmon, weakfish, redfish, fish under 15 pounds.

Rod: Stiff-action fiberglass trolling rod with hardwood butt and gimbal fitting, designed to work with 12- to 20-pound-test line. Roller guides and tip-top, chromed-brass reelseat.

Reel: Star-drag or small lever-drag model in 2/0 size, gear ratio about 3:1.

Line: Low-stretch monofilament, 12- to 20-pound-test.

Star-drag tackle, medium duty: Big bluefish, medium stripers, pollock, medium salmon, fish 15 to 40 pounds.

Rod: Stiff-action fiberglass trolling unit with hardwood butt and gimbal fitting, designed to work with line in the 30-pound class. Roller guides and tip-top, chromed-brass reelseat.

Reel: Star- or lever-drag model, 3/0 size, 3:1 gear ratio.

Line: Low-stretch monofilament in 30-pound-test class, or quality 30-pound-test Dacron.

Star-drag tackle, heavy duty: Trophy stripers and salmon, king mackerel, school tuna, amberjack, yellowtail, fish to 80 pounds.

Rod: Stiff-action fiberglass trolling model with hardwood butt, gimbal fitting, designed to work with 50-pound class line. Roller guides and tip-top, chromed-brass reelseat.

Reel: Star or lever drag, 4/0 size, 2.8:1 gear ratio.

Line: Low-stretch monofilament to 50-pound test, or quality Dacron in same weight class.

Lead-core, braided, and solid wire lines are included in the following tackle list. They have been described in detail in the chapters on lines. The backing line commonly used under a shot of wire is usually good-quality Dacron or monofilament. A few anglers still use linen or braided nylon line for backing. In any case, backing should average 20 to 25 percent stronger than the wire being used.

Tackle for deep trolling with wire lines

Maximum effective depth vs. line length:

Water depth	Lure depth	Wire length
10 ft.	8 ft.	64 ft.
20 ft.	17 ft.	136 ft.
30 ft.	26 ft.	200 ft.
40 ft.	35 ft.	280 ft.
50 ft.	44 ft.	350 ft.

The table above is for solid soft-drawn Monel wire line, standard lure with a one-ounce lead head, and trolling speed of three to four knots. Average ratio of line length to lure depth is about 8:1.

Light-duty fishing: Bluefish, small stripers, small salmon, mackerel, weakfish, redfish, all fish under 15 pounds.

Rod: Soft-action fiberglass trolling rod designed to work with lines of 20-pound maximum test. Specially hardened roller guides and tip-top, chromed-brass reelseat, light gimbal fitting on hardwood butt.

Reel: Star-drag trolling model in 2/0 size with wide, open spool and not over 3.5:1 gear ratio.

Line: Lead-core, braided stainless wire, or soft-drawn solid Monel wire not over 20-pound test. Backing, if used, should be at least 25-pound test.

Medium-duty fishing: Big bluefish, medium stripers and salmon, pollock, all game fish 15 to 40 pounds.

Rod: Soft-action fiberglass trolling rod designed to work with lines up to 35-pound test. Hardened roller guides and tip-top, chromed-brass reelseat, trolling gimbal on hardwood butt.

Reel: Star-drag trolling model in 3/0 size with wide, open spool and not over 3:1 gear ratio, harness rings.

Line: Lead-core, braided stainless steel, or soft-drawn solid Monel wire between two- and 30-pound test. Backing, if used, should be about 50-pound test.

Heavy-duty fishing: Trophy stripers and salmon, king mackerel, school tuna, wahoo, amberjack, yellowtail, all food and game fish 40 to 80 pounds.

Rod: Soft-action fiberglass trolling rod designed to work with 50-pound-test lines. Hardened roller guides and tip-top, chromed-brass or stainless-steel reelseat, gimbal on hardwood trolling butt.

Reel: Star-drag model in 4/0 size with gear ratio not over 3:1. Wide, open spool, harness rings.

Line: Lead-core, braided stainless steel, or soft-drawn solid Monel wire testing to 50 pounds. Backing, if used, should be at least 60-pound test.

Very heavy duty fishing: Similar equipment using reels of up to 6/0 and 9/0 size, wire lines to 70- to 80-pound test, occasionally are used for very large fish in very deep water. In the Gulf of Mexico, snapper-fishing boats frequently use electric-powered star-drag reels with 60- to 70-pound-test wire.

Harry Clemenz gaffs a Montauk striper taken on 45-lb.-test solid Monel wire line, a Penn #68 Long Beach reel, and fiberglass rod with Carboloy ring guides, roller tip-top.

When tournament angler Elwood Harry puts pressure on a freshly hooked potential record, he expects his tackle to perform to the highest peak of efficiency.

15 Tackle for Big Game and Record Hunting

The International Game Fish Association's tackle classes, ranging from six-pound-line test to 130-pound test, have given many experts an excuse to fish for big game with tackle that ordinary fishermen consider ridiculously light. Each man to his own game. Tackle for record hunters is covered later in this chapter. The opening section deals with equipment that most fishermen agree is standard for the species being discussed.

These species include all of the billfishes, tunas over 100 pounds, sharks, giant sea basses, and other large, exotic fishes that anglers occasionally seek. Fish of different species, but with the same fighting ability, are grouped together under classes of tackle appropriate for taking them under average conditions.

Years ago, big-game fishing was considered to be a test of physical endurance. In some instances it still is, but in most cases, personal fishing skill with modern tackle has become much more than a marine weightlifting contest. To satisfy anglers who consider themselves to be more or less skilled than the average, two other classes of tackle are suggested for each group of fishes, one lighter and one heavier.

BIG-GAME TACKLE

Light tackle, big game (30-pound line)

spearfishes
white marlin
Atlantic and Pacific sailfish
striped marlin under 150 pounds
blue marlin under 150 pounds
black marlin under 150 pounds
swordfish under 150 pounds
game sharks under 150 pounds
other sharks under 200 pounds
giant sea bass under 150 pounds
rays under 200 pounds
sawfish under 200 pounds

Rod: Medium-action fiberglass trolling rod built to match 30-pound-class line. Roller or ceramic guides, roller tip-top. Hardwood butt, chromed-brass reel-seat, gimbal fitting.
Reel: Star- or lever-drag 4/0 model with gear ratio of about 3:1, harness rings.
Line: Good-quality 30-pound-class monofilament or Dacron; double line not over 15 feet long.
Options: Lighter, 20-pound-class matched tackle; heavier, 50-pound matched tackle.

Top: This is the kind of tension Australians put on their tackle while stand-up fishing for yellowfin tuna at The Peak, 7 miles off the Down-Under city of Sydney. **Center:** Twin 50-lb. outfits and a 30-pounder in an unusual rod-holder arrangement on the fighting chair of Gene Watters' Hatteras sport fisherman, "My Gena." **Bottom:** West Coast angler fights a giant black sea bass standing up with typical medium-heavy tackle, 80-lb. Dacron line, 9/0 Senator reel, fiberglass rod with roller guides.

Medium-light tackle, big game (50-pound line)

Pacific sailfish over 150 pounds
tuna 100 to 300 pounds
striped marlin over 150 pounds
blue marlin 150 to 400 pounds
black marlin 150 to 400 pounds
swordfish 150 to 400 pounds
game sharks 150 to 500 pounds
other sharks 200 to 600 pounds
giant sea bass 150 to 300 pounds
rays 200 to 600 pounds
sawfish 200 to 600 pounds

Rod: Medium-action fiberglass trolling rod to match 50-pound-class line. Roller guides and tip-top. Hardwood or aluminum butt, chromed-brass or stainless-steel reelseat, gimbal fitting.

Reel: Star- or lever-drag 6/0 model with gear ratio of about 3:1, harness rings.

Line: Good-quality 50-pound-class Dacron (preferred), or equal quality low-stretch monofilament; 15-foot double line.

Options: Lighter, 30-pound-class matched tackle. Heavier, (1) stiff-action 50-pound rod with 7½/0 reel filled with 50-pound-class line; (2) standard 80-pound matched tackle with 9/0 star- or lever-drag reel.

Medium-heavy tackle, big game (80-pound line)

tuna 300 to 600 pounds
blue marlin 400 to 700 pounds
black marlin 400 to 700 pounds
swordfish 400 to 700 pounds
game sharks 500 to 800 pounds
other sharks 600 to 1,000 pounds
giant sea bass over 300 pounds
rays 600 to 1,000 pounds
sawfish over 600 pounds

Rod: Medium-action fiberglass trolling rod to match 80-pound-class line. Roller guides and tip-top. Hardwood or aluminum butt, stainless-steel reelseat, gimbal fitting.

Reel: Lever- or star-drag 9/0 model with gear ratio of 2.5:1 or 2:1, harness rings and front tension yoke.

Line: Good-quality 80-pound-class Dacron; up to 30 feet of double line allowed.

Options: Lighter, 50-pound-class tackle with stiff-action 50-pound rod. Heavier, (1) 10/0 reel with 80-pound-class line on stiff-action 80-pound-class rod; (2) 10/0 reel with 130-pound-class line on medium-action 130-pound-class rod.

Heavy tackle, big game (130-pound line)

tuna over 600 pounds
blue marlin over 700 pounds
black marlin over 700 pounds
swordfish over 700 pounds
game sharks over 800 pounds
other sharks over 1,000 pounds
rays over 1,000 pounds

Rod: Medium-action fiberglass trolling rod built to match 130-pound line,

June Rosko finds the harness a bit loose as she fights an Atlantic blue marlin, somewhere off Bimini, with a 12/0 Fin-Nor reel with lever drag and 130-lb. Dacron line.

roller guides, hardwood or aluminum butt, gimbal fitting.

Reel: Lever- or star-drag 12/0 model with gear ratio of about 2:1, harness rings and front tension yoke.

Line: Good-quality 130-pound-class Dacron line; double line up to 30 feet long permitted.

Options: Lighter, soft-to-medium-action 130-pound rod with 10/0 reel filled with 130-pound line. Heavier, stiff-action 130-pound rod with 14/0 reel filled with 130-pound line.

Unlimited class (line over 130-pound test)

This group includes all fish over 1,000 pounds. While IGFA does not publish records of game fish caught on line testing more than 130 pounds, it does preserve such records, provided all tackle and operating rules have been observed and the necessary application has been made, and the line sample provided does not test over 180 pounds. Unlimited-class tackle was popular until a few years ago among anglers who fished for the very largest game fish. An unlimited-class outift would be something like the following:

Rod: Extra-heavy action, matching 150- to 180-pound-test line. Fiberglass construction, possibly double-built, with roller guides and tip-top, stainless-steel reelseat, aluminum butt, gimbal fitting.

Reel: Lever-action 14/0, 16/0, or larger model with harness rings and front tension yoke. Gear ratio of 1:1.

Line: Heaviest Dacron line consistent with the overall tackle combination, not over 180-pound test if IGFA recognition is sought.

With the present degree of perfection of tackle in the 130-pound class, and with vastly improved baits and fish-fighting techniques available, very few modern anglers are tempted to experiment with tackle in the unlimited class. The reels and rods are quite heavy in themselves, and anglers find themselves expending as much energy fighting the heavy tackle as they do fighting the fish.

A stiff-action 130-pound-class rod mounting a modern 12/0 or possibly 14/0 lever-drag reel is about as heavy a piece of tackle as even a strong fisherman may wish to handle.

TACKLE FOR THE RECORD HUNTER

Record hunters are a special breed of angler. Tackle that satisfies most other fishermen often leaves them cold. But tournament tackle, as record-hunting tackle is sometimes called, does not have to be extremely expensive to do its job. In fishing, where you are competing against established records or against other anglers in a true contest of skill, tackle must be as closely balanced to optimum efficiency as possible. This means that the rod should exactly, not approximately, match the line in power and type of action. The reel should be big enough, but no bigger and heavier than is needed to hold the required yardage of line. The line itself must be of top quality.

As has been mentioned, the International Game Fish Association recognizes saltwater game-fish records taken on lines that do not test over 6, 12, 20, 30, 50, 80, and 130 pound breaking strain. This means that a record hunter must make sure that the line he uses is of "tournament" rating, not standard rating. As was mentioned in the chapter on lines, standard commercial ratings of lines guarantee that the line will not break at *less than* the advertised breaking strain.

A "tournament-rated" line, on the other hand, is one that is guaranteed not to break at *more than* the advertised line class. To be on the safe side, manufacturers of tournament-grade line usually select a line that consistently tests five to 10 percent under the allowed breaking strain. If you couple this with the fact that nylon monofilament tends to lose up to 10 or 15 percent of its dry strength when thoroughly wet, you could wind up with line testing 20 to 25 percent under the maximum allowed breaking strain for the line class being used after a long, hard day on the water.

This explains why a competitive fisherman using tournament tackle and putting maximum pressure on his equipment for quick kills or releases may find himself breaking lines on fish that he confidently expects will add to his score. It's popular to give names to tackle classes, and the names most commonly used to designate the various IGFA line classes are as follows.

Class name	IGFA line class
Ultra-light	6 lb.
Very light	12 lb.
Light	20 lb.
Medium light	30 lb.
Medium	50 lb.
Medium heavy	80 lb.
Heavy	130 lb.

Of course, these definitions are relative only to themselves. What may be light tackle for black marlin may be heavy tackle for sailfish. Rather than go through a long list of tackle recommendations that would repeat suggestions already made, let us look at the problems of the record hunter from the viewpoint of the special problems he encounters, with a few special tackle suggestions inserted where they are needed.

One segment of saltwater sport fishing that attracts many record hunters is that of light-tackle billfishing. The Atlantic and Pacific sailfishes, the sporty little white marlin of the Atlantic, the audacious striped marlin of Indo-Pacific waters, and the rare and exotic spearfishes are perfect for light-tackle fishing without the stigma of stunt angling.

This is usually stand-up fishing, and the lighter the weight of the tackle without sacrificing power and action, the easier it is on the angler. Interestingly, IGFA recently has created several new species divisions in the small tuna category, and tackle designed for light billfishing is perfect for taking these recent non-billfish additions to the IGFA list.

Light tournament-grade trolling tackle: IGFA line classes 6, 12, 20, 30

sailfish
white marlin
spearfish
striped marlin
small blue marlin
small black marlin
small swordfish
non-billfish under 200 pounds

Rod: Top-quality medium- to stiff-action fiberglass or graphite-fiber model designed for the indicated line class. Roller guides and tip-top, except where rod may be used for casting, in which case, guides and tip-top should be ceramic. Hardwood, aluminum, or fiberglass butt with length adjusted to individual angler's preference for use with gimbal-equipped fishing belt and light shoulder harness. Chromed-brass or light stainless-steel reelseat and metal butt gimbal fitting. Rod to be used with Dacron line only may be medium action.

Mrs. Daniel J. W. McCarthy, former president of the International Women's Fishing Association, favors very light tackle for top sport in tournament competition.

Hawaiian angler Rufus Spalding caught his record 240-lb. ahi (yellowfin tuna) with medium-duty 50-lb.-test line, fiberglass rod, and 9/0 Fin-Nor lever-drag reel.

Reel: Star- or light lever-drag model in following size relationships; six-pound-line class, 1/0; 12-pound-line class, 2/0; 20-pound-line class, 3/0; 30-pound-line class, 4/0. Gear ratio 3:1 to 4:1. Ultra-smooth drag, harness rings.

Line: Tournament-grade monofilament in six- to 20-pound-line classes, option of monofilament or tournament-grade Dacron in 30-pound-line-class. Up to 15-foot double line permitted.

Auxiliary equipment: Comfortable shoulder harness and gimbal-equipped fishing belt for stand-up fishing.

The 50-pound-line class would appear to be a stepchild when it comes to making game-fish records, but a look at the record book shows that the 50-pound-line class slots are well populated with quite a few really big fish. One problem, from an average angler's viewpoint, is that 50-pound-class tackle is seldom considered to be potential record tackle unless it is designated as acceptable light tackle in some tournament that awards extra points for light-tackle captures, or somebody happens to luck into an exceptional fish while fishing with this class of equipment.

Another problem is different. This is the fact that 50-pound-line class tackle seems to be halfway between what most people consider stand-up or sit-down tackle. Few anglers have difficulty fishing standing up with tackle of 30-pound-line class or less. Tackle in the 80-pound and 130-pound-line classes requires a fighting chair to enable the angler to utilize the strength of the line and power of the rod to full advantage.

It takes a strong man or woman to fight a game fish standing up, working 50-pound tackle to its full capability. By the same token, using this gear in a fighting chair seems to smack of beating a bass drum with a wet sponge. Nevertheless, medium-duty 50-pound-line-class tackle does take a lot of trophy fish and has a surprising number of IGFA record potentials, so let's scrutinize it from the viewpoint of a record-conscious fisherman.

Medium tournament-grade trolling tackle: IGFA line class 50

giant sea bass, jewfish
blue, black, striped marlin
swordfish
hammerhead shark
Atlantic-Pacific bigeye tuna
southern bluefin tuna
all new IGFA species divisions

Rod (stand-up fishing): Lightweight, medium-action fiberglass or graphite-fiber model, one- or two-piece construction. Fiberglass butt tailored to angler's required length for use with belt, harness. Chromed-brass or stainless-steel reelseat, roller guides and tip-top, cork or composition grips, light gimbal fitting.

Rod (fighting-chair fishing): Medium-duty, medium-weight fiberglass model, conventional two-piece trolling construction. Hardwood or aluminum straight butt, or curved metal butt for heavy-duty fishing, gimbal fitting. Roller guides and tip-top, chromed-brass or stainless-steel reelseat, cork or composition grips.

Reel (stand-up fishing): Star-drag model, 6/0 size, with one-piece metal spool, 3:1 gear ratio, harness rings, rod yoke.

Reel (fighting-chair fishing): Lever-drag model, 6/0 size, with 2.5:1 to 3:1 gear ratio, harness rings, rod yoke.

Line: Tournament-grade 50-pound-class Dacron; 15-foot double line permitted.

Auxiliary equipment: Top-quality fishing belt with gimbal, vest-type harness adjustable to the angler.

Modern fishing techniques are such that bigger fish are now being taken on medium-heavy 80-pound-line-class tackle than were being caught a few years ago on heavy 130-pound equipment. The heavier the tackle, the harder the angler has to work just to use the equipment, and the smaller store of energy he has left for fighting the fish. But at the same time, when it comes to fighting the very largest billfish, super-giant bluefin tuna, and great game sharks, there is no substitute for tackle that is built to work at the very top of an angler's physical and psychological ability.

Considerable controversy has developed over the merits of the curved butt. Some purists even claim that it gives the angler an "unfair advantage" over the fish. Originally, all game-fish rods had straight butts. As fighting chairs became better designed over the years, the advantage of locating the chair gimbal cup on a vertical member that provided for vertical adjustment became apparent. Thus, longer or shorter butts could be accommodated to a given chair by a few moments of work with a wrench or screwdriver.

One of the major problems of fishing for super-large game fish is having to pump up the fish in deep water. If the rod somehow could be angled down into a more horizontal position, lifting would be easier. Early versions of the bent-butt rod had an adjustable joint in the butt just below the reelseat. With the advent of the first bent-butt rods came a fresh discovery. If the lower portion of the butt

Tackle of the 50-lb. class is about the heaviest that can be used for stand-up fishing from a boat. Lacking a harness, this angler may have to use a chair.

Using medium-heavy tackle with 80-lb. line, a 9/0 Fin-Nor reel, and rod with bent butt, Jack Rounick took three swordfish in one day at Montauk, N.Y., with Capt. Jack Pierpont.

were made longer, the gimbal cup could be dropped lower, increasing the effective lever distance that the angler could use in pulling with his hands or harness against the gimbal's fulcrum, while not increasing the distance the angler would have to reach with his arms to handle the rod and reel effectively.

Floridian Jim Hardie shows the strain of battling one of Nova Scotia's big bad bluefins, using a 12/0 Penn Senator and 130-lb. line.

Rods with adjustable butt joints are no longer made. Instead, the curved butt is made of machined cast aluminum with an offset angle of 30 to 35 degrees at the bend. The bend radius is located about six inches below the lower extremity of the reelseat and about 21 inches above the lower extremity. This increases the angler's effective working leverage from an average of about 18 inches to about 27 inches, or by about 50 percent. Naturally, a chair with a very low gimbal cup adjustment is required.

Not all big-game anglers use or even like the curved butt. But it has proved extremely effective on very large fish that tend to dive deep, requiring all of the angler's muscle power to bring them to the surface. Its use is sanctioned by IGFA, and it is employed almost exclusively on 80- and 130-pound-class tackle.

Heavy tournament-grade trolling tackle: Medium-heavy, IGFA line class 80; Heavy, IGFA line class 130

trophy black and blue marlin
Chilean swordfish
super-giant bluefin tuna
game sharks over 1,000 pounds

Rod: Heavy-action "unlimited"-grade fiberglass big-game rod for 130-pound line, or heavy-action fiberglass rod built for 80-pound-class line. Aluminum curved butt, stainless-steel double extra-strong reelseat, roller guides and tip-top, composition grip.

Reel: Lever drag in the following sizes: for 80-pound-class line, 9/0 or 10/0 model with 2:1 gear ratio; for 130-pound-class line, 12/0 or 14/0 model with 2:1 or 1:1 gear ratio. Rod tension yoke, harness rings.

Line: Tournament-grade Dacron line in class specified; up to 30-foot double line allowed.

Auxiliary equipment: Individually fitted kidney or seat harness with parachute-quality nylon web straps. Canvas gloves for line-tending.

Big-game rods usually are called trolling rods, even though they are frequently used with drifted or deep-fished live or natural bait. Once the fish is hooked, the fighting tactics are the same as for fish hooked while trolling.

When it comes to record fishing with casting tackle, the same general suggestions about trolling tackle apply. The thoughtful angler is sure that his line will not test over the limit set by the line class. If he is not sure, he tests his own line by loading a sample piece of it with a bucket and a spring balance and gradually adding water or sand until the true breaking strain reveals itself.

The great danger to line in casting tackle is a worn, cracked, or grooved guide. Both rod and reel should be washed carefully after each day's use in salt water. Dacron line is relatively impervious to ultraviolet damage from sunlight, but nylon monofilament loses strength after prolonged exposure to sunlight.

Not many anglers are able to say, "I went fishing for a new record and I caught one!" Most record fish are just ordinary fish when they are hooked. But if a fish is really big, and may be a record for the class of tackle being used, excitement quickly mounts until the fish is either gaffed or gains its freedom. The record hunter fishes with tackle that is always record-ready. He treats each fish as a potential record. This way, when a real record comes along, he doesn't die of stage fright before bringing the beauty to the side of the boat.

Karl Osborne favors a full-size surf spinning outfit with a cut-down butt for casting metal lures in the Hatteras region for fish like this 60-lb. channel bass.

16 Tackle for Boat and Surf Casting

Although most surf casters will deny it, there are probably as many casters working from boats as from the beach. Surf casters themselves are taking to small boats, because boats provide the range and mobility the anglers lack ashore.

Boat casting tackle is often identical with that used on the beach, but frequently there are subtle differences. In a few instances, distinctive tackle has been developed for particular types of boat casting. Generally speaking, the combinations of rod action, reel size and power, line quality, and terminal tackle that boat casters employ are dictated by the fish they are after, the conditions under which they fish, and local preferences.

Also generally speaking, boat casting on salt water can be broken down into four major categories: northern 'longshore casting, southern 'longshore casting, Florida-Bahamas flats casting, and offshore game-fish casting.

Let us look at each of these categories in turn, breaking them down further in terms of heavy-, medium-, and light-duty fishing and including the major species of game fish against which each distinctive type of boat-casting tackle is most effective.

BOAT CASTING TACKLE

Northern 'longshore boat casting

Heavy duty: Trophy stripers, channel bass, black drum.

Rod: Medium-action long-range or Hatteras Heaver type of surf spinning rod designed to work with lines to 30-pound test, fiberglass butt-and-tip construction, boat rod butt with gimbal fitting rather than surf-length butt. Chromed stainless-steel or ceramic guides and tip-top, chromed-brass reelseat, 9½ to 10 feet overall length.

Reel: Large-capacity surf spinning reel with multidisc drag and about 3.5:1 gear ratio.

Line: Surf-grade, low-stretch monofilament in 20- to 30-pound-test range, depending on working conditions.

Alternate outfit: Similar rod equipped to work with top-quality, large-capacity, star-drag, revolving-spool surf-casting reel, braided Dacron line in the 25- to 36-pound-test range, depending on conditions.

Medium duty: Medium stripers, bluefish, pollock.

Rod: Medium-action eight- to nine-foot fiberglass surf-rod tip with boat rod or cut-down surf butt, designed to work with lines in the 18- to 25-pound-test range. Chromed stainless-steel or ceramic guides and tip-top, chromed-brass reelseat, light metal gimbal fitting on butt.

Reel: Medium-capacity surf spinning reel in 15- to 20-ounce weight class, capacity 300 to 400 yards of 20-pound monofilament.

Line: Surf-grade, low-stretch monofilament in 18- to 25-pound-test range.

Alternate outfit: Similar medium-action surf rig built around a medium-

The typical Florida boat casting outfit resembles a light surf spinning stick with a shortened butt for boat work. Lines go from 8 to 20 lbs. breaking strain.

duty star-drag casting reel, 20- to 30-pound line.

Light duty: Weakfish, mackerel, redfish, small stripers.

Rod: Light-action surf spinning tip with cork grip boat-style butt end, 7½- to 8½-foot overall length, single or two-piece fiberglass construction. Chromed stainless-steel or ceramic guides and tip-top, chromed-brass or anodized-aluminum reelseat, light gimbal butt fitting. Designed to match 12- to 18-pound-test line.

Reel: Medium-light spinning reel in 12- to 16-ounce weight class. Capacity 300 to 350 yards of 18-pound-test line. About 4:1 or 4.5:1 gear ratio.

Line: Low-stretch, surf-grade 12- to 18-pound monofilament.

Alternate outfit: Similar outfit built around a light star-drag regular or level-wind reel and 15- to 20-pound Dacron squidding line.

Southern 'longshore casting

Heavy duty: Big red and black drum, cobia, sharks.

Rod: Heavy-action version of southern-style saltwater spinning rod, fiberglass construction with length of nine to 9½ feet, designed to work with lines in the 20- to 30-pound-test range. Cork grips, chromed stainless-steel or ceramic guides and tip-top, chromed-brass reelseat, light gimbal fitting at butt end.

Reel: Large-capacity surf spinning reel with 4:1 gear ratio, multidisc drag.

Line: Surf-grade, low-stretch monofilament in 20- to 30-pound-test range.

Medium duty: Snook, bluefish, barracuda, big jacks.

Rod: Medium-action, southern-style two-handed fiberglass spinning rod in one- or two-piece construction, designed for work with lines in the 18- to 25-pound-test range. Cork grips, chromed-brass or anodized-aluminum reelseat, chromed stainless-steel or ceramic guides and tip-top, light metal gimbal fitting on butt. Length 7½ to 8½ feet.

Reel: Quality medium-duty spinning reel in 15- to 20-ounce weight class, 4.5:1 gear ratio, multidisc drag preferred. Capacity 300 to 400 yards of 25-pound-test line.

Line: Quality low-stretch 18- to 25-pound monofilament.

Light duty: Snappers, mackerel, pompano, ladyfish.

Rod: Light-action one- or two-handed southern-style fiberglass spinning rod 6½ to 7½ feet long, designed to work with lines of 12- to 18-pound test. Cork grips, chromed stainless-steel or ceramic guides and tip-top, anodized-aluminum or Delrin reelseat.

Reel: Quality medium light duty spinning reel in 12- to 14-ounce weight range, 5:1 gear ratio. Capacity 250 to 300 yards of 18-pound line.

Line: Quality low-stretch 12- to 18-pound monofilament.

Tackle for Boat and Surf Casting   135

Bonefishing on a very light spinning outfit with 8-lb.-test line will test the skill of any angler. Either shrimp bait or artificial lures may be used.

Alternate outfits: Top-quality, long-tip, heavy-, medium-, or light-duty saltwater bait-casting outfits in proper line class, or saltwater fly-casting tackle (see related chapters).

Florida-Bahamas flats fishing

Heavy duty: Big tarpon, very large barracuda, sharks.

Rod: Medium-action southern two-handed spinning rod in eight- to nine-foot length, designed to work with 18- to 25-pound-test line. Cork grips, chromed stainless-steel or ceramic guides and tip-top, chromed-brass reelseat, metal butt cap.

Reel: Medium heavy duty quality spinning reel with 3.5:1 gear ratio, multi-disc drag. Capacity 300 yards of 25-pound-test monofilament.

Line: Quality low-stretch, 18- to 25-pound-test monofilament.

Medium duty: Permit, large snook, trophy bonefish.

Rod: Medium-action southern two-handed spinning rod in fiberglass construction, length seven to eight feet, designed to work with lines of 12- to 18-pound-test. Cork grips, chromed-brass or anodized-aluminum reelseat, chromed stainless-steel or ceramic guides and tip-top, plastic or metal butt cap.

Reel: Medium light duty 12- to 18-ounce spinning reel with 4.5:1 gear ratio. Capacity 400 yards of 18-pound-test line. Multidisc drag preferred.

Line: Quality low-stretch, 12- to 18-pound-test monofilament.

Light duty: Bonefish, ladyfish, small permit.

Rod: Medium-light action, southern-style one- or two-handed fiberglass spinning model, length 6½ to 7½ feet, designed to work with eight- to 12-pound-test lines. Chromed stainless-steel or ceramic guides and tip-top, anodized-aluminum or Delrin reelseat, cork grips, plastic or metal butt cap.

Reel: Top-quality, light-duty, 10- to 12-ounce spinning model with 5:1 gear ratio. Capacity 300 yards of 12-pound-test line.

Line: Top-quality, low-stretch, eight- to 12-pound-test monofilament.

Alternate outfits: Top-quality, long-tip, heavy-, medium-, or light-duty saltwater bait-casting outfits in proper line class, or saltwater fly-casting tackle (see relevant chapters).

Offshore game-fish casting

Heavy duty: Trophy dolphin, yellowfin tuna, trophy wahoo.

Rod: Heavy-action fiberglass southern- or northern-style spinning rod, boat-casting type of tip and butt, designed to work with 25- to 30-pound-test lines, length 8½ to 9½ feet. Hardwood butt or cork grips, stainless-steel or chromed-brass reelseat, chromed stainless-steel or ceramic guides and tip-top, light metal gimbal fitting on butt.

Reel: Large-capacity, multidisc, heavy-duty spinning reel. Capacity 300 to 400 yards of 30-pound-test line.

Line: Low-stretch, 25- to 30-pound-test monofilament.

Milt Rosko used his northern-style boat-casting spinning outfit with 12-lb. line and a light bucktail lure to entice a little tuna with a well-placed cast.

Medium duty: Yellowtail, bonito, school dolphin, wahoo.

Rod: Medium-action fiberglass, southern- or northern-style spinning rod, boat-casting tip and butt, designed to work with line in the 18- to 25-pound-test range, length 7½ to 8½ feet. Cork grips, chromed-brass or anodized-aluminum reelseat, chromed stainless-steel or ceramic guides and tip-top.

Reel: Medium-capacity spinning reel in 12- to 18-ounce class. Capacity at least 400 yards of 18-pound line, 4.5:1 gear ratio.

Line: Low-stretch, 18- to 25-pound-test monofilament.

Light duty: Small dolphin, small jacks, bluefish.

Rod: Light-action southern- or nothern-style spinning model, length 6½ to 7½ feet, fiberglass one- or two-piece construction, designed to work with lines in the eight- to 12-pound-test range. Cork grips, anodized-aluminum or Delrin reelseat, chromed stainless-steel or ceramic guides and tip-top, light metal or plastic butt cap.

Reel: Light-duty spinning model in the 10- to 12-ounce weight class, 4.5:1 to 5:1 gear ratio. Capacity 300 yards of 12-pound-test line.

Line: Low-stretch, eight- to 12-pound-test monofilament.

Alternate outfit #1: Cut-down (boat style) surf rod with star-drag casting reel and braided Dacron line in the equivalent line class.

Alternate #2: Saltwater quality long-tip bait-casting rod with appropriate star-drag level-wind reel and line in equivalent line class.

There is a great deal of regional variation in boat casting tackle. Before investing for the first time in this kind of equipment, by all means find out what the local fishermen consider best for the fish at hand. The suggestions here should serve as a guide, but being able to fine-tune one's casting tackle for maximum efficiency very often is the result of seeking and following good local advice.

To remove any misunderstanding about the meaning of the terms *northern-style spinning tackle* and *southern-style spinning tackle*, below are the definitions.

Northern-style spinning tackle: Features a medium- to heavy-action type of rod tip, one-piece construction with shaft extending through the butt section. Where converted to boat casting use, the long, fairly heavy tip is retained, and a hardwood or cork-finished butt section carrying the reelseat is added to the separate tip.

Southern-style spinning tackle: This usually is two-piece tackle, both pieces of equal length. Butt section is shorter, cork-gripped, and designed primarily for boat casting, although frequently used from surf or shore. Tip action is on the light side, compared with the northern variety. For surf work, full-length single-piece rods of this medium-light type of action are often preferred, especially where smaller fish like pompano are the target.

On the West Coast, examples of both northern and southern spinning and conventional casting tackle are found, usually with a tendency toward the West-Coast preference for long, slim, progressive-taper rods. The latter have long,

Tackle for Boat and Surf Casting 137

Angler-illustrator Ray Prohaska caught this magnificent 50-lb. striper at Montauk, N.Y., using an 11-ft. Hatteras Heaver rod, Penn Squidder reel, and 36-lb. linen line.

shaft extending to lower butt end. Chromed stainless-steel or ceramic guides and tip-top, chromed-brass or stainless-steel reelseat, plastic or rubber butt cap. Average length 11 to 11½ feet.

Reel: Large-capacity, heavy-duty surf spinning model in 18- to 24-ounce weight range. Capacity of at least 400 yards of 30-pound-test monofilament. Multidisc drag. Some anglers prefer manual line pickup.

Line: Braided surf-quality Dacron 30- to 36-pound test, or surf-quality, low-stretch monofilament in 30-pound test.

Hatteras Heaver heavy-duty conventional surf tackle

Rod: Heavy-action fiberglass 10- to 10½-foot one-piece model with stainless-steel or ceramic guides and tip-top, designed for use with star-drag, revolving-spool casting reel. Shaft extends to lower butt end. Chromed-brass or stainless-steel reelseat, rubber or plastic butt cap.

springy tips for fast casting action, and a stiff, powerful lower shaft section. Mastering any one of these types of tackle is merely a matter of practice. All produce fish equally well for those who use them properly.

TACKLE FOR SHORE AND SURF CASTING

Surf casters are perhaps the most independent, self-reliant, and self-assured of anglers. Certainly their tackle has come a long way since the days of the 14-foot hardwood or Calcutta rod and the knuckle-buster reel. Following are the types of surf tackle most likely to be encountered on a trip down our sand beaches and jetties.

Hatteras Heaver heavy-duty spinning tackle

Rod: Heavy-action fiberglass spinning stick in one-piece construction, rod

On the Pacific Coast, as in the East, the standard surf outfit is spinning tackle, here employed to good effect by angler-writer Larry Green of California.

Reel: Penn Squidder #145 or equivalent star-drag reel.

Line: Braided Dacron surf-quality squidding line in 30- to 36-pound-test class.

Medium-duty surf spinning tackle

Rod: Medium-action fiberglass surf model, either one piece or with detachable hardwood spring butt, designed to work with lines of 20- to 30-pound-test range, 9½ to 10 feet long. Ceramic or chromed stainless-steel guides and tip-top, chromed-brass reelseat, plastic or rubber butt cap.

Reel: Medium-large surf spinning reel in 16- to 22-ounce weight range, minimum capacity 350 yards of 25- to 30-pound-test surf-grade monofilament. Multidisc drag.

Line: Low-stretch, surf-quality monofilament in the 20- to 30-pound-test range.

Medium-duty conventional surf tackle

Rod: Medium-action, 8½- to 9½-foot model designed to work with star-drag reel and lines of 20- to 30-pound test. One-piece or detachable butt construction. Hardwood spring butt with chromed-brass reelseat if detachable. Rubber or plastic butt cap. Chromed stainless-steel or ceramic conventional-style guides and tip-top.

Reel: Penn Squidder #145 or equivalent star-drag reel.

Line: Braided surf-grade Dacron squidding line in 20- to 30-pound-test range.

Light-duty surf spinning tackle

Rod: Light-action, surf spinning model eight to nine feet long in one-piece, butt-and-tip, or equivalent two-piece construction, designed to work with monofilament lines of 12- to 18-pound range. Light hardwood spring butt if needed. Chromed stainless-steel or ceramic guides and tip-top, spinning style. Chromed-brass reelseat, plastic or rubber butt cap.

Reel: Medium-light (12 to 18 ounce) spinning reel with 4:1 or 4.5:1 gear ratio. Capacity 350 to 400 yards of 15-pound-test surf-grade, low-stretch monofilament.

Light revolving-spool and spinning surf outfits are popular in Florida waters for such heavyweights as black drum, fished with bait not far from shore.

Light-duty conventional surf tackle

Rod: Light-action surf model 7½ to 8½ feet long, designed to work with star-drag reel and casting line in the 15- to 20-pound-test range. Butt-and-tip, two-piece construction, light surf-length spring butt, chromed-brass reelseat, rubber or plastic butt cap. Chromed stainless-steel or ceramic guides and tip-top, conventional style.

Reel: Penn Surfmaster #100M, #150M, or equivalent star-drag model.

Line: Surf-grade braided Dacron casting line in the 15- to 20-pound-test range, or equivalent monofilament.

Ultra-light surf spinning tackle

Rod: Light-action, one-handed or two-handed spinning model, 6½ to 7½ feet long, designed to work with lines of eight-pound-test maximum. Two-piece construction. Cork grips; stainless-steel or ceramic guides and tip-top; chromed-brass, anodized-aluminum, or Delrin reelseat; rubber or plastic butt cap.

Reel: Any quality light spinning reel.

Line: Surf-grade, low-stretch monofilament, six- to eight-pound-test range.

Bait-casting tackle for the surf

Rod: Medium-action, 6½- to seven-foot bait-casting rod with extended two-handed grip, designed to work with line in the 20- to 30-pound-test range. Quality saltwater construction.

Reel: Saltwater quality level-wind bait-casting model with star drag. Capacity of at least 300 yards of 20- to 30-pound-test line.

Line: Quality heavy-duty braided or monofilament line in 20- to 30-pound-test range to match the rod.

Western long-line surf tackle

Rod: One-piece fiberglass heavy-action model 11 to 13 feet long, designed to work with lines of 30- to 40-pound test. Chromed stainless-steel or ceramic guides and tip-top. Special Alvey reelseat.

Above: *Alain Wood-Prince enjoys superlative light-tackle fishing with an ultra-light spinning outfit, used for longfin pompano in the shallows of a Bahamian beach.* **Below:** *The single-action Alvey side-cast reel is an Australian import. After casting, the reel is turned on its seat so the line can be reeled in as with other tackle.*

Reel: Australian Alvey reel with or without drag, or similar Scarborough model.

Line: Low-stretch, surf-grade monofilament in the 30- to 40-pound-test range.

17 Special-Purpose Tackle

Sometimes it seems that just about every kind of tackle can be called "special-purpose tackle." Refinements to older styles of tackle have become so numerous that one is hard put to keep abreast of what's new. But having thus far covered a very wide range of tackle for specific fishing purposes, we wind up with three types of tackle that most fishermen will agree can be called special-purpose equipment. They are: fly tackle for salt water, tackle for kite fishing, and tackle for the traveling man.

Saltwater fly tackle is enjoying a boom. Many anglers now are attracted to the quality of the fishing, and the challenge of taking the fish by a very exacting method rather than the older concept of making each fishing trip an exercise in weight lifting.

Kite fishing is also growing in popularity. The kite is a tool for presenting live baits to exceptionally wary fish. While the tackle used is not radically different from other light tackle, the way it is used is often quite different.

Finally, modern sportsmen do a lot of traveling, and carting along a collection of large and cumbersome rods and tackle boxes can be a real chore. Fortunately, new travel kits of light tackle have been developed to put versatile, multipurpose equipment in the hands of the angler who, by preference or necessity, wants to travel light.

FLY TACKLE FOR SALT WATER

As was mentioned earlier, fly tackle is divided into a number of weight classes, depending on the weight in grains of the first 30 feet of the casting line. The formula for determining the weight class of any fly line, and thus the tackle designed to handle the line, is given in Chapter 11.

Saltwater fly fishing employs tackle in the weight classes of Weight-7 (W7) and up. For the purpose of this study, we can divide this tackle into three general classifications.

Light: tackle using lines of Weight-7 and Weight-8.

Medium: tackle using lines of Weight-9 and Weight-10.

Heavy: tackle using lines of Weight-11 and Weight-12.

These weight divisions do not correspond to similar weight divisions commonly used to describe freshwater fly-casting equipment. Because the construction of the fly rod is largely dependent on the weight class of the line for which it is designed, there is not as much variation in power and appearance among fly rods of a class as there is among conventional and spinning rods of an equal class.

Weight-11 and Weight-12 rods, however, do tend to be rather beefy in build and fast in action, due to the need to im-

The fly rod has become increasingly popular with saltwater anglers, like this Florida Keys bonefisherman about to release a fish taken on a fly.

Californians Larry Green and George Cox were early leaders in using the fly rod to take striped bass and other game fish in the San Francisco Bay region.

prove their weight-lifting and fish-fighting ability. Any attempt to introduce weight-lifting power into the lower section of a fly rod also tends to make its action faster. Good casters learn to compensate for this situation.

Mark Sosin clears his line after hooking a school tarpon on Weight-9 saltwater fly tackle, somewhere in the mangrove country of South Florida.

Light saltwater fly tackle: Bluefish, weakfish, redfish, bonefish, bonito, school stripers, fish up to 15 pounds.

Rod: Fiberglass, impregnated bamboo, or graphite fiber eight-foot rod, slow-to-medium action, four to 4½ ounces, designed for W7 and W8 lines. May have short extension butt.

Reel: Saltwater quality star-, lever-, or disc-action-drag model with capacity of W7 or W8 line, plus 200 yards of 20-pound-test Dacron backing. Single-action or 2:1 gear ratio. Positive non-reverse spool feature.

Line: Weight-forward, saltwater-taper, or similar W7 or W8 casting line with floating, slow-sinking, or fast-sinking quality, depending on fishing requirements.

Medium saltwater fly tackle: Trophy stripers, very large bluefish, school tuna, sailfish, large permit, tarpon, game fish 15 to 50 pounds.

Rod: Fiberglass, impregnated bamboo, or graphite fiber nine- to 9½-foot rod, medium action, five to six ounces, designed for W9 and W10 lines. Should have short extension butt.

Reel: Saltwater-quality star-, lever-, or disc-action-drag model with capacity of W9 or W10 line plus 250 to 275 yards of 20-pound-test Dacron backing. Single-action or 2:1 gear ratio. Positive non-reverse on spool.

Line: Weight-forward, saltwater-taper, or similar W9 or W10 casting line with floating, slow-sinking, or fast-sinking qualities, depending on requirements.

Heavy saltwater fly tackle: Trophy tarpon, sailfish, small marlin, sharks, any game fish over 50 pounds.

Rod: Fiberglass or impregnated bamboo 9½- to 10½-foot rod designed to cast W11 or W12 lines, medium-to-fast action, six to eight ounces. Should have medium extension butt.

Reel: Largest capacity saltwater fly reel with star-, lever-, or disc-action drag, positive nonreverse spool, capacity of W11 or W12 line, plus 300 to 350 yards of 20-pound-test Dacron backing. Single-action or 2:1 gear ratio.

Line: Weight-forward, saltwater-taper, or similar casting line in W11 or W12; floating, slow-sinking, or fast-sinking, depending on requirements.

For special casting situations and very long casts, a shooting head may be substituted for the regular casting line. (As was explained in Chapter 11, a shooting head is a fairly short, quite heavy section of fly line that has the same weight characteristic as the first 30 feet of normal fly line. It usually is attached to about 100 feet of 20- to 30-pound-test monofilament, which, in turn, is fastened to the normal backing line.)

Anglers fishing for records under Salt Water Fly Rodders of America (SWFROA) rules should use single-action reels. SWFROA rules do not permit geared fly reels or separate insertable rod-extension butts.

KITE FISHING TACKLE

Fishing with a kite is both one of the oldest and one of the newest of modern game fishing systems. Basically, the kite is used to position bait, preferably alive, well away from the boat. The kite thus becomes a sort of super-outrigger with certain distinct advantages.

Properly rigged, the live bait is the only thing in the water near the game fish. Even the leader is lifted and supported by the kite. The bait is free to take evasive action when the game fish zeros in on it, yet it cannot get away completely, being tethered under the kite by the leader and line. This results in very exciting surface action, as the game fish tries to capture the bait and the bait tries to escape.

Tackle for kite fishing is usually on the light side, and while there may be considerable variation in what individual anglers may prefer for this kind of fishing, it does fall into a definite overall class.

Tackle for kite fishing. Sailfish, bonito, small-to-medium tuna, dolphin, large barracuda, small-to-medium marlin, am-

Proof of the pudding! Stu Apte whipped this record 154-lb. tarpon near Key West, fishing a heavy-duty saltwater fly rod outfit with 12-lb.-test tippet.

Above: *The fishing kite, with its tremendous reach, enables one to place live baits close to wary fish without bringing the boat into the immediate strike zone.* **Bottom:** *Tackle for kite fishing must be light, and stand-up fishing is standard. Here a Florida sailfish jumps clear almost at rod's tip on 20-lb.-line-class tackle.*

berjacks, game sharks, wahoo, and similar species.

Rod: Medium- to stiff-action fiberglass trolling or cut-down surf-casting rod designed to work with 12-, 20-, or 30-pound-test line. May be either spinning or revolving-spool type, with the latter usually preferred. Cork grips or light hardwood butt construction; chromed-brass, anodized-aluminum, or Delrin reelseat; chromed stainless-steel, ceramic, or roller guides; roller tip-top. Light metal butt gimbal fitting.

Reel: Lever or star drag, or large spinning reel designed for the class of line being used. Top-quality drag; gear ratio of 3:1 or more in star- and lever-drag reels, 4.5:1 to 5:1 in spinning reels. Capacity at least 400 yards of the class of line chosen.

Line: Top-quality, low-stretch monofilament or top-quality Dacron, depending on type of reel and personal choice.

Auxiliary equipment: Complete kite-fishing kit consisting of proper kite for the wind situation, kite line with at least two line-release devices, kite-line reel attached to the boat. Kite line may be ordinary 50-pound-test or heavier monofilament. Gimbal belt and light shoulder harness for the angler.

A medium- to stiff-action rod is selected, because the boat has little or no real motion with respect to the bait, and hook-setting line tension is entirely up to the angler. It is easier to set a hook in a fish with a stiff rod than a light-action rod when boat motion does not help the angler.

Special-Purpose Tackle   145

Kite-fishing tackle, like that shown here, is a medium- to stiff-action rod, high-speed star-drag or large spinning reel, and tournament-quality 12- to 20-lb.-test line.

manufacturers (which are noted in the Manufacturers' Index in the back of the book).

TACKLE FOR THE TRAVELING MAN

When it comes to traveling long distances and taking advantage of good fishing if it happens to be available, the modern angler is in something of a dilemma. First, there are scores of good fishing spots not too far from logical targets of business or pleasure travel, but how in the world do you transport fragile fishing tackle without receiving a pile of matchwood at your destination?

A number of manufacturers are selling so-called trail-fishing kits and pack-rod kits, which knock down into small, easily stowed packages. Unfortunately, while these outfits are great for light freshwater fishing, they don't do much for the saltwater angler. Some serious tournament anglers go to the trouble of

Because light tackle is employed, a fishing belt with rod butt gimbal and a light shoulder harness usually are used, even with tackle up to 50-pound class. Kite fishermen usually prefer to bring their fish in from a "dead boat," meaning that the boat's operator is not allowed to assist the angler by backing down or running up on the fish.

Depending on wind conditions, a light-weather, medium-weather, or heavy-weather kite may be used. In nearly windless weather, the boat may create "wind" by trolling across or into the existing breeze. In windy weather, the boat can reduce the wind effect by running downwind. However, excessive boat motion through the water tends to change the bait-presentation situation from a live-bait condition to a trolling condition, which may not help the fishing.

Kites are used to a limited extent to carry baits and lures farther out from the shore or beach when there is an offshore wind of the proper strength and direction. Kite kits are available from several

If you love both to fish and to travel, equip yourself to take advantage of opportunities such as pompano fishing on the pink sands of Bermuda.

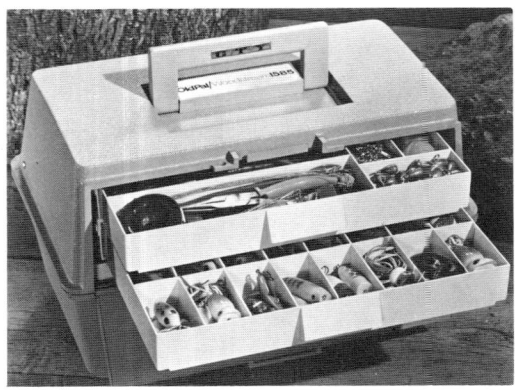

With carefully chosen contents, a modern tackle box can keep an angler properly equipped for light-tackle fishing almost anywhere he chooses to travel.

providing themselves with large telescopic rod caddies that will hold three or four medium- to big-game rods and straight butts, plus special foam-rubber-filled tackle boxes for their expensive game-fishing reels.

This is great for tournament fishermen who insist on using their own tackle, but it doesn't do much for the average angler who doesn't want to be burdened with a string of long rod caddies and small-tackle trunks that have to be checked into and out of airline baggage departments. Fortunately for the everyday fisherman, there are other options.

Faced with this situation, I have settled for two dual-purpose rigs, neither of which is advertised extensively except by its maker. The first is an eight-foot, two-piece Shakespeare light surf rod that is a fine casting rod when it is used with a spinning reel and line of about 15-pound test; it doubles as a useful trolling or jigging rod for a saltwater-quality, level-wind star-drag reel loaded with 20-pound monofilament. The big spinning guides have been replaced with smaller ceramic guides, retaining low line friction for casting and making it easier to pack the rod in a light rod caddy.

The second outfit is a dual-purpose, impregnated bamboo Orvis combination spinning-fly-casting rod that works with W5 or W6 fly lines. It handles a light spinning reel and six- to eight-pound-test monofilament. The rod is in two pieces, totaling 6½ feet. Both rods store in the same caddy. If serious fly fishing appears to be a possibility, there is room in the caddy for a two-piece, eight-foot Battenkill fly rod that does a notable job with W8 lines.

These three outfits, two dual purpose and one for light-to-medium saltwater fly casting, cover the spectrum as far as fly casting, light and heavy spinning, jigging, plug casting, bottom fishing with bait, or trolling are concerned. The lower section of a large, professional-model photography gadget bag is ample for reels and other necessities. Bag and rod caddy can be carried on board an airliner, and the baggage inspectors usually grant easy passage when they discover that the reel bag does not conceal hand grenades.

Following are the specifications on this tackle.

Dual-purpose casting-trolling outfit

Rod: Shakespeare fiberglass model SS890, two-piece eight-foot surf rod, light action, ceramic guides and tip-top (add-

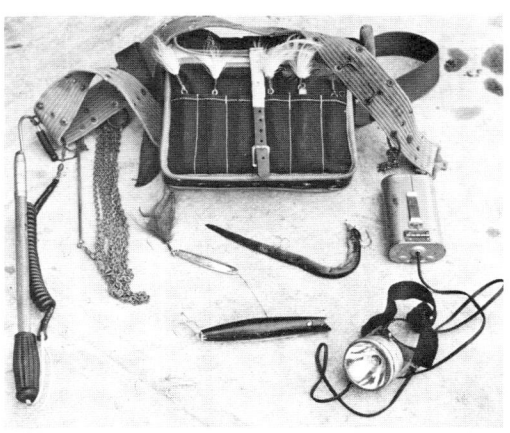

Not counting the rod and reel, which usually can be rented on the spot, the surf fisherman's essentials can be carried on a web belt and in a small lure caddy.

Above: *The answer to many a traveling angler's prayer is the telescoping Powerscopic rod, available in spinning, spin-cast, fly, and fly-spin fiberglass models with stainless hardware.* **Below:** *A more sophisticated outfit is this eight-in-one fly-spinning-bait-casting combination offered as a travel pack by Berkley and Company, tackle manufacturers.*

Special-Purpose Tackle 147

ed), cork grips, plastic butt cap, designed to work with lines of 15- to 18-pound test. Chromed-brass reelseat.

Reel #1: Shakespeare no. 2081A spinning reel, 3.2:1 gear ratio. Capacity 250 yards of 15-pound monofilament.

Reel #2: Pflueger Bond #2955 stardrag; level-wind reel. Capacity 300 yards of 20-pound monofilament.

Line: Quality low-stretch monofilament.

Dual-purpose spinning-fly-casting outfit

Rod: Orvis impregnated bamboo Rocky Mountain Fly-and-Spin model, 6½ feet, 3-1/8 ounces. Fly reelseat, spinning reel rings on inletted cork foregrip. Stainless wire guides. Two-piece construction. Medium action.

Reel #1: Orvis #50A lightweight spinning reel.

Reel #2: Orvis CFO III fly reel.

Line: Six-pound-test monofilament for spinning; low stretch. WF6F or equivalent fly line with 50 yards of light Dacron backing for fly casting.

All-purpose fly-casting outfit

Rod: Orvis Battenkill impregnated bamboo two-piece rod, eight-foot length, 4-3/8-ounce weight for W8 lines. Slow action.

Reel: Fin-Nor #2 saltwater fly reel with disc drag and single action; or Bogdan Medium with 2:1 gear ratio, lever drag.

Line: Any quality WF8, saltwater-taper, W8 shooting-head, or similar fly line with suitable 20-pound Dacron backing.

The specific recommendations of trade names and model numbers do not have to be followed exactly to produce an all-purpose or dual-purpose traveling tackle outfit. The important points to remember are these:

• Analyze your expected fishing requirements. If a very good single-purpose outfit appears best, by all means get top-quality equipment in the style of tackle you need. No dual- or all-purpose outfit can ever quite match a top single-purpose piece of tackle.

• However, if broad-banded tackle is needed, equipment that can do a variety of jobs reasonably well, follow the general ideas suggested here.

• Make a spinning-trolling rod from your old favorite two-piece spinning stick by replacing old metal guides with new, smaller ceramic guides and tip-top.

• You can convert a Weight-8 fiberglass fly rod into a light spinning rod by removing the butt cap and inserting a light fiberglass rod blank into the fly rod butt end to increase the stiffness to handle spinning lures. Make it removable so it won't spoil the rod for future fly casting.

• Pare your supply of traveling flies, lures, and other tackle to the bare essentials.

• Look over the tackle market for equipment that you can use directly or adapt to your special requirements.

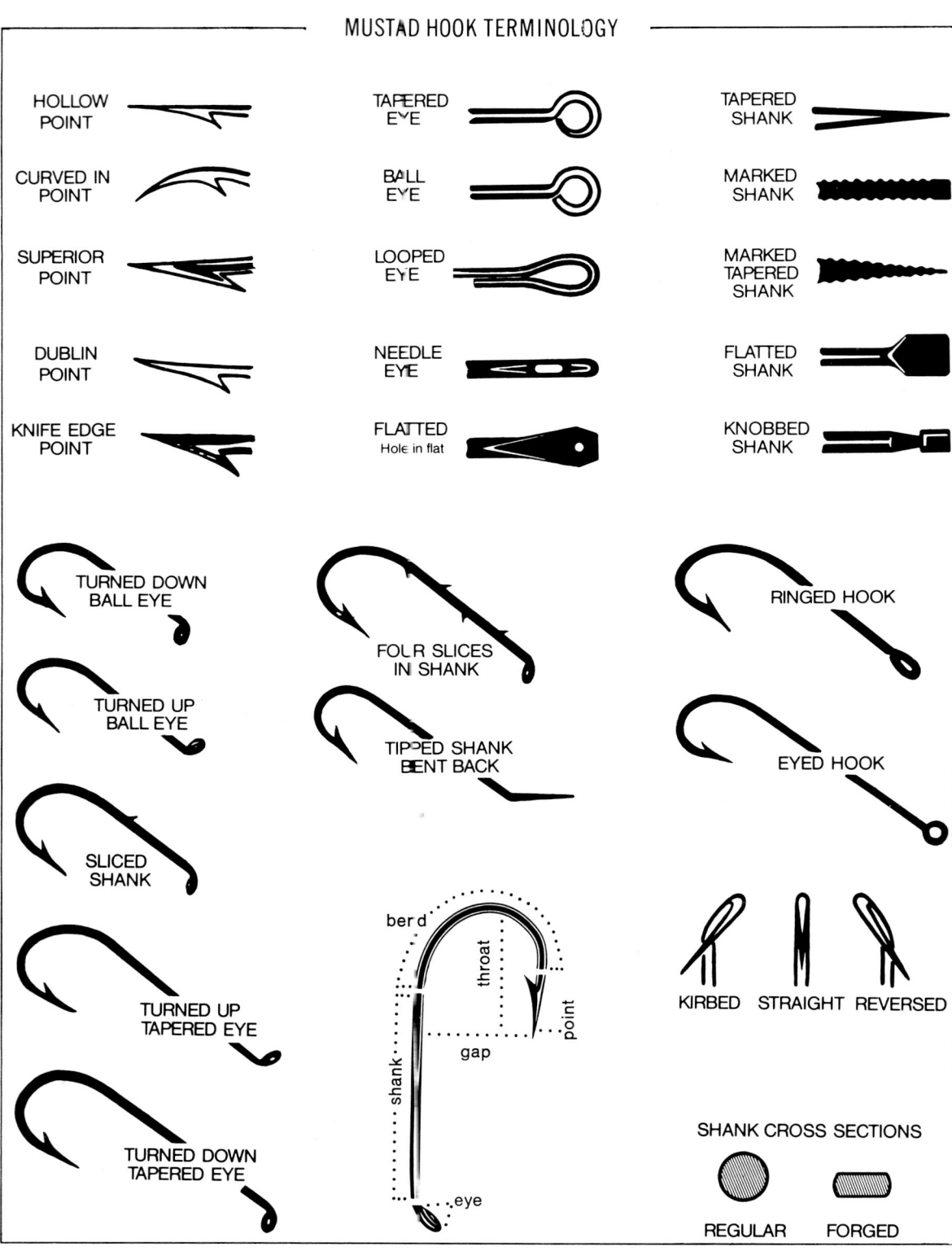

18 Hooks and Terminal Tackle

Even experienced fishermen are frequently baffled by the many names that are applied to various styles of hooks. The naming of hook styles began more than 500 years ago. The well-known Kirby pattern, for example, is named after one Charles Kirby, a Londoner who developed a distinctive style of hook in 1651, and at the same time perfected a manufacturing process that is little changed today.

Hook patterns have been developed to perform specific tasks or to fulfill particular requirements. The almost circular hooks used by tuna long-liners, for instance, are designed for great holding power after the fish has hooked itself. Other patterns of hooks provide solutions to other problems. Fortunately for sport fishermen, a few well-known patterns cover a wide variety of fishing situations.

The popular O'Shaughnessy pattern is about as close to a universal hook pattern as one can get. It works well on fishes with hard and soft mouths, fishes that jump, and fishes that bore down deep and make long runs. It has good penetration and holding power, and it is available in many wire diameters and shank lengths for specialized situations.

The Siwash or Pacific Salmon pattern, with its very long point and extra-deep barb, is excellent for small- to medium-size fish with soft mouths that jump a lot. This fish group includes the salmons, trouts, bluefish, weakfish, and some members of the mackerel family.

The strikingly similar American Eagle Claw and Mustad Beak hook patterns have proved very effective for all kinds of bait fishing. The in-curved point of the Eagle Claw and the Mustad Beak patterns places the axis of the hook's point penetration almost exactly in line with the natural line of pull of the combination of hook and line. This facilitates quick setting of the hook in situations where the angler must strike the hook into the fish with his rod.

Fish with small, tough, fleshy, or leathery mouths—like that popular northeastern pan fish, the tautog or blackfish—require a small, almost circular hook with a short, quick-penetrating point and a strong barb. This combination is found in the Virginia pattern.

Flatfish present a double problem. Summer flounders (or fluke, as they are often called) have mouths with a horizontal rather than a vertical gape, very narrow jaws, and small, sharp teeth. Fluke hooks, therefore, are usually long shanked, with a kirbed or reversed point. A kirbed point is one that is bent sideways to the right—as viewed from the top of the hook with the eye toward the viewer. A reversed hook is similarly bent at the point, but to the left.

Winter flounders, on the other hand, have tiny, round, soft, sucking mouths. This calls for a long-shanked hook of the Chestertown pattern, also kirbed or reversed.

(Continued on page 159)

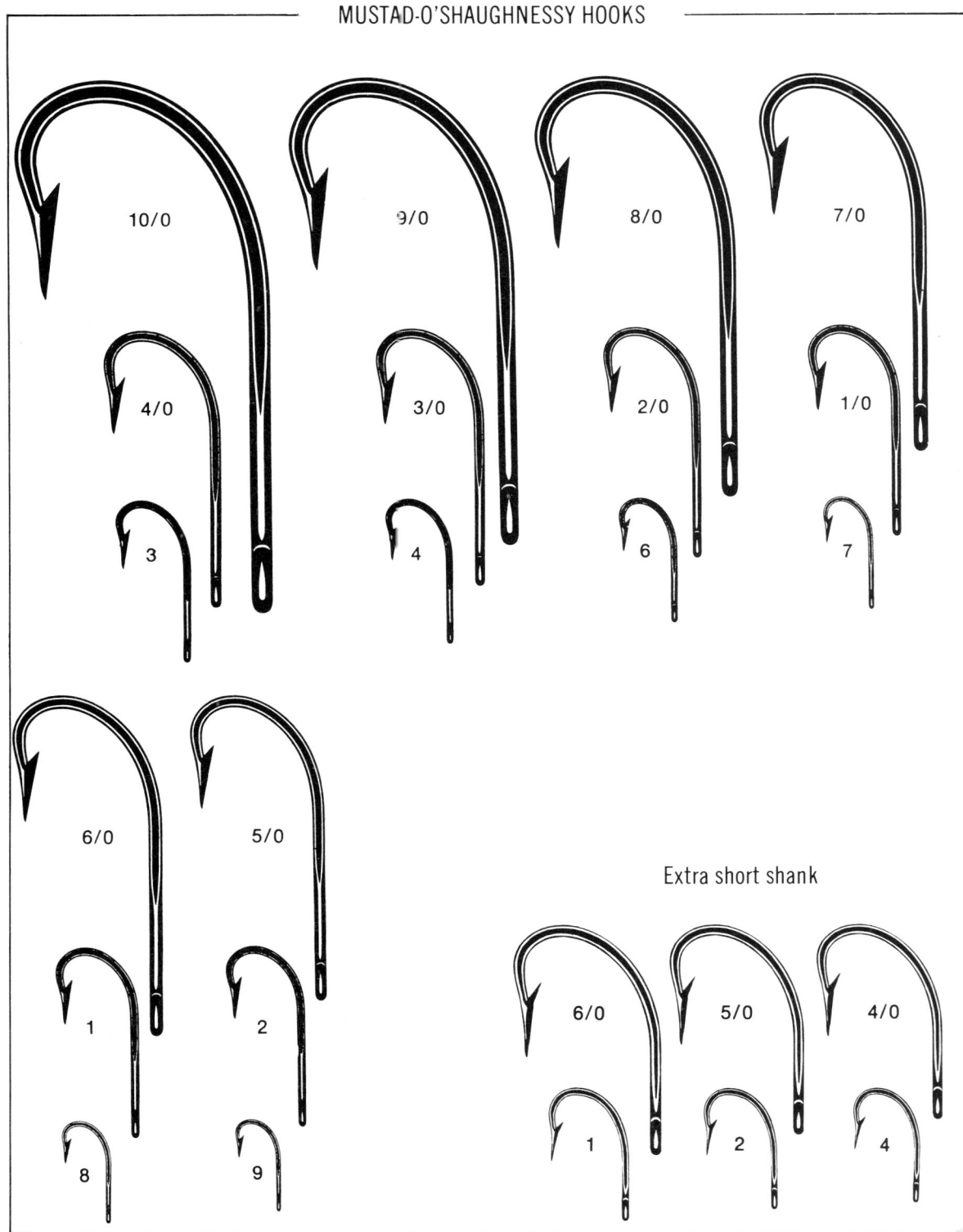

Hooks and Terminal Tackle 151

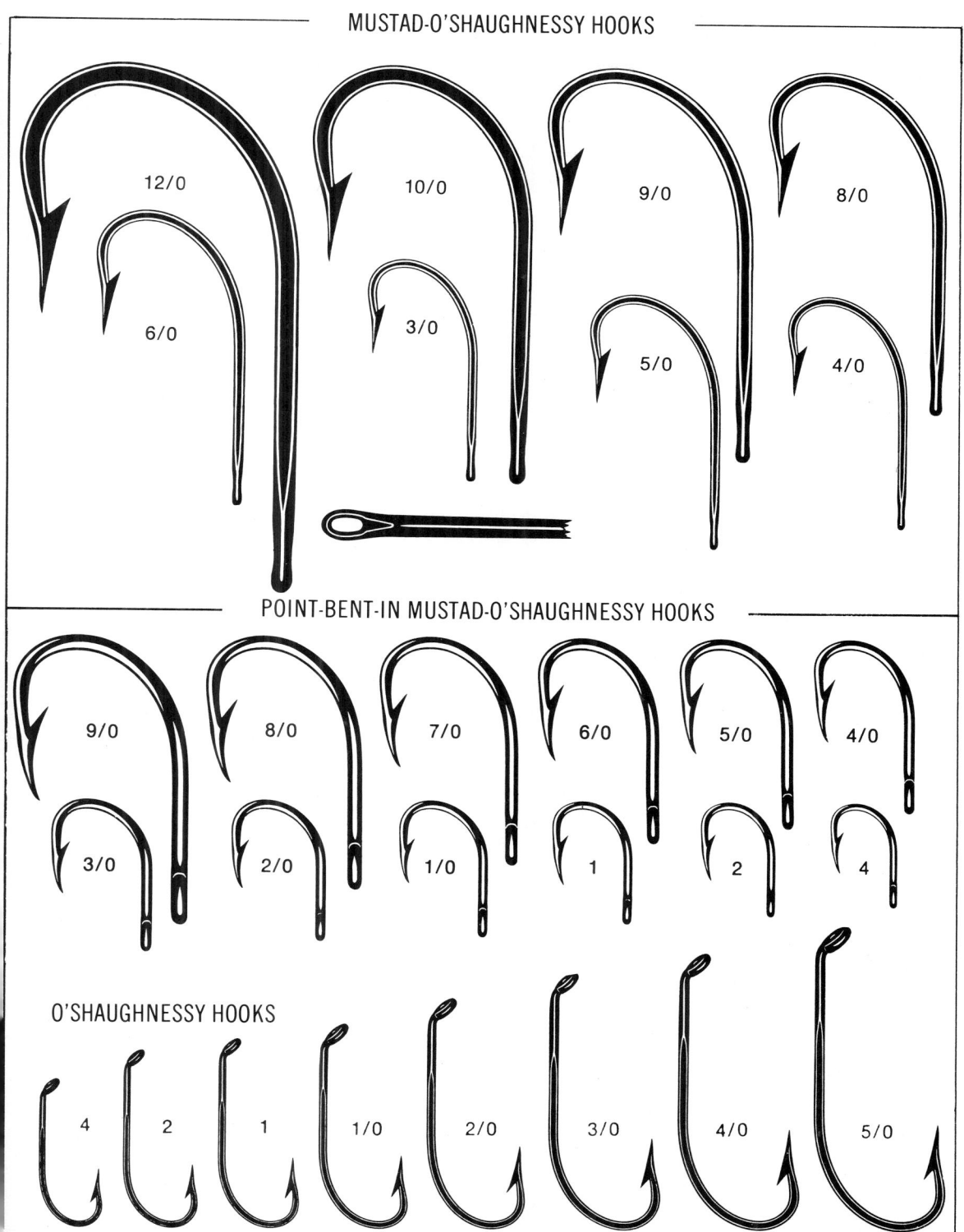

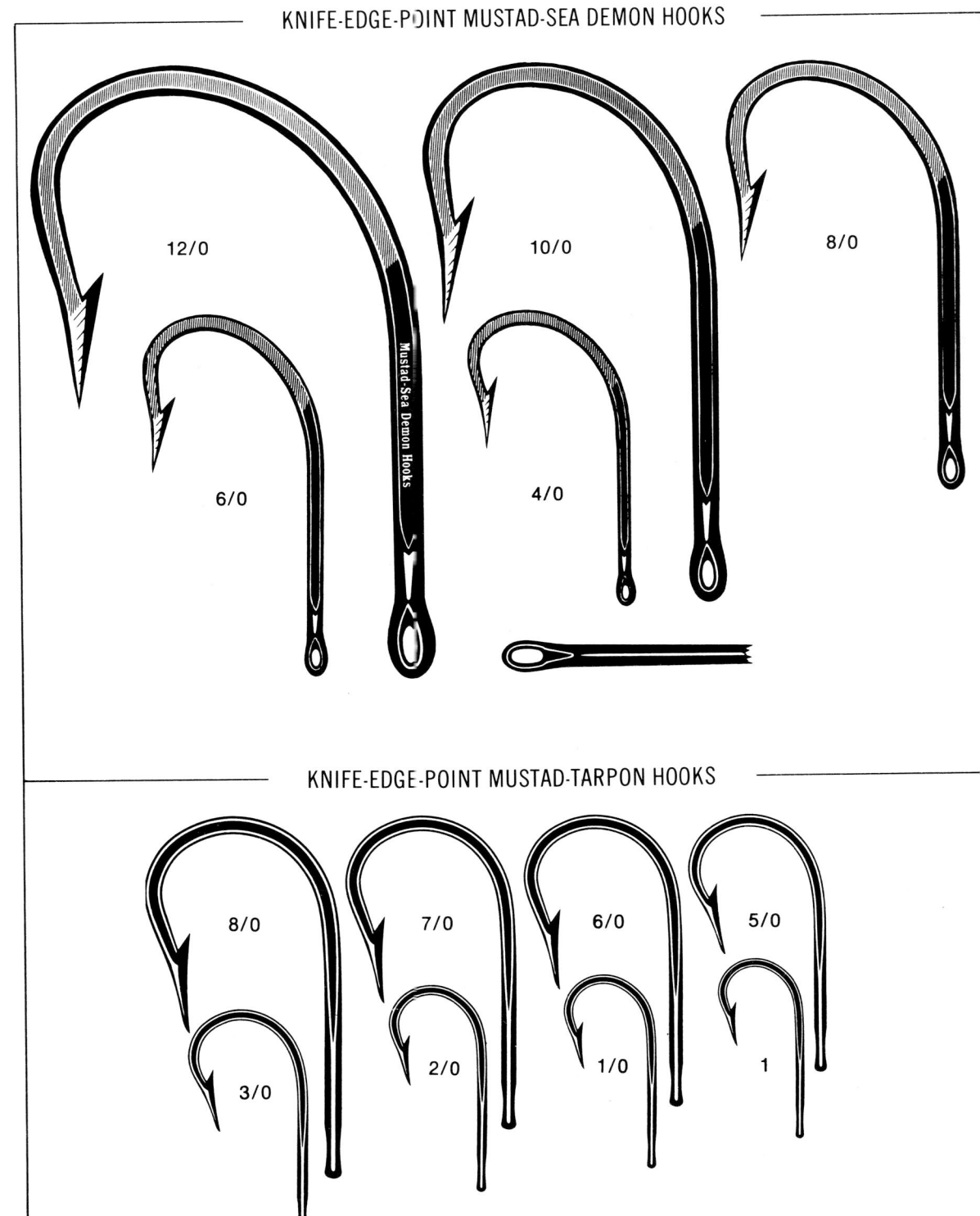

Hooks and Terminal Tackle 153

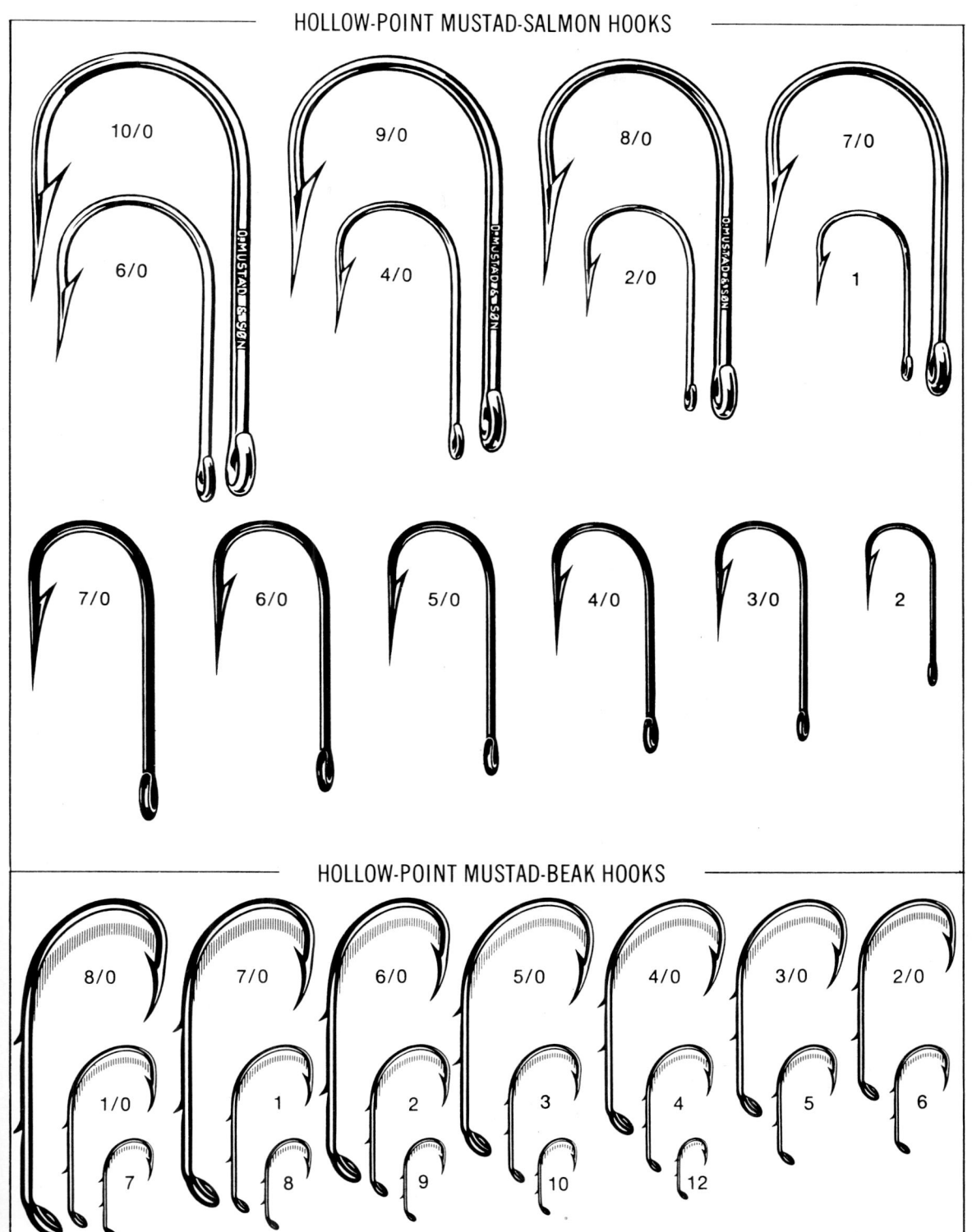

154 MODERN SALTWATER FISHING TACKLE

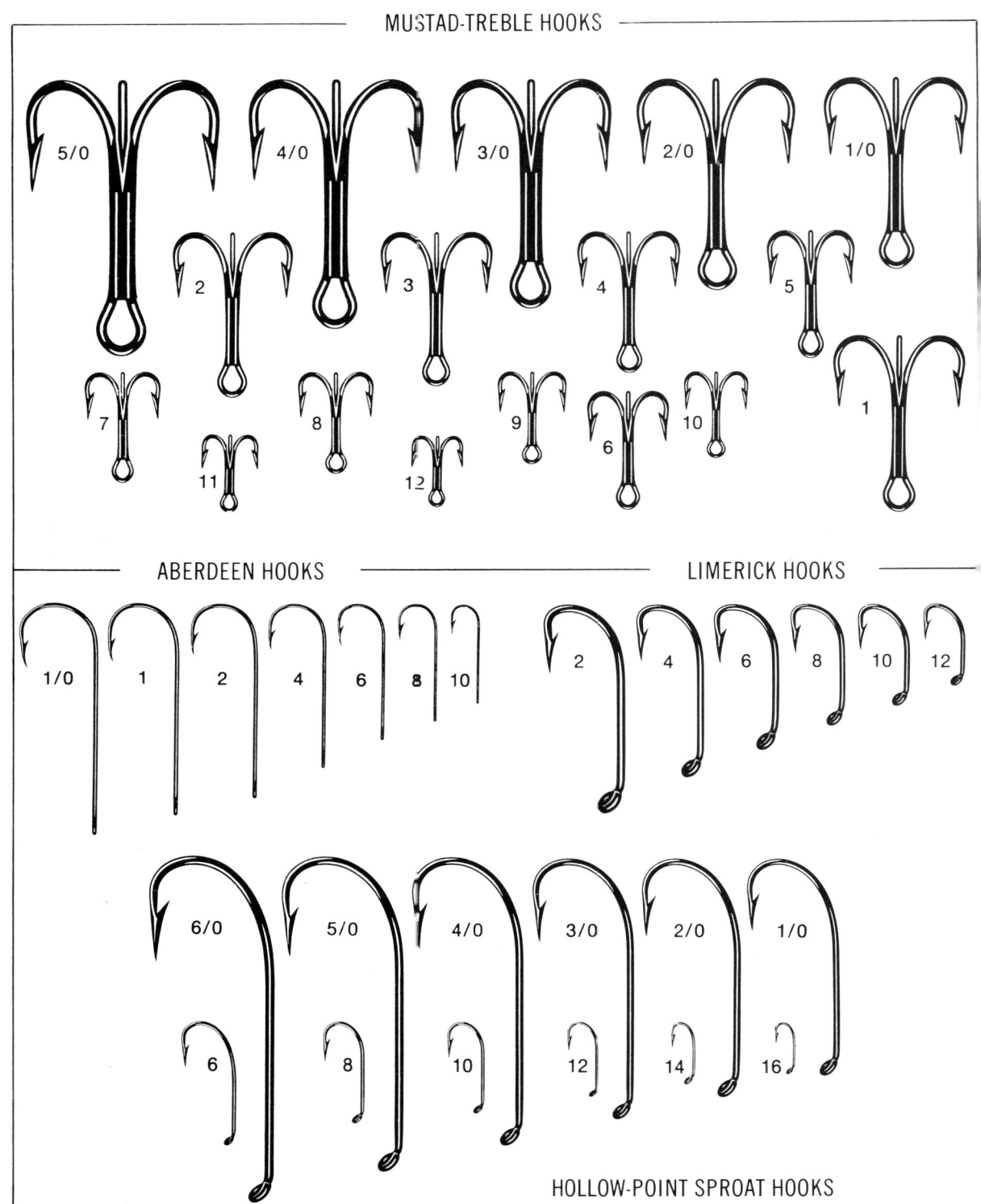

Hooks and Terminal Tackle 155

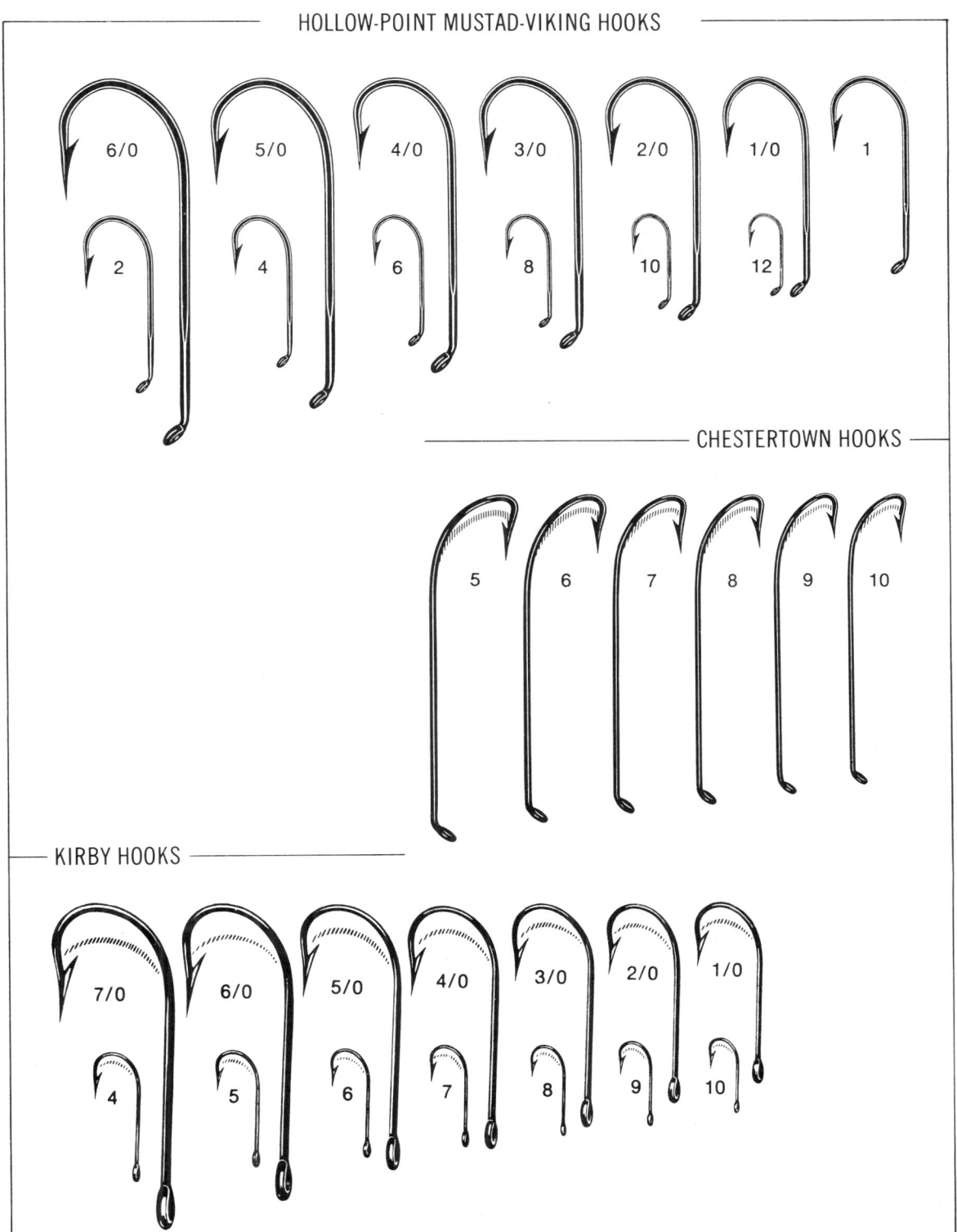

156 MODERN SALTWATER FISHING TACKLE

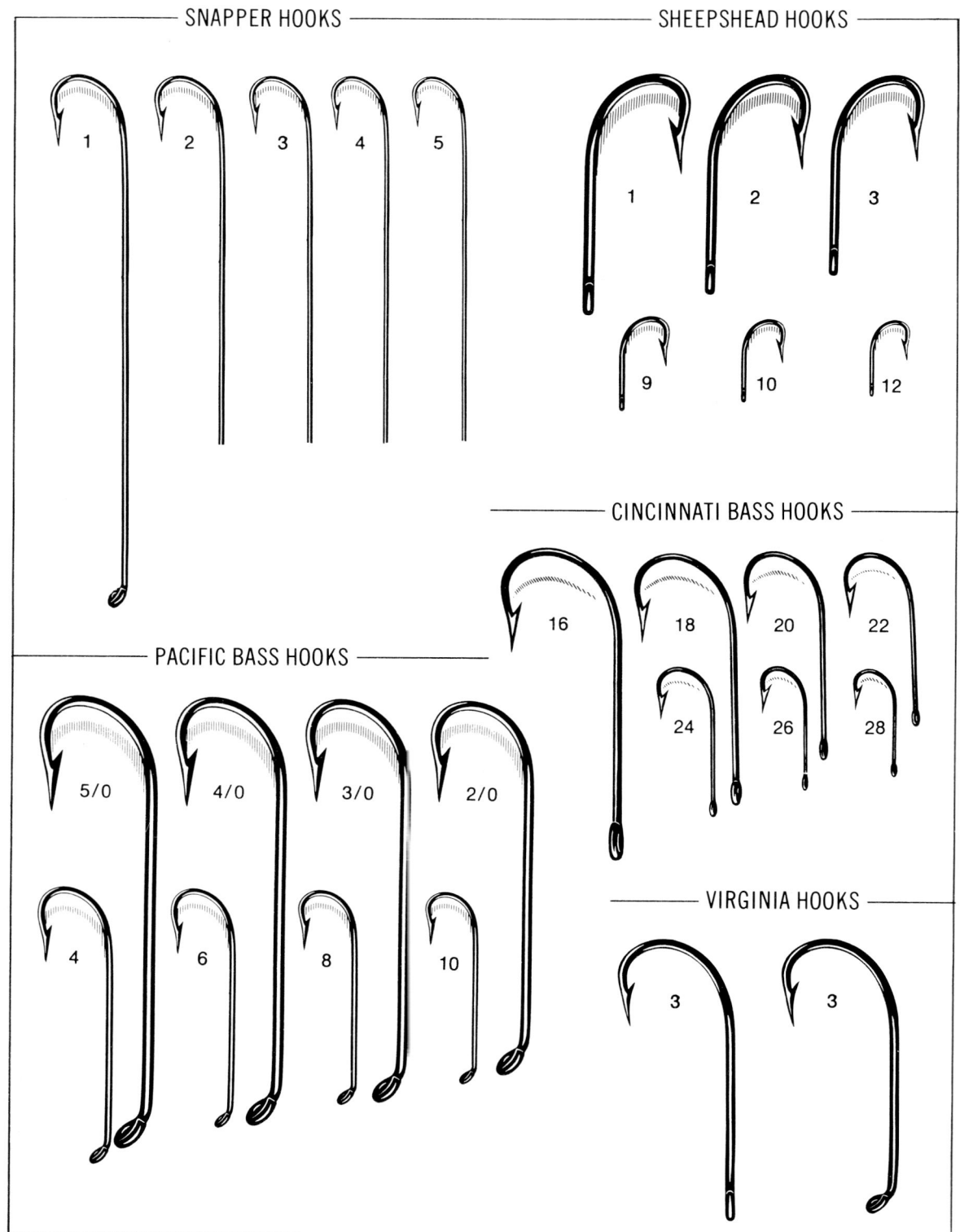

Hooks and Terminal Tackle 157

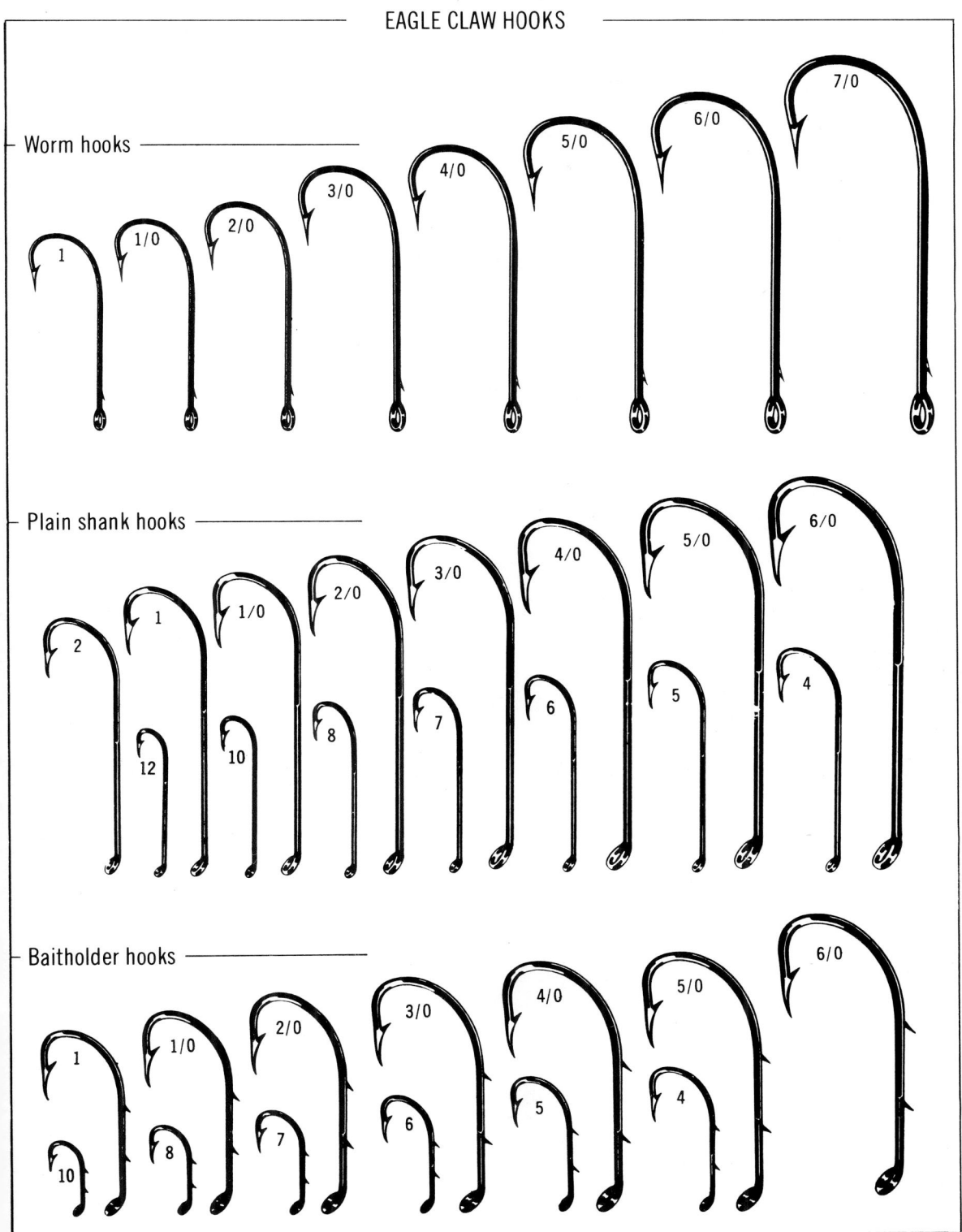

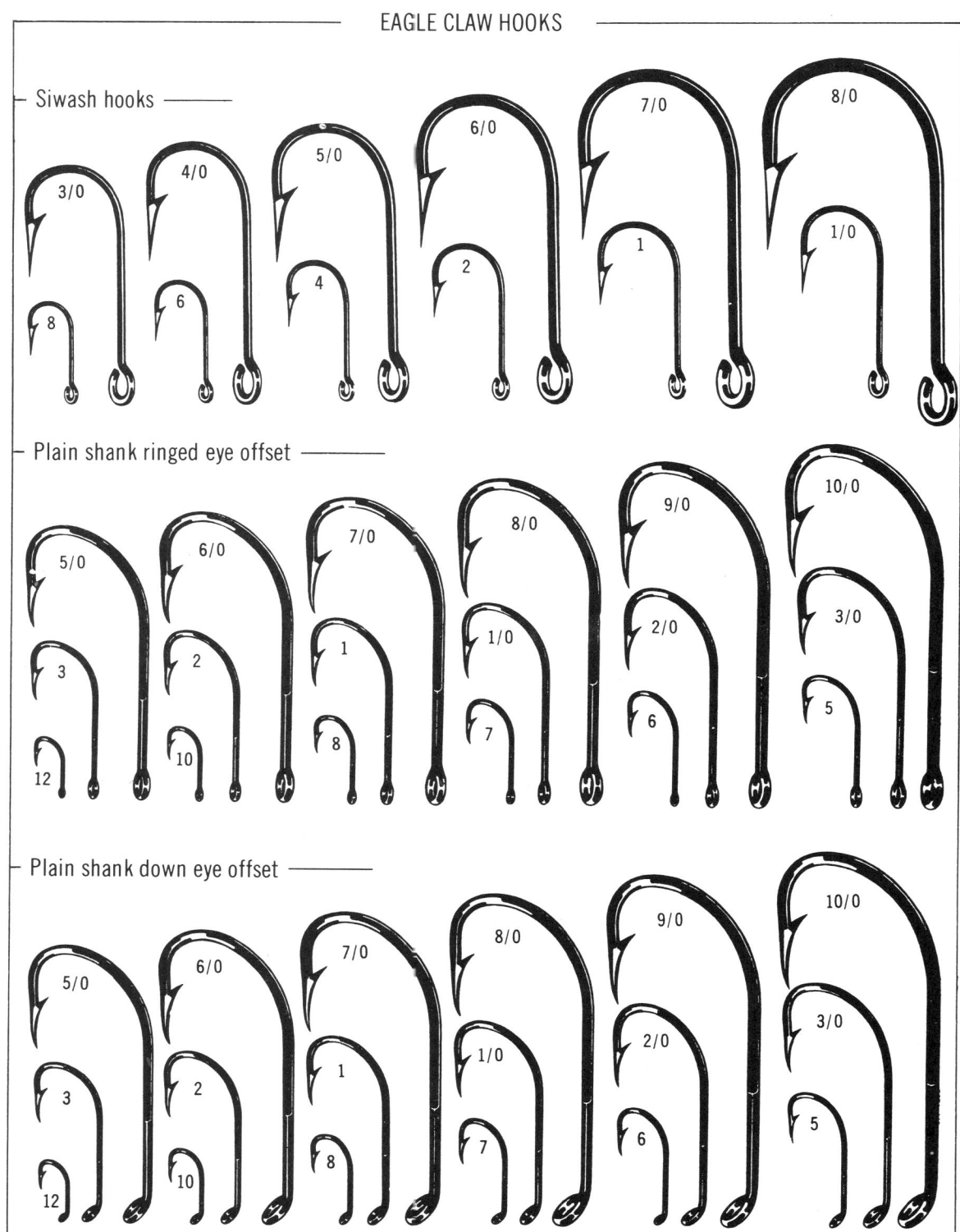

Hooks for big game have an additional problem in that they need to withstand tremendous bending stress when the hook is struck into the fish's hard, bony jaw, and when the fish uncorks a long, fast run. When an angler decides to tackle big game with very light equipment, his problems of hook choice become compounded. A hook of one type may be "good" because it is very strong, especially with medium to heavy tackle. But it may also be more difficult to strike into a fish with very light line than a different model that may not be quite as strong in the sense of resisting bending.

Likewise, a kirbed or reversed hook may hook more flatfish on the bottom, but its offset hook point tends to make an artificial lure revolve when it is trolled or retrieved after casting, so most hooks used with artificial lures do not feature kirbed or reversed points.

A perfectly round wire hook, when properly tempered, has a definite value in terms of the pull at which it starts to bend open. Tempering causes it to spring back into its original shape when the tension is relieved. But if the wire of the hook is hammered slightly flat, or forged, along the shank and bend before tempering, the same hook becomes considerably stronger. For this reason, almost all big-game hooks are forged.

Now let us consider some of the special characteristics of hooks.

Wire size

It is not necessary to know the actual measured diameter of the wire used to make a hook. It is more important to know how the wire size or diameter of a particular hook relates to the wire size of larger or smaller hooks. For example, a standard hook of standard pattern, size, and wire diameter is named by its pattern name, overall hook size, and the word *regular*, which designates that the wire is standard for this combination. Example: Mustad Viking #8 Regular.

If the wire of the hook in question happens to be thinner or thicker than normal for that size and pattern of hook, then the word *regular* is replaced with the letter X and the word *fine*, to designate a thinner wire; or *stout*, or *strong*, for a thicker wire. Mustad Viking #8 1X Fine, for example, means a hook with a wire equal in thickness to the next smaller size, or #9, hook. (Numbers increase as hooks get smaller, except in the "O" hook sizes.) Mustad Viking #8 2X Stout means a hook with a wire equal in thickness to a hook two sizes larger, or #6 hook.

Hooks are not usually made in wire diameters finer than 3X Fine or 4X Stout. Finer hooks usually have better penetration, but they bend more easily. Stouter hooks are harder to strike into a fish, but they resist bending or breaking. In live-bait fishing, a light wire hook is preferred, because it does not injure the bait as much as a standard hook, and it gives the bait more freedom to move about.

The hook shank

Each size and pattern of hook has a standard length of shank, but hooks with longer or shorter shanks are also available. Here again, the difference in shank length is expressed with an X. The number before the X indicates the size of hook larger or smaller than the one in question, with respect to shank length. The word following the X is either *long* or *short*, to describe the relative length of the hook in question. Mustad Viking #8 1X Short, for example, is a hook with wire of standard diameter for size #8, but with a shorter shank equal in length to the shank of the next smaller size, #9. Mustad Viking #8 2X Long is a hook with wire of standard diameter for size #8, but with a longer shank equal in length to the shank of a hook two sizes larger, or size #6.

Hooks are not normally manufactured in sizes more than 6X Long or 5X Short, although special orders can be taken. A short-shank hook is more easily hidden in a bait, and it is lighter where hook weight is important, as in making flies. A long-shank hook is good for fish with sharp teeth and for making lures like streamer flies, which require a long, stiff body section.

Seven types of shank shapes are commonly used in saltwater fishing
(1) Straight shank: straight from eye to bend
(2) Humped shank: shaped to hold a plug body
(3) Sliced shank: small barbs to hold bait
(4) Central draught shank: for penetration
(5) Curved-down shank: to help penetration
(6) Bent-down shank: shaped to hold jig body
(7) Step shank: for tying weedless keel flies.

The hook eye

The various types of eyes commonly used are depicted in the Hook Terminology illustration. Each type has a specific purpose.

Tapered eye: The end of the wire is tapered so the eye is formed of wire of decreasingly small diameter, saving weight. This is sometimes important for tying small flies.

Ball eye: The end of the wire is full diameter. In big-game models, the wire end may be brazed or welded to the shank for extra strength. The "open" ball eye is made with the eye end detempered so it can be closed with pliers around a ring or other lure fitting.

Looped eye: The end of the wire is laid back along the shank and usually is tapered. Used primarily in making salmon flies.

Needle eye: The eye is shaped like that of a needle and is useful for making up many kinds of baits. This eye is quite strong and is preferred by many big-game fishermen.

Flatted eye: The shank end is flattened and a small hole is drilled in the flat part. Not frequently used by sportsmen.

The hook point

Five of the most popular types of hook points are illustrated on page 148.

Hollow point: While the axis of the point is straight, the inner profile is curved or hollowed, giving the point a long, tapered shape for quick penetration.

Curved-in point: Also known as the Eagle Claw and the Mustad Bent point. Axis of the point curves inward toward

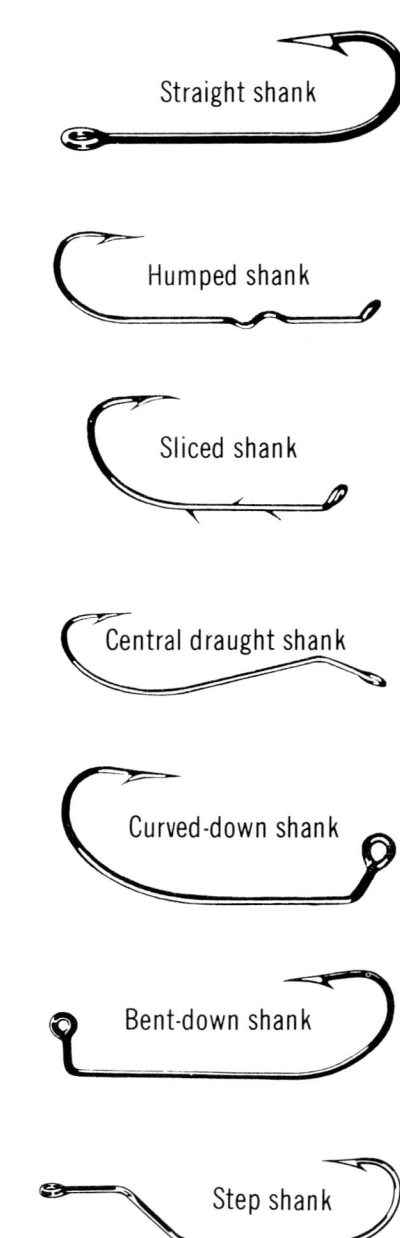

HOW TO SNELL YOUR OWN HOOKS

Cut the leader material about four inches longer than the length you'll require when the snell is finished. Pass one end through the eye of the hook so it extends along the shank about as far as the turn and barb.

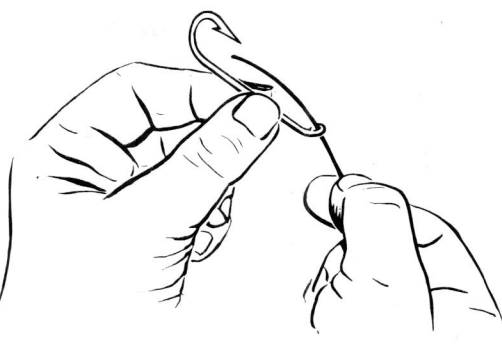

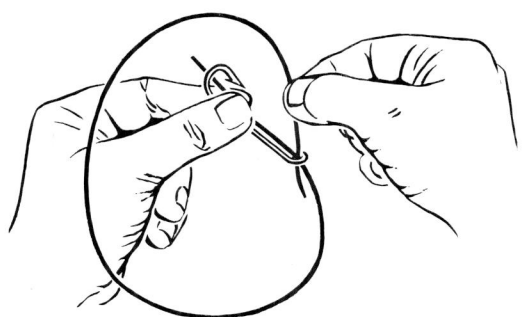

Pass the other end of the leader through the eye in the opposite direction and let it extend an inch or two beyond the hook eye.

Hold the two pieces of leader along the shank with the thumb and forefinger of the left hand. Take the leg of the loop that hangs down from the eye and wind a tight spiral coil around the shank and the two leader ends you are holding. Wind from the eye toward the hook.

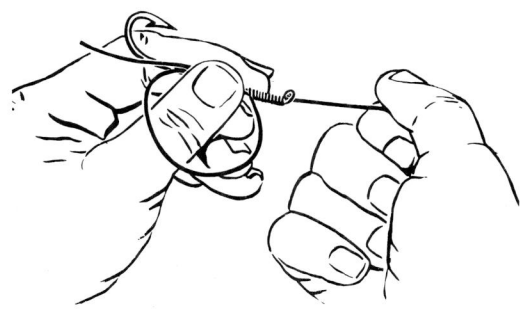

After taking 10 to 15 turns around the shank, hold this tight coil in place with the thumb and forefinger of the left hand. Grasp the leader end protruding from the eye and pull steadily until the entire leader has passed under the coil and straightened the coil on the shank.

Use pliers to pull the leader end that extends toward the hook. Pull it good and tight. Snip off this end flush with the last coil and tie a loop in the other end of the leader.

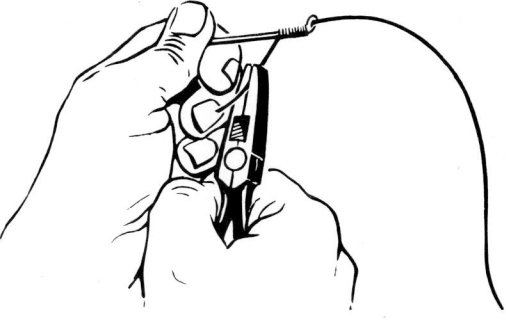

the location of the hook eye, bringing the point axis almost parallel with the axis of line pull through the eye for easier penetration.

Superior point: Sometimes called the spear point, this forged point is easy to manufacture and has good penetrating qualities. It is usually found on heavier grades of hooks.

Dublin point: A fast-penetrating point frequently used with fairly thin wire.

Knife-edge point: Four sides of the point are ground to form a knifelike penetrating point. Fairly wide, flat surface to the barb for extra holding power. Requires a strong pull to set, but preferred for most big game.

The axis of the point may have any one of four common positions with respect to the axis of the hook shank.

Straight point: Axis of the point is parallel to the shank axis, one of the most common styles.

Rolled point: The tip of the point from just below the notch of the barb is rolled inward toward the shaft.

Bent-in point: The entire point from just above the notch of the barb to the point itself is rolled or curved in toward the shaft.

Bent-out point: The point, from a location a little below the barb notch, is rolled outward away from the shaft to increase the speed of first penetration. This style is found frequently in big-game hooks.

Hook sizes

While all manufacturers grade their hooks by size, unfortunately there is no general agreement among manufacturers on an overall standard of sizes. The hook samples in this book are shown full size for the hooks named. There are noticeable differences in size between hooks of the same size rating.

Starting with hook size 0, hooks become smaller as the numbers increase from #1 to #22 or #24. Conversely, hooks become larger as numbers progress from 1/0 to 16/0 or larger. To be completely accurate, a hook should be compared to its twin in pattern name and manufacturer's identification if its true size is to be determined.

Recommendations of hook styles and sizes for many different kinds of baits, lures, and fishing conditions are made in Chapters 24 and 25.

SWIVELS AND CONNECTORS

Swivels are used in terminal tackle mainly to prevent a spinning or revolving lure or bait from twisting the fishing line. Connectors are designed to join two parts of the line-leader combination in a quick, sure manner. Very often the two functions are combined in snap swivels or connector swivels of relatively simple design.

Swivels and connectors also are sometimes incorporated with trolling sinkers or weights. A keel sinker, for example, is frequently placed above or in front of a Bead Chain swivel and connector to prevent the fishing line from twisting when a spinner or spoon is used as a trolling lure. Planers and downriggers are often thought of as terminal tackle, and when attached directly to the fishing line and supported by the line and rod, they are true terminal tackle. But when used in the manner of an underwater outrigger, they are auxiliary equipment. (Planers and downriggers are discussed in Chapter 20.)

Ordinary brass swivels soon lose their swiveling ability after salt water has started metal corrosion on their friction surfaces. Ball-bearing and Bead Chain swivels stand up better under saltwater conditions. All swivels have maximum ratings assigned by the manufacturer. These are usually breaking strains. To work effectively, no swivel should be loaded beyond 50 percent of its manufacturer's rating, and a 30 or 40 percent limit is even better.

Swivels that depend on sliding friction to achieve swiveling action usually start to bind as tension increases beyond

(Continued on page 167)

Hooks and Terminal Tackle 163

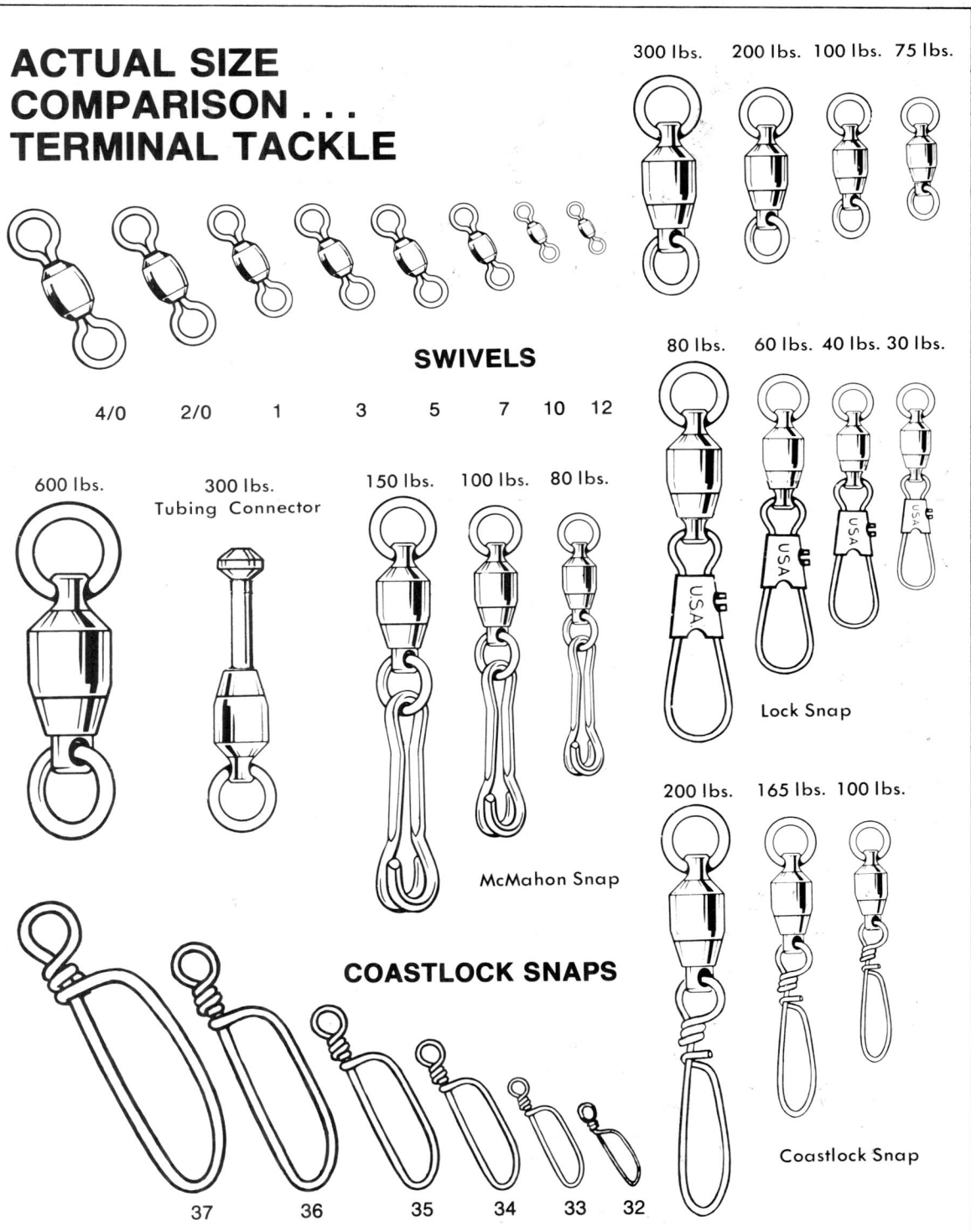

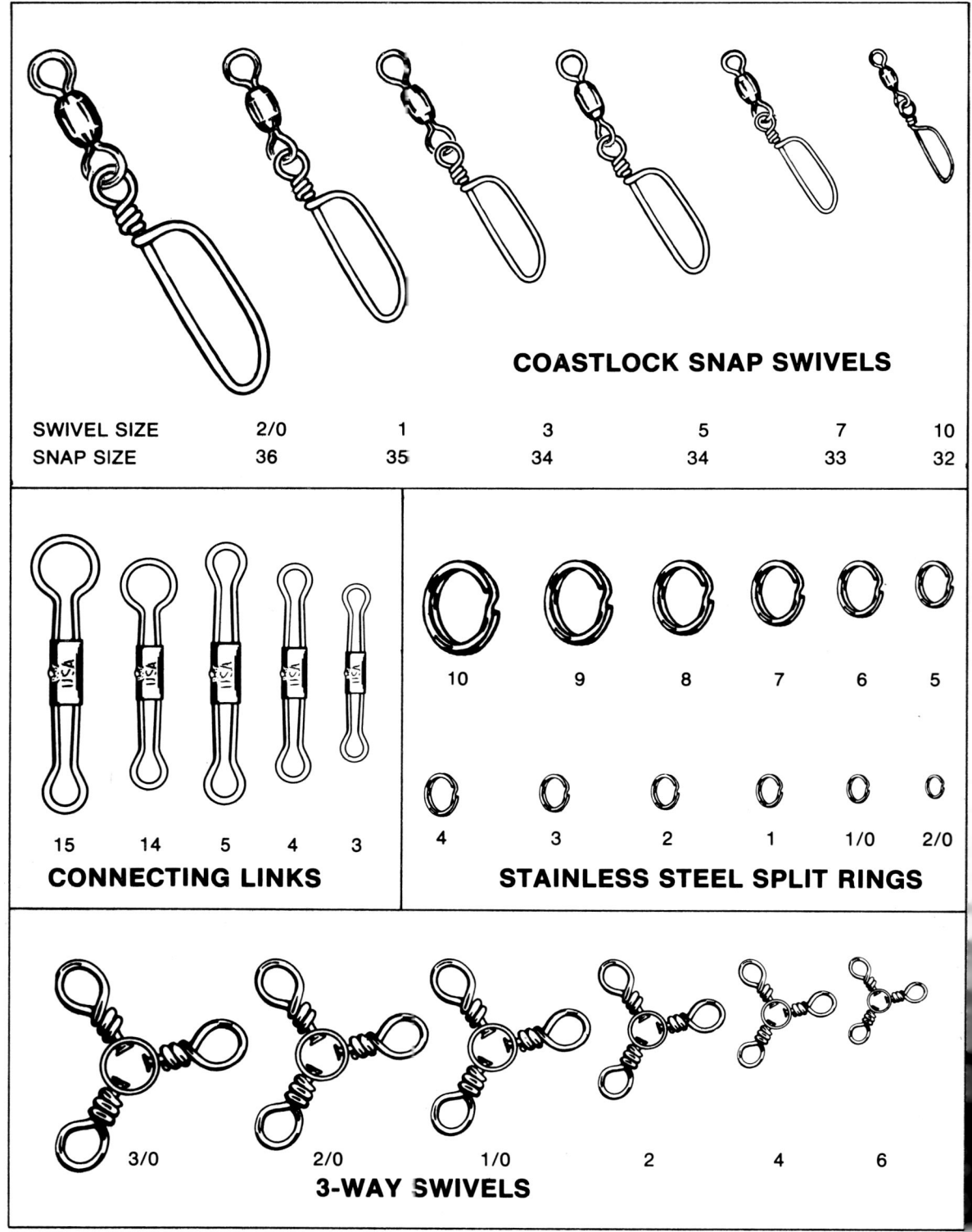

Hooks and Terminal Tackle 165

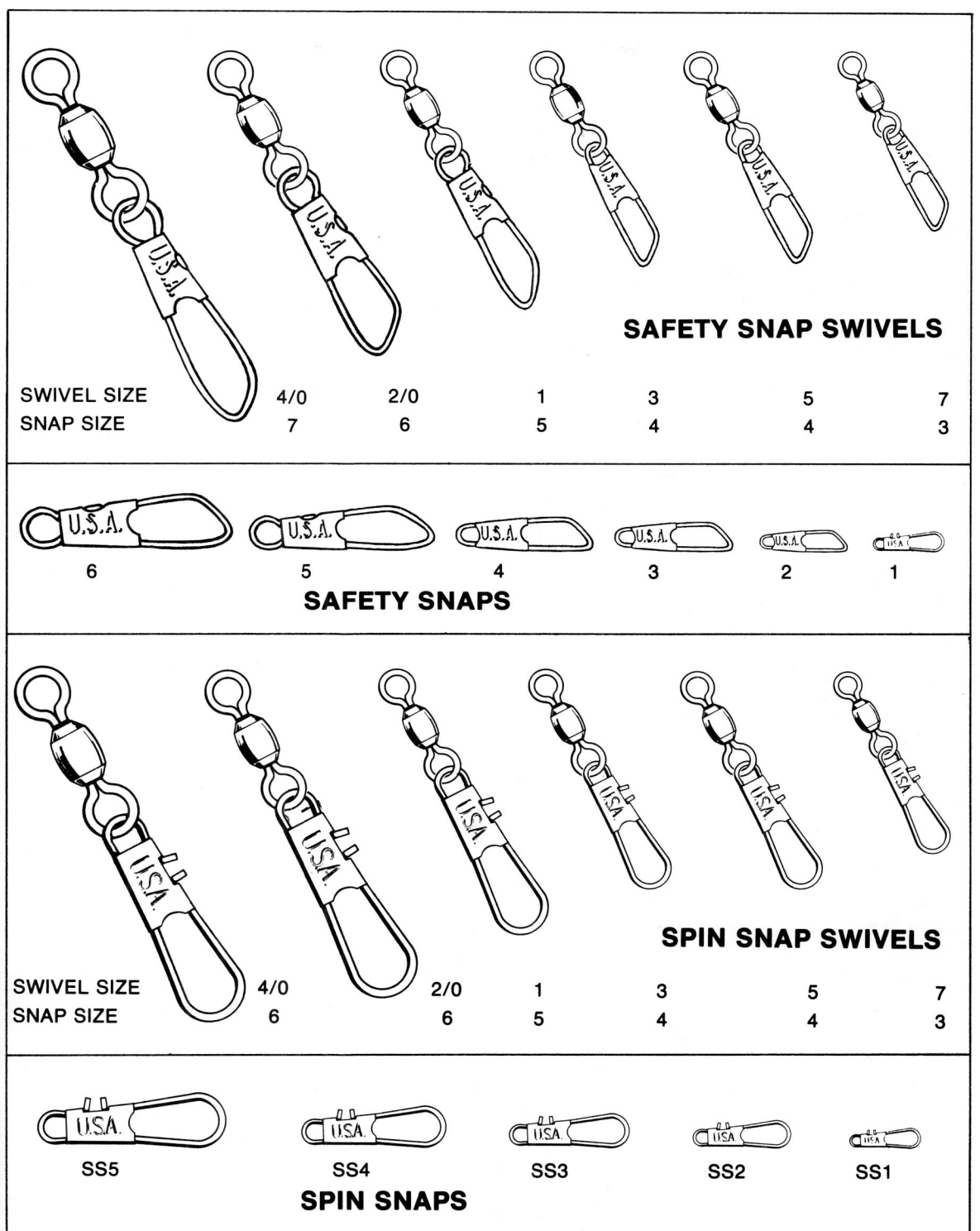

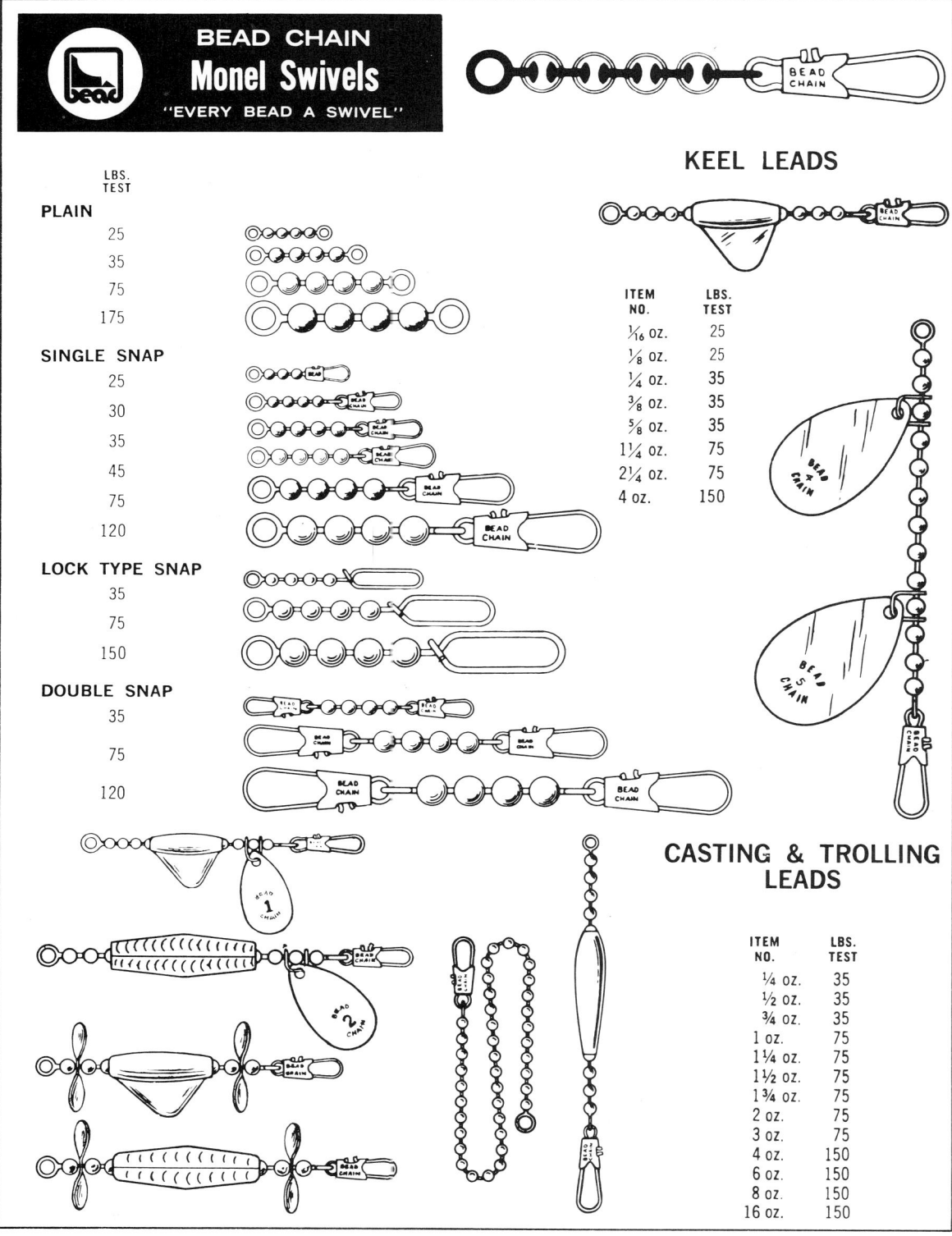

a low percentage of the manufacturer's rating. You can test the relative efficiency of swivels yourself this way:

(1) Take two identical swivels and join them with a short piece of strong leader wire.

(2) Hook one swivel's outer eye to a strong hook in the wall, or place it between the jaws of a bench vise.

(3) Hook a "De-Liar" type of fish-weighing scale to the other swivel's outer eye.

(4) Insert a thin bait-rigging needle into the inner eye of the outer swivel at right angles to the line of pull.

(5) Pull on the scale, increasing your pull by one-pound increments. At each increased degree of pull, turn the swivel with the rigging needle. Note the increased friction as line-pull increases.

What does this test accomplish? Nothing great, scientifically, but it does give you a method of measuring directly the efficiency of swivels. If you need a swivel that really swivels, and one that isn't just another kind of connector, this test may help you decide what model of swivel is best for your purposes.

Experienced anglers follow certain rules in selecting connectors and swivels for various kinds of fishing:

• Don't use a swivel-connector combination where you only need a connector.

• Select connectors that are strong, light, and easily worked.

• When spinners and spoons are used as trolling lures, always place a keel sinker, followed by a good swivel, between the fishing line and the lure leader.

• If sharp-toothed fish try to bite chrome-plated swivels or connectors, severing lines or leaders, spray the shiny metal with flat black paint.

• Store swivels and connectors in tackle-box compartments marked with the working rating (line class) that each style can handle.

• Equip the working end of each of your trolling and casting lines with a suitable connector or snap swivel to facilitate quick changing of lures and leaders. Select the smallest connector or snap swivel that will stand up to the breaking test of your line.

SINKERS AND DRAILS

Practically everybody knows what a fishing sinker is, although not many fishermen can name all of the various sinker styles. Few people, however, know that the word *drail* is applied to a special type of heavy trolling sinker shaped somewhat like a thick turkey leg with an offset neck of lead sticking up from the thicker end. Drails originally were used for commercial trolling with handlines, in order to get the lines down deep. Nowadays they occasionally are used as makeshift downrigger weights (see section on downriggers).

A number of popular styles of sinkers, trolling sinkers, and drails are illustrated. Most of these can be purchased in various weights in tackle stores, but many anglers like to cast their own sinkers from scrap lead. Metal molds for casting sinkers, drails, lure heads, and other special bits of terminal tackle can be ordered from manufacturers listed in the Manufacturers' Index in the back of the book.

Many anglers prefer to attach trolling sinkers directly to the fishing line rather than resort to a downrigger or wire line for deep trolling. The following table gives approximate trolling sinker weights needed to take a one-ounce leadhead lure down to a desired depth on 30-pound-test monofilament at an average trolling speed of three or four knots and a line length of 80 to 100 feet.

TROLLING SINKER WEIGHT/DEPTH TABLE

Sinker weight	Lure depth
4 oz.	8 ft.
8 oz.	12 ft.
12 oz.	16 ft.
16 oz.	20 ft.
20 oz.	24 ft.

Naturally, greater depths will be achieved at slower trolling speeds, and some lures and fishing lines have more water drag than others, which affects trolling-lure depth. Smart anglers experiment with standard sinker-lure-line-length combinations when fishing is slow, in order to establish their own vital statistics for times when fishing becomes hot and there is no opportunity for experimentation.

What sinkers should you stock for what kind of fishing?

Bank sinker: The general, all-purpose sinker style, available in weights from ½ ounce to 16 ounces and more. Its shape helps keep it from rolling on smooth bottom in a strong current.

Ball sinker: Usually available with a cast-lead ring eye rather than a brass wire eye. A favorite of anglers who fish rocky bottom, but it rolls on hard, smooth bottom. Available in lower weights not much over four ounces.

Pyramid sinker: Available in weights up to four or five ounces, this angular sinker resists rolling strongly and has a tendency to dig into soft sand. A favorite of bait-fishing surf anglers.

Cigar sinker: Its symmetrical, tapered, cigarlike shape, plus eyes or Bead Chain swivels cast into either end make it the ideal trolling sinker for non-revolving lures. Available in weights from ½ ounce up to 16 to 24 ounces.

Keel sinker: With its weight offset from the line of pull, it strongly resists the twisting effect of spinner lures and certain spoons that tend to revolve. A favorite of West Coast salmon trollers who habitually use cut baits and plugs designed to spin when trolled. Available in weights from ½ ounce to eight ounces or more.

Pinch sinker or split shot: Very light ball or cigar sinkers that are split nearly through with a knife, so they can be squeezed onto a line or leader with pliers to add a carefully regulated small amount of weight. Used primarily by light-tackle spinning or fly casters.

Drilled-barrel sinker: Shaped like a fat little cigar or a miniature barrel, this

A *Deep sea cod-pollock rig.*
Line: 30-50 lb. monofilament or Dacron.
Sinker: 8-20 oz. bank sinker.
Upper hook: 7/0-8/0 O'Shaughnessy or Eagle Claw on 50-60 in. snell of 40-50 lb. mono, rigged 4-6 ft. above sinker.
Lower hook: 6/0 O'Shaughnessy or Eagle Claw on 12-16 in. snell of 40-50 lb. mono, rigged 8 in. above sinker.
Baits: clam on lower hook, squid upper.

B *Flounder rig with spreader.*
Line: 12-20 lb. monofilament.
Sinker: 4-8 oz. ball or bank sinker.
Spreader: standard 12 in. brass wire.
Hooks: two #10-#6 Chestertown hooks on 30-lb.-test monofilament snells.
Baits: blood/sand worm, clam, mussel.

C *Tandem-hook flounder or tautog rig.*
Line: 15-30 lb. monofilament.
Sinker: 4-8 oz. ball or bank.
Hooks (flounder): two bridled #10-#6 Chestertown, 4 in. above sinker.
Hooks (tautog): two #6-#2 Virginia, bridled, rigged 4 in. above sinker.
Baits: worms, clam, mussel, crabs.

D *High-low sea bass and porgy rig.*
Line: 13-30 lb. test monofilament.
Sinker: 4-10 oz. bank sinker.
Upper hook: 4/0-6/0 Sproat or similar pattern, 15 in. mono snell, rigged 12 in. above lower hook.
Lower hook: 3/0-5/0 Sproat or similar pattern, 15 in. mono snell, rigged 4-6 in. above sinker.
Baits: clam, squid, mussel, worm, crab.

E *Fish-finder surf bait-fishing rig.*
Line: 18-30 lb. monofilament.
Sinker: 4 oz. pyramid sliding on line above stop swivel. Brass wire eye.
Hook: 4/0-6/0 Eagle Claw baitholder on 30-36 in. of 30-40 lb. monofilament.
Bait: clam, worms, squid, crab, fish.

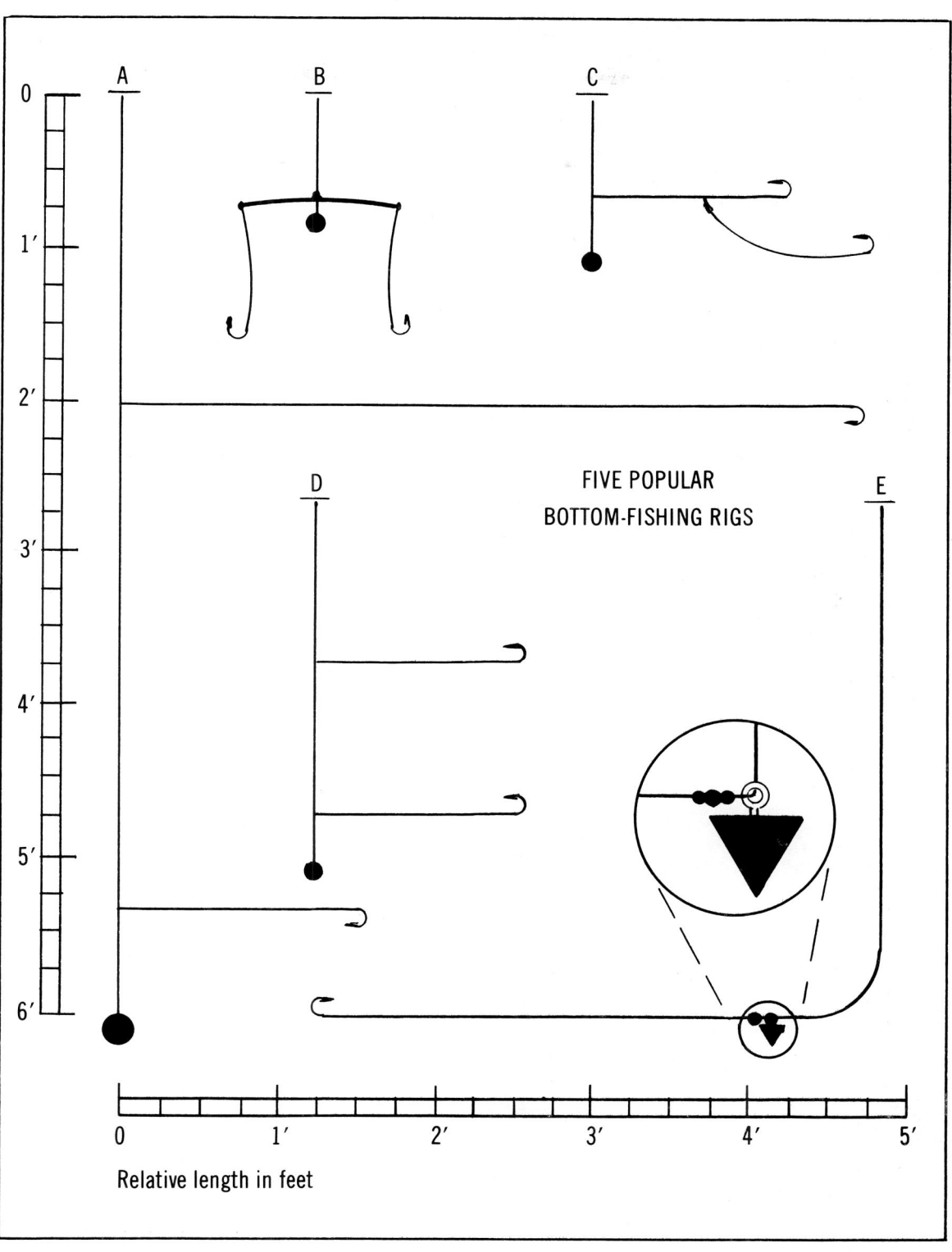

sinker has a hole drilled or cast through its center, end to end, so it can be strung on wire or line. Several together can be used as a jury trolling sinker. Frequently used by bait riggers to add weight to mullet and other baits designed to be trolled in the swimming position. Original use was as a foot-rope weight on light seine nets. Weights of ½ ounce to four ounces.

Gooseneck drail: The old commercial handline deep-trolling sinker. Handline to the boat is tied to the gooseneck swivel ring; handline to the lure or bait is tied to the tail swivel ring. When the drail is used as a makeshift downrigger weight, a snap-jaw clothespin or small line-release clip is tied to the tail swivel ring with heavy fishing line or light leader wire. Weights of one pound to eight pounds.

How much weight do you need to hold bottom in a tidal current? This depends largely on the thickness and smoothness of the fishing line. Thin-diameter, ultra-smooth monofilament is the best of the nonwire lines. While exact figures cannot be determined for all lines and all currents in all fishable depths of water, the following table, figured for average smooth-finish monofilament of 30-pound test and depths from 10 to 100 feet of water, gives suggested sinker weights for currents of one, two, and three knots.

Depth	1 Knot	2 Knots	3 Knots
10 ft.	1 oz.	2 oz.	3 oz.
20 ft.	2 oz.	4 oz.	6 oz.
30 ft.	3 oz.	6 oz.	9 oz.
40 ft.	4 oz.	8 oz.	12 oz.
50 ft.	5 oz.	10 oz.	15 oz.
60 ft.	6 oz.	12 oz.	18 oz.
70 ft.	7 oz.	14 oz.	21 oz.
80 ft.	8 oz.	16 oz.	24 oz.
90 ft.	9 oz.	18 oz.	27 oz.
100 ft.	10 oz.	20 oz.	30 oz.

One secret of successful bottom fishing in a strong tide is to use only enough sinker to hold bottom. The clever cod fisherman, for example, may start off with a 20-ounce sinker to hold bottom during the full strength of a tide, but he may wind up using only six ounces of sinker at slack water. Too much weight on the line is tiring, and it destroys the sensitivity of "feel" that one needs to convert nibbles into substantial hookups.

19 Leaders for Game Fishing

Five major types of material are used for making up game-fishing leaders: solid stainless-steel wire, plain or tinned steel piano wire, nylon-sheathed stainless cable, plain stainless cable, and nylon monofilament. Of these, monofilament is by far the most popular in the lower-test ranges. Solid and cable stainless steel are preferred for big-game fishing, although heavy-gauge monofilament is sometimes used for big billfish.

Cable-laid stainless material comes in three varieties, designated 1 × 7, 6 × 19, and 6 × 37: 1 × 7 means the cable is a single strand of seven wires twisted together; 6 × 19 is cable made up of six strands of 19 wires each; 6 × 37 is cable made of six strands of 37 wires each, and it is the softest and most flexible of all wire leaders. Nylon-clad cable has a thin outer sheath of nylon over the cable.

Monofilament of up to 600-pound test is now used by some anglers for big-game leaders, but 400-pound-test mono seems to be about the top strength in regular use. With a density only slightly more than that of water, large-diameter mono leaders do not sink as quickly as wire or cable leaders. Heavy-caliber monofilament is difficult to knot, so leader eyes are often made up with metal crimp sleeves pressed in place with special crimping pliers.

Cable is measured by diameter in fractions of an inch and sometimes also in thousandths of an inch. All solid stainless-steel and common-steel piano wires are designated by size numbers that correspond to definite diameters in thousandths of an inch. The following table gives the diameter and breaking strain for the solid-wire sizes most commonly used. Plain and tinned piano wire are not used frequently in salt water because of the corrosion problem.

WIRE SIZES AND BREAKING STRAINS

Wire size	Diameter (inches)	Piano wire (pounds test)	Stainless wire (pounds test)
#2	.011	28	27
#3	.012	34	32
#4	.013	39	37
#5	.014	46	44
#6	.016	60	56
#7	.018	76	69
#8	.020	93	86
#9	.022	114	104
#10	.024	136	128
#11	.026	156	148
#12	.028	184	176
#13	.030	212	202
#14	.032	240	232
#15	.034	282	272

The 14 wire sizes can be divided into five major categories.

Ultra-light. Wire sizes #2 to #4. Primary use is to make short end sections to protect casting flies and other light-tackle lures from being cut by sharp teeth.

Light. Wire sizes #5 to #7. Wire of

The leader (or trace, as it is often called in Europe) is literally the connecting link between the hook and the fisherman. Heavy nylon monofilament is favored by many anglers when the fish in question do not have sharp teeth, and where low visibility in the water is an important factor.

Leaders for Game Fishing

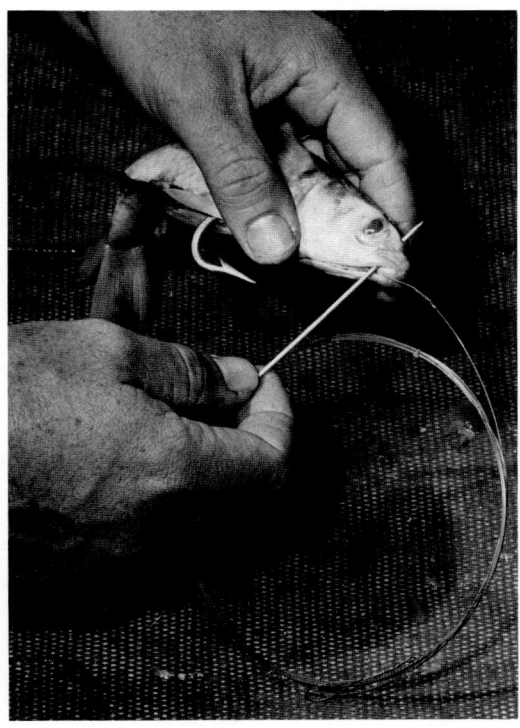

Wire leaders have been used for many years, and they are a necessity for fish with sharp teeth. Most popular wire leader on salt water is stainless steel, shown here with a mullet bait.

Unless the wire leader eye is "married" by twisting the two parts together as a twisted-pair, the eye may render under heavy strain, causing the wire to break at the hook.

this category is used either full length in leaders, or as part of composite leaders made up with a primary length of mono.

Medium. Wire sizes #8 to #10. Used full length in leaders for a wide variety of game fish from sailfish and white marlin to school tuna, big stripers, sharks, etc.

Light-heavy. Wire sizes #11 to #13. Normally used full length and sometimes as double twisted strands for fish worthy of 80-pound-class tackle: billfish, tuna, etc.

Heavy. Wire sizes #14 and #15. Any wire leaders heavier than these become so stiff as to defeat their own purpose. Used for the largest billfish, tuna, and game sharks.

Knots for monofilament are described in Chapter 12. Solid-wire eyes are made with the inappropriately named haywire twist, following this sequence of action.

(1) Double four or five inches of the end of the wire back on its main part, making the 180-degree bend small and smooth. Hang the hook eye or lure eye on this bend if a hook or lure is to be applied.

(2) Grasp the bend with parallel-jaw pliers and, with a twisting motion of the thumb and forefinger of the other hand, twist the wire end and the main part of the wire firmly around each other to "marry" them for at least eight half-turns. The wire end must not be wrapped around the main part; the two parts must be twisted together equally.

(3) Shift the grip of the pliers to the twisted portion. Take four or five close finishing turns of the wire end around the main part of the wire.

(4) Finish off by bending an L into the end of the wire. Using the L as a lever, break the wire cleanly at the last turn. The finished eye should not render under heavy strain, and it should hold 80 to 90 percent of the strength of the plain wire.

Cable leaders and very heavy grades of monofilament have eyes made up with cable crimp sleeves, as was mentioned earlier. Crimp sleeves come in sizes to accommodate various sizes of wire or mono. Take special care, when crimping sleeves on monofilament, to avoid injuring the mono by crimping too heavily. A cable eye may call for one or two crimps, whereas a mono eye should have at least two or three sleeves applied under slightly less pressure.

Following are directions for making up a number of specific wire, mono, cable, and composite leaders. (See also the recommended leader particulars in the table, The Bait Rigger's Handy Guide, in Chapter 24.)

Light billfish monofilament leader
Fish: swordfish, marlin up to 200 pounds
Tackle class: 30-, 50-pound line
Length: 14 feet 6 inches maximum
Material: 100- to 150-pound-test monofilament
Eye ends: Bimini Twist, Surgeon's Knot
Hook: 5/0 to 8/0 ringed-eye Sea Demon

Medium billfish monofilament leader
Fish: swordfish, marlin 200 to 400 pounds
Tackle class: 80-pound line
Length: 29 feet 6 inches maximum
Material: 250-pound-test monofilament
Eye ends: knotted or crimped
Hook: 8/0 to 10/0 ringed-eye Sea Demon

Heavy billfish monofilament leader
Fish: swordfish, marlin over 400 pounds
Tackle class: 80- to 130-pound line
Length: 29 feet 6 inches maximum
Material: 400-pound-test monofilament
Eye ends: crimped
Hook: 10/0 to 14/0 ringed-eye Sea Demon

Light billfish-shark wire leader
Fish: billfish, sharks under 200 pounds
Tackle class: 12-, 20-, 30-pound line
Length: 14 feet 6 inches maximum
Material: #6 to #8 stainless-steel wire
Eye ends: haywire twist
Hook: 4/0 to 6/0 needle-eye Sea Demon, Sobey, O'Shaughnessy, ringed-eye Eagle Claw

Medium billfish-shark wire leader
Fish: billfish, sharks 200 to 500 pounds
Tackle class: 50-pound line
Length: 14 feet 6 inches maximum
Material: #10 to #11 stainless-steel wire
Eye ends: haywire twist
Hook: 6/0 to 8/0 needle-eye O'Shaughnessy, Sobey, or Sea Demon

Medium-heavy billfish-shark wire leader
Fish: billfish, sharks 400 to 700 pounds
Tackle class: 80-pound line
Length: 29 feet 6 inches maximum
Material: #13 to #14 stainless-steel wire
Eye ends: haywire twist
Hook: 8/0 to 10/0 needle-eye Sea Demon or Sobey

Very heavy billfish-shark wire leader
Fish: billfish, sharks over 700 pounds
Tackle class: 130-pound line
Length: 29 feet 6 inches maximum
Material: single #15 or double-twisted #12 stainless-steel wire
Eye ends: haywire twist
Hook: 12/0 to 16/0 Sea Demon or Sobey

Light billfish-shark cable leader
Fish: billfish, sharks under 200 pounds
Tackle class: 12-, 20-, 30-pound line
Length: 14 feet 6 inches maximum
Material: 40- to 90-pound test, nylon-covered 1 × 7 or 6 × 19 stainless-steel cable
Eye ends: crimped
Hook: 4/0 to 6/0 ringed-eye Sea Demon, Sobey, O'Shaughnessy, or Eagle Claw

Medium billfish-shark cable leader
Fish: billfish, sharks 200 to 500 pounds
Tackle class: 50-pound line
Length: 14 feet 6 inches maximum
Material: 150-pound-test plain or nylon-covered 6 × 19 stainless-steel cable
Eye ends: crimped

Hook: 8/0 to 10/0 ringed-eye Sea Demon or Sobey

Medium-heavy billfish-shark cable leader
Fish: billfish, sharks 400 to 700 pounds
Tackle class: 80-pound line
Length: 29 feet 6 inches maximum
Material: 240-pound-test 6 × 19 stainless-steel cable
Eye ends: crimped
Hook: 8/0 to 10/0 ringed-eye Sea Demon or Sobey

Very heavy billfish-shark cable leader
Fish: all fish over 700 pounds
Tackle class: 130-pound line
Length: 29 feet 6 inches maximum
Material: 400-pound-test 6 × 19 or 6 × 37 stainless-steel cable
Eye ends: crimped
Hook: 12/0 to 16/0 Sea Demon or Sobey

Standard sailfish wire leader
Fish: sailfish, white marlin, spearfish
Tackle class: 12- to 30-pound line
Length: 14 feet 6 inches maximum
Material: #4 to #7 stainless-steel wire
Eye ends: haywire twist
Hook: 4/0 to 6/0 needle-eye O'Shaughnessy, Sobey, or Sea Demon

Tournament release sailfish leader
Fish: sailfish, all small marlin
Tackle class: six-, 12-, 20-pound line
Length: 14 feet 6 inches maximum overall
Material: composite; bait made up on 18-inch section of #3 stainless-steel wire; remainder of leader is 40- to 50-pound-test monofilament, snap swivel connector
Eye ends: wire, haywire twist; mono, Improved Clinch Knot to connector, Surgeon's Knot or Bimini Twist at the fishing-line end loop
Hook: 3/0 to 6/0 needle-eye O'Shaughnessy, Sobey, or Sea Demon

Light tuna chumming wire leader
Fish: bluefin, other tuna to 300 pounds
Tackle class: 50-pound line
Length: 14 feet 6 inches maximum
Material: #10 stainless or piano wire

Leaders for Game Fishing 175

Eye ends: haywire twist
Hook: 8/0 to 10/0 Sobey or Sea Demon

Medium tuna chumming wire leader
Fish: bluefin tuna 300 to 700 pounds
Tackle class: 80-pound line
Length: 29 feet 6 inches maximum
Material: #13 stainless or piano wire
Eye ends: haywire twist
Hook: 10/0 to 12/0 Sobey or Sea Demon

Heavy tuna chumming wire leader
Fish: bluefin tuna over 700 pounds
Tackle class: 130-pound line
Length: 29 feet 6 inches maximum
Material: double-twisted #12 stainless or piano wire, or single #15 wire
Eye ends: haywire twist
Hook: 12/0 to 14/0 Sobey or Sea Demon

Light tarpon monofilament leader
Fish: tarpon to 100 pounds
Tackle class: six-, 12-, 20-pound line
Material: monofilament; 36-inch lower shock section of 50-pound mono; remainder made up of 30-pound monofilament
Knots: Improved Clinch Knot on hook, Blood Knot between sections, Surgeon's Knot or Bimini Twist for leader eye
Hook: 4/0 to 6/0 Sobey or Eagle Claw

Heavy tarpon monofilament leader
Fish: tarpon over 100 pounds
Tackle class: 30-, 50-pound line
Length: 14 feet 6 inches maximum
Material: monofilament; 36-inch lower shock section of 80-pound mono; remainder made up of 40- to 60-pound mono, depending on whether 30- or 50-pound line is used
Knots: Improved Clinch Knot on hook or lure, Blood Knot between the sections, Surgeon's Knot or Bimini Twist for eye
Hook: 5/0 to 7/0 of pattern to suit

Universal bluefish leader
Fish: all sharp-toothed fish to 30 pounds
Tackle class: 12-, 20-, 30-pound line
Length: five feet to 14 feet 6 inches maximum
Material: composite; 6-inch #6 stainless-

steel wire to the hook, plus remainder of 30- to 40-pound mono, depending on line
Eyes, Knots: haywire twist in wire; Improved Clinch Knot in mono on a split ring between mono and wire, Surgeon's Knot or Bimini Twist for mono eye
Hook: 3/0 to 6/0 Siwash, O'Shaughnessy, Eagle Claw, or other desired pattern

Light striped-bass trolling leader
Fish: stripers, etc., to 25 pounds
Tackle class: 12-, 20-, 30-pound line
Length: five feet to 14 feet 6 inches maximum
Material: 40-pound-test monofilament
Knots: Improved Clinch Knot to hook or lure, any good loop knot to the eye
Hook: 3/0 to 6/0 per desired pattern

Heavy striped-bass trolling leader
Fish: stripers, etc., over 25 pounds
Tackle class: 50-pound line
Length: 14 feet 6 inches maximum
Material: 60-pound-test monofilament
Knots: Improved Clinch Knot to hook or lure, any good loop knot to the eye
Hook: 6/0 to 8/0 per desired pattern

Universal kite-fishing leader
Fish: any game fish to 150 pounds
Tackle class: 20-, 30-pound line
Length: 14 feet 6 inches maximum
Material: 50-pound-test monofilament
Knots: Improved Clinch Knot to hook, any good loop knot to the eye
Hook: 5/0 to 8/0 Eagle Claw

There are a number of instances when no leader at all is used, since the line is tied directly to the hook. In those cases, the line might be called a self-leader.

Live bait for stripers
Tackle class: 20-, 30-pound line
Bait: mackerel, herring, eel
Hook: 5/8 to 8/0 Eagle Claw

Worm drifting for stripers
Tackle class: 20-pound line
Bait: sand or blood worms
Hook: 2/0 to 4/0 Eagle Claw

Live bait for yellowtail, tuna
Tackle class: 30-, 50-pound line
Bait: anchovy, sardine, squid
Hook: 4/0 to 6/0 Eagle Claw

Live shrimp for redfish, sea trout
Tackle class: 12-, 20-pound line
Bait: live shrimp
Hook: 1/0 to 3/0 per desired pattern

Live shrimp for bonefish
Tackle class: 6-, 12-, 20-pound line
Bait: live shrimp
Hook: 1/0 to 3/0 per desired pattern

Live crab for permit
Tackle class: 12-, 20-pound line
Bait: small crabs
Hook: 3/0 to 5/0 Eagle Claw

Live bait for cobia, channel bass
Tackle class: 50-pound line
Bait: pinfish, grunts
Hook: 6/0 to 8/0 Eagle Claw

The use of line as a self-leader is limited to those fish that do not have particularly large, sharp teeth and that normally shy away from a bait presented with a leader. In a few instances, the use of a hook with an extra-long shank helps keep the line from being cut by sharp teeth. In other cases, a very short tooth leader of light wire or heavier monofilament may be added to the line between line and hook. In this case, line and tooth leader are tied together with no swivel or connector between.

LEADERS FOR SURF AND BOAT CASTING

Trolling anglers very often take advantage of the full 15 feet of double line allowed under IGFA tackle rules for lines of 50-pound test and under, but surf and boat casters find the long double line of no real value to their work. In fact, many habitual casters do away entirely with the double line and knot a suitable length of heavier monofilament directly to the fishing line. This is called a shock leader, and it performs three tasks:

(1) It takes the sudden tremendous shock of casting the lure, a shock that puts great strain on the first few feet of line between rod tip and lure.

(2) It counteracts the tendency of a light line to rub and scrape against the rough-scaled body of a fish after the fish is hooked.

(3) It gives the angler a much stronger section of line with which to control the fish close to the boat or in the surf just prior to netting or gaffing.

The preferred knot for joining monofilament line and shock leader is the Blood Knot or, in the case of line that is very much smaller than the shock leader, the Stu Apte or Improved Blood Knot. In the latter, the end of the lighter line is doubled back on itself before the knot is made. Typical shock-leader characteristics, compared to fishing line, are given below.

Line test	Leader length	Leader test
6 lb.	3 ft.	20 lb.
12 lb.	4 ft.	30 lb.
15 lb.	4½ ft.	36 lb.
20 lb.	5 ft.	40 lb.
25 lb.	5 ft.	50 lb.
30 lb.	6 ft.	60 lb.

The exact length of the shock leader is a matter of convenience to the fisherman. Some casters tie a swivel or snap to the working end of the shock leader. Others prefer to tie the end of the shock leader directly to the lure or hook. It really doesn't make much difference, as long as the angler is satisfied and the rig catches fish. But many anglers do think that extra hardware between leader and hook or lure just helps to confuse the fish, which is not the purpose of fishing.

If you are after fish with sharp cutting teeth, like bluefish, you will need at least a short tooth section between leader and hook or lure. Many casters make up short wire leaders in wire sizes of from #5 to #9 and lengths of six to 18 inches. In this instance, a snap or connector tied to the end of the shock leader or line is a great help when it comes to changing lures. Tackle stores sell made-up casting leaders of light nylon-covered stranded wire; these serve the same purpose. A number of different lengths, wire tests, and connector styles are available in various combinations. Whether fish appreciate their neatness is a question, but these leaders certainly do help to unclutter the tackle box.

How heavy should a casting leader or shock leader be? For spinning and conventional casting tackle, the lighter the better. Weight and windage are factors that cut down casting distance and accuracy. If you suspect that your cast-

Jack Fallon uses a 5-ft. leader of 50-lb. monofilament between the plastic float and the live eel bait of this casting rig, designed for big Cape Cod striped bass.

Capt. Cal Cochran (right) gaffs a big Florida Keys tarpon taken on saltwater fly tackle by light-tackle specialist Bob Stearns. Fly leaders require special construction.

ing terminal tackle is too heavy, try cutting down on the weight and length of leaders and shock sections a bit at a time, until you achieve the lightest combination consistent with adequate functioning of the tackle on fish.

The fish will appreciate light, unobtrusive leaders also, and they will reward you with more and stronger bites.

FLY-CASTING TERMINAL TACKLE

The leader of any fly-casting line, on fresh or salt water, is designed to be a sort of mechanical-energy transformer between the relatively heavy fly line and the practically weightless fly. In saltwater fly casting, a small element of lure weight does creep in. Hooks are bigger and heavier, and the plugs, poppers, streamers, and other lures used are more air-resistant.

The typical nine-foot freshwater leader is either a carefully engineered piece of tapered monofilament or an equally carefully calculated length of mono made up of successively thinner pieces tied together. The purpose of the tapered leader is two-fold:

(1) To enable the line and leader to roll out effortlessly, presenting the fly to the fish without fuss or splash.

(2) To place the thinnest part of the leader close to the fish, where it will have the least disturbing effect.

Following are specifications for several successful representative saltwater fly leaders. All are made up from measured sections of monofilament of the designated test. Sections are joined by Blood Knots, which are streamlined with Pliobond cement so they will pass easily through the rod guides.

Joe Brooks nine-footer: lines of W7, W8, W9
Butt section   24 in. 30-lb. mono
2nd section   18 in. 25-lb. mono
3rd section   18 in. 20-lb. mono
4th section   18 in. 15-lb. mono
Tippet section   12 in. 8- to 10-lb. mono
Shock section   18 in. 30-lb. mono

Bob Zwirz nine-footer: lines of W6, W7, W8
Butt section   30 in. 25-lb. mono
2nd section   30 in. 20-lb. mono
3rd section   24 in. 14-lb. mono
Tippet section   12 in. 6- to 10-lb. mono
Shock section   12 in. 30-lb. mono

Bob Zwirz 12-footer: lines of W8, W9, W10
Butt section   36 in. 30-lb. mono
2nd section   30 in. 25-lb. mono
3rd section   30 in. 20-lb. mono
4th section   24 in. 15-lb. mono
Tippet section   12 in. 8- to 12-lb. mono
Shock section   12 in. 40-lb. mono

Simplicity nine-footer: lines of W8 through W12
Butt section   72 in. 40- to 50-lb. mono
Tippet section   12 in. 8- to 15-lb. mono
Shock section   24 in. 50- to 60-lb. mono

Simplicity six-footer: lines of W7 through W10

Butt section	48 in. 30- to 40-lb. mono
Tippet section	12 in. 6- to 10-lb. mono
Shock section	12 in. 40- to 50-lb. mono

Big-game nine-footer: lines of W10, W11, W12

Butt section	30 in. 40-lb. mono
2nd section	30 in. 30-lb. mono
3rd section	24 in. 20-lb. mono
Tippet section	12 in. 10- to 15-lb. mono
Shock section	12 in. 50- to 60-lb. mono

Lefty Kreh tapered 10-footer: lines of W7, W8, W9

Butt section	24 in. 30-lb. mono
2nd section	12 in. 25-lb. mono
3rd section	12 in. 20-lb. mono
4th section	8 in. 18-lb. mono
5th section	8 in. 15-lb. mono
6th section	8 in. 12-lb. mono
Tippet section	24 in. 10-lb. mono
Shock section	24 in. 60-lb. mono

Lefty Kreh utility leader: lines of W9 through W12

Butt section	24 in. 40-lb. mono
Tippet section	12 in. 10- to 15-lb. mono
Shock section	12 in. 60- to 80-lb. mono

Lefty Kreh, the old master of the fly rod, claims that a long, tapered leader is unnecessary for many species of saltwater fish. For sensitive fish like bonefish, however, he recommends a tapered leader. The short "simplicity" and "utility" leaders described above are very often used for fish like tarpon — the ability to get off a quick, accurate cast to 40 or 50 feet is more important than a delicate presentation at 60 or 80 feet. Medium-soft monofilament makes the best saltwater leaders.

All of the fly leaders described can be "tooth-proofed" by the addition of a short section of leader wire between the end of the shock section and the hook. This should be not more than six inches long, and shorter if possible. Join the wire to the shock leader by first making a small eye in the end of the wire, using the haywire twist. Then tie the end of the shock leader to the wire eye with the Double Clinch or Improved Clinch Knot. Wire should be #3 to #5.

The diameter of the butt section of any leader has a direct relationship to the thickness of the end of the fly line. Generally, the butt section should have a diameter about two-thirds that of the line end. Line diameters vary, but the following table shows the range of butt-section diameters compared to standard lines of the weights normally used in saltwater fly casting.

Line weight	Mono leader test
#7 and #8	25 to 30 lb.
#9 and #10	40 lb.
#11 and #12	50 lb.

Terminal tackle is the most direct connection between fish and fisherman. Care exercised in its choice and use directly affects the outcome of the fishing.

Outriggers dress up a boat, but they also perform the very important task of giving lift and separation to bait trolling lines.

20 Outriggers, Kites, Downriggers

Outriggers and fishing kites are designed to accomplish the same task—to tow or present a prepared bait or lure at a distance from the boat. Outriggers do this by imparting lift and spread to the bait lines, placing the towed baits well outside the boat's wake and well behind the stern. To work properly, the boat must tow the outrigger baits at a speed somewhere between two and eight or nine knots.

The distance that baits can be trolling behind outriggers is definitely limited to not much more than 90 or 100 feet. Placing the bait before the fish requires maneuvering the boat. The angler may have some degree of control over the bait if the fishing line is rigged to render through the ring or arm of the line-release clip. But if the line is held tightly by the clip, all the angler can do to help a fish take the bait is to "knock down" the line to the fish by yanking it clear of the clip at the instant the fish is about to contact the bait.

Kites work differently. True, the general action is the same, in that the kite acts as a sort of super-outrigger, giving lift and separation to the bait, but there the similarity ends. The kite is usually flown from a drifting, stationary, or slowly moving boat. The boat's operator has considerable control over the kite by means of the length of the kite line and also by movement of the boat. Because the bait moves through the water only a little, compared to trolling, this is an ideal way to present live baits to game fish.

The kite supports both the line and the leader, so nothing is in the water but the bait. If an undesired fish like a shark appears, the angler can lift the bait clear of the water merely by reeling in some line. Eventually the kite will lower its flying altitude under this added weight, putting the bait back into the water, but the bait does not have to be in the air very long to frustrate a surface-swimming shark.

Outriggers and kites are very difficult to use at the same time, because they require entirely different operating conditions. But many game fishermen equip their boats with both outriggers and kite gear, so they will be able to take advantage of whatever bait-presenting situation looks best.

Outriggers used to be installed about amidships and "wung out" at right angles to the boat's side, like the wings of an old-fashioned airplane. This put the tips of the outriggers and their line-release clips somewhat forward of the anglers' fishing positions in the cockpit. This meant that the lines of the outrigger rods first had to lead forward and up before they could lead back to the trolled baits.

The result was that when the line was pulled clear of the release clip at the outrigger tip, quite a large loop or bight of loose line could fall into the cockpit from the windward outrigger, possibly fouling on a rod tip or some other obstruction. Correction of this condition proved to be relatively easy.

Nowadays it is standard procedure to mount the outriggers so they have a

181

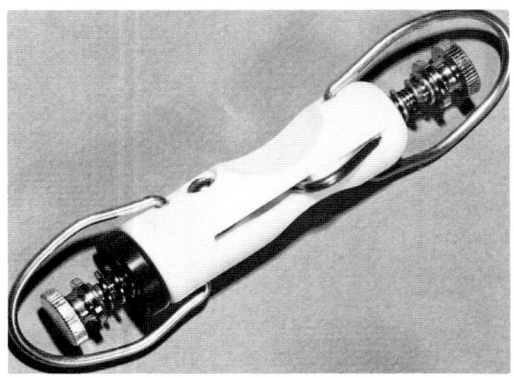

Above: The "Trip-Eze" adjustable outrigger release clip is excellent for a wide range of bait weights, line lengths, and trolling speeds. Parts are plastic and stainless steel. **Below:** Still popular is the spring-loaded wooden clip, here reinforced with rubber bands wrapped around the clip jaws. Clip resembles an overgrown snap-jaw clothespin.

Two types of surface outriggers exist, stiffened and unstiffened. Their characteristics are as follows:

Stiffened outriggers: These are very long shafts that are stiffened with metal or wooden spiders and wire stays. Only the outboard section, not more than a quarter of the total length, is left unstiffened. Stiffened outriggers are designed to tow heavy baits in rough water without causing the baits to jump clear of the water because of excessive bending of the outrigger shaft and its resulting "slingshot" effect on the towed bait.

Unstiffened outriggers: These are usually long fiberglass or aluminum shafts that do not have spiders and wire stiffeners. They are considerably less expensive than the more elaborate stiffened type, and they can tow heavy baits quite

strong after-rake in both the shipped and the operating positions. This places the release clips at a point abreast of or slightly aft of the boat's stern, giving the outrigger fishing lines an after lead rather than a forward lead from rod tip to release-clip position.

When the line is released, even the windward line falls clear of the boat, eliminating any possibility of fouling the loose, falling line on gear in the cockpit. This position of the release clip also simplifies visual inspection of the outrigger, the clip, and the fishing line.

The truss-built outrigger is designed to tow heavy skipping baits in choppy water without excessive plunging and diving of the bait. This all-metal model is equipped with double halyards and can tow two baits at one time.

Outriggers, Kites, Downriggers 183

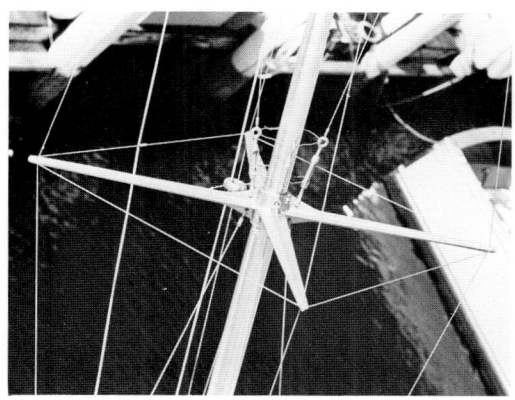

Above: *Close-up of one of the metal spiders of a modern truss-built outrigger. The spider is cast aluminum, tube is stainless steel, wires are also stainless steel.* **Below:** *Elbow-joint support strut locks like a human knee joint when outrigger is in the trolling position. Nylon safety rope is a common precaution against possible mechanical failure.*

Unstayed fiberglass small-boat outriggers are mounted in curved aluminum butt sections, can be attached to sunshade as here or thrust into standard side-deck flush rod holders.

well in smooth water. They tend to "slingshot" big baits as water gets choppy and rough. They are available as kits in lengths from 18 to more than 30 feet.

Under average conditions, outriggers are used to tow baits or special lures with the shafts held at about a 45-degree angle to the vertical. In Hawaii, however, where it is customary to tow two, three, or four large plastic Konahead lures for marlin and *ahi* (yellowfin tuna), at speeds up to eight or nine knots, the outriggers are rigged much higher, sometimes bolted permanently in the upright position. This is because Hawaiian custom places the lures or baits in Indian-file formation at distances of 60, 90, 120, and 150 feet behind the boat. In other regions, the common practice is to place the outrigger baits or lures abreast of each other, one on each side, at the proper distance behind the boat to achieve good skipping action.

Properly designed and installed outriggers can be lowered or raised by one person, merely by removing lock pins or loosening lock wheels. Struts should be arranged to be self-locking in the fishing position, so the outrigger cannot bounce up and down when the boat rolls. Careful skippers provide spliced-in safety lines of yacht-quality nylon rope to support an outrigger in case a lock pin or other support part fails.

Light outriggers for small boats are put into the fishing position by removing the shaft from a rod holder type of side deck support and rotating the shaft before reinserting it. The lower end of the shaft is metal with a 30- to-45-degree bend quite similar to the bend in a curved rod butt. A gimbal nock in the bottom of the shaft engages a fixed bolt or pin in the flush-mounted holder tube, usually providing three action positions: upright, winged out for fishing, and low rake back over the stern for passing under bridges.

Outriggers that double as radio antennas have been invented, but they do not always work well as antennas in the fishing position. Metal outriggers can be considered to be lightning rods of a type, and each metal outrigger should be bonded through its base to the boat's main ground system. Any competent marine electrician or radio technician can do this, or recommend how the owner can do it himself.

FISHING KITES

Excellent fishing kite kits are available from firms listed in the Manufacturers' Index. Three sizes and weights of kites

Above: *Mate Fred Harvey tends the kite line, which is heavy monofilament stored on a large wooden reel mounted on a piece of metal tubing designed to fit into a flush-mounted rod holder.* **Below:** *Capt. Bob Lewis of Miami, Fla., has perfected a complete kite-fishing kit, including reel, reel stand, plus light-, medium-, and heavy-weather kites for a wide range of fishing conditions.*

Florida charter skipper Capt. Angelo Durante specializes in using the fishing kite to bait game species like this sailfish. Tackle here is spinning gear with 18-lb.-test line.

are carried by the well-equipped kite fisherman: light-, medium-, and heavy-wind models. A light-wind model can be flown with normal baits and tackle in winds of as little as six to eight mph. Medium-wind kites are designed for winds of 12 to 18 mph. A small heavy-wind kite can be used in winds up to about 25 knots, provided the boatman assists the kite in strong puffs or momentary lulls.

The kite-line reel should be mounted where it is easy to use, but out of the way of fishing operations. Because this is largely light-tackle fishing, each angler should have his own personally adjusted gimbal belt and light shoulder harness. Ordinary snap-jaw clothespins can be used as line-release clips, or lightweight spring-loaded outrigger clips can be employed. The normal procedure is to pass the fishing line through a light plastic ring, which, in turn, is held by the release clip. This enables the angler to render his fishing line freely through the ring-clip combination, which is necessary for proper deployment of the bait. A quick yank of the rod pulls ring and line clear of the clip, as does a sudden strike from a fish.

As has been suggested, kites are used in a few localities to take baits or lures away from a shore where there is an off-shore wind.

DOWNRIGGERS AND PLANERS

The modern downrigger is nothing but an underwater outrigger that holds a monofilament or Dacron fishing line at the desired depth for deep trolling. In older days, some Montauk and other East Coast fishermen used heavy gooseneck lead drails or iron sash weights as downrigger

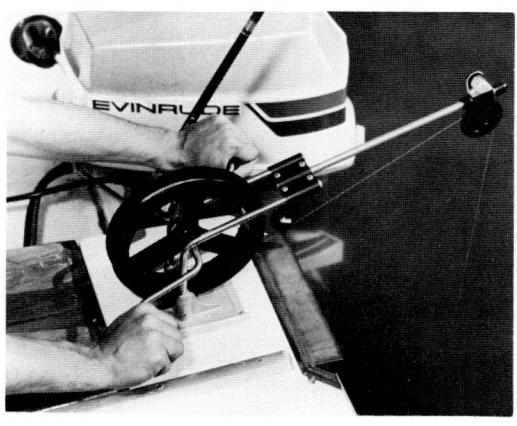

Above: *This Luhr Jensen downrigger is hand operated. A pair can be mounted on the stern of any boat.* **Below:** *Side-mounted Big Jon downrigger gives extra spread to the deep-trolling line arrangement.*

Downrigger works as an underwater outrigger. Trolling sinker (up to 10 lbs.) carries the fishing line and lure to any desired depth. When a fish strikes, the "Line Snatcher" (or any similar line-release device) releases the fishing line and the angler plays the fish without weight on his line. Meanwhile, the weight is hauled up and a fresh line and lure are made ready to lower away.

weights. The weight was equipped with a snap-jaw clothespin to act as a line-release clip, and it was hung on a separate piece of heavy, tarred handline.

Boats that did a lot of deep trolling for stripers, bluefish, pollock, and the like, hung a downrigger weight from a short pipe outrigger on each side of the boat and one or two more weights from the corners of the stern. This crude but simple deep-trolling system worked well in waters not over 40 feet deep.

Modern downriggers are considerably more sophisticated. Perfected in the Midwest for deep trolling in the Great Lakes for coho and Chinook salmon and lake trout, a modern downrigger consists of a hand-operated or motor-driven metal spool carrying a length of heavy Monel or

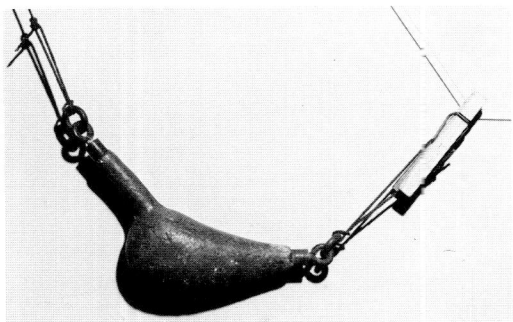

Above: *A simple downrigger can be made from a heavy lead drail, a piece of handline, and a snap-jaw clothespin to act as a quick-release device.* **Below:** *Electric-powered Riviera downrigger has an automatic line-out measuring counter. Some new models even incorporate a temperature-sensing device attached to the heavy weight and reading in the boat via an electric cable.*

stainless-steel wire line. The weight is a ball or bomb-shaped chunk of cast iron carrying a release clip on a short leader line.

In use, the lure is streamed a few feet behind the boat, and the line from the rod is then clipped into the weight's line-release clip. Both weight and fishing line are lowered to the desired fishing depth. Most downrigger models now have line-measuring devices to tell exactly how deep the weights are trolling, or the line itself may be color-coded. Once trolling depth is achieved, the rod is put in a handy rod holder until a fish strikes the lure and pulls the line clear of the downrigger weight clip.

Some anglers prefer to use the so-called planer, rather than a weight, to achieve depth. Originally, the planer was invented as a device that could be attached to the fishing line itself to achieve depth through its paravane shape and action rather than weight. A fish strike is sufficient to trip the planer out of the diving position and into a free-towing position. But the planer's usefulness as a downrigger depth vehicle was soon apparent.

Installing downriggers on a boat is largely a matter of individual choice in each instance. Some anglers do a great deal of deep trolling and install their downriggers as more-or-less-permanent cockpit equipment. Others arrange the installation so that the complete downrigger can be removed from the hold-down bolts or deck fitting and stowed away when not needed.

A specialized downrigger called a siderigger is now offered by some makers. This is nothing more than a downrigger frame and wire spool equipped with a fiberglass fishing-rod blank and special pulley fairleads for the wire. Rigged for trolling, it holds the weight wire four or five feet out from the side of the boat. One siderigger on each side of the boat, and one or two conventional downriggers on the stern, give a vessel tremendous deep-trolling capability.

An accurate electronic depth sounder is an absolute must for efficient use of downriggers. The sounder indicates the true depth under the boat, thus saving the weights from being hung up on bottom. If the sounder's transducer is located well aft, the weights themselves often can be monitored by the sounder, and quick changes of fishing depth can be made to accommodate the equipment to the depth of fish spotted on the sounder.

The ultimate trolling depth of a good downrigger setup may be more than 200 feet. In Lake Michigan, depths of 100 to 150 feet are fished regularly with downriggers for salmon and lake trout. Interestingly, the International Game Fish Association has specifically allowed downriggers for taking game fish with rod

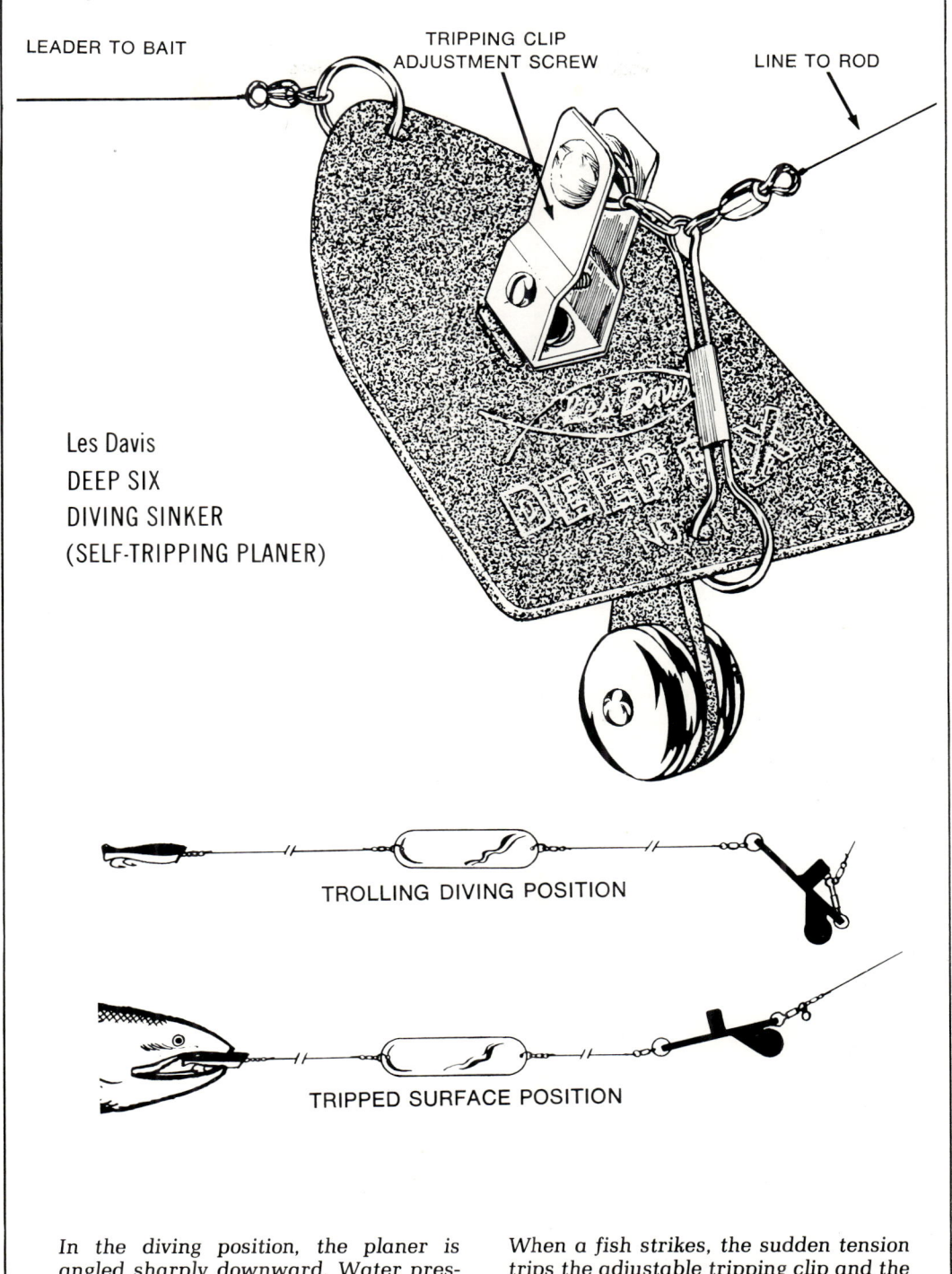

LEADER TO BAIT
TRIPPING CLIP ADJUSTMENT SCREW
LINE TO ROD

Les Davis
DEEP SIX
DIVING SINKER
(SELF-TRIPPING PLANER)

TROLLING DIVING POSITION

TRIPPED SURFACE POSITION

In the diving position, the planer is angled sharply downward. Water pressure from forward motion causes it to dive strongly, carrying the lure with it.

When a fish strikes, the sudden tension trips the adjustable tripping clip and the planer assumes a straight-line attitude with the fishing line and lure.

and reel, provided no wire line is used in the rod and reel equipment, aside from the length of wire or monofilament leader provided for in IGFA tackle rules. This means that up to 15 feet of leader plus 15 feet of double line can be used for tackle in the 50-pound-line class and lighter, and up to 30 feet of leader plus 30 feet of double line can be used for tackle of 80- and 130-pound-line class.

The depth-seeking fishing planer attached directly to the fishing line is less complicated to use on an individual basis and costs less, but it has certain inherent disadvantages. Consider the advantages and disadvantages from the viewpoint of an angler seeking trophy fish.

First, if you fish all alone with just one or two trolling lines out, planers may be a good way for you to achieve depth with IGFA-accepted tackle. Nothing in IGFA rules makes line-attached planers "illegal." One immediately visible disadvantage is that the planer puts a great deal of extra strain on the line and the rod, strain that is supported by the downrigger when that equipment is used. Another disadvantage is that this strain increases very rapidly as speed is increased, and an increase in speed is not always accompanied by a decrease in trolling depth. Until it is tripped, the planer just digs deeper as speed increases.

Downrigger-weight wire is usually at least 75 to 80 pounds in test. Because no strain is placed on the fishing line by the downrigger, it can be used for deep trolling with very light lines. The planer, however, puts enough strain on the fishing line to make the lower limit of line-breaking strain at least 20 pounds in many cases. A system for overcoming this deficiency is as follows:

(1) Rig the fishing line with a double line a full 15 feet long, attaching a snap swivel to the end.

(2) Make up a leader of heavy monofilament or light wire, which, when cut into two parts with a planer inserted between them, is not more than 15 feet long. This should satisfy the letter of IGFA tackle rules.

(3) Make the upper portion of the leader 10 feet long, attaching its upper end to the snap swivel of the line and its lower end to the planer.

(4) Make the lower part four feet long, to go between the planer and the lure. With this arrangement, the planer can work at the end of a double-line-plus-leader combination that will measure 15 + 10 = 25 feet. By keeping about five feet of double line in the guides of the rod, and down to one turn on the reel, there is still 20 feet of depth from rod tip to planer. Allowing two or three feet of lift for water drag, this will place the planer 17 to 18 feet deep if the rod tip is held down close to the water's surface. The planer may even act like an attractor to entice the fish.

Lures for deep trolling are discussed in detail in Chapter 25, but here is an important tip to bear in mind: neither downriggers nor planers permit rod action to be passed on to a lure, so it is wise to use only those types of lures that work best without jigging or other rod action. The lures also should be all one type for trolling speed. You waste valuable success percentages when you mix lures that call for different speeds for maximum fish-getting efficiency. Planer usefulness in on-line fishing is limited to depths of 40 to 50 feet.

21 Specialized Boat Equipment

FISHING AND FIGHTING CHAIRS

Most nonfishermen, and even quite a few anglers, do not realize that there is a basic difference between fishing chairs and fighting chairs. Below are the true definitions and uses of each variety.

A *fishing chair* is a fairly light chair, either fixed on a swivel pedestal or movable, equipped with a rod butt gimbal cup at the edge of the seat, but without a footrest. The seat height is such that the angler sits with his feet firmly planted on the deck. The chair may or may not have rod holders attached to the armrests. It is used primarily in light- to medium-tackle fishing with tackle of 50-pound-line class or lighter.

A *fighting chair* is usually of fairly heavy all-metal or metal-and-fiberglass construction, placed on a fixed heavy metal pedestal with swivel top and equipped with a footrest. The angler is thus able to raise his feet and place the power of his legs in direct opposition to the pull of the line. The chair back folds down or can be removed for fighting a fish, and the footrest length is adjustable. There are usually rod holders attached to the armrests. A friction brake governs the rotation of the chair on the pedestal and locks it in any desired position. The chair is used for big-game fishing with tackle of 50-pound-line class or heavier. Light fighting chairs are occasionally mounted on the reinforced tops of motor boxes of boats with stern drive units.

In planning the installation of a fighting chair, it is wise to follow these precautions:
- Locate the pedestal deck plate on the cockpit deck centerline far enough forward from the stern so a person can pass between the extended footrest and the stern or any stern fish box that may be placed there.
- Install a heavy hardwood or laminated plywood doubling piece under the deck where the deck plate is to be fastened. Fasten the plate with bronze or stainless-steel bolts, never brass fastenings, which may corrode and weaken after exposure to salt water.
- Test the strength of the deck plate and its fastenings periodically by bouncing your full weight on the extended footrest to make sure nothing will fail while you are fighting a very large fish under heavy pressure in rough water.

A popular way to arrange chairs on larger boats is to place one fighting chair in the after end of the cockpit, flanking it with two fixed or movable fishing chairs, one on either side and slightly forward of the fighting chair. In this flexible arrangement, the fishing chairs can be left behind if big game is the primary target, or the footrest of the fighting chair can be removed and the seat placed on a low pedestal to give the effect of three fishing chairs for comfortable small-game trolling.

Owners of boats of the center-console type sometimes mount a single

Specialized Boat Equipment   191

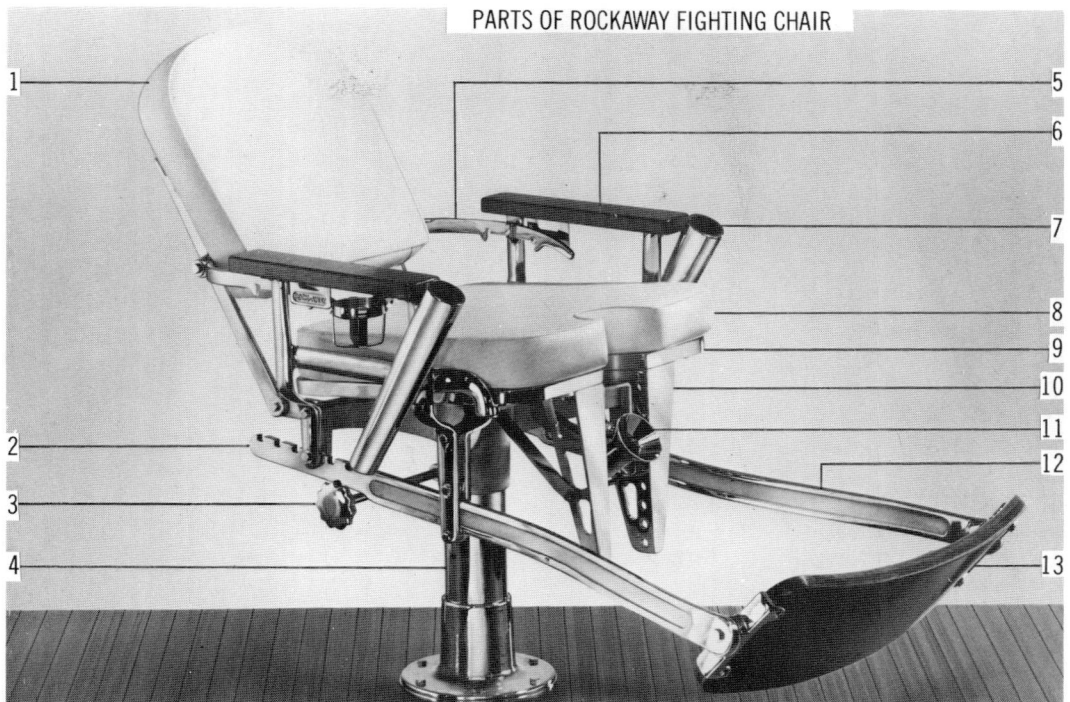

PARTS OF ROCKAWAY FIGHTING CHAIR

1 Back cushion
2 Footrest length-adjustment bar
3 Pivot friction brake knob
4 Chair stand (locks into deck plate)
5 Backrest angle-adjustment bar
6 Armrest (left and right)
7 Rod holder (left and right)
8 Foam-rubber seat cushion
9 Metal seat and chair frame
10 Adjustable rod gimbal riser
11 Rod gimbal cup
12 Footrest bar (left and right)
13 Adjustable-angle footrest

Left: Don Leek, on his Pacemaker sport fisherman, waits out the deep run of a Bahamian blue marlin. A modern fighting chair enables an angler to pit the full strength of his body against any fish, working the heaviest tackle to the limit of its endurance. **Below, left:** Another version of a fighting chair, this one by Tournament Marine, makers of chairs, outriggers, and related equipment. **Below, right:** Close-up of the gimbal cup riser of a typical Rockaway fighting chair. A number of vertical positions are provided for the cup bolts to accommodate straight or curved rod butts of various lengths. Adjustment should be made before fishing starts.

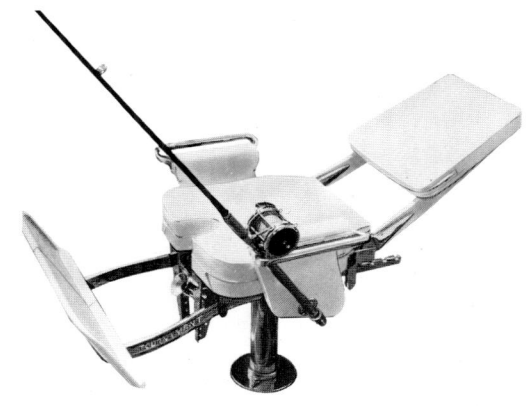

light fighting chair back aft. The footrest is knocked down and can be assembled and attached in a moment's notice if it is needed for a big fish. In other such boats, a light fighting chair is frequently mounted in the bow. The angler fights a hooked fish over the bow rather than over the stern, a considerable advantage with big fish in rough water.

Modern fishing and fighting chairs are usually high-expense items. Turnover of merchandise in this line is slow, and materials are expensive. It's possible to convert almost any light metal or heavy wooden fishing chair into a serviceable fighting chair that will take large fish. The accompanying series of photos shows how I accomplished such a conversion of a solid teakwood fishing chair.

If you contemplate following this procedure, there are a few precautions that must be taken:

- Wooden chair seats usually are built up of fairly narrow pieces of wood that are doweled and edge-glued together. This doweling and gluing cannot be trusted under the heavy strains of big-game fishing. Therefore, two strong cross members of wood or metal must be fastened to the bottom of the seat, and each wooden seat part is bolted to the cross members. The cross members also carry the pipe tubes, into which the footrest pipe members are thrust.

- Don't trust a common brass or bronze pipe pedestal that is screwed into a deck flange fastened to the deck. Get two flanges and have one bored out for a snug fit to the outside diameter of the pedestal pipe. Install this on the deck after drilling a centerline hole large enough for the pipe pedestal to pass through the deck and screw into the second pipe flange, located on a strong wooden partner fastened to the boat's bottom or across the keelsons, well under the deck. The lower plate supports the weight of the chair without having to overcome bending strains. The upper sleeve flange takes side thrust without having to support weight.

It is a mistake to try to crowd too many fishing or fighting chairs into a boat's cockpit. In some resort areas, you see charter craft with four or more chairs in the cockpit. These boats cater to transient anglers who aren't interested in fishing efficiency as long as they can sit comfortably while waiting for a fish to strike. This is fine if a group of friendly people are just out for a day's fun on the

The author used this homemade fighting chair for a number of years in his boat at Montauk, N.Y., taking numerous billfish and giant tuna. Rod holders were added to the armrests after this picture was taken.

Two light Pompanette fishing chairs serve double duty in this Mako inboard fishing boat.

Specialized Boat Equipment 193

Above: *A light Pompanette chair mounted on the stern motor box of this small fisherman performed well for Dennis Good of New Orleans, fishing marlin and large tuna off South Pass, Miss.* **Below:** *Joseph Teti adjusts the length of a flat-line on his fishing cruiser "Jomar III." The other rod is rigged to an outrigger bait.*

water. But if the fishing is competitive or for large, active game, more lines in the water and more chairs in the cockpit add up to more tangles and confusion when a fish finally appears.

There are a number of different chair designs available, and information on specific details and current prices can be obtained from the manufacturers listed in the Manufacturers' Index.

ROD HOLDERS

The rod holder is nothing new in saltwater fishing. What is new is the way clever makers of fishing equipment have adapted the old pipe or rubber hose rod holder to new tackle arrangements. Basically, there are now four major types of boat rod holders.

(1) The conventional tubing or open-frame cockpit-side rod holder, made of metal or plastic, which can be attached to the woodwork.

Above: Sally Rice and Aka Hodgins have just set four heavy outfits in the staggered trolling pattern typical of trolling with Konahead lures for blue marlin off the Kona Coast of Hawaii. **Below:** Rod with curved butt in rod holder made for either curved or straight butts, part of the armrest of a fighting chair. (1) Straight-butt rod position (2) Curved-butt rod position. Gimbal fitting of the rod butt fits into a separate swiveling gimbal (not shown), mounted on side of the chair seat.

(2) The newer, rubber-lined, metal, flush-mounted rod holder, which is inserted into the stern or side deck with only the rounded upper lip showing above the deck surface. The main tube of the holder is below the deck line.

(3) The fighting-chair rod holder. Here there are two varieties. The older type looks like a conventional rod holder of the tubing sort. The newer type is actually part of the armrest, a curved piece of pipe or metal rod placed in such a way that, combined with a separate gimbal socket, it can be used with either straight or curved butt rods. Chair rod holders are almost always installed in pairs.

(4) The "rocket launcher," or multiple rod holder, for light-tackle stand-up fishing. The launcher is so-called because it resembles a launcher for military rockets when the four individual holders are filled with rods. This handy item is composed of four flush-mounted rod holders attached to a flat board that, in turn, is usually mounted on a fairly high tubing support. This support is often placed on the deck plate of the fighting chair. The rocket launcher is ideal for light-tackle tournament fishing, where a fighting chair is hardly necessary.

The primary rules of rod-holder placement are:

• Locate the holders in a pattern that gives good spread to the flat-line trolling tackle, preventing tangles while under way.

• Keep holders within easy reaching distance of chairs.

• In big-game trolling, locate the outrigger rods at the fighting chair, one in each chair holder. Locate flat-line tackle in cockpit side holders.

• In small-game fishing, many anglers prefer to hold their rods in their hands, awaiting the thrill of the strike. Rod-storage rod holders should be located away from the primary scene of fishing action, so stored rods will not interfere with proper use of fishing tackle.

• During active fishing, rods in rod holders should have the reel drag set at a low tension to forestall breakage of a rod or butt in case there is an unexpected strike. Careful anglers attach a safety

Above: "Rocket launcher" is positioned atop the fighting-chair pedestal in this Florida fisherman, preparing for a light-tackle sailfish tourney. Note the side-mounted gin pole for big fish. **Below:** New England bass expert Frank Woolner uses special homemade horizontal rod holders to store extra tackle in a ready-to-fish condition on his Boston Whaler bass boat.

line to each outfit, so that if a butt breaks on a sudden strike, the entire rod and reel won't be lost.

ON-DECK FISH BOXES

Nothing messes up a boat more quickly than fish and bait kicked around underfoot. The day of the built-in stern fish box is about over, but modern fiberglass deck fish boxes are available in a number of sizes and shapes. Most are insulated to preserve ice for keeping the fish cool, and they are available with attractive teak trim.

The drainage system for these boxes consists of one or more flexible rubber or plastic tubes that can be attached to permanent drain fittings or thrust out through a handy deck scupper. The teak or plastic top usually is finished to act as a boarding step when the boat is backed up to the pier. Some models have interior baffles or extra compartments for icing beverages and food. When the boat is not being used for fishing, the fish box can be left on the pier as a storage locker, or it can be kept on board as a cockpit gear locker.

UNDER-DECK FISH WELLS

The under-deck fish well is a carry-over from old commercial fishing days, when boats were sail-powered and did not carry ice. As fast as the fish were caught, they were popped into the commodious wet well, where seawater, flowing in through holes in the hull planking, kept much of the catch alive.

The modern under-deck wet well seldom uses the old hole-in-the-planking method of obtaining circulating water, but its location under the deck increases effective deck space, especially on smaller boats. If you are thinking of putting a wet well in your boat for fish and/or live bait, here is a plan of action that has worked for many boat owners.

(1) Measure your under-deck area to find out how much space you can devote to a built-in under-deck fish-and-bait well. The space between the sister keelsons and/or engine bed stringers may be satisfactory. For a box to be effective, it should have a capacity of at least five or six cubic feet.

(2) Mock up a dummy box in corrugated paperboard to see if your proposed box will fit. Don't cut deck beams or planking until you are sure you are doing it right.

(3) Figure out where the water inlet will be located and how drainage will be arranged. Allow enough space for a sea cock on each through-hull fitting; place each one where it can be operated from a deck hatch.

(4) Design your box with side walls sloping inward about 15 degrees toward the top to minimize splashing. Also design adequate support members if necessary.

(5) Build the box of marine plywood, coated inside with fiberglass. Installing the box may necessitate cutting deck timbers, or the box may be slid into place via the main engine space or a deck hatch.

(6) Make sure the box is fastened strongly to the bearers so it can't slide around in rough weather. Make the deck hatches big enough so the box can be cleaned after use.

LIVE-BAIT WELLS AND BOXES

The most important factor in the well-being of live anchovies, shrimp, and similar bait is a plentiful supply of clean seawater to supply needed oxygen and to remove contaminants like blood and slime from injured fish. The popular West Coast style of on-deck bait tank features a built-in circulating pump and insulation from heat and sunlight. All you have to do is hook up the electric power and the hoses for water supply and drainage.

In large sport-fishing boats, the bait tanks often involve a built-in custom installation, but many smaller fishing boats now come with bait tanks molded into their fiberglass hulls. When looking over boats with built-in bait tanks, keep the following questions in mind.

• Will the tank have proper water circulation when the boat is anchored or drifting?

• Is the bait compartment big enough for the quantity and types of bait you intend to use?

• Does the tank have any blind cor-

Specialized Boat Equipment 197

Above: An insulated, fiberglass combination deck fish box and live-bait well, by Frigibar. **Below:** This custom-made stainless-steel deck well doubles as a live-bait well and a fish well for small fish, such as these bonitos. Valves control water inflow and overboard discharge.

ners into which bait fish or shrimp can crowd together and suffocate?

• Is the bait easy to reach from the fishing location?

Owners of very small boats frequently have to make do with a specialized minnow or shrimp bucket instead of a built-in tank. This works well, provided you change the water often. There are electric air pumps or aspirators that shoot a stream of bubbles into the bait-bucket water. The water still should be changed frequently to remove blood and slime washed into the water from injured bait fish.

Are oxygen pills or pellets effective in a bait bucket? Results seem to be inconclusive. Some fishermen seeking aquarium specimens are successful in transporting home small live fish in plastic containers into which a few whiffs of pure oxygen have been puffed. Temperature appears to be very important, as does uncontaminated water. A change of a few degrees of temperature may put the fish under heavy stress, and many fish are very susceptible to the toxic effect of fish blood in water.

REFRIGERATION

For owners of small fishing boats, the handiest type of bait and fish refrigerator is one of the popular lightweight insulated beverage coolers in one- to three-cubic-foot size. Both bait and fish should be placed in separate watertight plastic containers in the box, so ice or melted ice water will not come in contact with fish or bait. Some anglers place crushed or chipped ice in plastic bags or watertight containers in the larger-size ice chest to keep ice and contents separate.

Should meltwater be drained away as it forms? One train of thought follows the claim that meltwater encourages ice to melt faster, thereby reducing the length of time that a load of ice may be effective. Another theory is that as long as there is cold water in the box, there is some refrigerating value left, and some is better than none, especially on a hot day.

An ice chest should never be kept in the sun. Radiant heat from the sun or any other source of infra-red rays will penetrate any non-metallic ice chest and go to work on the contents. But even a thin wall of shiny aluminum foil will reflect a large proportion of radiant heat. The most effective portable ice chests, therefore, are those that combine adequate thermal-transfer insulation with radiant-reflective insulation.

Tournament-class sport-fishing cruisers very often feature a built-in freezer with a capacity of several cubic feet. Trolling baits can be prerigged, then frozen. A day's supply is removed from the freezer at one time, thawed, and affixed to proper leaders. Ready for use, these baits are kept on chipped or block ice in a cockpit ready box of the portable beverage type.

Thawed baits often will keep well overnight if they are wrapped in plastic sheeting or aluminum foil and placed on ice, but refreezing damages the bait tissues and renders the baits too soft for more than a few minutes' towing the second day. The preservation of specific baits is discussed in more detail in Chapter 24.

A number of companies offer seat-type and upright boat freezers as compact units, and freezer kits that can be adapted to existing hulls. See the Manufacturers' Index for details on these companies.

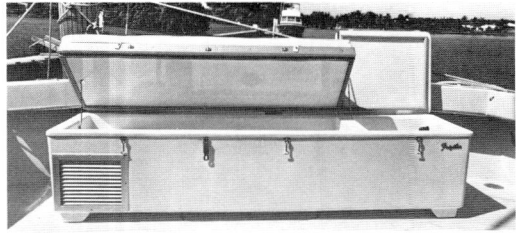

Another Frigibar unit — a combination portable deck freezer and live-bait well. Several companies offer a variety of deck fish and freezer boxes in seat-high and stand-up models.

A properly installed side-mounted gin pole will handle fish up to 1,000 lbs. This 550-lb. tuna was taken off Nebraska Shoal, R.I., during an Atlantic Tuna Tournament.

GIN POLES, HOISTING DAVITS, AND STERN DOORS

A handy device for lifting very large fish from the water is a side-mounted gin pole. The origin of the name is obscure, but a gin pole is essentially a vertical mast or king post attached to the after end of the cabin side or the rear corner of the deckhouse overhang. It is equipped with a block and fall for lifting heavy weights.

A serviceable gin pole can be made from a clear fir four-by-four 12 to 14 feet long. Ash is even better, since it is light and strong. Oak is used frequently. Some gin poles have been built like a hollow spar with spruce or selected white pine.

In any event, the pole should be long enough to provide at least eight feet of clear lifting space between the cockpit side-rail top and the hook of the lower fall block when the fall is in the two-block position. If you allow 18 inches for the fall blocks and their attachment to the pole, and 30 inches for the distance from cockpit deck to side deck surface, the pole has to be 12 feet tall to provide the eight feet of free lift needed to haul in a long fish over the rail.

The gin pole should be stepped in a separate hardwood block or pad and fastened to the cabin top or deckhouse overhang with a stout U-shaped strap of heavy brass, bronze, or stainless steel. Some companies that make fishing hardware now offer a pivoting davit head of strong metal that can be mounted atop an aluminum or stainless-steel pipe about three inches in diameter and as tall as a standard gin pole. The davit head swings outboard for lifting and inboard for dropping a big fish on deck.

Follow this simple system for preparing the rope fall, and you won't go wrong.

(1) First determine the lifting power you need. For example, a fall made up of two two-sheave blocks rigged as illustrated will handle fish up to 600 pounds quite comfortably. A fall made with two three-sheave blocks will handle 1,000 pounds with the same amount of pulling power on the rope. Use only top-quality nylon 1/2-inch yacht rope and blocks to match.

(2) Next estimate how much rope you need. Measure the height of the top block above the waterline. If this is 14 feet, let us say, multiply this height by the number of block sheaves plus one. A fall made up of two two-block sheaves will yield the following line-length formula: 14 feet x 5 (four sheaves plus one) = 70 feet of line.

(3) Add five feet of line for splicing, etc. This means you will need a total of 75 feet of line, which will result in a fall that will reach from pole top to waterline, with enough extra line at the pulling end for comfortable pulling.

(4) When splicing nylon rope, fuse the strand ends with a cigarette-lighter flame so the strands won't ravel during splicing. Three tucks is standard for manila rope, but four tucks is better for nylon.

The stern door is a hinged door or panel in the boat's transom that can be swung open so big fish can be slid in on deck without having to be lifted. Quite a few manufacturers of larger sport-fishing boats now offer stern doors as standard

Rockaway fish hoisting davit has a ball-bearing swivel top, easing the job of swinging a very large fish into the boat.

June Rosko is elated as Capt. George Seaman helps to slide her freshly caught blue marlin through the stern door of George's boat "Mitchell II."

Nova Scotians like the direct approach to pulling fish into the boat. The low freeboard of their Cape Island boats helps when it comes to muscling in a 600-pounder.

or optional features. It is definitely better to plan a stern door before the boat's final construction than to try to alter an existing hull.

Unless the boat's cockpit deck is exceptionally high above the waterline, a block and fall usually is not needed for hauling in even the biggest fish. If the deck is so high that a tackle is needed to bring in fish through the stern door, a side-mounted gin pole or fish-boating davit might be the more efficient way of getting big fish aboard.

How do you boat a fish if you don't have lifting gear or a stern door? The Nova Scotians regularly pull in tuna weighing up to 800 pounds head-first over the rails of their Cape Island boats. These vessels, of course, are blessed with a low, sweeping sheer line and low freeboard amidships. On the West Coast, some anglers take advantage of the popular stern platform for boating big fish. This is fine, provided the platform's fastenings to the hull are strong enough to take the weight of a very large fish.

As a last resort, be prepared to tail-rope a fish that's too big to lift, and then tow it home. This is often done with sharks, which are slow to die and constitute a definite danger if taken into the boat alive. A dock line makes a good tail rope.

TUNA TOWERS

The so-called tuna tower is an elevated boat control station atop a light metal framework. It is designed to improve the boat operator's ability to spot and follow fish swimming underwater. Towers originated in the Florida-Bahamas area and were used first for spotting and following migratory bluefin tuna as the fish passed over the shallows of the western edge of the Bahama Banks. Towers soon proved to be effective in spotting and following such underwater swimmers as swordfish, marlin, and sharks.

A tower improves underwater visibility in two ways. First, elevating the eye level above water tends to reduce the effect of surface ripples and glare. Second, the higher the eye, the greater the circle of observable nearby undersurface water. The accompanying photo illustrates how the observable area increases as the square of the increase of eye elevation.

From any position of elevation, the minimum angle of eye penetration into the water is about 40 degrees from the horizontal. This may vary according to light and surface conditions, but it remains a fairly accurate rule of thumb. The photo illustrates graphically how increased eye-level height enlarges the observable area at a rate equal to the square of the increase in height.

THE TOWERING PROBLEM. *How elevation increases underwater viewing area. Length of boat: 42 ft. Height of eye on flying bridge: 14 ft. Height of eye on tower: 25 ft. Assuming the same downward angle of observation, the man on the bridge can spot underwater fish within a circle with a radius of 24 ft., or a circle of 452.4 sq ft. The man on the tower, on the other hand, can search a circle with a radius of 42 ft. and an area of 1385.4 sq. ft., or 306 percent larger. Height also diminishes loss of underwater vision caused by surface ripples and sky reflection.*

Originally, towers were thought of as equipment for fairly large boats. Now, even open outboards as small as 24 feet overall can be equipped with towers built in proportion to their smaller size. Such towers place the operator's eye height about equal to that found on a 40-footer's flying bridge, but even this increase is extremely helpful to the operator of a small boat engaged in tournament fishing.

Modern towers are built primarily of welded aircraft-quality aluminum alloy or stainless steel. Several companies now specialize in making up standard or custom-designed towers. In earlier days, home-built towers made up of aluminum pipe and heavy cast-aluminum awning fittings were popular. Insurance companies do not encourage such construction, largely because the bond between the various members is not a weld, but the bite of a stainless-steel set screw into softer metal pipe.

Maximum tower height, even on very large fishing cruisers, should be not much more than 30 or 35 feet above the water. A point is quickly reached beyond which motion becomes rather difficult, even in larger boats. Provided a tower is not overloaded with human weight, the structure does not put any great strain on a well-built hull and superstructure. Towers are designed to be entirely self-supporting without additional struts or stays. A well-built tower can support at least two persons in any manageable sea condition, yet it does not raise the center of gravity of a boat by more than a tiny fraction of a percentage point.

Towers do present something of a windage problem to some boats, especially underpowered single-screw boats of shallow draft. But for the average adequately powered sport-fishing boat, the wind drag of a tower is no great problem. Prudence indicates that all metal towers and outriggers be bonded electrically to the boat's primary ground system for protection against possible lightning strokes. Any competent marine electrician can do this.

A tower makes an ideal location for a radar antenna, and also for various types of radio antennas. The addition of a tower to an existing boat usually will require retuning of the radio transmitter, but it should not alter the transmitter's final power output.

Towers built of aluminum alloy profit by being anodized with gold or some other appropriate color. Stainless-steel towers usually are given a brushed finish. The interior of the belly rail atop the tower stand should be padded with vinyl-covered foam rubber for comfort and safety. The ladders for climbing the tower usually are part of the structural system.

If the tower is to be fully effective, there should be complete steering and motor controls at the tower control station, plus a compass, radio remote-control box, and sometimes a duplicate set of important engine instruments. Some owners also put in an intercom system to facilitate conversation between tower and cockpit. This beats loud shouting exchanges on a windy day.

The seat harness used by Jack Rounick to fight a Montauk swordfish puts the line of pull of the harness straps at or just below the level of his beltline, enabling him to put heavy body weight pressure on the tackle without unduly tiring the body muscles.

22 Tackle Box and Cockpit Equipment

No mechanic can work without adequate tools, and no fisherman can prepare baits, lures, or terminal tackle without a well-equipped tackle box. Not every item in the following list can be crammed into just one tackle box, but all of the items are intimately connected with preparing tackle for fishing. Asterisked (*) items are suggested for the beginner's basic tackle box, outlined in Chapter 13.

THE COMPLETE TACKLE BOX

*Bernard parallel-jaw fisherman's pliers
 Needle-nose side-cutting pliers
*Bait-cutting and filet knives
 Broad-blade butcher knife
*Oilstone for knives
 Small oilstone for hooks
*Reel wrenches and spare parts
*Reel lubricant
*Screwdriver set
 Bait-cutting board
 Bait needles (long and short)
 Backbone remover
*Leader material (mono and wire)
*Spare fishing line
 Ferrule cement
 Small propane torch
*Snap swivels, plain swivels, connectors
*Assorted sinkers, as needed
*Assorted hooks, as needed
*Assorted lures, as needed
*Fish-scaling tool
*Fishhook remover
 Friction and plastic tape
 Outrigger release clips
 Prepared pork rind
 Crimping pliers, crimp sleeves
 Fish-weighing scale
 Emergency rod-winding silk
 Lacquer silk preserver
*First-aid kit
 Thermometer for water temperature
 Gloves for handling leader wires
 Dacron line-splicing tool

Until recently, only the larger, more expensive big-game fishing boats could boast the luxury of a special tackle locker and bait-rigging station. On smaller boats, the skipper or mate had to (and often still does) make do with a scrap of plywood in lieu of a bait-rigging station. Now some boat manufacturers incorporate a specially designed tackle locker and work station, usually an optional extra, into the layouts of their fishing models.

Successful fishing often depends on an adequate supply of baits or lures prepared in advance of a spell of fast action. Few things can be more frustrating than having to fumble for fresh baits or lures from raw materials while hungry fish are searching the nearby water for something to eat.

The ideal tackle locker and work area is located in the cockpit or fishing area, but out of the way of direct fishing action. It is protected from sun, spray, and back-and-forth traffic. In larger boats, the top of the deck bait freezer or tackle-storage locker makes a good work area. This locker is often placed under the flying bridge access ladder or the after

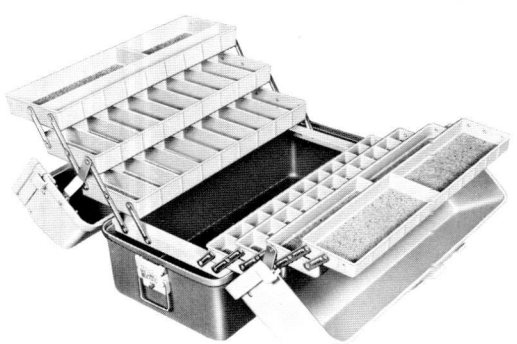

A typical modern tackle box from the Plano Molding Company. Large compartments have non-skid material applied to tray surfaces.

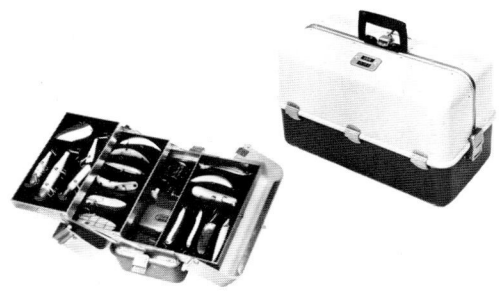

This Umco tackle box is designed to carry a sizable selection of different kinds of casting lures, plus other items of tackle.

overhang of the deckhouse. In small boats, some sacrifice of fishing space often has to be made to accommodate the tackle work area.

Tackle-box requirements vary widely among anglers. Some fishermen are able to get by with a single all-purpose box and a supply of spares at home. This system is great for the small-boat angler, the surf caster, or the traveling fisherman, but it requires careful weeding of equipment before starting out on a fishing trip.

Other anglers prefer to stock different types of materials in separate boxes. Tools, for example, are heavy, so they may call for a metal box. Plugs come with hooks attached, and nothing is more troublesome than a box with several loose plugs tangled together by their sharp hooks. Fortunately, tackle-box manufac-

turers very often are also fishermen, and ingenious boxes have been created expressly for storing an assortment of plugs of various sizes and shapes.

Bulky items—like large spools of line or wire, spare reels, coils of leader wire, line-driers, fishing belts and harnesses, and the like—should be stored in large boxes designed for the purpose, or in built-in tackle lockers in the boat's cabin or deckhouse. The supply of sinkers should be kept separate from other equipment, preferably in a box or locker close to the deck, where the weight of the sinkers won't damage anything if they fall during a spell of rough water.

Information on manufacturers of tackle boxes and related equipment is provided in the Manufacturers' Index. A box for just about every imaginable purpose can be found in the catalogs of these manufacturers.

Not all fishermen are good housekeepers. Tackle boxes tend to become catchalls for loose gear, engine tools, and a host of nonfishing items. The way to prevent a tackle box from becoming an unsightly mess is to take just a few minutes after each trip to put the box and its contents into shipshape order.

GAFFS, NETS, COCKPIT GEAR

Gaffs come in a variety of sizes and shapes, ranging from the stub-handled surf-caster's gaff to the powerful big-game flying gaff with its six- to eight-foot handle. There are four important gaffs.

Stub gaff: The lower portion of the hook itself is part of the gaff handle. A wooden or plastic filler piece is cemented to the gaff-hook tang, and it usually is fitted with a rubber bicycle-handlebar grip cemented in place. Stub gaffs are the preferred weapons of surf casters; they are used occasionally by small-boat fishermen with surf-fishing experience.

Common boat gaff: The gaff hook usually is made of stainless steel, without a barb, and it is fastened by wire wrappings to a stout hardwood or light metal handle three to four feet long. In most

Above: *The common boat gaff is the quickest and surest tool for boating an 18-lb. cod like this specimen taken jigging in Nova Scotia.* **Below:** *This Yankee surf fisherman used a stub gaff to nail a school striper taken on a plug from Nova Scotia's Annapolis River.*

cases, the hook is curved 180 degrees, with a slight outward bend to the sharp point. One variety is the so-called pick gaff, on which the hook is shorter than on the common gaff; it is curved only a little beyond the 90-degree angle to the handle. The pick gaff usually has a perfectly straight point.

The common gaff is thrust into the fish with a quick lifting motion of the arm. The pick gaff, on the other hand, is struck into the fish with a hammer stroke of the forearm, as one would drive a nail into wood with a hammer. The pick gaff is effective against fish with large, thick scales, such as school tarpon and very large striped bass. It is an adaptation of an old commercial fishermen's model.

Long-handled gaff: This is a heavy-duty version of the common boat gaff, with a wooden or metal tubing handle up to eight or more feet long. The hook is often side-forged for extra strength. This gaff is used to lift big fish up to the decks of large party boats, or to secure fish taken in the surf when the angler cannot

Gaffing a big fish on slippery rocks at night can be dangerous. Milt Rosko solves the problem with a long-handled gaff.

Flying gaff with stout safety rope lies ready on the stern of the author's boat while Ray Bizzigotti fights a swordfish. Pillow stuffed into the kidney harness is an emergency solution to the problem of harness straps too long for the tackle combination.

get into the water to take the fish with a shorter gaff.

Flying gaff: The flying gaff is so-named because of its detachable or "flying" head. The entire hook end is arranged to fit into a metal sleeve on the end of the gaff handle. A stout rope or light, flexible wire cable is spliced into an eye welded onto the hook shank. With the gaff fastened to the handle, the angler strikes the gaff point into the fish by lifting and pulling simultaneously on the handle and the rope. The hook is secured to the handle by one turn of light fishing line. After the fish is gaffed, a strong pull on the handle alone breaks the turn of fishing line, and the angler controls the fish by means of the rope attached to the gaff head. For fish like swordfish, giant tuna, or large marlin, the rope is usually 1/2-inch yacht-quality nylon rope. Wire cable is used for sharks. IGFA tackle rules permit a flying-gaff rope of up to 30 feet in length.

Scoop and throw nets: The scoop or dip net is better than a gaff for some species of fish, notably weakfish, small stripers, and any fish the angler may wish to unhook and return to the water. The length of the hardwood or metal handle depends largely on the distance one has to reach down to net a fish from the cockpit of the boat. Short-handled trout nets are better than nothing, but they seldom are useful in any but the smallest boats.

In the Florida Keys and other southern areas, the circular throw net is widely used to gather live mullet and similar fishes for bait. A description of the art of using the throw net is beyond the scope of this book, but adequate instruction usually can be found where such nets are sold.

Cleaning gear: Boat housekeeping equipment can hardly be categorized as fishing tackle, but a clean boat is a happy boat, and all fishing boats get dirty when they fish. Cleaning gear includes scrub brushes, buckets, sponges, and detergent. One very important item is a source of wash water. In the good old days, when a 10-knot boat was a fast one, a bucket on a draw rope was good enough. Smart anglers quickly learned how to snatch up a bucket of seawater without dislocating a shoulder.

Nowadays, many owners install a small electric pump down below with a garden-hose discharge valve on deck. Scales and gook wash away easily if they are attacked while fresh.

Fishing rod storage: Two kinds of rod racks are now quite popular: the

Paul Johnson, chief of tackle research for Berkley & Company, nets a trophy bonefish for the author in the Florida Keys. Their sunglasses have special tan lenses to accentuate the contrast of fish in the clear water.

Throw-net is widely used in many southern areas to collect live mullet and other small fish for bait for larger fish.

Right: *Overhead rod storage rack in an offshore big game cruiser stores unrigged rods not needed for the fishing of the moment.* **Below, right:** *Woman on a California party boat uses a light shoulder harness and gimbal belt to fight a 60-lb. yellowfin tuna standing up with 30-lb. class tackle, 4/0 Penn Senator reel.*

overhead hanging type found in many larger boats' cabins, and the side locker variety built into many smaller, open-console fishing craft. Rod racks are primarily for storing rods that are not rigged for immediate action. Rods needed for spares for the fishing at hand are usually carried fully rigged in spare rod holders in the cockpit.

PERSONAL EQUIPMENT

Harness and rod belt: As was mentioned earlier, a fishing harness is a real necessity for using a fighting chair to full advantage, and a light shoulder harness is an indispensable aid to stand-up fishing for medium-to-large game fish. The three major types of harnesses are worth careful scrutiny.

Oldest in terms of fishing service is probably the shoulder harness. This is a sort of vestlike garment, usually made of leather or leatherlike material, that fits across the angler's shoulders. Strong straps over and under the shoulders terminate in clip hooks that are clipped into the lift rings of the game-fish reel.

The shoulder harness places the major strain of the fish and the tackle fairly high on the angler's body, so it can be tiring to use, especially if it is not fitted perfectly to the angler's frame, the length of the rod butt, the depth of the seat gimbal from the seat surface, and the relative position of the reel and its lift rings with respect to the fisherman's body. All harnesses work by transferring the pull of the fish and the line from the rod to the angler's back and body, leaving both hands free to manipulate the reel and handle the line.

The second variety of big-game harness is the kidney harness. This is a wide, padded corset or a broad strap that fits around the central and lower part of the angler's back, depending on the pull of the harness straps attached to the reel to maintain position. Because the major strain of the pull is placed lower on the angler's back, the kidney harness is less tiring to use.

The third variety is the seat harness, which is nothing more than a low-fitting kidney harness sewed or fastened to a stout canvas seat arrangement in which the angler sits while fighting the hooked fish. The line of direct pull of the seat harness is very low, usually not higher than the angler's belt level. A properly adjusted seat harness is the most powerful and least tiring harness you can use in a prolonged fight with a very powerful fish, if you are using heavy tackle and a fighting chair.

The advent of light-tackle tournament fishing has brought about a renewal of the popularity of the shoulder harness for stand-up or fishing-chair angling. Tackle up to the 50-pound-line class, and sometimes heavier, is often used by anglers fishing from small, open boats to take tuna, marlin, swordfish, and sharks weighing well into the hundreds of pounds.

A fishing belt with a gimbal cup is not needed if there is an adequate fishing or fighting chair handy, but for stand-up fishing afloat or on the beach, a good belt is a real necessity. There are many models available. Some have metal gimbal cups, others have plastic ones. In use, the belt is adjusted for a loose fit, with the gimbal shield covering the angler's pubic region. This is not for modesty, but because it provides the best leverage for handling the rod and reel.

Reels as small as 2½/0 are now available with harness rings. Some anglers adapt spinning tackle to harness use by passing one strap under the rod's reelseat just ahead of the spinning reel foot stem and clipping it into the clip of the other, shortened, strap.

Binoculars: To be useful on the water, where there is always a good deal of boat motion, and especially if one fishes at night, binoculars should have large objective lenses. One popular type is the 6x30 power rating, in which six-power magnification is teamed up with a 30-mm objective lens. The power-to-lens-diameter ratio is the key to night light-gathering ability. Binoculars of 7x50 power rating have a ratio of about 1:7, better than the 1:5 ratio of the 6x30 instrument.

Binoculars of more than seven-power magnification are hard to use from a boat because of the motion. Salt water corrodes the aluminum or magnesium used in most lightweight binocular bodies, so make sure the instrument you buy is designed for use on the ocean.

Sunglasses: Polarizing sunglasses have long been recognized as important for spotting underwater fish. This is especially true in dark water with a high degree of surface glare from summer haze or overcast skies. In the Florida Keys, where bonefish, tarpon, and permit are sought against an almost pure white or light yellow coral sand background in very strong sunlight, fish-sighting has been extremely successful with American Optical Company's Cosmotan sunglasses.

Cosmotan glasses are not polarizing glasses, but they have the ability to increase the visual contrast of anything that has a touch of green. Bonefish, permit, and tarpon appear to be almost colorless, yet their backs and fins have a flush of pigment containing green. Cosmotan lenses have the ability to make this green pigment stand out in contrast to the light sand background, substantially increasing the chances of spotting these elusive fish. Cosmotan glasses are available in plain or prescription form from most optometrists.

First aid: Anglers catch other anglers with hooks. Sunburn irritates tender skin. Seasickness spoils many a happy party, and shoreside maladies sometimes go to sea. So—below are the important ingredients of a first-aid kit.

- Side-cutting pliers for cutting hook shanks
- Band-Aids and light compress bandages
- Surgical tape
- Mercurochrome or other good antiseptic
- Analgesic burn ointment
- Tourniquet to control massive bleeding
- Antiseasick pills or tablets

- Aspirin for relief of minor pain
- Smelling salts for fainting or shock

People who handle fish and bait, especially squid, often develop a septic skin condition loosely called fish poisoning. This can be painful and potentially serious if it is allowed to get out of hand. Below is a proven preventive routine.

(1) Scrub hands and fingers thoroughly with soap, hot water, and a soft-bristle brush.

(2) Next, draw a fresh basin full of water as hot as you can stand. Into this, pour two tablespoons of a standard household disinfectant, like Lysol or CN.

(3) Finally, mix the solution with your hands, soaking them in the hot solution for at least five minutes. Rinse lightly with fresh water and dry.

The hot disinfectant destroys bacteria and counteracts fish and bait slime that has soaked into the outer layers of the skin. It also toughens the skin against cuts from fin spines and rough fish scales.

Clothing: Clothing is largely a personal matter, but a few special items are useful for most anglers. At the top of the list, as well as the body, is a good fishing cap or hat. My own favorite fishing cap has a medium-size peak and a special neck flap that can be turned up when not needed, or turned down to ward off the sun on a very hot day.

Topsider and similar nonskid canvas shoes are great for warm weather. The same nonskid soles are available in knee and hip hoots. A suit of light foul-weather gear is a real necessity when fog or rain threatens.

Fishing from boats is always accompanied by the possibility that someone might fall overboard. The Coast Guard now requires all vessels to have on board one PFD (personal flotation device) for each person. These devices are available as sleeveless vests and as windbreakers that can hardly be distinguished from nonflotation clothing. Where there is a choice, the flotation type of windbreaker makes the most sense.

23   Electronics for Fishing

In a narrow sense, electronic devices are not actually fishing tackle. But in a broader sense, anything that helps a fisherman find and catch fish can be considered as part of his tackle. What is the single most important electronic device a fisherman can put on his boat? Captain Benjamin Franklin Rathbun, skipper of the veteran fishing boat *Anna R* of Noank, Connecticut, answered that question this way:

"If I could afford only one piece of electronic gear, the piece I'd select would be a good combination flasher-recorder sounding machine. My sounder does three things for me. First, it keeps me off the rocks in narrow passages like Wicopesset Passage when the fog is thick. Next, it helps me find good bottom where the fish I'm after congregate. Finally, it spots live fish in places where I'd never stop to fish without a sounder to reveal their presence."

SOUNDERS AND FISH FINDERS

Before looking at specific types of sounders for particular fishing jobs, let us review how sounders work. All electronic sounders work on the so-called sonar principle of projecting a beam or cone of high-frequency sound pulses toward the bottom and then receiving, amplifying, and displaying the returning echoes in terms of feet or fathoms of depth beneath the transducer.

The transducer is a special device that has the ability to convert electrical pulses into mechanical sound waves of the same frequency, and vice versa. It usually is located on the outside of the hull next to the keel and is connected to the control and amplifying electronic box by a coaxial cable passing through a watertight through-hull connection. In operation, the sounder works as follows:

A timing device creates electrical pulses that have a pulse *frequency* between 30 and 90 kHz (kilocycles per second), a pulse *duration* of a tiny fraction of a second, and a pulse *repetition rate* of anywhere from one second to a fractional part of a second. As each pulse is created, it is instantly converted to sound waves that blast downward from the transducer at the speed of 4,900 feet per second, the velocity of sound in water. Because the pulses are quite short and properly separated in time by longer intervals of silence, there is plenty of time for an echo from the bottom to return to the transducer before the next pulse occurs. The returning echoes are detected by the transducer and amplified to a degree of power that enables them to be displayed as an indication of depth.

There are four major display systems. One is the flasher system, in which a neon bulb on a rotating arm flashes at the zero mark of a circular scale and then flashes again at any point along the circular scale that corresponds to the indicated depth.

Bridge of the 63-ft. catamaran sport fisherman "Bo Ann" is a full-fledged communications and navigating center equipped with sounders, radar, RDF, loran, VHF/FM, and SSB.

Electronics for Fishing

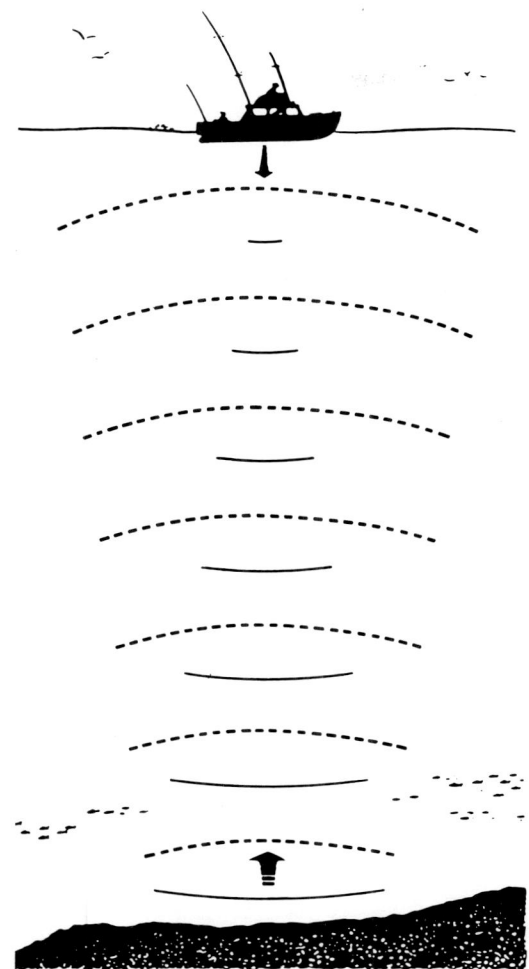

Sounders work by projecting a shaped beam of high-frequency sound pulses toward the bottom, then detecting, amplifying, and displaying the echoes in terms of depth.

A second type is the recorder system, in which a moving stylus marks the surface of a slow-moving paper tape. The marks form a continuous and permanent record of the depth under the boat. The paper is overprinted with special lines that give direct readings of depth plus the relative position of fish under the boat.

A third type is the digital-readout system, in which depth is displayed as numbers formed by LED (light-emitting diode) units. The fourth and last system is the meter system, in which a moving meter hand points to the corresponding depth on a printed scale of feet or fathoms. Some very modern instruments now add a special depth scale expressed in meters, a bow to the impending changeover to the metric system, which can be expected to overtake us in the not-too-distant future.

How do sounders help fishermen find fish? As mentioned in the previous remarks of Captain Rathbun, they help to keep a boat off the rocks, and they are a tremendous help in confirming a navigational fix by supplying a corroborating depth of water. More important, they often give direct evidence of the character of the bottom, in addition to the depth under the boat. In this respect, recorders are probably the best, followed by flashers with adequate power and sensitivity. Digital and meter-readout instruments give few clues as to the character of the bottom.

Finally, both flashers and sounders are quite capable of indicating schools of small fish or individual larger fish between the boat and the bottom. Light-emitting diode and meter-readout instruments are not equipped to display all of the information contained in the returning echoes. Learning to recognize fish marks on a tape or fish flashes on a flasher's dial takes some practice, but skilled observers seldom miss a good sign of fish, and some skippers claim they can determine the species of fish being observed by the size and relative density of the marks on a tape and their distance from the bottom or surface.

What should a sport fisherman look for in a sounder? This depends on how and where he fishes, the fish he is after, the size and type of his boat, and how much money he has to spend. That may not be a very satisfactory answer when one is after specific advice, so let us look at the types of sounders available, with an eye to suggesting which types may be best for specific circumstances. (Costs must be adjusted to compensate for pos-

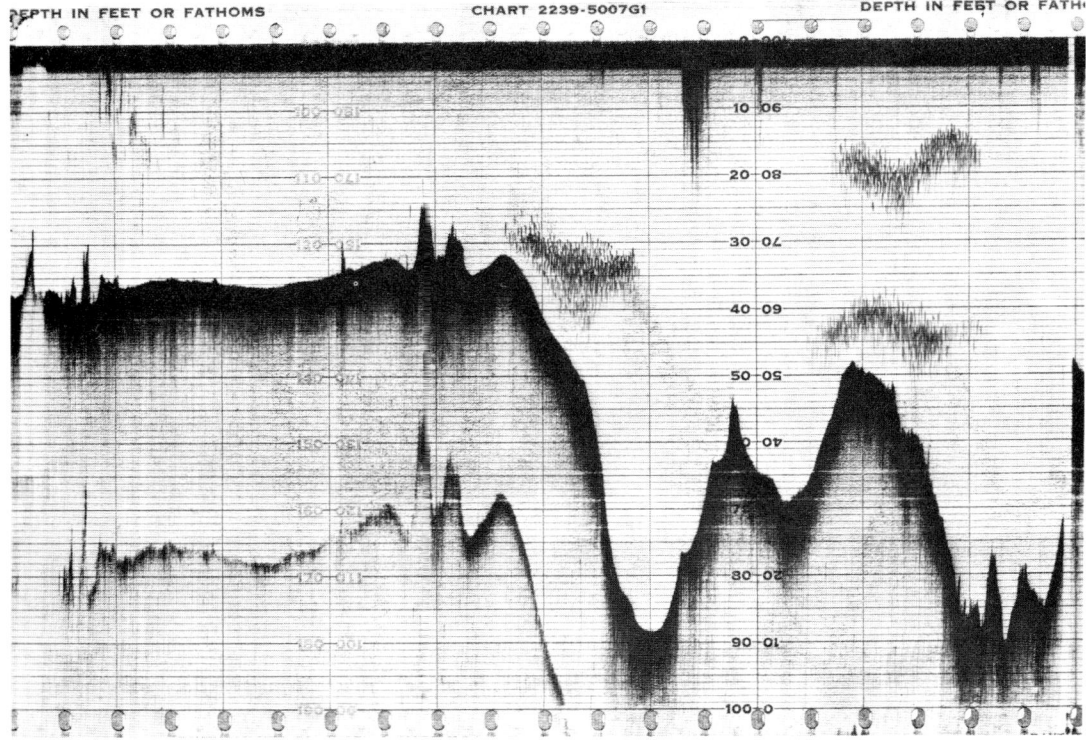

Above: The paper tape of a Raytheon multirange depth recorder displays three schools of fish at various depths, along with their relationship to the bottom. **Below:** Lowrance portable self-contained "lunch-box" sounder can be used from boats as small as this 14-ft. cartopper. It locates both free-swimming fish and productive bottom areas.

sible inflation after the 1975-1976 sample period.)

Portable shallow-water flashers. These so-called "lunch-box" instruments are self-powered by batteries and can be used in boats as small as the eight- to 12-foot cartop class. The depth range usually is at least 100 feet, and fish resolution may vary from poor to excellent. The cost averages from about $100 to nearly $200, depending on size, power, and the quality of engineering and electronic components.

These small, lightweight sounders have proven quite popular among inland bass fishermen and along ocean coasts wherever small fishing boats work. In salt water, they are useful in locating rocky bottom that may harbor blackfish, sea bass, scup, cod, groupers, snappers, and other rock-loving species. They are also capable of indicating sand or soft mud bottom that may harbor flatfish. Some models have proven useful in locating schools of larger fish, like stripers, bluefish, and salmon.

Flashing sounders are particularly useful for small boats at night, for staying on a trolling reef or rip in fog or darkness, and where light weight and low power consumption are important considerations.

Permanently installed flashers. These have many of the characteristics of portable flashers, but they usually feature depth ranges of 300 to 600 feet, more power, and greater sensitivity and selectivity. The transducer is usually hull-mounted beneath the bottom planking. The cost varies from about $150 to a little over $300, and power consumption is usually quite low. Many large fishing boats utilize a separate flasher at the flying bridge or tower-control station as a backup to a permanent recording sounder.

Combination flasher-recorders. These versatile instruments are very popular with owners of boats of the center-console type, up to the vest-pocket offshore class. Depth capability is 600 to 1,200 feet in the better models, usually in two or more depth-range scales. Combination flasher-recorders utilize a single electronic section to obtain both flashing and recording modes of depth indication. The cost varies from about $400 to over $600, depending on model, depth range, and other factors. This type of sounder is particularly well suited to sport-fishing boats in the 25- to 35-foot-length class.

Permanent recorders. Many models of permanently installed recording sounders are available, some expressly designed for fish location. They feature fast and slow pulse rates, fast and slow paper-tape motion, and some are capable of more than one pulse frequency. Depth

Above: *Humminbird Mark IV flasher installed on the console of a modern bass boat. Unit is powered by boat's 12-volt electrical system and can be dismounted for storage.* **Below:** *Ray Jefferson Model 5300 is typical of the new combination flasher-recorders. Unit works on either mode and has three separate depth-recording ranges to 150 ft.*

COMMUNICATIONS

Back in the "bamboo age" of saltwater sport fishing, before and immediately after World War II, it was a rare fishing boat that boasted a radiotelephone. Most interboat communications consisted of loud shouting when boats happened to pass on the water, and long-range spying with binoculars trying to dope out what the other guy was up to.

What became known as The Great Boating Boom of the 1950s also spawned an equally great expansion of the use of marine radio. Within two decades, the airwaves became so crowded with yacht, ship, and fishing-boat traffic that the Federal Communications Commission saw fit to promulgate new regulations, based on an international agreement, that in 1972 provided for the phasing out of the older AM (amplitude modulation) "double-sideband" type of marine radiotelephone communication and the institution of new VHF/FM radio for short-range communications, and SSB (single sideband) emission for long-range telephone work.

All old AM marine sets are prohibited as of January 1, 1977, and new marine mobile stations (meaning boat stations) may be licensed only with VHF/FM and SSB equipment. The law requires that before you can have your boat station licensed for long-range SSB equipment, you must first have it licensed with a type-approved VHF/FM unit.

Oddly enough, nothing in the new regulations prevents a boat owner from having a duly licensed Citizens Band (CB) unit on his boat, even though the CB outfit operates by the old AM mode of transmission. To eliminate possible further confusion, let us look at each of the communications systems mentioned to see how they work and how they fit into the saltwater sport-fishing picture.

Old-fashioned AM (amplitude modulation), the outmoded marine system, is exactly like ordinary commercial broadcast radio in wave-form, but it is limited to a "power input" of 150 watts and operation in the 2 to 3 MHz (megacycle) band.

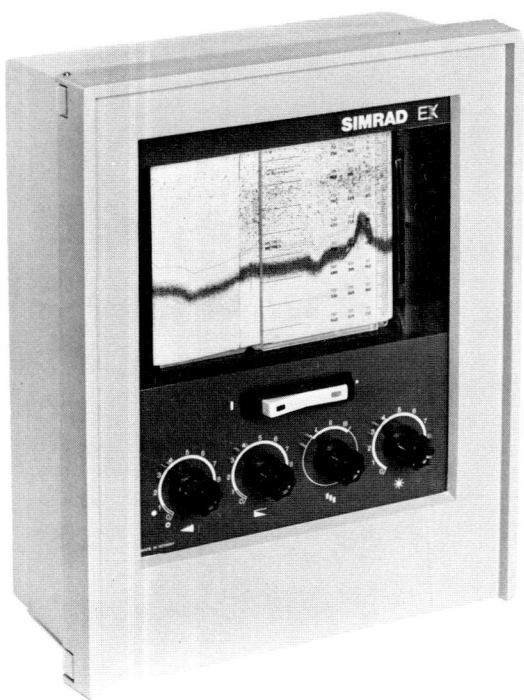

Simrad EX is a permanently installed depth finder with special tuning refinements to detect and display fish either in midwater areas or close to the ocean's bottom.

capability is usually at least 600 to 1,200 feet. Some models are designed to sound to depths three or four times as great. Sensitivity and selectivity are usually excellent, and there usually is an electronic provision to separate bottom-dwelling fish from the actual ocean bottom. The cost ranges from a little under $1,000 to more than $3,000, depending on design, capability, and quality of circuits and components. This type is ideal for larger tournament and long-distance cruising sport-fishing boats.

Digital and meter-readout sounders. The great advantage of these two types is their light weight, low power consumption, and small size. They are popular among sailboat owners, but their inability to define fish or the character of the bottom limits their usefulness to anglers.

VHF/FM is radio shorthand for "very-high-frequency/frequency-modulation." This short-range system is largely line-of-sight in operation, and it is limited to 25 watts output. There are 68 designated ship-to-ship, ship-to-shore, weather, emergency, and special-purpose channels. Older VHF/FM sets were crystal-controlled to stay on transmitting and receiving frequencies. Newer sets make use of "synthesized frequency" circuits, made possible by the development of micro-circuits.

This system is limited to ranges of eight to 30 miles for intership traffic, and two to possibly three times these distances for ship-to-shore work. Units cost from about $250 to over $1,000, depending on power, number of channels, and other factors. Good for small-boat short-range traffic, and required before any marine SSB long-range equipment may be licensed, VHF/FM is winning friends rapidly among fishermen.

SSB is a type of radio propagation in which the original carrier wave has been suppressed and only one of the two original audio sidebands is amplified and transmitted. This effectively cuts the signal band-width in half, to approximately 3 MHz, permitting twice the number of working channels in a given portion of the radio spectrum. It also permits effective amplification of talk power up to about six times that of AM radio, without an increase of the original transmitter's final amplifier power. The resulting signal sounds like Donald Duck on AM receivers, but it comes in loud and clear on receivers designed to handle the SSB signal.

Operating on several bands between 2 and 8 MHz, SSB marine radio can provide transoceanic communications where needed. Power limitations for marine use are 300 watts PEP (peak envelope power) for most applications. Depending on power, number of channels, and other factors, SSB units cost from under $1,000 to over $3,000. Solid-state circuit design has greatly reduced the size, weight, and power requirements of SSB equipment. SSB is now the only radiotelephone system legally available for new marine stations that plan to operate beyond the range of VHF/FM equipment.

Citizens Band radio enjoyed a boom on boats in the early 1970s, when the further installation of AM marine radio sets was outlawed. CB operates in 28 designated channels in the 27 MHz band, with a legal maximum power input of five watts. Both AM and SSB modes are allowed on CB radio, with AM vastly more popular. The maximum range is up to 30 miles between boats over water, although the average working range may be one-third to one-half of the 30-mile value.

The CB frequencies now are terribly overcrowded, and one authority estimates that at least half of all CB units on the air are unlicensed stations. Nevertheless, CB is a valuable, inexpensive communications link for boats in areas where competing traffic is not too heavy. Sets cost from a low of under $150 to a high of

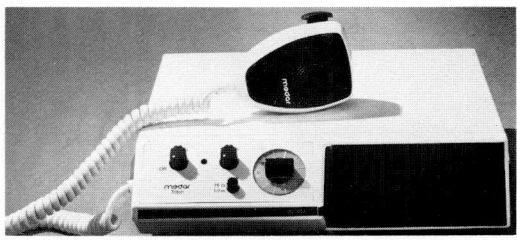

Above: *The Modar Triton is one of a family of VHF/FM marine radiotelephones ranging from 10 to 30 watts output power for ship and coast base station marine communications.* **Below:** *Northern Radio's Model N570 is a modern SSB (single sideband) marine radiotelephone with round-the-world contact capabilities when equipped with the proper frequencies.*

over $500, depending largely on the sophistication of the design. The Coast Guard does not monitor CB, and cannot use CB under present law, but a CB licensee may have units in his boat house, car, and airplane if he wishes, making this a popular interservice communications system.

While every fisherman must catch his own fish, modern fishermen have learned to use communications to good advantage to facilitate fleet search operations for tuna and other widespread species, for safety, and for traffic in important fishing information. Fishermen may talk more now than they ever did, but they probably tell fewer lies.

NAVIGATION

The time probably never will come when sport fishermen will use satellite electronic navigation to find out where they are on the ocean. There are now less expensive and remarkably accurate systems that plot positions instantaneously and constantly as a boat moves through the water.

Three such systems in common use in the United States known as Loran-A, Loran-C, and Omega. All three are signal-matching electronic systems in which a pulsed radio signal is emitted by a master station and is picked up and echoed by one or more slave stations. The receiver, in each case, picks up the incoming pulses, discriminates between master and slave emissions, compares their differences in real time and electrical phase, and produces a digital readout that can be transferred directly to numbered hyperbolic lines on a navigation chart.

Loran-A has been in operation on the East and Gulf Coasts for a number of years, but it is not widely used on the West Coast because of a lack of baseline stations. It operates in the 1800 to 2000 kHz band and has a practical position accuracy of one to two miles, under average ground-wave conditions and within a distance of about 400 miles from the baseline between stations.

Overhead navigation module on K. C. Li's fishing cruiser "Anna Lee" contains twin Loran-A-C units, automatic direction finder tuner and bearing display instruments.

Loran-C is a refinement of the basic loran concept. It has been accepted by the Coast Guard as the official United States coastal confluence radio navigating system. It operates in the low 100 kHz range and is said to have an average accuracy of 1/4 to 1/2 mile within a ground-wave range of up to 600 miles from the station baselines.

Omega is an international electronic navigation system that operates at very low frequencies, so low that the space between the earth and the radio refraction layers of the ionosphere acts as a wave guide, making true ground-wave reception possible at very great distances. Its accuracy is said to be in the nature of two to four miles under open sea conditions, and as fine as 1/2 mile under special coastal signal-interpretation conditions.

As fishermen view dollars, these systems are not cheap. Least expensive is Loran-A, which averages between $900 and $1,800 per solid-state receiver. Next comes the hybrid Loran-A-C combination receiver, with a cost between $1,500 and $2,500. A pure Loran-C receiver costs between $2,000 and $4,000, depending on model, type, and sophistication of circuits. An Omega receiver runs $3,000 to $4,500 per unit.

Much less expensive is the marine radio direction finder (RDF), which comes in a variety of portable, manually controlled, and automatic models. So-called all-band RDF receivers are usually equipped to provide radio bearings on transmitters operating in the low beacon band (275 to 325 kHz), the commercial broadcast band (550 to 1600 kHz), and the 2 to 3 MHz marine band.

Costs range from a low $150 to $200, for a small, portable beacon-band RDF unit, to over $2,000 for a permanently installed high-quality automatic all-band ADF receiver. The accuracy of any direction-finding receiver is a function of the distance from the transmitting station, the sensitivity and selectivity of the receiver, and the skill of the operator. It may vary from two or three degrees of angle in good conditions to as much as ± 10 or 15 degrees under difficult conditions of distance and atmospheric interference.

Present-day RDF units generally are designed to work on the ground-wave portions of AM radio signals. With AM marine radio rapidly becoming a thing of the past, electronic engineers are bending efforts to develop RDF receivers that will be compatible with AM, FM, and SSB signals. At least one VHF/FM direction-finding system is now available.

Boat owners contemplating the purchase of new and possibly costly electronic equipment should bear one cardinal fact in mind: the electronics business is highly competitive, and there are seemingly wide variations in price for apparently similar items. But in electronics, as in other competitive lines, you get what you pay for. Barring accident, the more expensive of two similar models usually delivers better service under marginal conditions, which is when you really need the best possible performance from your equipment.

WATER TEMPERATURE

In recent years, anglers have become increasingly conscious that many fish are highly sensitive to changes in water temperature, preferring to remain in what is called their temperature comfort zone. Surface temperature readings are easy to obtain if one's boat is fitted with a temperature-sensing device, usually placed in the main raw-water engine-cooling intake. A dial or meter at the main control station tells the operator exactly how warm or cold the surface water may be.

In many areas, a thermocline, or temperature-change zone, develops between warm surface water and cold water below. In a thermocline, the temperature change is usually quick and large. A number of combination depth-temperature devices have been invented, most of which incorporate some sort of thermistor or temperature-sensitive unit at the end of an insulated electrical conductor wire. The wire may be color-coded

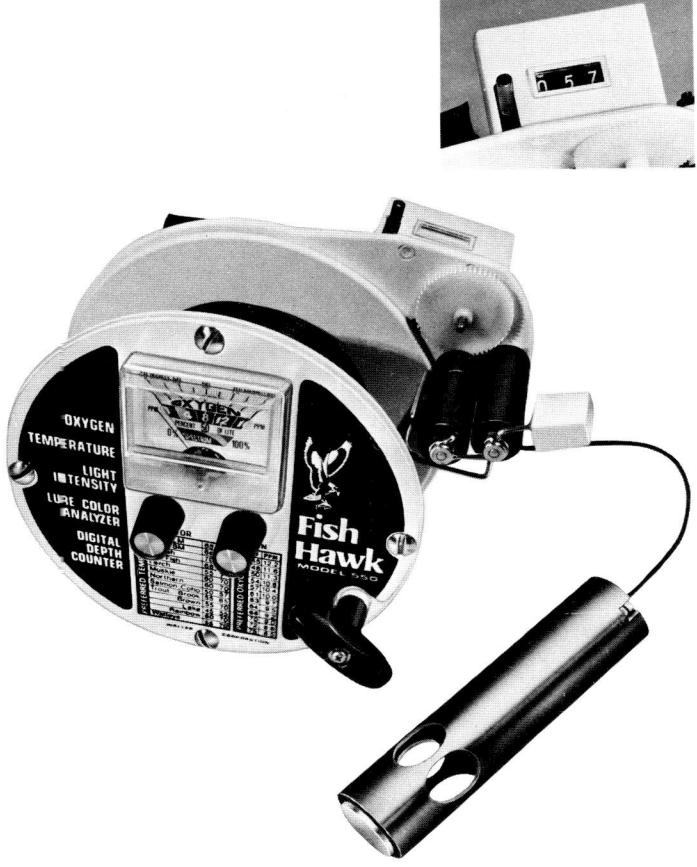

The Fish Hawk Model 550 instrument is a combination depth, temperature, oxygen content, light intensity, and lure color analyzing meter with digital and meter function readouts.

for depth, or it may run from a direct-reading depth-metering spool. A separate temperature meter finds the desired comfort zone or thermocline.

If you lack a fancy electric gadget, it's easy to dip up a bucketful of surface water and take its temperature with a small thermometer. It's also surprisingly easy to find the depth of a thermocline with nothing more elaborate than a small thermometer, a small bottle, and a measured length of heavy fishing line.

Ballast the bottom of the bottle with a few sinkers and some melted paraffin. Fit the bottle with a watertight cork or rubber stopper that can be pulled out with a single, quick tug. Screw a good-size eye screw into the top of the stopper, and tie the stopper loosely to the neck of the bottle with strong fishing line, so that when the stopper is yanked out at the desired depth, the bottle will hang by the line between the stopper eye screw and the neck.

Obtain a small thermometer that will fit into the bottle when the stopper is inserted. Tie a long piece of strong fishing line to the eye screw of the stopper. Measure the line carefully and mark it with india ink or colored nail polish at suitable intervals, about every five feet.

To find the temperature at any depth, cork the bottle with the thermometer inside, lower it to the desired depth, and remove the cork from the bottle with a quick yank on the fishing line. Hold the bottle at that depth for a few seconds, so it will fill with water. Then pull up the bottle and its water sample and read the temperature.

The cork-and-thermometer gambit may not quite fit into the definition of electronics for fishing, but it does show how ingenuity can solve a problem. I first saw it used by marine biologist Jack Casey while shark-tagging off Montauk Point, New York, and I later used the same method to find a thermocline while salmon fishing in Lake Michigan.

Mackerel rigged by a Chilean guide is a prime skipping bait for large billfish such as swordfish or blue marlin. Leader is double #15 stainless wire with 14/0 hooks, to be used with 130-lb.-line class tackle.

24   Natural Baits for Game Fish

Natural baits are divided into three primary groups: dead baits rigged to move naturally through the water for trolling and casting; dead baits prepared for still fishing; and live baits for trolling, drift fishing, and kite fishing. Dead baits for trolling are further subdivided into baits that skip on the surface when trolled and baits that "swim" under the surface in a fairly lifelike manner. A special category includes materials of natural origin, like pork rind, which are prepared to enhance artificial baits and lures.

Surface skipping baits
Balao (ballyhoo)
Bonito
Bonefish
Eel
Mackerel
Mullet
Squid
Strip bait

Swimming baits
Mullet
Squid
Eel

Motionless dead baits
Clam
Squid chunks
Cut bunker
Fish chunks
Whole small fish
Anchovy
Sardine
Crab, shrimp
Ground fish meal

Live baits
Shrimp, crab
Mackerel
Pinfish, grunt
Worms
Runner
Eel
Anchovy
Sardine
Squid

Enhancement bait
Prepared pork rind
Mullet strip
Squid strip

Tools and supplies for rigging trolling baits are relatively simple:
Cutting board (plywood or hardwood)
Filet knife
Deboning tool (for removing backbones)
Bait needles (sail needles will do)
Sewing twine (shoemaker's thread)
Egg and split sinkers
Hooks as required
Leader wire (solid stainless steel)
Leader monofilament
Fishing pliers
Swivels, connectors

Rigging baits with superior fish-catching ability is something of an art. Good bait riggers are painstaking people, selecting only the firmest, least damaged baits, and exercising care through every step of rigging. With very few exceptions,

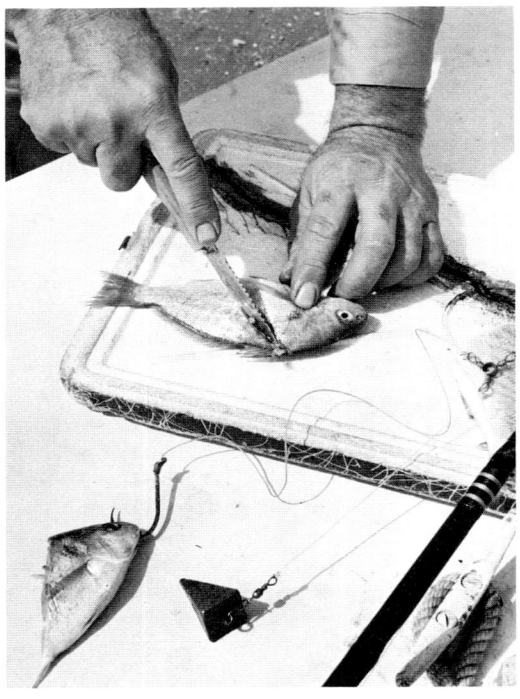

Above: A 10-lb. bonito or skipjack tuna, rigged "Catalina style" with the hook external of the bait's forehead, is another potent big-game trolling bait. It can be used as a skipping or swimming bait, depending on boat speed. Leader is stainless cable. **Below:** Three popular skipping baits are (top to bottom): black eel, whole squid, ballyhoo. These baits are rigged on 100-lb.-test monofilament for sailfish and white marlin.

Above: Dead baits like grunts or porgies, when cut in half, make prime baits for channel bass and black drum. Hooks are Eagle Claw models on heavy monofilament leaders. **Below:** Live crabs are the best bait for permit, some tarpon, and other large inshore species. Eagle Claw or Siwash hook is tied on monofilament.

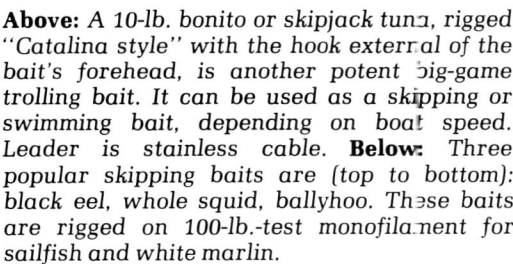

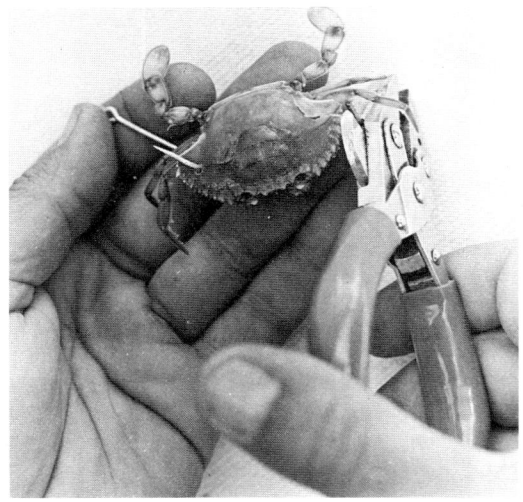

Natural Baits for Game Fish 227

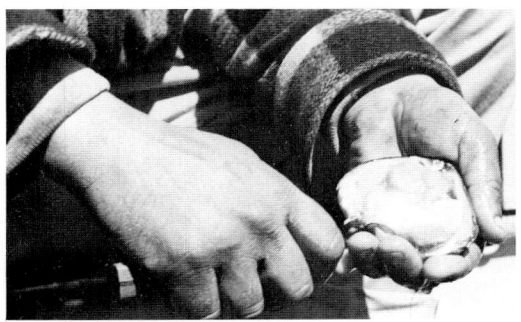

Above: *The ubiquitous skimmer or surf clam is good bait for bottom feeding species like cod, sea bass, and porgies.* **Below:** *A lip-hooked shiner, small shad, or similar live bait is extremely effective on many types of game fish from bluefish, stripers, and salmon to groupers, barracuda, big jacks, and even sailfish or white marlin.*

a properly rigged trolling bait does not spin or turn when trolled. Skipping baits are carefully sewed, so the strain of being towed through the water does not cause the bait to come apart prematurely.

While most bait-rigging tools are standard fishing items, a few are specialized. Deboners and rigging needles, for example, are not available in every tackle shop, and frequently they must be made by the angler himself. Here's how to make these special items.

Bait deboner

The deboner is a tubular tool that is used to core out the backbone of a mullet or similar bait to make the bait more flexible for lifelike action when trolled. A typical deboner can be made from a 12- to 15-inch-long piece of thin-walled hard aluminum, stainless steel, or similar tubing with an inside diameter of 1/2 to 5/8 inch.

With a hacksaw and triangular file, cut a number of saw-teeth into one end of the tube, so it will act as a circular core-cutter when it is twisted down the length of a bait's backbone. The other end should be left hollow. It can be given a handle of rod corks cemented on and shaped, or just a good wrapping of friction tape.

In use, the deboner is thrust in through the fish's open mouth or gill slot, and the backbone is removed by coring it out with the hollow tube. The 1/2- to 5/8-inch tube is large enough for mullet and other small baits. For big bonito and other very large baits intended for large billfish, a deboner of 18 to 24 inches length and 3/4 to one inch tube diameter may be necessary.

Rigging needles

Curved upholsterer's or sailmaker's needles are great for sewing up bait bellies, gills, and hook slits, but longer needles are needed for stringing eels and for passing leaders through very large baits. Extra-long needles can be made in any desired length from brass, bronze, or stainless-steel welding rod of suitable

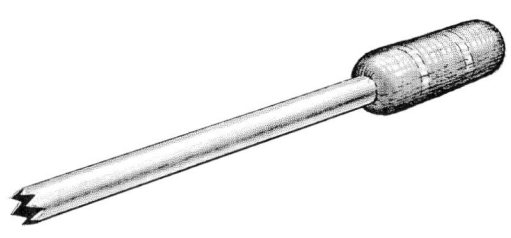

A deboner is an important bait-rigging tool.

Popular West Coast live baits (top to bottom): two large sardines, two anchovies, two squids.

diameter. Sharpen one end by grinding or filing. Strike a flat on the other end with a hammer and anvil. Drill a small hole in the flat to take the end of a leader wire or sewing twine. Typical eel or big bait needles are about 18 inches long.

In a pinch you can make a serviceable eel or big bait needle from a length of stiff leader wire. Make a small eye in one end to hold the wire or twine that must be drawn through the bait. The needle can be pulled through with pliers if you can't get a good grip on it with your fingers.

The Bait-Rigger's Handy Guide

This table gives specific bait, hook, and leader combinations for a great variety of game-fishing situations and all IGFA tackle classes from six- to 130-pound line. If you discover slight differences between the recommendations in this table and those given in Chapters 18 and 19, don't let this worry you. Both sets of recommendations will catch fish. Their differences serve to point up the fact that successful bait riggers follow flexible rather than inflexible rules.

THE BAIT-RIGGER'S HANDY GUIDE

Species	Weight	Bait	Line	Hook	Leader Material	Speed
ATLANTIC AND PACIFIC BLUE OR BLACK MARLIN	100-300 lb.	Strip bait, ballyhoo, or mullet	6 lb.	3/0	15' #3 wire or 30 lb. monofil	3-5 knots
			12 lb.	4/0	15' #4 wire or 40 lb. monofil	
			20 lb.	5/0	15' #6 wire or 50 lb. monofil	
	300-600 lb.	Mullet or mackerel	30 lb.	6/0	15' #8 wire or 80 lb. monofil	3-5 knots
			50 lb.	8/0	15' #10 wire or 120 lb. monofil	
	600-900 lb.	Mackerel or bonito	80 lb.	10/0	30' #12 wire or 200 lb. monofil	3-6 knots
			130 lb.	12/0+	30' #15 wire or 300 lb. monofil	
	500-1500 lb.	Artificial plastic lures	50 lb.	2-12/0	15' #12 wire or 200 lb. monofil	8 knots
			80 lb.	2-14/00	30' #15 wire or 300 lb. monofil	
			130 lb.	2-16/0	30' 2 × #15 wire or 500 lb. mono	
	500-1000 lb.	Live bonito or runner	50 lb.	10/0	15' #10 wire or 120 lb. monofil	3 knots
			80 lb.	12/0	30' #12 wire or 200 lb. monofil	
			130 lb.	14/0	30' #15 wire or 300 lb. monofil	
STRIPED MARLIN	100-300 lb.	Strip bait, ballyhoo, or mullet	6 lb.	3/0	15' #3 wire or 30 lb. monofil	3-5 knots
			12 lb.	4/0	15' #6 wire or 40 lb. monofil	
			20 lb.	5/0	15' #6 wire or 60 lb. monofil	
			30 lb.	6/0	15' #8 wire or 80 lb. monofil	
			50 lb.	8/0	15' #10 wire or 120 lb. monofil	
ATLANTIC SAILFISH	30-140 lb.	Strip bait, ballyhoo, or mullet	6 lb.	3/0	2' #3 wire + 12' 30 lb. monofil	3-5 knots
			12 lb.	4/0	2' #4 wire + 12' 40 lb. monofil	
WHITE MARLIN	40-160 lb.		20 lb.	5/0	2' #6 wire + 12' 60 lb. monofil	
			30 lb.	6/0	2' #8 wire + 12' 80 lb. monofil	
PACIFIC SAILFISH	40-220 lb.		50 lb.	8/0	2' #9 wire + 12' 90 lb. monofil	
BROADBILL SWORDFISH	40-100 lb.	Live bait, squid, or mullet	6 lb.	4/0	15' #3 wire or 30 lb. monofil	Drift or 3-4 knots
			12 lb.	5/0	15' #5 wire or 50 lb. monofil	
			20 lb.	6/0	15' #7 wire or 70 lb. monofil	
	100-300 lb.	Squid or mackerel	30 lb.	6/0	15' #9 wire or 90 lb. monofil	Ditto
			50 lb.	8/0	15' #10 wire or 120 lb. monofil	
	300-1000 lb.	Squid or mackerel	80 lb.	10/0	30' #12 wire or 200 lb. monofil	Ditto
			130 lb.	12/0	30' #15 wire or 300 lb. monofil	
BLUEFIN TUNA	50-175 lb.	Mullet	30 lb.	5/0	15' #9 wire or 90 lb. monofil	Chum or 3-8 knots
	100-400 lb.	Squid	50 lb.	6/0	15' #10 wire or 120 lb. monofil	
	300-700 lb.	Mackerel	80 lb.	8/0	30' #12 wire or 200 lb. monofil	
	500-1000 lb.	Herring	130 lb.	10/0	30' #15 wire or 300 lb. monofil	
GAME SHARKS	50-150 lb.	Squid	30 lb.	5/0	15' #8 wire or 80 lb. monofil	Chum or 3-4 knots
	100-300 lb.	Mackerel	50 lb.	6/0	15' #10 wire or 120 lb. monofil	
	300-500 lb.	Herring	80 lb.	8/0	30' #12 wire or 200 lb. monofil	
	500-1000 lb.	Whiting	130 lb.	10/0	30' #15 wire or 300 lb. monofil	

USING NATURAL TROLLING BAITS

As any live-bait fisherman will tell you, nothing beats a live, natural forage fish when it comes to enticing predatory game fish. But to be perfectly honest, opportunities to use effective natural live baits do not come as often as opportunities to use dead baits that have been rigged to look and act like the live creature. It is this lifelike appearance and action that makes a rigged dead natural bait so effective.

One of the first rules of using natural baits successfully is to select a type of bait that you know will be appealing to the game you are after. Here are a few examples.

Sailfish and white marlin are relatively small, surface-feeding predators that are enticed by small, fast-moving, surface-skipping or surface-running baits. The balao, or ballyhoo, is a prime example. So is the skipping or swimming mullet. Oddly enough, mullet are seldom found in the stomachs of sailfish or white marlin, yet these small billfish take them readily. The inference is that it is the action of the bait that triggers the billfish's feeding rush, rather than recognition that this is a "familiar" forage fish.

Swordfish are bottom feeders throughout most of their vast oceanic ranges. Their huge eyes are specially adapted for feeding in dim light. Yet, in temperate continental-shelf waters, they frequently appear at the surface, "finning out" as they swim along slowly. Stomach contents of swordfish taken by rod and reel and long-lines reveal a good percentage of squid in the diet. Squid are deep-swimming bait. A large squid is an excellent rigged bait for a surfaced swordfish.

But it is dangerous to build generalizations on skimpy evidence. Experienced swordfish anglers know that these unpredictable predators will often ignore a fresh squid to rush a rigged balao, small dolphin, eel, or mackerel in true surface-feeding style.

Big blue and black marlin prefer larger baits, such as cero or Spanish mackerel, bonefish, scaly mackerel, bonito, and the like. While these baits in the wild condition are very different in their appearance and actions from surface-running balao, they are extremely effective when rigged and trolled as skipping baits.

Bluefin, yellowfin, bigeye, and other tunas show what can best be described as an opportunistic attitude toward potential prey. They will take a surface skipping bait, a surface swimming bait, a deep-drifted still bait, or a live bait, depending on the local circumstances. Some tunas, notably albacore, are highly temperature-conscious. Others, like the bluefin, seem to be able to tolerate a wide range of temperature differences. Water temperature is important in all game fishing, and there is a definite comfort zone and optimum temperature, as per the following table.

Species	Range	Optimum Temperature
Albacore	60°-66°	64°
Amberjack	60°-72°	65°
Barracuda	70°-82°	75°
Bluefish	56°-79°	68°
Bonefish	70°-82°	75°
Bonito	60°-80°	64°
Cod	40°-58°	48°
Dolphin	72°-82°	75°
Fluke	56°-70°	66°
Flounder	48°-64°	54°
Kelp bass	60°-70°	65°
Marlin, black	68°-80°	70°
Marlin, blue	70°-82°	75°
Marlin, striped	65°-80°	72°
Marlin, white	65°-80°	70°
Permit	70°-82°	75°
Pollock	40°-60°	50°
Red snapper	50°-62°	57°
Sailfish	70°-82°	79°
Salmon (basic)	48°-60°	52°
Shark (basic)	50°-80°	70°+
Skipjack (aku)	65°-82°	73°
Striped bass	54°-70°	60°+
Swordfish	50°-68°	58°
Tarpon	70°-82°	76°
Tuna, bigeye	62°-68°	64°
Tuna, blackfin	70°-82°	74°
Tuna, bluefin	50°-78°	68°
Tuna, yellowfin	64°-80°	72°
White sea bass	60°-70°	67°
Yellowtail	60°-70°	67°

Every bait, be it balao, bonito, eel, mullet, or mackerel, has a particular boat speed at which it works best. Some, like squid and big eels, work most effectively at relatively slow speeds. Others, like swimming mullet, small black eels, and balao, are often most productive at relatively fast trolling speeds. The speed ranges quoted in The Bait Rigger's Handy Guide reflect the speeds at which various baits produce the most strikes from game fish.

One fact should be quickly apparent. It does not pay to mix trolling baits that work best at radically different trolling speeds. This suggests the first rule of successful bait trolling:

Always choose a mixture of baits that work well at the same trolling speed.

Another fact is not as easily seen. This is the fact that the speed of a fish is relative to its size, not to our terms of measurement in knots or miles per hour. This has been demonstrated by scientific observation of the way fish school together in groups of the same body size.

A baby zero-year-class tuna, for example, may be only a foot long. It can uncork a tremendous burst of speed in an emergency, probably as fast as an adult tuna, but its normal *cruising speed* is a function of its body length, not its top speed potential. Thus, larger tunas in the 100-pound class, for example, swimming at the same speed in proportion to their body length, are actually swimming at several times the speed of the baby tuna in terms of miles per hour.

The small tuna keep to themselves, because their relative speed for food gathering is not competitive with the relative speed of the larger fish. This suggests another rule for trolling baits:

Always relate your trolling speed, and therefore your choice of trolling baits, to the relative size and swimming speed of the fish you are after.

But here again you must guard against sticking blindly to arbitrary rules. When you consider that slow trolling is two or three knots and fast trolling only six to nine knots, you don't have much speed variation to tinker with in terms of your boat's potential top speed, which may be well over 20 knots. But a very small speed variation often produces surprising results.

Furthermore, there is ample evidence that each boat has its own best speed for each particular species of game fish, and this speed may vary rather widely from boat to boat. We cannot explain this phenomenon, except to speculate that the boat's combined sound and pressure-wave field in the water may exercise a stronger reactive force on the fish at some speeds than at others, and that the field of each boat is distinctive and different. This proposes a third rule for success with trolling baits:

Use controlled experiments to try to discover the best speed range of your boat for each species of game fish.

When you know from experience that your boat raises marlin, for example, at a speed rather slower than most of the other boats, you have learned a most valuable bit of information.

Finally, there are two different types of fishing situations that you should be able to recognize. The first is the situation in which you are out with a group of friends to catch whatever may be in the water ready to chase your baits. Here you are wise to put over a pair of large, medium-speed baits on the outriggers for larger game and two or three small, medium-speed baits on flat lines over the stern.

The second situation is the one confronted by the competitive tournament fisherman who is after one prime species or just a few of the many species that may be available in the water. If you put

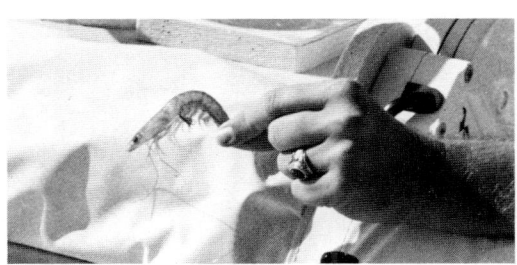

Live shrimp are top baits for bonefish, snook, sea trout (weakfish), redfish (channel bass), and kindred small inshore game fish.

over the mixed array of baits suggested for the first situation, you are like the deer hunter who never bags a deer because he can't resist blazing away at every rabbit that scampers up from underfoot. The fourth rule of successful bait trolling is:

Use only the baits that will attract the special fish you are after when you are fishing competitively.

Why are some boats and crews so much more successful than others? The following suggestions may yield some clues.

- Keep your hooks needle-sharp. You'd yell if the doctor jabbed you with a dull needle. Hone your hooks with a file or whetstone before each use and after each strike.

- Troll only live-looking baits. Change baits before they become washed-out by long towing, or whenever the smallest blemish appears on the bait body.

- Keep your anglers awake. Nothing is as frustrating as to raise a good fish and miss the strike because some deadhead isn't paying attention to what's going on.

- Train your anglers. Tell them ahead of time what to expect and what to do. Encourage them to ask intelligent questions about the fishing. Be patient with them when they miss a strike.

- Don't fish too many lines. You are fishing too many lines and baits if you have a Chinese fire drill every time a fish appears in the wake. Two or three well-fished lines are vastly better than five or six that catch nothing but shouting, confusion, and tangles.

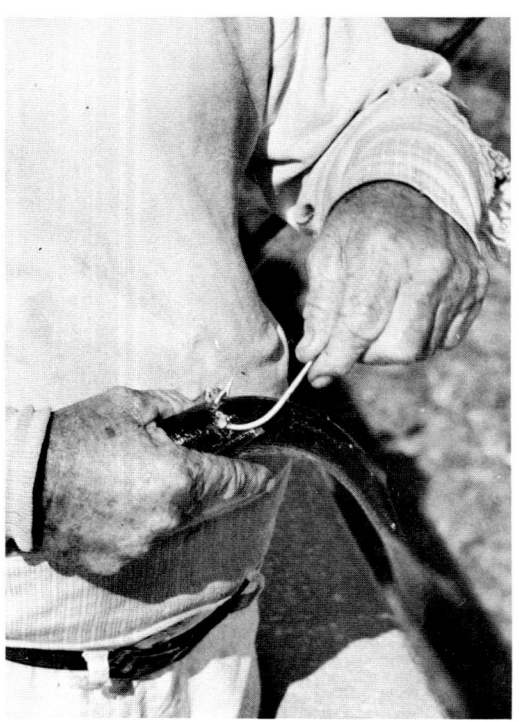

Live mullet hooked through the back attracts a wide variety of game fish, whether fished deep directly from a boat, or on the surface under a fishing kite. Hook is an 8/0 O'Shaughnessy on 60-lb.-test monofilament.

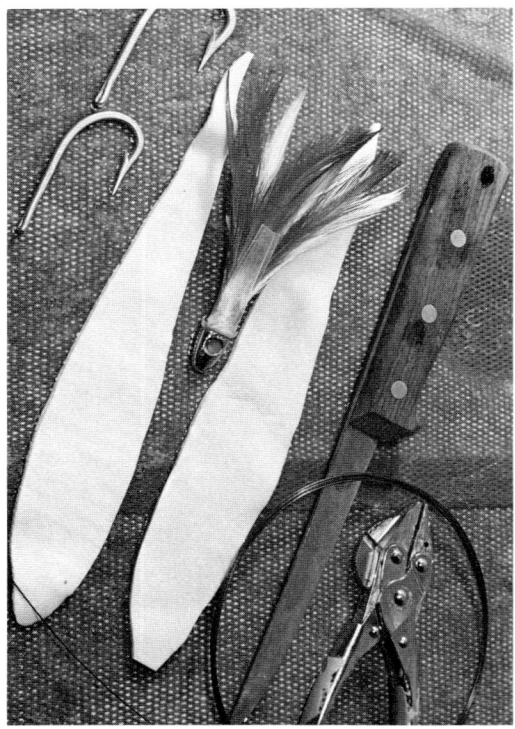

Pork rind strips make good strip baits, or add to the attractiveness of artificial lures.

- Keep your baits and hooks scrupulously clean. Fish refuse to strike at baits with grass or weed on the hooks. Observe the water. If shoestring grass and other weeds are evident, haul in each bait frequently to remove bits of weed and other debris. This may seem like a very minor thing, but strict attention to grass removal very often is the only "secret" that seemingly lucky anglers use to out-fish lazier fishermen.

Check The Bait Rigger's Handy Guide and the chapter on Terminal Tackle for rigs for live and dead natural baits for kite fishing, drifting, and still fishing.

25 Artificial Lures and Baits

It's easy to see that cleverly made plastic artificials may closely imitate natural fish baits in shape, color, flexibility, texture, and sometimes even taste, but this does not account for the fish-catching ability of many types of nonimitative baits and lures. What makes the nonimitators attract and catch fish?

Modern anglers like to have a logical explanation for the mysteries of fish behavior. Some lure manufacturers have gone so far in answering this desire as to describe their products as "sexy." One gets the impression that big bass are supposed to lurk lecherously under lily pads waiting for a hula-skirted lure to go waltzing by so they can mutter, "I love my wife, but oh, you kid!"

Actually, fish have one-track minds and find it difficult to mix food and sex. Sex is something that happens to them only at lengthy intervals, but food, predation, curiosity, and the territorial imperative are everyday facts in their lives. It is a mistake to presume that fish think as we do. They don't have the mental equipment. But nature has compensated for this deficiency by building sensitive reactive processes into their bodies and their genes.

Biologists experimenting with lower animals have discovered that many of these creatures have stereotyped physical reactions built into their nervous systems. A toad, for example, has a special nerve circuit that biologists call its "bug perceiver"—it links the eyes and the brain. Tap this circuit with the input of an oscilloscope, and you observe a voltage peak on the scope whenever a bug is brought within the toad's vision. A certain pattern of such voltage peaks triggers feeding reaction in the toad. Much the same mechanism is presumed to work in fish.

What are the external stimuli that trigger feeding behavior in receptive fish? Four can be named.

Vision: including object shape, color, light pattern, and physical action.

Taste: including what we call smell.

Sound: ranging from ultra-high frequencies through the spectrum available to humans down to very low vibrations.

Electric potential: a little-understood phenomenon that has been observed in electric eels and torpedo rays and may be present in many other species to a lesser and currently unknown degree.

Imitative artificial baits and lures play heavily on "fooling" the fish's vision with an article that closely resembles a live bait fish or other food in appearance, color, action, and texture. When imitative baits and lures fail, it is usually because something about the lure or bait appears "wrong" to one or more of the fish's other senses, triggering inhibition of the feeding response. This negative reaction is present in all fish, and it is a fundamental natural defense mechanism.

Closely resembling bait fish in size, color, and action, this Rapala deep-swimming plug is a deadly artificial lure for fish like striped bass.

Nonimitative lures excite various combinations of the four major senses into triggering a feeding response by stimulating the appropriate perceiver circuits. Fish that live in clear water depend heavily on visual perception to identify food or to warn against dangerous or phony objects. Fish that live or prefer to feed in water of low visibility (striped bass, for instance) depend more heavily on sound, taste, and possibly electrical potential than they do on sight to identify food.

When nonimitative baits and lures fail, it is usually because some small but vital part of the lure's combination of audio-visual-electric attractiveness is missing or has gone haywire. What are the sights, sounds, tastes, and electric potentials that should be built into lures to make them attractive to fish? Let's take a look at representative types of artificials to see what really makes them tick.

PLASTIC IMITATOR BAITS

The development of soft, durable plastics has given us a new family of fishlike and baitlike artificials with amazingly realistic color, flexibility, texture, and action. Included are all sorts of artificial baits, from worms and shrimp up to eels, mullet, herring, balao, and squid. The advantages of these baits are obvious. They don't need refrigeration, they are easily rigged, and they are durable.

There are also disadvantages. Taste and mouth texture are different from the natural bait, and this may be an inhibiting factor after the game fish has

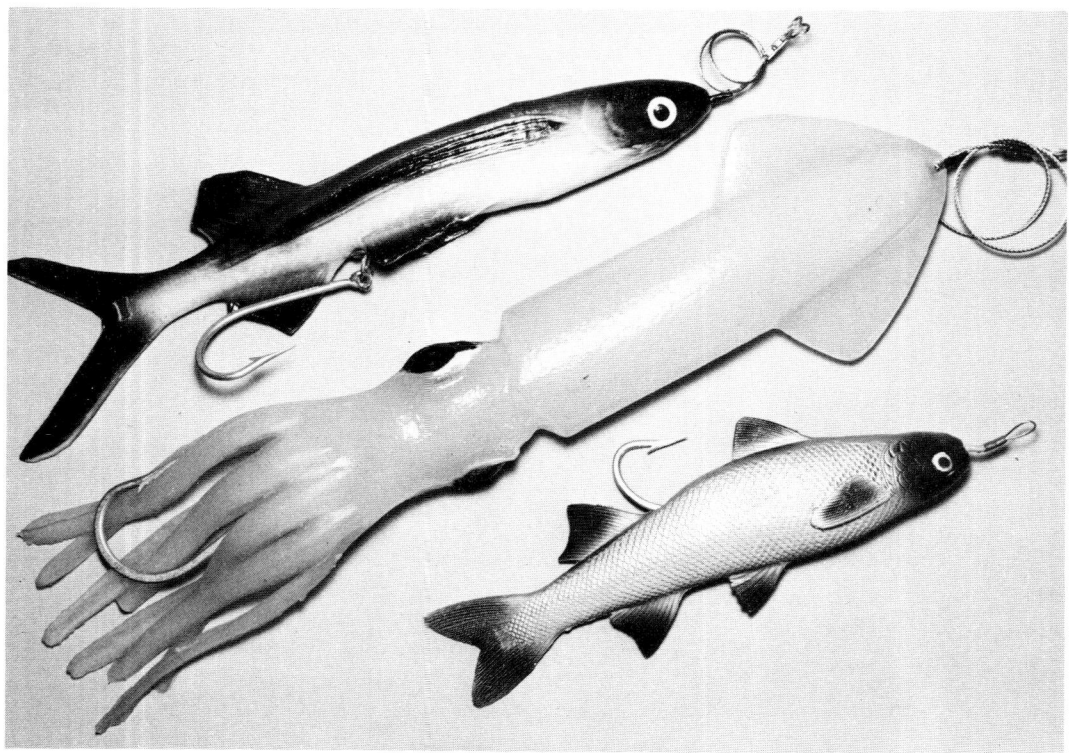

Artificial soft plastic lures for big game are (top to bottom): flying fish, squid, mullet. Soft plastic comes very close to simulating the actual bait in shape, color, texture, and trolling action.

finally picked up the bait in its mouth. This suggests that the angler should strike quickly to set the hook before the fish can drop the bait. One uncertainty is that the sound field created by the trolled bait may not exactly match that of a natural bait. Two disadvantages from the human side are the reluctance of some anglers to try something new, and the relatively higher unit cost of the artificials.

Certain game-fish species show definite partiality to artificial imitator baits.

Artificial mullet or balao (trolling)
sailfish	dolphin
white marlin	amberjack
striped marlin	school tuna
blue marlin	albacore
black marlin	wahoo

Artificial squid (trolling)
sailfish	large tuna
white marlin	striped bass
striped marlin	dolphin
swordfish	game sharks

Artificial eel (trolling, casting)
striped bass	amberjack
bluefish	barracuda
school tuna	dolphin
white marlin	sailfish

Artificial shrimp (casting)
redfish	bonefish
sea trout	weakfish
school tarpon	jacks
striped bass	snook
snappers	bluefish

Tubing eel (trolling, casting)
striped bass	barracuda
bluefish	weakfish
pollock	school tuna

Soft plastic artificial worms have registered great success on freshwater species such as largemouth bass. A few experimenters have used these worms or parts thereof in salt water and have had notable success with bonefish, snappers, small tarpon, snook, school stripers, bluefish, weakfish, and the like. Further experimentation will probably open a whole new field of worm fishing to light-tackle saltwater fishermen.

A semi-imitator artificial casting bait that has proved highly effective on sea trout, weakfish, and similar inshore food-game species is the so-called "wiggle-tail." It resembles a shrimp with a small lead casting head. The 3/0 to 4/0 hook is cast into the head, which is usually painted pink, yellow, white, or pale orange. The soft plastic shrimp body is threaded onto the hook and fastened to the rear end of the head by means of a small internal anchor cast around the hook shank. The body usually has a highly flexible tail, which gives the lure amazingly lifelike action when trolled or retrieved by bumping over the bottom.

These shrimp imitators come in white, yellow, pink, chartreuse, red,

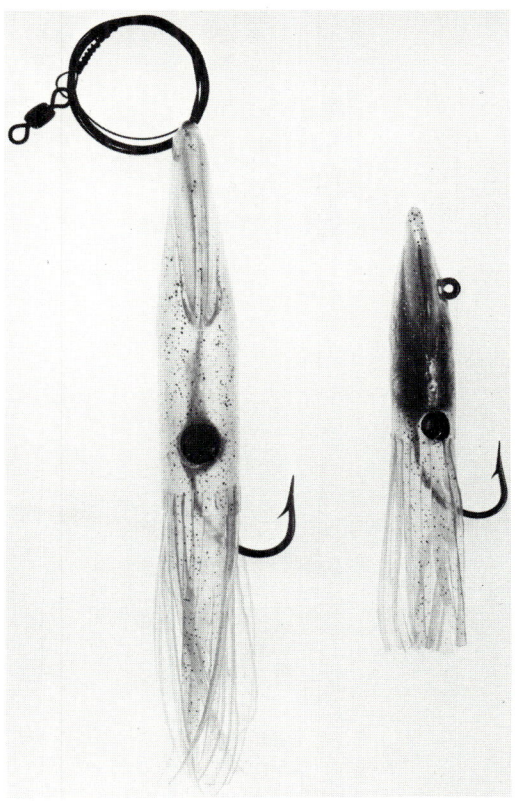

Small plastic squids make natural-looking trolling lures that appeal to many species of game fish.

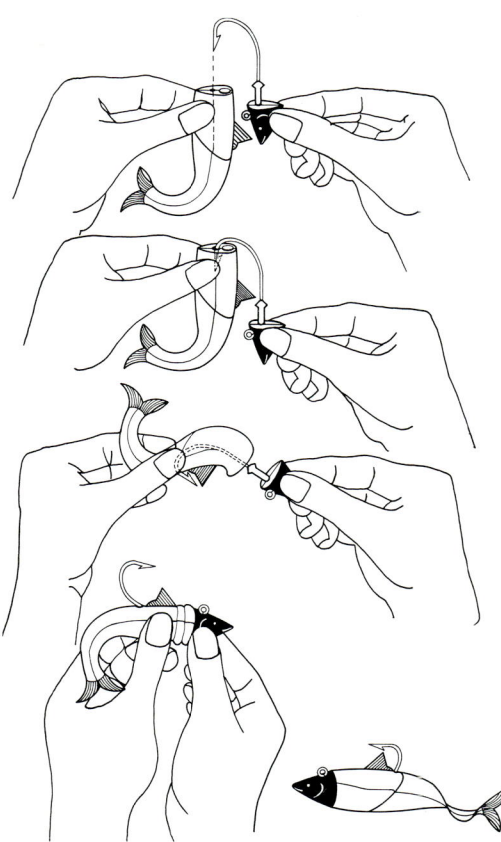

Method of replacing soft plastic "wiggle tail" lure on lead casting-trolling head. Replacement plastic bodies can be bought in bulk, like bait.

visible, with practically identical action to rigged natural baits when trolled or retrieved after casting. Colors do not fade, and plastic does not become stiff, thus changing action, as does the flesh of some natural baits after long towing.

Taste: Results of experiments are inconclusive. The taste and texture of plastic certainly are different from natural baits, but this does not seem to bother many fish, and it may even be a beneficial factor in some cases. Manufacturers could easily add taste factors to the plastic mix when they prove helpful.

Sound: Test results are inconclusive. Certainly, the gross sound of a plastic or a natural mullet skipping or swimming on a line appears to be the same. Whether fish can detect significant differences is a moot question.

Electrical potential: Too little is known about the electrical properties of

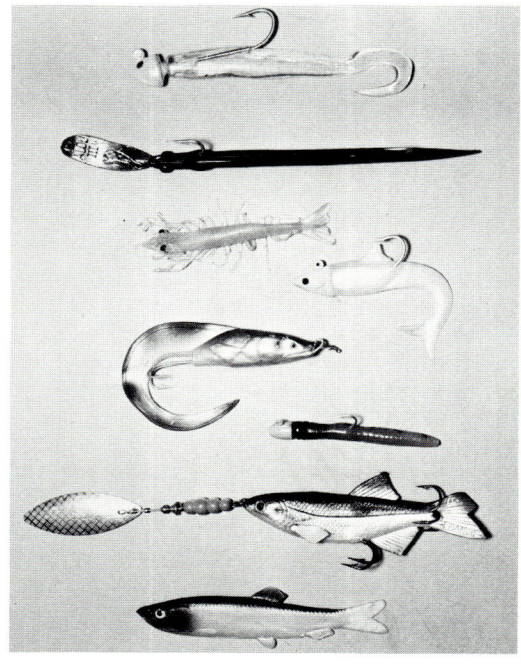

Soft plastic lures for small to medium game include (top to bottom): leadhead plastic tail jig, plastic black eel, artificial shrimp, another leadhead plastic tail jig, plastic worm, artificial minnow on spinner-and-bead combination, soft plastic minnow.

silver, and other colors. The secret of ultimate success appears to be the use of a short, quick type of rod action while trolling or retrieving the lure.

Experimentation with plastic imitator baits is still in its infancy. As use and production increase, unit costs no doubt will go down. This already has proved true with worm and shrimp imitators. The leaders, hooks, and other terminal tackle chosen for plastic lures should follow closely those recommended in Chapter 24 for the corresponding natural baits.

Here is how plastic imitators appear to score against the four major physical senses mentioned earlier.

Vision: Plastic lures are highly

natural or artificial fish bodies in water to venture a guess in this department, but this could be a fruitful area for scientific investigation.

Practical conclusions: Used with imagination, plastic imitator baits could easily be a secret weapon for anglers who master the nuances of their use, and they certainly are a very useful type of bait to have around when natural baits are unavailable.

CASTING AND TROLLING PLUGS

Although some plugs perform excellently as trolling lures, practically all plugs are designed primarily for casting. In the great family of artificial lures, plugs fall about halfway between the imitators and the nonimitators. Most of them imitate (and sometimes exaggerate) the swimming motions and surface action of bait fish. They are painted and colored to simulate fish. But most of them do not duplicate specific fish in their details, and they are made of materials that are not the least bit fishlike.

Five basic types of plugs are universally recognized.

Popper: a tail-heavy floating plug with a dished or concave front end, designed to splash or "pop" when the line is jigged energetically with the rod. It is a surface-action plug that depends on strong audio-visual appeal to attract fish; it is good for rough, dirty water and when large bait is active on the surface.

Darter: a floating plug with a long, sloping surface planed into the top of the front end, making the plug directionally unstable when retrieved at slow-to-moderate speed. Action is erratic, side-to-side darting. Best used in calm water or slight-to-moderate chop. Attraction seems to be mainly visual, and it is most effective in clear water.

Swimmer: a floating or sinking plug with an adjustable front nose plate or lip that causes the plug to undulate or "swim" rapidly from side to side as it is trolled or retrieved at moderate speed. Attraction is both visual and sonic. Rapid changes of course probably set up pulsing rhythms or vibrations in the water that attract predatory fish, bringing them within visual range in dirty or roily water.

Diver: a floating or sinking plug, usually long and slim, with a long nose lip that forces the plug to dive deep when trolled or retrieved at constant speed. Attracts fish by sonic means until they are within visual range.

Countdown plug: this sinking plug has a known rate of sink, making it possible to predetermine its working depth by a mental or stopwatch countdown after casting. Usually rigged to swim at a constant depth when retrieved. Sonic attraction brings fish within visual range.

A sixth type of plug, sometimes known as a "bait carrier," is a plug of any type that has a hollow interior for holding some sort of bait, such as ground-

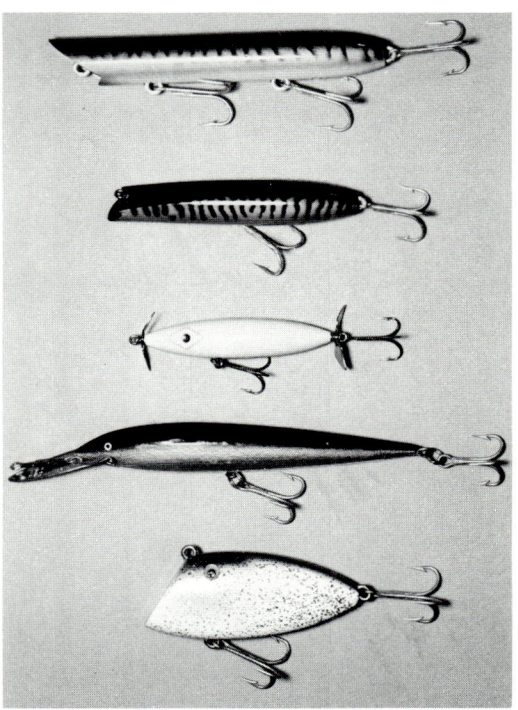

Five standard types of plugs are (top to bottom): Gibbs full-size popper; Gibbs spinning-size darter; propeller-action swimmer; Rapala floating deep diver; Salty Bogie count-down vibrating diver.

fish catfood. While the theory of a tasty plug sounds excellent, not many plugs of this type are found in the plug caddies of fishermen.

How sonic are plugs? Plenty, when you stop to consider those gang hooks gnashing around on their metal eyes, the water gurgling around the diving lip, and the splash and vibrations set up by popping or strong, erratic darting and swimming. Some plugs now are manufactured with a small metal or plastic ball inside a cavity in the body. This clicks around in the plug's body, avowedly making the plug "sonic." Whether the clicking ball catches more fishermen than fish is an unanswered question.

Because the final stimulus of a plug to a fish is visual (after it has been lured within range by the plug's sonic attraction), choice of color and pattern can be critical. Plugs are offered in a great profusion of color combinations, often generating great confusion in the mind of a beginning angler. Fortunately, it's possible to boil down the basic color and pattern requirements to just a few primary combinations, depending on the color and state of the water, the time of day or night, and the quality of light.

For example, on dark days with heavy clouds, a dark, mackerel-finish plug seems to work best. If the water has some color from beach sand and sediment, a good plug is a white one, or a yellow one with touches of red. At night, it's best to use very dark or very light colored plugs. A true secret weapon on a moonless night is a jet-black plug. Sonic? It has to be! Visual? Yes, if there's a trace of phosphorescence in the water.

In bright sunlight with clear water, a medium-dark plug with a few bright spots of contrasting accent color is good. For bottom-grubbing, a diving plug with a dark brown or black back and a yellow or silver-gray belly works well. Silver "glitter" glued to the plug body increases the percentage of strikes, as does a strip or two of the new, self-adhesive, prismatic fish-scale sheet material. Californians recently discovered the effectiveness of luminous plastic strips fastened to plugs for nighttime use.

On the stimulus score sheet, artificial plugs seem to add up this way:

Vision: The plugs are highly visible once the game fish has come within the limit of visibility of the local water. Visual attractiveness includes shape, color, contrast, pattern, and the curiosity value of something out of the ordinary.

Taste: This has negligible value, except for the rare instances in which a plug carries bait or is given a special scent.

Sound: This probably is the most important attraction feature. The fuss and commotion of surface action and the low-frequency vibrations of diving and swimming seem to be particularly attractive to many species of fish.

Electric potential: This has been neglected completely in present plug and fish behavior research. Could a fish find happiness with a plug whose external AC or DC electric field is supplied by an internal battery?

Practical conclusions: While some plugs seem to catch fish almost automatically, plugs in general require considerable personal skill to be used to maximum effect. Skill is evident in the way an angler selects shape and color combinations to match water, weather, and light conditions. It is also evident in the way he modifies plugs to meet special conditions, and how he alters known retrieval rhythms to change the sonic and visual impact on the fish.

It is important to remember to look for the combinations of stimuli that reinforce each other in exciting the predatory fish's interest. Here are some samples couched in words that smack strongly of reading human motives into fish behavior, but ones that explain the situation more clearly than muddy scientific or psychological terms.

"*Looking over the new girl in town*" (satisfying basic curiosity about something strange and novel). Any plug that combines sonic attraction with high color or contrast and seductive surface or swimming action is a curiosity-arouser. Nose and tail propellers, flap-tail plates, flash panels, "glitter," popping or chugging surface action, sudden deep dives followed by surface drifts, built-in sound effects—all these are strong curiosity-provoking stimuli.

"*Exercising territorial imperative*" (chasing the rascals out). Large, noisy plugs that imitate the form and action of fish that resident fish consider "intruders" often excite action in fish with a strong territorial sense. Such plugs require realistic shape and color, slow, deliberate action, and relatively large size.

"*Yielding to hunger competition*" (being stimulated by the feeding action of other fish). A plug chosen to copy the size, color, and action of bait observed in the water is often best during a period of competitive feeding.

"*Browbeating the overdressed dandy*" (yielding to a tendency toward aggression). Some fish exhibit what appears to be direct aggression toward lures that are exaggerated in shape, color, contrast, and action. This probably is an extension of curiosity into a drive toward aggressive action.

"*Catching the sneak thief*" (response to the intrusion of a quiet, low-key lure). A slow-action lure with low visual contrast and little sound sometimes triggers action where noisy, gaudy lures fail. The basic reactions of fish to the artificial plugs described here apply also to trolling and jigging lures, casting lures, and any baits rigged for trolling or casting.

The accompanying tables outline standard plugs, lures, and jigs used in several styles of fishing for a number of popular saltwater species.

THE PLUG RIGGER'S HANDY GUIDE

Species	Plug type	Weight	Hooks	Leader	Best color	Depth	Retrieve action
Barracuda	Diving	1-3 oz. floater	2 3/0 gang	12" #7 wire	White-red or green-yellow	Midwater	Slow, variable reeling action
Bluefish	Popping	2-3 oz. sinker	2 4/0 gang	6" #7 wire	Yellow or mackerel	Surface	Quick, erratic pop-and-reel
Dolphin	Swimming	½-2 oz. floater	2 2/0 gang	20" 40-lb. mono	Yellow, white, blue-yellow	Surface	Quick, steady reeling action
Jack cravelle	Swimming	½-2 oz. sinker	2 2/0 gang	15" 40-lb. mono	Blue, green, or mackerel	2-4 ft.	Moderate, steady reeling action
Pollock	Popping	3-4 oz. floater	5/0 gang	20" 40-lb. mono	Red squid or mackerel	Surface	Slow, variable pop-and-reel
Redfish	Swimming	½-2 oz. sinker	2 2/0 gang	20" 30-lb. mono	Red-yellow, pink	Midwater	Moderate, steady reeling action
Sea trout (weakfish)	Swimming	½-1½ oz. sinker	2 2/0 gang	15" 30-lb. mono	Red squid or mackerel	Midwater	Moderate, variable reeling speed
Snook	Popping	1-2 oz. floater	2 3/0 gang	6" #7 wire	Blue-yellow + glitter	Surface	Slow, erratic pop action and retrieve
Striped bass	Popping	3-4 oz. floater	5/0 gang	50-lb. mono shock	Red squid or mackerel	Surface	Quick, erratic pop-and-reel
Striped bass	Swimming	3-4 oz. floater	2 5/0 gang	50-lb. mono shock	Mackerel or blue-white	1-2 ft.	Very slow, erratic swimming action
Striped bass	Diving	2-3 oz. floater	2 5/0 gang	50-lb. mono shock	Red squid or mackerel	Up-down	Fast-stop-slow for up-down swimming
Yellowtail	Countdown	4-6 oz. sinker	2 5/0 gang	50-lb. mono shock	Green-yellow, blue-white	Variable	Countdown to depth, high-speed retrieve

THE TROLLING RIGGER'S HANDY GUIDE

Species	Lure	Head wt.	Hook	Leader
Albacore	Japanese feather	1-2 oz.	4/0-6/0	60" 60-lb. mono
Amberjack	Japanese feather	2-3 oz.	8/0	60" #8 wire
Barracuda	"Parrot" feather	1 oz.	6/0	6" wire + 60-lb. mono
Bluefish	Nylon eel	1 oz.	6/0	6" wire + 50-lb. mono
Bonito	Japanese feather	½-1 oz.	4/0	36" 50-lb. mono
Dolphin	Leadhead jig	½-1 oz.	4/0-6/0	60" 50-lb. mono
Mackerel, Boston	Mackerel jig	¼-½ oz.	2/0	36" 30-lb. mono
Mackerel, king	Drone spoon	—	8/0	60" #9 wire
Marlin, blue	Konahead lure	½-1 lb.	12/0	30' #15 wire
Marlin, white	Nylon eel	1 oz.	5/0 treble	15' 100-lb. mono
Marlin, striped	Japanese feather	1-2 oz.	7/0	15' 150-lb. mono
Pollock	Japanese feather	1 oz.	7/0	40" 50-lb. mono
Salmon	Spoon or cutplug	—	1/0-3/0	60" 40-lb. mono
Snook	Swimming plug, 4"	—	1/0-2/0	60" 30-lb. mono
Striped bass	Plastic eel	2-3 oz.	4/0-6/0	60" 50-lb. mono
Striped bass	Eelskin	1-2 oz.	5/0-7/0	60" 50-lb. mono
Striped bass	Nylon eel	1 oz.	7/0	60" 60-lb. mono
Striped bass	"Parrot" feather	1 oz.	7/0	60" 50-lb. mono
Striped bass	Bunker spoon	4 oz. keel	10/0	15' 80-lb. mono
Tarpon	Swimming plug, 10"	—	5/0	15' 80-lb. mono
Tuna, blackfin	Japanese feather	½-1 oz.	4/0	36" 50-lb. mono
Tuna, bluefin	Japanese feather	1-3 oz.	5/0-7/0	60" 80-lb. mono
Tuna, yellowfin	Konahead lure	4-8 oz.	6/0-8/0	60" 80-lb. mono
Wahoo	Drone spoon	—	8/0	60" #9 wire
Weakfish	Nylon jig	¼-½ oz.	2/0-4/0	40" 30-lb. mono

Skirt	Best color	Strip	Speed
Nylon or feather	Red-white or yellow	None	7-9 kn.
Feather	White, yellow	Mullet	2-3 kn.
Feather	White or yellow-white	Mullet	2-3 kn.
5" nylon	Blue, white, or yellow	Tailhook pork	3-4 kn.
Nylon or feather	White, yellow, green-yellow	None	5-7 kn.
Nylon or feather	Yellow, white, green-yellow	Squid	4-6 kn.
Nylon or Mylar	White or silver	Mylar	3-4 kn.
None	Silver	None	3-4 kn.
Nylon	Yellow-green or red-white	None	8-9 kn.
12" nylon	Black-white, blue-white	None	4-5 kn.
Nylon or feather	White, yellow, green-yellow	None or squid	5-6 kn.
Nylon or feather	White, yellow, green-yellow	Squid	3-4 kn.
—	Silver or red-yellow	None	2-3 kn.
—	Blue-silver-orange	None	2-3 kn.
—	Black, amber, or clear	None	2-3 kn.
—	Natural	None	2-3 kn.
12" nylon	White or tangerine	Pork or squid	3-4 kn.
Feather	White or yellow	Pork or squid	3-4 kn.
—	Silver	None	3-4 kn.
—	Red head, white body	None	3-4 kn.
Nylon or feather	Yellow, white, red-white	None	5-6 kn.
Nylon or feather	White, yellow, red-white	None	4-6 kn.
Nylon	Yellow or yellow-green	None	5-7 kn.
—	Silver	None	3-4 kn.
Nylon	Silver, pink, white, yellow	Squid	2-3 kn.

LEADHEAD LURES AND CASTING JIGS

Trolling, casting, and jigging lures of the leadhead variety are bait-fish simulators rather than imitators. For the sake of definition, an imitator is a bait or lure that tries to duplicate the exact appearance, texture, and action of a natural bait fish. A simulator, on the other hand, gives the *illusion* of being a bait fish without being an exact copy.

Leadheads perform three functions: (1) They cause a lure to troll beneath the surface. (2) They provide weight for casting and deep jigging. (3) They are a durable front end to which a suitable skirt can be tied. In many instances, a strip of squid, pork rind, or fish flesh hung on the hook adds attractiveness to the lure.

Skirt materials vary from dyed chicken feathers to nylon fibers, plastic strips, and natural bucktail hair. There is little tendency to mix types of materials. Mylar, a thin, silver-finished plastic, is often cut into thin strips. A few such strips added to the skirt material give the lure considerable flash and make it extremely competitive.

Jigs with fixed hooks cast into the head are used for both casting and trolling, and often for deep jigging. Lures with free-swinging hooks are almost invariably used for trolling. All-metal casting jigs usually have free-swinging single or gang hooks, but a few have single or double hooks cast into the lure body.

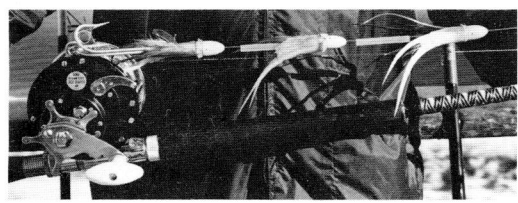

Three Japanese-style feathered jigs are rigged in tandem for tuna trolling. Separators are short pieces of light-colored plastic tubing.

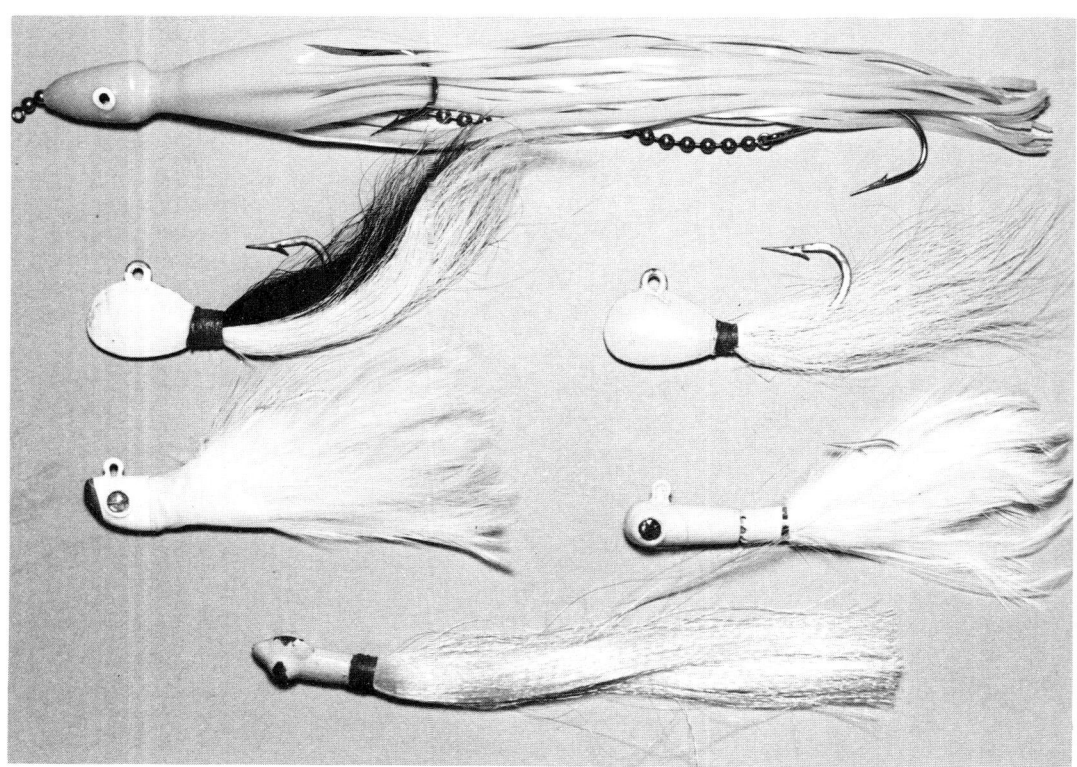

Casting-trolling leadhead lures include (top to bottom): Psychotail artificial eel; two varieties of Upperman bucktail jigs; parrot-head and bullet-head feathered jigs; nylon Jigit eel.

THE JIG CASTER'S HANDY GUIDE

Species	Jig type	Weight	Hook	Leader	Best color	Depth	Retrieve action
Bluefish	Metal squid	1½-3 oz.	4/0-6/0 single	6" #7 wire	Bright tin or chrome	Variable	Fast, erratic rod-pumping action
Bonefish	Leadhead feather	½ oz.	4/0 single	None	White-red or all pink	Bottom	Variable bottom-bumping action
Bonito	Leadhead nylon	1-2 oz.	4/0-6/0 single	50-lb. mono shock	Yellow-white, green, blue	Surface	Fast retrieve, no rod action
Channel bass	Metal Hopkins	1½-3 oz.	6/0-8/0 single	50-lb. mono shock	Hammer-finish stainless	Midwater	Quick countdown, moderate retrieve
Dolphin	Leadhead feather	½-1 oz.	3/0-5/0 single	40-lb. mono shock	Yellow, green, white-red	Surface	Fast retrieve, no rod action
Fluke	Leadhead nylon	¼-½ oz.	2/0-3/0 single	6" #4 wire	Silver-white + Mylar	Bottom	Slow bottom-bumping rod action
Jacks	Leadhead bucktail	¼-½ oz.	2/0-3/0 single	6" #4 wire	White, yellow, or blue-green	Midwater	Fast retrieve, no rod action
Pollock	Metal lead	3-4 oz.	6/0-8/0 single	50-lb. mono shock	Bright metal, chrome	Up from bottom	Drop to bottom, retrieve slowly
Snappers (southern)	Leadhead bucktail	½-1 oz.	3/0-4/0 single	15" 40-lb. mono	White, yellow, or pink	Near bottom	Fast retrieve, easy rod action
Striped bass	Metal squid	2-4 oz.	5/0-7/0 single	50-lb. mono shock	Chrome or bright tin	Midwater	Variable retrieve, easy rod action
Tarpon	Leadhead hackle	1 oz.	5/0-7/0 single	80-lb. mono shock	Red, orange, or pink	Midwater	Moderate retrieve, slight rod action
Weakfish (sea trout)	Leadhead bucktail	¼-½ oz.	2/0-3/0 gang	None	White or pink + Mylar	Midwater	Moderate retrieve, easy rod action

Leadhead trolling and casting jigs and lures with feather, nylon, bucktail, or fiber skirts are pretty much of a class and, within limits, they exhibit much the same attraction values.

Vision: Most leadhead jigs and lures are quite visible, especially when contrasting or complementary colors are used. Yellow is a very successful color, having excellent underwater penetration value. Performance of most leadhead lures is improved when rod-jigging action is applied.

Sound: Any lure passing through water creates sound and low-pressure waves. These waves are accentuated by the skirt fibers and also by the strip of squid, pork rind, or other material that is frequently added to the hook. Sound quality appears to be that of small bait fish.

Taste: This appears to be a relatively negligible factor, especially since little if any genuine testing has been done. Squid does seem to work better than pork rind, however, in a significant number of instances.

Electric potential: Dissimilar metals, such as the lead of the head and the tinned or cadmium-plated metal of the hook, could set up a small electric field, but there is no hard evidence that such a field exists, or if it exists, that predatory fish take advantage of it.

Conclusions: Leadhead lures are best used in a general mass-feeding situation, but some specialized lures have been developed to the point of being true secret weapons.

SPOONS

For several reasons, spoons are extremely useful lures. First, they are attractor-type lures that combine visual flash with considerable noise. Second, there is a possibility that a weak electric field may exist around some spoons, generated by the battery effect of dissimilar metals immersed in an electrolyte, water.

Spinners can be classed with spoons, in that their action and points of attraction are the same, although on a smaller scale. Salmon fishermen of the Pacific Coast and many inland lakes are in the habit of using huge sheet-metal dodgers or attractors a few feet ahead of the spoon or lure that carries the hooks. Saltwater anglers after other species might profitably experiment with multispoon or dodger-and-spoon combinations.

Next, spoons are almost indestructible, and they require no special preservation or refrigeration. When a spoon loses its original finish, it can be restored

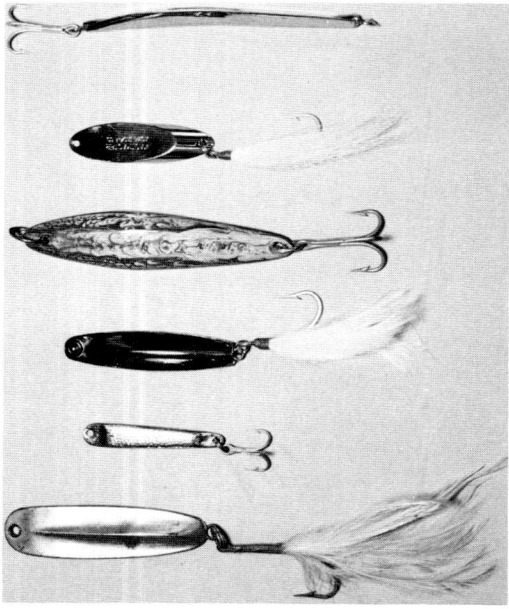

Above: *Six effective casting-jigging metal lures (top to bottom): Vi-Ke eel-type chromed lead lure; Auto-Cast chromed brass casting lure; West Coast style enameled casting and deep-jigging lure; chromed lead keel casting jig; Hopkins hammered-finish jig; block tin satin-finish keel casting jig.* **Below:** *Pressure-sensitive plastic scale-flash material adds flash and glitter to this Tony Accetta Pet spoon.*

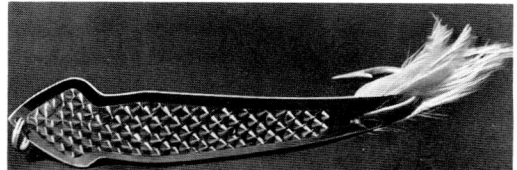

THE DEEP-JIGGER'S HANDY GUIDE

Species	Jig type	Weight	Hook	Leader	Best color	Depth	Action
Bluefish	Diamond	3-5 oz.	4/0 gang	15" #7 wire	Chrome plus pork rind	Near bottom	Countdown, then lift-jigging action
Cod	Diamond	5-8 oz.	6/0 gang	30" 50-lb. mono	Chrome plus squid strip	5' above bottom	Hit bottom, lift 5', lift-jigging action
Grouper	Leadhead feather	1-2 oz.	6/0 single	50-lb. mono shock	Yellow, white, yellow-green	Near bottom	Countdown, intermittent lift-jigging
Kelp bass	Enameled lead	3-4 oz.	4/0 gang	50-lb. mono shock	Green-blue, red squid	Midwater	Countdown, lively lift-jigging
King mackerel	Leadhead feather	2-3 oz.	6/0 gang	50-lb. mono shock	White-red, yellow	Up from bottom	Hit bottom, retrieve with jigging action
Pollock	Diamond	5-8 oz.	6/0 gang	50-lb. mono shock	Chrome plus squid strip	15' above bottom	Hit bottom, lift 15', lift-jigging action
Porgies (scup)	Diamond	2-3 oz.	3/0 gang	20" 30-lb. mono	Chrome plus bucktail	Midwater	Countdown, constant fast lift-jigging
Sea bass	Diamond	3-4 oz.	4/0 gang	20" 30-lb. mono	Chrome plus squid strip	5' above bottom	Hit bottom, lift 5', constant easy jigging
Striped bass (school size)	Diamond	3-4 oz.	5/0 gang	30" 40-lb. mono	Chrome plus hair-Mylar	Midwater	Countdown, lift-jig at various depths
Tautog (blackfish)	Diamond	3-4 oz.	3/0 gang	20" 30-lb. mono	Plain chrome	3' above bottom	Hit bottom, lift 3', slow lift-jigging
Yellowfin tuna	Metal Hopkins	3-4 oz.	6/0 gang	80-lb. mono shock	Hammer-finish stainless	Midwater	Countdown, retrieve with jigging action
Yellowtail	Enameled lead	8-10 oz.	6/0 gang	80-lb. mono shock	Green-blue, red squid	Midwater	Countdown, retrieve with jigging action

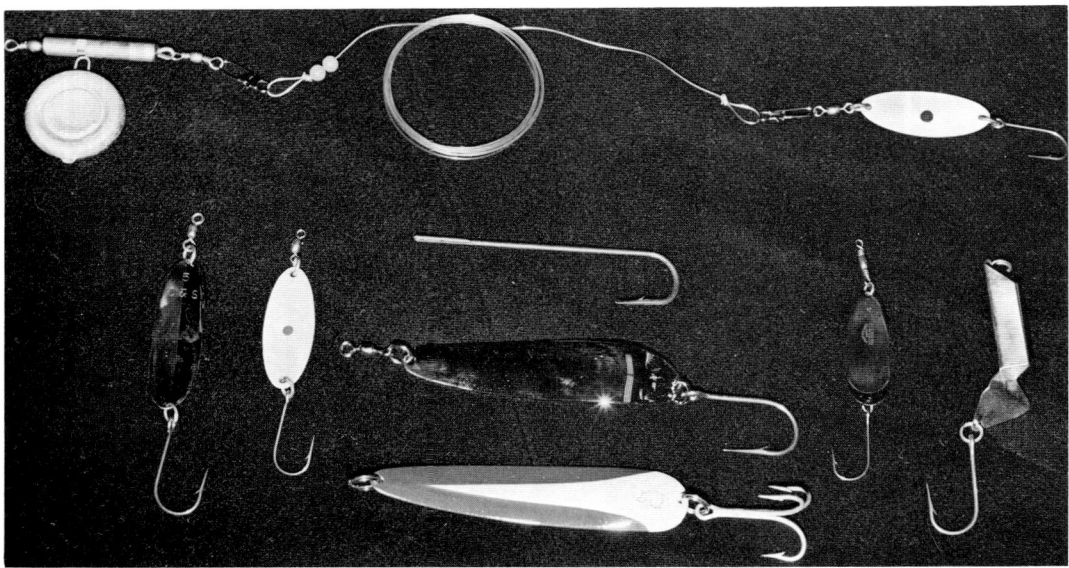

Weight-dropping deep-trolling rig for West Coast salmon features painted and bright metal spoons.

to new life with a few quick sprays of colored enamel. In fact, many now-effective spoon color combinations are the direct result of someone's attempt to get more mileage out of a battered but still useful old spoon.

Finally, spoons cast surprisingly well with light tackle and form more or less of a secret weapon in the tackle boxes of many traveling anglers. As one old-timer put it, "Give me a red-and-white spoon and I'll catch fish anywhere in the world!"

All-metal jigs, casting lures, and spoons are a special class of lures, with the following attraction score:

Vision: The flash of a highly polished metal surface is extremely visible and it works to attract fish from beyond the limits of normal in-water visibility. This flash is often enhanced by a hammer finish simulating scales, or by rubbing a texture pattern onto unchromed metal lures with steel wool.

Taste: This is negligible, except for the possible addition of squid.

Sound: Spoons, especially, are noisy in the water, as skin divers have reported. Heavy metal casting lures also trail air bubbles that help to create noise. Flash and noise combine for maximum attraction effort.

Electric potential: There is a strong possibility of a weak electric field around all-metal spoons and jigs where dissimilar metals are immersed in water, especially salt water. Research is needed to develop this idea.

Conclusions: Practical fishermen recognize the importance of all-metal lures for casting and trolling. The metallic flash principle is very old, and it is used in nonmetallic lures by the addition of flash plates, glitter, shiny plastic coatings, and scale-textured self-adhesive plastic sheeting.

Remember that the combinations of lures, hooks, leaders, and recommended actions in the previous tables are by no means the final word. They are known to be successful, so they are suggested to give anglers starting points for personal experimentation.

THE SPOON RIGGER'S HANDY GUIDE

Species	Type	Size	Hook	Leader	Finish	Technique	Speed
Black drum	Chum or drone	7"	8/0 single	50-lb. mono shock	Bright or blue-white	Deep trolling	2-3 kn.
Bluefish	"Pet"	#13	5/0 single	6" #7 wire 40-lb. mono	Chrome + pork rind	Deep trolling	2-3 kn.
Bonito	Chum or drone	4"-5"	6/0 single	36" 50-lb. mono	Chrome or blue-white	Surface trolling	3-5 kn.
Channel bass (redfish)	Hopkins	Large	7/0 single	60" 60-lb. mono	Hammered stainless	Deep trolling	2-3 kn.
Grouper	Drone	6"	7/0 single	80-lb. mono shock	Bright or yellow-red	Deep trolling	2-3 kn.
Mackerel, king	Chum or drone	7"	8/0 single	60" 80-lb. mono	Bright or blue-white	Deep trolling	2-3 kn.
Pollock	Chum	5"	7/0 single	36" 50-lb. mono	Bright or red squid	Deep trolling	3-4 kn.
Salmon	DarDevle	4"-5"	5/0-6/0 single	36" 40-lb. mono	Yellow or red-white	Deep trolling	2-3 kn.
Spanish mackerel	"Pet" or drone	4"-5"	4/0 gang	36" 40-lb. mono	Chrome or mackerel	Deep trolling	3-4 kn.
Striped bass	Bunker	15" + 4-oz. keel	8/0 gang	15' 80-lb. mono	Bright	Deep trolling	3-4 kn.
Wahoo	Drone	7"	8/0 single	60" #9 wire	Bright or blue-white	Deep trolling	3-4 kn.
Weakfish	Willow leaf	2"-3"	2/0 gang	40" 30-lb. mono	Bright or pink	Deep trolling	2-3 kn.

The powerful 46-ft. Bertram Convertible Sport Fisherman is typical of the fast, long-range fishing boats designed to be floating bases for deep-sea tournament fishing.

26 Boats as Fishing Tools

The idea of considering a boat as a fishing tool may seem ridiculous to nonfishermen, but experienced sport anglers know that the boat a fisherman selects may spell the difference between failure and success. Boats were invented originally as a means of transportation over the water. They carried fishermen to the fishing grounds and then it was up to the fishermen to catch the fish through luck or skill.

Boats designed specifically as fishing tools came into the hands of fishermen only recently, but within two or three decades they have expanded into a number of specialized families. Some are generalized types that perform surprisingly well under a wide variety of fishing situations. Others are quite specialized, the result of experimentation and refinement in particular fisheries. But regardless of how they are described, modern sport-fishing boats, large and small, have certain characteristics in common:

- The capability of handling more than their share of rough water.
- Cockpit or open-hull working spaces specifically laid out with fishing operations in mind.
- A provision for installing and operating such important auxiliary equipment as electronic sounders, radiotelephones, outriggers, downriggers, fishing chairs, fish-hoisting gear, bait and tackle stowage, effective navigating equipment, and a reasonable provision for personal comfort.
- The absence of nonessentials that do not add to fishing efficiency. Perhaps it is in this last characteristic that boats designed for sport fishing differ most noticeably from the general run of pleasure runabouts and family cruisers. Fishing boats are distinctive because they are designed to be functionally efficient, not because they must follow the latest trends in boat fashion. In fact, the functional good looks of certain types of sport-fishing boats now are being copied by builders of nonfishing boats.

What makes modern sport-fishing boats tick? One important characteristic is versatility. Take the very modern open or semiopen center-console boat as a prime example. Its length may vary from 17 feet to nearly 30 feet, but it universally features a very large amount of safe working area for fishing and related activities. Depending on how you rig the boat, you can use it for almost any type of fishing, from drifting the Florida Keys flats for tarpon or bonefish or trolling baits for sailfish, to plug casting for stripers off Montauk, or deep-trolling for salmon on Lake Michigan or in the Pacific Northwest.

Another characteristic is stability and ease of control, whether the boat is running at full speed or slowed to a crawl for trolling. Fishermen are critical users of boats, and they will not long abide a boat that cannot maintain a good turn of speed in rough water, or one that rolls the passengers to the point of seasickness when slowed to trolling speed in a beam or following sea. Nor, in these days, will they abide a boat that does not make efficient use of fuel.

Still another requirement of a sport-fishing boat is the ability to bring together many different pieces of fishing equipment into a smooth-working whole. Outriggers must troll their baits properly at sea, but they must not be in the way when the boat is being brought back into its berth. Rod holders and fishing or fighting chairs must be installed to provide quick access to the working tackle when fish are raised, while the trolling lines are held in a nontangling spread. Electronic equipment must be instantly accessible to the skipper, but protected from spray and rough-water accidents.

Fortunately, most manufacturers of modern sport-fishing boats have listened to the suggestions of expert boat fishermen and usually can offer boat-and-equipment combinations well suited to generalized or specialized fishing Below is a breakdown of the eight major classes of sport-fishing boats now available, in ascending order of size. Prices suggested are averages for 1975-1976, and they should be readjusted for any subsequent inflation.

Cartop portables, eight to 12 feet long. These small one- or two-man open boats can be carried atop a Jeep, ordinary car, recreational vehicle, or light trailer. Several styles of cartop boat-loading devices are available, most of which can be operated by one person.

Power is usually 10 to 20 horsepower outboard. Because of their small size and low fuel capacity, cartoppers are restricted to protected waters or nearby inshore ocean waters not far from suitable launching sites. These boats can and frequently are launched directly from ocean beaches in good weather. Mobility is provided by their land-operating carriers. The cost of the hull and motor combined varies from around $800 to over $1,500, depending on hull size and engine power.

Cartop portables are especially

The lightweight 10-ft. Aluma-Craft skiff is a perfect boat for inshore one-man angling. Requiring only low power, it can be carried atop almost any car or station wagon.

The Avon Inflatable boat, with an outboard motor of modest power, can be transported easily by trailer or cartop to remote inland or shoreside fishing areas.

suited to: live-bait fishing for striped bass, bluefish, and similar species; bottom fishing in protected waters; 'longshore trolling and plug casting in good weather; fishing rivers and small lakes inland. While they are not ideal for Florida Keys flats fishing, they can be used for stalking bonefish, permit, and tarpon where specially designed flats-fishing boats are not available.

Inflatable portables, eight to 14 feet long. Oceanographer Jacques Cousteau has popularized the use of inflatable outboard boats for skin diving and research work from his research vessel, *Calypso*. They are easily adapted to some types of light-tackle sport fishing, and they can be transported on land, either inflated or deflated, by any suitable vehicle.

Power may be any outboard from eight to 20 horsepower that does not overpower the boat in question. They also are carried aboard easily and launched from large sailing or power cruising yachts and big sport-fishing boats. Their range of operations is restricted to approximately that of the eight- to 12-foot cartoppers, although the larger sizes of inflatables have proved capable of operating in open-sea situations, accompanied by a mother vessel.

The cost varies from around $800 for the smallest models with a three-horsepower motor to over $2,500 for larger models with appropriate power. Their extremely shallow draft lets them drift or operate in very shallow water, but they are more vulnerable to damage than boats with metal or fiberglass hulls.

Small, trailable skiffs, 12 to 16 feet long. These are the favorites of ocean surf casters for beach-launching at inaccessible locations. They are ideal for two-man light-tackle operations in protected waters.

Power averages 10 to 25 horsepower. Auxiliary equipment can include a portable "lunch-box" sounding machine, walkie-talkie CB units for boat-to-boat or boat-to-shore communications, one or two light downriggers for deep trolling. Complete units, including motor and light trailer, average from $1,400 to $2,500, depending on hull size, motor power, and trailer capacity.

Outboard skiffs of this class are quite popular for family fishing in sheltered waters, for 'longshore casting and

Chrysler's 15-ft. aluminum outboard skiff can handle two anglers and their gear in smooth water, drives well with 15 hp., and can be launched from its lightweight trailer.

With raised forward-deck and center-console controls, the 17-ft. Mako outboard fiberglass skiff develops speeds over 35 knots, yet it is easily transported by automobile trailer.

surface trolling, for deep trolling in good weather on salt water and on the Great Lakes, and occasionally as tenders to long-range fishing and cruising vessels. Trailer mobility helps to compensate for limited endurance on the water.

Large, trailable skiffs, 16 to 20 feet long. This is one of the most popular sport fishing boat classes, both inland and along our ocean coasts. Depending on size, these larger open skiffs can accommodate two or three anglers in safety and relative comfort.

Power is generally outboard from 30 to 80 horsepower, although there are a few stern-drive inboard (I/O) models offered. A significant outgrowth of this class has been the very popular freshwater bass boats developed for inland conditions. These generally have less beam than saltwater models, but they are suitable for inshore ocean fishing under good weather conditions.

The cost, including power and trailers, ranges from a low of about $2,500 to over $6,000, depending on size, power, and carrying capacity of the components. Added equipment can include:

Boats as Fishing Tools 255

Above: *Aquasport's Model 240 is a 24-ft. outboard fisherman capable of carrying a tower and outriggers for sustained offshore small- and big-game fishing in moderate weather.*
Below: *The Pro-24 by Pro-Line features a walk-through windshield effect forward and stern-drive power. Options include outriggers, Bimini top, rod holders, and even a small tower.*

Power varies from twin outboards, totaling slightly over 200 horsepower, to single or twin stern-drive or straight inboard motors of up to about 400 total horsepower. Fuel tanks are built in, and they provide endurance of over 400 miles in some diesel-powered models.

The cost, not counting a suitable trailer, averages from slightly under $5,000 for smaller, single-outboard models to at least $15,000 for the larger, twin-inboard models. Auxiliary equipment may include outriggers; downriggers; a complete control tower; plastic-enclosed under-tower deck space; fishing or fighting chairs; flashing and/or recording sounders; CB, VHF/FM, and SSB (single sideband) radiotelephones; gin pole for hoisting big fish; built-in tackle, bait, and fish storage; limited cruising and personal comfort accommodations.

The most efficient cruising speeds are often in excess of 30 knots, and the endurance of these highly developed boats is equal to that of the most physically rugged fishermen.

Vest-pocket offshore fishermen, 25 to

portable electronic sounder; portable RDF; CB or VHF/FM radiotelephone; light surface outriggers; at least two downriggers; built-in tackle stowage; permanent fuel tanks; side or center control console; permanent rod holders; extra batteries for night-fishing safety. The endurance of this class of boats is 50 to 90 percent greater than that of the smaller classes.

Big center and side console models, 20 to 28 feet long. These are the largest trailable sport-fishing boats. Some have small cuddy cabins forward, and a few carry low towers that place the operator at a level above the water equal to the height of the flying bridge of a 40-foot tournament-class fishing cruiser.

Twin inboard motors and minimal cruising accommodations distinguish this Bluefin 26-ft. light tournament fisherman, which is designed for competitive fishing.

35 feet long. These condensed versions of the larger offshore fishing cruisers offer both cruising accommodations and complete fishing equipment. They are widely used for family fishing, and they often are employed in tournament competition.

Power is usually straight inboard, although a few stern-drive models exist. Power averages 300 to 450 horsepower in twin-screw models or 150 to 225 horsepower in single-engine boats. Endurance is good: usually at least 300 miles in twin-motor fishermen and sometimes as much as 450 miles in the most efficient single-engine hulls.

The costs vary widely, depending on hull size, type of construction, and choice of power. Smaller, single-motor models can be bought for under $20,000. Larger, twin-screw boats may exceed $50,000, not counting electronic and fishing gear. Top speeds vary from under 20 knots for some single-engine examples to over 40 knots for the fastest twin-engine boats.

Special equipment may include a tower, outriggers, fishing and fighting chairs, and full electronics for communications, navigation, and fish location. Built-in bait and food freezers and air-conditioning are found in larger models.

Tournament fishermen, 35 to 55 feet long. The term *tournament fisherman* is often applied to a variety of sport-fishing cruisers in this size class. Cruising accommodations are more luxurious, although they are seldom designed for more than six or eight persons.

Power is almost universally straight inboard, usually diesel. Endurance averages better than 400 miles, and it may be extended to 600 miles with auxiliary fuel tanks. Top speeds average 22 to 28 knots, and the fishing and electronic equipment is usually quite extensive.

The cost depends on size, power, and construction, and it may vary from around $40,000 for some smaller models to well over $100,000 for larger vessels. Auxiliary equipment may add as much as 50 percent to these amounts. Engine power ranges between 400 and 800 horsepower. Because of their complexity, many boats of this class are designed to be operated by professional crews, for whom separate cabin accommodations are provided.

Super-cruisers, 55 to 80 feet long. These palatial fishing yachts are relatively rare, and they usually are built in the style of fast, long-range power cruisers adapted to fishing rather than as pure fishing machines. Some carry small, open-outboard or stern-drive fishing boats for light-tackle fishing in suitable locations.

Power is universally twin diesel of 800 to 1600 horsepower, providing cruising speeds of 18 to 25 knots and a range of 500 to 800 miles. The cost is high, frequently exceeding $200,000 for a basic vessel without auxiliary fishing and electronic equipment. Boats of this class, however, are capable of cruising to and fishing at all but the most remote game-fishing areas.

Selecting your boat is not difficult if you follow a logical plan of action.

- Define your practical fishing goals.
- Determine how much you can afford to invest in the boat and her equipment, and how much you can spend each year in operating costs, maintenance, and upkeep.
- Reach a reasonable compromise between what you want to do and how much you can afford to spend.
- Visit the big boat shows in your area and find out what other people in your category are using in the way of fishing boats.
- Select a boat type that is compatible with your fishing goals and comes within your price and budget range.
- Within this type, look for the particular model that appears to offer the most in functional design, efficiency, looks, and relatively carefree operation.
- Test each candidate before making your final choice.
- Don't overlook the used-boat market if you can't find a new vessel that meets your requirements. But don't buy a used boat until you've had her inspected by a completely competent and honest surveyor or other qualified person.

Above: *True offshore capability in almost any fishable weather, plus long-range cruising potential, are features of the 34-ft. welded aluminum Striker "Canyon Runner," with twin diesel power.* **Center:** *Cruising range of 2,000 miles at 20 knots is the boast of this 85-ft. Huckins super-fisherman with worldwide cruising and fishing ability on a completely self-contained basis.* **Bottom:** *Ultra-modern in appearance and equipment is Trojan's 44-ft. Tournament sport fisherman, built of fiberglass with diesel power for speed and efficiency far from home.*

Above: A New England specialty is the 32-ft. Wasque fisherman, a fiberglass version of the famous Down East lobster-boat hull. It offers seaworthy efficiency with diesel power. **Below:** The 60-ft. "Pacific Clipper," from the Willard Boat Works of southern California, is an archetype of the large, long-range Pacific live-bait-fishing sport-fishing cruiser.

Above: *The late, great Capt. Tom Gifford designed the layout of this 30-footer with twin stern-drive power, planned for charter fishing in tropical Puerto Rican waters.* **Below:** *The 19-ft. Cape Kawanda dory from Oregon is a type developed for launching from ocean beaches. The outboard motor is housed in an inboard well, aft of the console.*

Making and repairing fishing tackle is an absorbing pastime. This lad is attaching new wings to a saltwater streamer fly, using a fly-tying kit from the Worth Tackle Corp.

27 Repairing Tackle

It would take another book the size of this one to show all the ways in which clever anglers repair and build their own tackle. Lacking the space, I'll do the next best thing and consider those aspects of tackle repair that are important from the viewpoint of the practical fisherman who repairs and maintains tackle in the field and during the season.

Many of the necessary tools have already been mentioned in the list of tackle-box equipment and in other parts of the book, but a few additional items should be listed.

Special tools

- Workbench with all-purpose vise
- Propane torch or small gas stove
- Plumber's lead-melting pot
- Large and small hacksaws
- Vise-grip pliers or small pipe wrench
- Grinding wheel or set of metal files
- Molds for casting sinkers and lure heads
- Hand or electric shop drill

Special supplies

- Rod ferrule heat-setting cement
- Weldwood or similar wood glue
- Assorted colors of rod-winding thread
- Liquid-silk color preserver
- Rod varnish or winding finishing liquid
- Quick-setting epoxy mix
- Cellophane tape
- Scrap lead for sinkers, etc.
- Assorted stainless hose clamps
- Sail needles
- Rubber cement
- Electricians' and friction tape

If you expect to take up rod winding as a hobby or for rejuvenating old but useful rods, you'll need some sort of rod-winding equipment. I adapted the jig pictured on page 262 from a rod-winding kit purchased from the Orvis Company and a variable-speed electric hand drill.

The drill mount was put together from scrap lumber. A remote foot switch enables the operator to control the rotation of the rod with one foot. Thin rod tips are chucked directly into the chuck of the drill. For larger rods, a tapered wooden mandrel in the drill chuck is forced into the hollow large end of the rod shaft. The mandrel was homemade, using the drill as a simple lathe.

EMERGENCY ROD REPAIRS

Even the most rugged fishing rods are vulnerable to accidents. When rods are stored in a hot attic, for example, the wood of rod butts and foregrips becomes dried out and shrinks, with the result that tight-fitting joints or ferrules on the rod shafts or butts tend to become loose. Ferrules usually are cemented to their rod components with heat-setting ferrule cement.

If the loose ferrule cannot be completely separated by hand, heat the metal ferrule over a small gas stove or propane torch flame until the hot ferrule can be pulled easily from the rod tip or butt with a pair of pliers. The wax cement melts at a temperature below that of solder, so you don't have to worry about melting out soldered joints if you keep the flame low. With an old knife blade, scrape away any loose, dry flakes or crusts of old ferrule cement. Clean out the inside of the ferrule with the iron tang of an old file. Try the ferrule on the shaft to see if the fit is slightly loose or very loose. If the fit is only slightly loose, as it should be, then recement with the following procedure:

(1) Pass the end of a stick of ferrule cement through the stove or torch flame to soften the cement. Daub some soft, hot cement onto the part of the rod shaft or butt that will go into the ferrule. Smear it on as evenly as you can.

(2) Holding the metal ferrule with a pair of pliers, heat it carefully in the stove or torch flame. The ferrule is hot enough when it actively melts the cement as the ferrule is pressed on over the end of the rod shaft or butt. You can estimate this by spitting lightly onto the hot ferrule. When the saliva jumps from the hot metal with a small popping sound, the ferrule is hot enough.

(3) Quickly press the rod shaft or butt end fully into the hot ferrule. Excess cement may well up from inside the joint. Leave this on until the joint has cooled.

(4) Cool the joint by plunging it into

Author's rod-winding jig is powered by a reversible, variable speed 3/8"-chuck electric drill. A variable foot switch controls the drill, leaving both hands free for maintaining winding-thread tension and making the finishing tucks of the thread. Center stand of the jig can be reversed and equipped with a removable tail-stock, transforming the winding jig into a small hand wood-turning lathe for making plugs and other small items of fishing tackle.

cold water. Clean away excess cement with a dull knife blade. It will chip away easily.

What about a joint that has an extremely loose, sloppy fit? The extra space between the shaft and the ferrule has to be taken up with some kind of material. A favorite method of rod builders is to cut or tear strips of heavy gauze or light unbleached muslin and drape these over the end of the shaft or butt, spotting them in place with daubs of hot ferrule cement. Then apply enough cement over the strip-covered end to form a good bond when the hot ferrule is forced on, as described above.

Jointed rods should be broken down at the ferrules at regular intervals, so the male and female parts of each pair of ferrules can be cleaned and lubricated. This prevents the joints from freezing tight through salt corrosion. If the male and female ferrule parts do become frozen, the smartest thing to do is to replace them with a new pair.

Frozen ferrule pairs sometimes can be unfrozen by soaking the frozen unit in kerosene or penetrating oil. Then, by applying heat carefully to the outer or female ferrule, and twisting the pair with two pairs of pliers, you may be able to force apart the frozen joint. Dressing the corroded parts with steel wool may bring them back into usable shape, but all too often the corrosion has removed enough of the metal from the male and female units to give them a loose and sloppy fit after they are cleaned. The fit should be snug and tight, but easily broken with hand pressure when the two joined parts are twisted and pulled apart.

The best ferrule lubricant is a light grease that does not oxidize or evaporate in time. Some anglers use wax. Others depend merely on cleaning and drying the ferrule carefully after every use. Only a very thin film of grease is needed. Too much grease may make the tackle sticky and prone to collect dirt.

A broken rod butt sometimes occurs when the rod is forced down beyond the swinging limits of the butt gimbal of a fighting chair. This can put a big-game outfit out of action unless the broken butt can be repaired. Not much can be done if the break is straight across straight-grained wood, but if the wood of the broken butt is not straight grained, and the break is at an angle, giving two sloping broken ends that can be "fished" or spliced, the butt may be salvaged. The procedure is as follows:

(1) Make several thin splints of hardwood, each about 1/2 inch wide, 3/8 inch thick, and five or six inches long.

(2) Scrape away the varnish for several inches from the broken sections of the butt.

(3) Prepare to apply quick-setting epoxy to the broken pieces. Obtain two stainless-steel hose clamps that will fit over the broken butt shaft, and slide one over each part.

(4) Apply quick-setting epoxy to the broken surfaces and mate them together firmly. Tighten the hose clamps around both ends of the break to hold the butt together until the epoxy sets.

(5) When the epoxy has set, remove the hose clamps and scrape or sand away the excess epoxy.

(6) Finally, apply the prepared wooden splints lengthwise to the broken section with epoxy under each splint. Clamp the splints tightly in place with hose clamps until the epoxy is set firmly.

(7) After cleaning, you may wish to wrap the entire splice strongly with heavy fishing line in the manner of a rod wrapping. The resulting splice may not be pretty, but it should be at least as strong as the original butt was before it broke.

Ring or roller tip-tops frequently become grooved or frozen, necessitating replacement. Keep a few tip-tops handy in the tackle box, in sizes that will fit your rods. A tip-top is removed by heating the metal with a flame until the tip-top can be pulled off with pliers. Then a little cement is hot-daubed onto the rod tip, the new tip-top is carefully heated to the spit-popping stage, and the tip-top is twisted

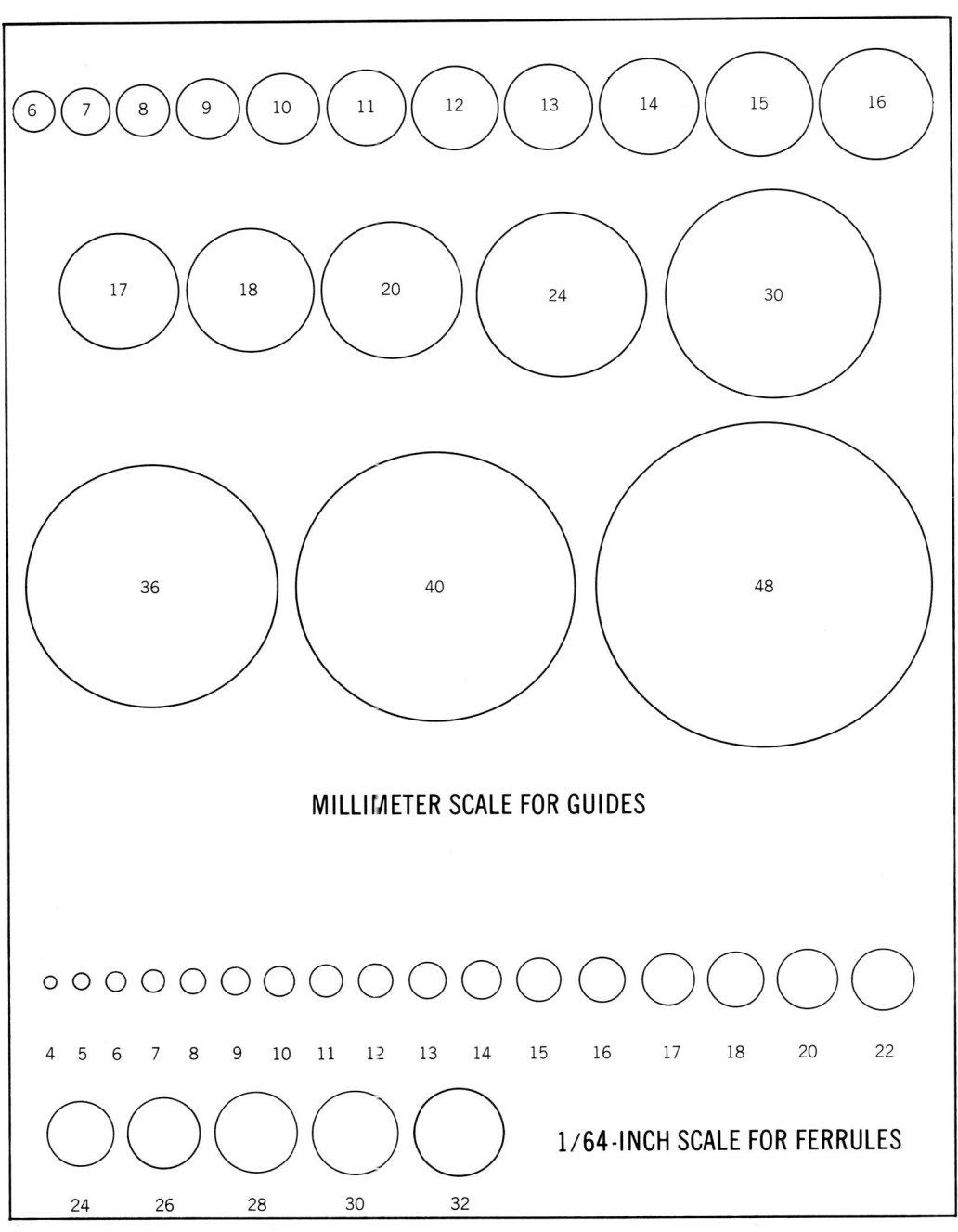

Rod guides are measured in millimeters of inside measure of the ring. Rod ferrules and tip-top ferrules are measured in sixty-fourths of an inch of inside ferrule diameter. Matching rings and ferrules to the figures given will give the correct diameter of unmarked ferrules and rings.

carefully and pressed into place with pliers. Make sure the tip-top is aligned with the rest of the rod guides before you quench it with cold water.

A rod guide that has been crushed or twisted out of shape very often can be bent back into shape with pliers. *Don't use any rod with one guide missing.* This completely upsets the loading of the rod shaft, and it may result in a broken rod. If the guide is damaged beyond repair in the field and you have to use the rod, you can tape into place a similar guide borrowed from another rod, wrapping a temporary winding of light fishing line or monofilament over the tape.

The process of making rod wrappings is described and illustrated in detail later in this chapter.

A broken rod shaft or tip can be mended, but the success of the mended rod will depend largely on where the break is located and how the mending is done. For example, if the tip is broken somewhere between the tip-top and the first or highest rod guide, you may be able to salvage the rod by cutting away and removing the top rod guide, filing down the tip at that point to accept the original ring or roller tip-top, and cementing the tip-top in this new location. The rod will be a few inches shorter and will probably be a little stiffer in apparent action, but it will have no broken portion anywhere on its shaft, and it can be used in a pinch quite satisfactorily.

A break in the middle of a tip, on the other hand, is a different matter. If you are lucky and the rod is worth salvaging, even for less than tournament use, you may be able to obtain a joint ferrule set that can be applied to the shaft at the broken spot, effectively making the one-piece shaft into a two-piece unit.

If you lack a ferrule set, but you have an old rod blank or shaft of suitable diameter, you can repair the break as follows:

• Carefully measure the exact diameter of the broken shaft above and below the break. Trim the broken ends.

• Cut out a section of the sacrificial shaft that has an interior diameter to slip

Well-known fishing writer C. Boyd Pfeiffer put together this well-equipped workshop in the basement of his home. Fly-tying table is at center. Workbench at right is for heavier work.

over the outside of the broken shaft in the manner of a circular splint about four inches long.

- Cut a portion of sacrificial rod shaft that is thin enough to be forced into the inside of the broken shaft for a few inches at the broken spot, forming an interior splint.
- Assemble the two broken halves, using the interior and exterior circular splints, cementing them in place with quick-setting epoxy.
- Apply a tight wrapping of heavy winding silk or light monofilament for two or three inches above and below the patch to strengthen the shaft. Finish with rod varnish or epoxy-type finishing liquid.

A rod repaired this way will be almost as strong as the original. There will be a small lump of resistance to bending at the point of the patch, but with normal care, the rod should stand up to almost any fishing situation. The important thing to remember is to achieve a snug, tight fit of the inner and outer splints, and to make sure the epoxy cement coats all the meeting surfaces thoroughly.

REPAIRING PLUGS AND LURES

It's amazing how fish will respond to some beat-up, tooth-scarred plugs and lures. Smart anglers recognize this situation when it happens and, not wishing to spoil a good thing, make no repairs to such a lure except to renew the hooks when necessary. But by and large, battered plugs and lures catch no more fish than new or freshly overhauled ones, and there is a good deal of satisfaction in knowing how to repair and refinish old, reliable lures, making them as good as new.

Hooks are usually the first parts of a plug or lure to wear with use, especially in salt water. Stainless-steel hooks definitely help to lick the rust and corrosion problem, but relatively few lures come from the store with stainless-steel hooks. It is definitely a mistake to replace a plug's or lure's original hooks with new hooks that are larger or heavier, except in a few specific instances. Manufacturers usually do a pretty good job of achieving good balance between hook size and lure size and weight.

Old hooks with solid eyes should be cut away by cutting the hook eyes with a pair of sharp side-cutters, or with a pair of parallel-jaw fishermen's pliers. Replacements usually have an open eye that can be pinched shut with the pliers. Very seldom will a fish exert enough strain to open a replacement hook eye. Dress the points of your hooks with a fine file or hook-stone before use. Sharp hooks catch more fish.

Small aerosol cans of lacquer or quick-drying enamel are ideal for applying fresh body coats to old plugs. Mackerel finish is applied by wrapping the plug body with a single layer of hex-weave fine screening and spraying the desired portion of the plug body with a contrasting color. "Glitter" can be sprinkled onto the fresh paint before it dries. If you have never refinished plugs before, experiment with a few old ones before trying your hand at the best models in your plug caddy.

Some plastic lures are made with color mixed into the body material. The shine or luster of old plastic plugs can be restored by washing and drying them, then spraying on a coat of clear, colorless lacquer. A secret weapon that is hardly secret anymore is the self-adhesive scale-finish reflective sheet material that some lure makers apply directly to the surfaces of their lures. You can buy this reflective material in most tackle stores and then use scissors to cut strips or blocks of it to the shape desired. The protective backing is peeled off before the material is applied.

Lead and block tin casting jigs rapidly become corroded and dark, but they can be restored to pristine quality by rubbing with a bit of double-O or triple-O steel wool. One real secret of using steel wool on metal lures is to rub the length of the body to give the lure a luster finish. Then accent bands are rubbed across the body of the lure with a tiny wad of steel wool. This produces a sort of band-effect that many predatory fish seem to like tremendously.

The action of plugs and lures can be modified by adding or cutting away weight, rebending a nose lip, changing the location of the hooks, and changing the location of the eye to which the leader is fastened. The best anglers are constantly fiddling with the adjustment of their best lures, seeking combinations of color and action that will increase the average of successful strikes.

The cost of leadhead casting and trolling lures has increased along with everything else, and refurbishing lures of this kind is one way the clever angler can really save money. Instead of throwing away old lure heads, put them aside until you have a fair supply, then remove the old paint from the heads with paint remover and a final rinse in turpentine.

Bucktail, feathers, plastic skirting material, and a great variety of other lure embellishments are available in many tackle stores. It's smart to retie lures in standard patterns that are known to produce fish, although experimentation may yield surprising results. One real secret of making successful casting and trolling lures is to include a few strands of Mylar tinsel in the skirt mix. The flash produced by the shiny Mylar is irresistible to many fish.

Standard colors for dipping the lure heads are white, chrome yellow, orange, pink, red, blue, and green—about in that order. Some experimenters swear by Day-Glo enamel. Others are successful at night when their lures have heads dipped in luminous paint.

The next step is to cast your own lure heads; for this, you will need a lead-melting outfit consisting of a melting pot, a good burner or a plumber's melting torch, a supply of scrap lead, and molds for casting the lure heads or sinkers. Block-tin casting jigs have gone out of style, except among a few surf-fishing specialists, probably because of the soaring price and scarcity of scrap tin. Tin is lighter than lead, and it has a higher melting point when it is pure, but when cast into jigs, it will bend into a new shape where a lead jig will usually break. A block-tin casting squid with the steel wool banded luster previously described will outfish almost any other lure or plug when bluefish and school stripers are feeding on fast surface bait.

Fly-fishing enthusiasts will want to add a tying vise and allied fly-tying tools to the list of tackle-building equipment. There are a number of excellent models offered by leading tackle stores and supply houses. Particularly helpful is one of those many-compartmented, plastic, small-parts boxes or chests for storing hooks, fly-tying materials, and all the other small stuff of tackle repairing.

REPAIRING REELS

A good bit already has been said in this book about maintaining reels, but a recap of essentials would not be amiss here. Reel repairs are best done in a workshop, but sometimes they must be accomplished in the field. The most frequent accidents with reels are these:

- Binding of the spool caused by spreading of the ends until they come in contact with the side plates. Carry a couple of extra spools for reel models that have this fault.
- Cracking or breaking of a plastic side plate when reel is dropped. Carry spare right and left side plates for impor-

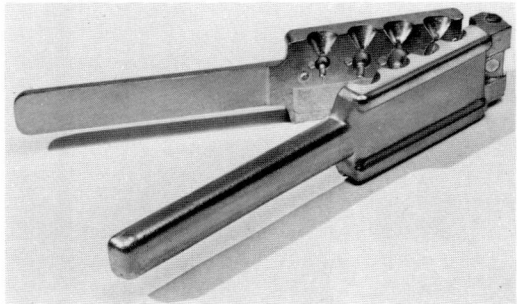

Sinker mold from Cordell Tackle Co. is one of many types of lead and plastic molding devices available for home manufacture of sinkers and lures.

tant models, or salvage some from old but undamaged reels.

- Excessive wearing of internal gears. This happens on many inexpensive models in which the gears are overloaded with line of too-heavy breaking strain. Obtain new gears and install them when the drive train gets "grindy."
- Grabbiness of drag washers, usually caused by overheating or prolonged dry storage with drag screwed down tight. Install proper new washers.
- Bending of the reelseat foot and frame. Usually caused by using a harness, too-heavy line, and lack of tension yoke under the forward section of the rod shaft. Obtain new reelseat foot from builder, preferably a foot made of stainless steel rather than soft brass.
- Corrosion of chromed parts. Mainly the result of not washing and cleaning the reel after use in salt water.
- Breaking or bending of reel handle. Improper winding technique.
- Clogging of lubrication holes. Oxidation of the lubricant and mixture with water clogs holes. Clean reel more often.

While most reel maintenance and repairs can be done by the owner, some manufacturers claim that it is much better to send complicated or expensive reels back to the factory for periodic overhaul. This is especially true with some lever-drag models in which the tolerances are fairly fine, and successful adjustment may depend on the knowledge of an expert. Tackle shops that advertise overhauls of specific makes and models of reels are usually good at this work.

The degree to which any individual undertakes tackle repairs and rebuilding depends largely on personal choice, enjoyment of the work, and space available to set up a small but efficient workshop. As in any other activity involving the use of tools, you learn by taking things apart and putting them back together again. There is special satisfaction in using good equipment that one has adapted and modified and found to be superior to the original product.

Likewise, there is great satisfaction in being recognized as an angler who takes pride in catching fish with his own tackle that he, himself, keeps in top shape.

WINDING ROD GUIDES

One facet of fishing rod construction that remains in the realm of hand work is the winding of thread to hold the line guides to the rod shaft. This also adds decorative appeal to the finished rod. Until recently, pure silk thread in appropriate colors was used universally, but nylon thread is now standard.

Rod winding can be very enjoyable, once the fairly simple procedures have been mastered. Many anglers design and assemble their own rods from kits purchased from rod manufacturers. A few have become so proficient that they wind rods professionally for tackle shops that specialize in custom-made tackle.

The accompanying step-by-step winding photos are taken from a special booklet on rod winding prepared by the Gudebrod Line and Silk Company, manufacturers of fishing lines, tackle-winding threads, and a good selection of other tackle components.

The first step in preparing a rod to receive windings and guides is to locate the spots on the shaft where the guides should go. In the spinning rod illustrated, the lower guide usually is placed about one-third of the way from the reel to the tip-top, in a position that brings the line, when stretched from reel to tip, just tangent with the outer portion of the inside of the guide ring.

The remaining guides, in sequence of reducing size, are placed along the shaft at slightly reduced intervals. This takes a little moving and adjusting to achieve a smooth, good-looking distribution of guides down the tip. The extremities of the winding spaces are then marked on the rod shaft with ink or grease pencil. The length of the windings should be proportioned to the size of the guides, and the size should diminish slightly, going from the lower to the upper end of the shaft. The final, finished rod should have a smooth, progressive bend when the line is reeved through the guides and tension is put on the line.

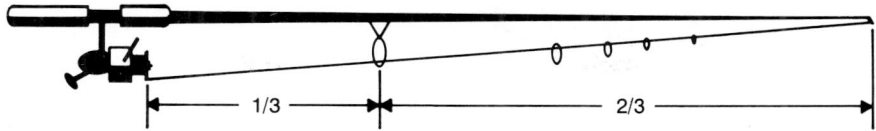

Lowest rod guide is located about one-third of the way from the reel to the tip. Space remaining guides evenly along the tip in descending order of size, and with reduced distances between guides. Experiment to achieve a smooth, well-spaced sequence of locations.

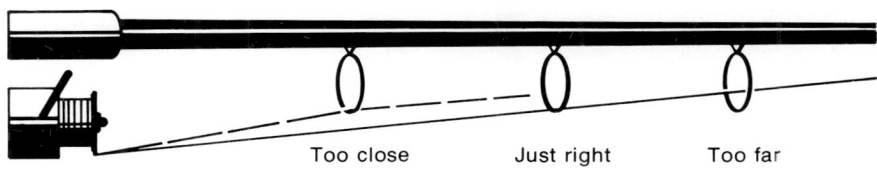

Correct location of the lowest guide is as shown when the line is stretched tight between the reel and the tip of the rod. Line coming from outside edge of reel spool should just touch outside edge of the guide ring. Fasten guides temporarily with masking tape.

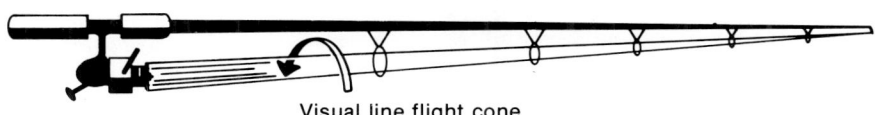

With the guides fastened temporarily in place with tape strips, about as shown, turning the reel handle should form a line flight cone within the various rings as indicated in the sketch. Very slight variations from an exact line flight cone are acceptable.

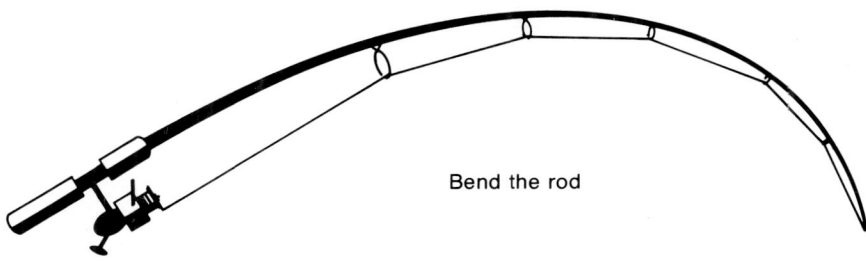

Before winding the guides in place, check the bend of the rod by reeving the line through the guides and tip-top and applying moderate tension to the line. The arc of the rod should be smoothly progressive with no significant humps or hollows in the stretched line.

Bottom and ends of the guide feet must be filed smooth so thread will wind smoothly and evenly up over feet. Feet should be bent gently into shape to fit parallel onto the rod shaft when taped in place before winding.

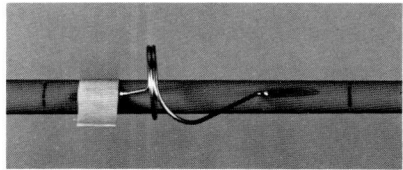

When exact guide locations have been found, mark the extremities of the windings with ink or grease pencil, allowing the winding to extend at least ¼″ beyond the end of the respective guide feet.

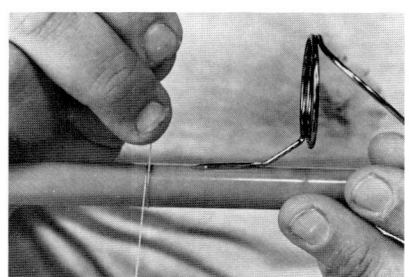

With guide held firmly in place by a wrapping of tape around shaft and one foot, start the first wrapping of winding line exactly on the mark on the shaft, taking a full turn of the thread around the shaft as shown.

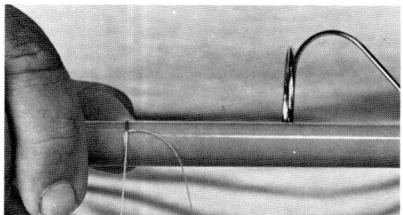

Clinch the end of the winding thread under the first and second turns of the thread, letting the end pay off toward the guide at right angles to the winding. Keep winding tension even and turns closely spaced.

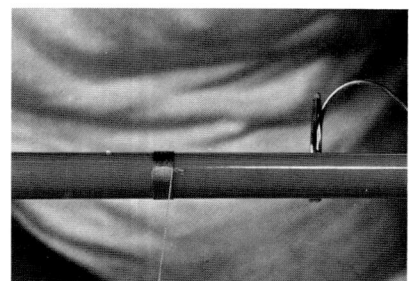

Take at least 10 or 12 turns of winding on top of the end of the winding thread before clipping off the extra thread. Bury the end under the winding by continuing to wind thread smoothly and evenly toward the guide.

Winding should move smoothly up over the filed end of the guide foot. Continue winding until you judge there is space to wind on 10 or 12 more turns. At this spot, start wrapping in a pull-through loop of thread.

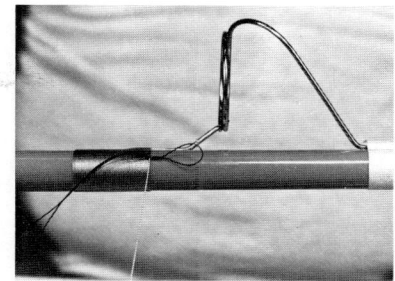

Continue wrapping the winding thread over the loop of pull-through thread until 10 or 12 wraps are taken, or winding reaches the expected terminal spot. Then clip the winding thread and thrust the end through the loop.

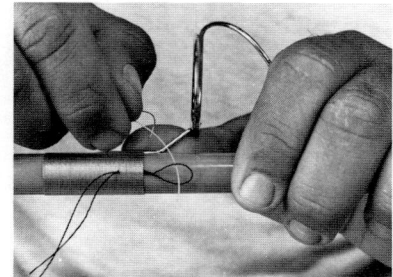

Keeping light tension on the clipped end of the winding thread, start pulling on the pull-through loop. This will pull the end of the winding thread under the winding, locking the clipped end in permanent position.

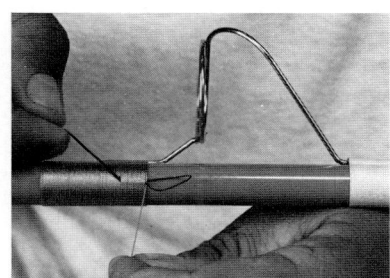

Pulled partway through, the pull-through loop is pulling the clipped thread end under the end of the winding. Pull evenly on both parts of the pull-through thread so the clipped end will come completely through.

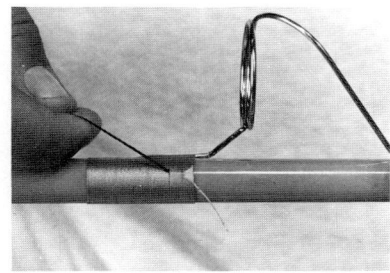

The locked-in end of the winding thread should look like this when pulled completely through. Do not worry about uneven spacing of winding turns at this point. You'll have an opportunity to smooth them out later on.

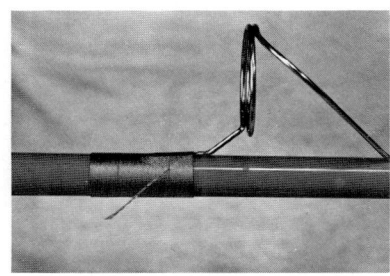

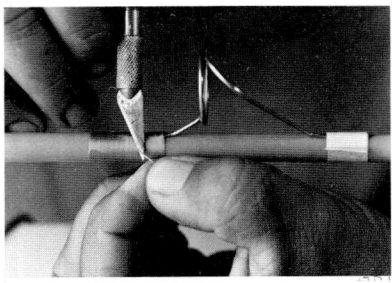

Using a sharp X-acto knife or razor blade, carefully cut off the excess of the end of the winding thread where it emerges from the winding. Be extra careful not to nick any of the winding turns with the blade.

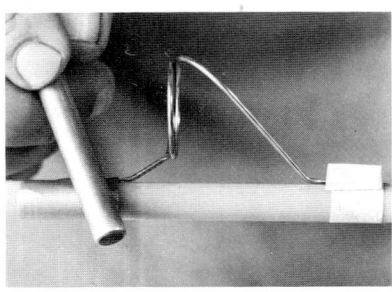

Now you can smooth out any tiny gaps in the wrapping by running it back and forth gently with any smooth, round implement like a used joint ferrule. Finished winding should have evenly spaced turns with no gaps.

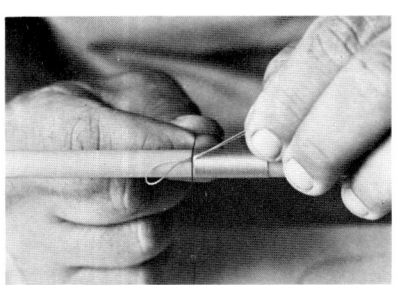

If you want to add a small ring of contrasting color to the end of the winding, start the first turn of the color winding directly over a pull-through loop of thread with loop pointing away from guide, as shown.

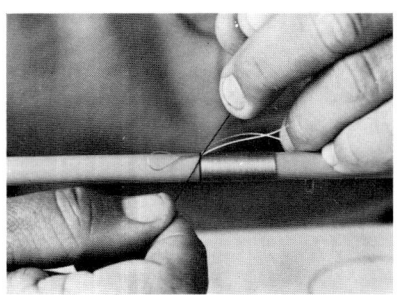

After securing the pull-through loop under the first full turn, cross the winding side of the thread over the tag end to bind the tag end under the turns as you did in starting the original winding.

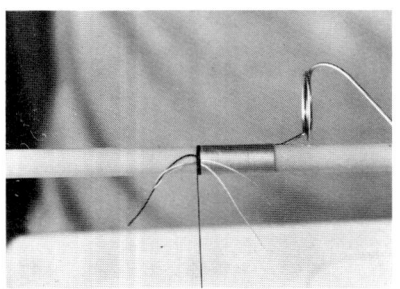

Continue winding the color contrast thread, moving outward over the color thread's tag end and the pull-through loop. A narrow band of contrasting color is more effective and classier than too wide a band of color.

A typical color band may be six to eight turns wide. When you still have two turns to go, clip off the end of the color thread that lies under the windings, using a sharp blade. Bury the end by taking the two turns.

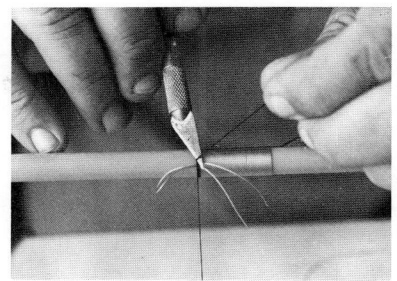

Pass the working end of the winding thread through the loop of the pull-through loop. When winding end color bands, take pains to keep the buried ends of the color thread from being too close together in the winding area.

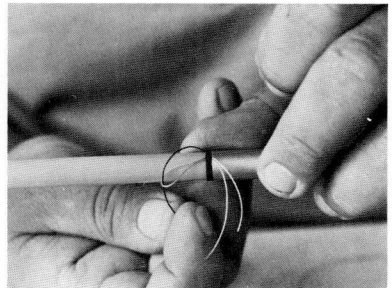

Carefully pull the end of the color winding thread through with the pull-through loop. Because the color band has only a very few turns, these turns should be wound on somewhat tighter than the turns of the main winding.

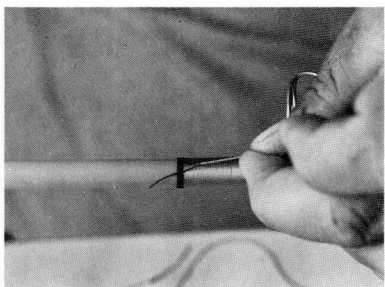

Carefully slice away the pulled-through end of the color-band thread with a sharp blade. Then smooth out the turns, removing any tiny gaps by rubbing a smooth ferrule over the turns, rubbing toward the foot of the guide.

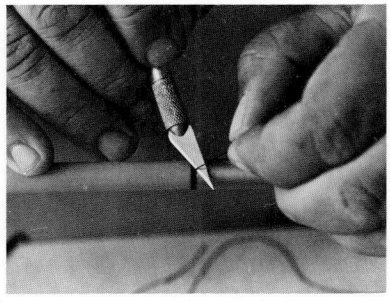

The completed winding, with its contrasting ring of color, is smooth, with evenly spaced turns and no riding turns. It now should receive at least four coats of color-preserving lacquer before the final coat of rod varnish.

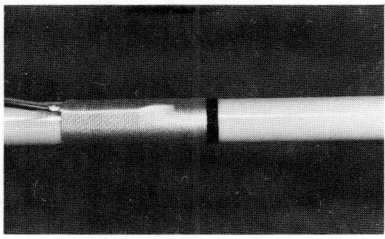

Tackle development engineer Paul Johnson (right) and Capt. Bob Marvin display a small blacktip shark caught by Johnson on an experimental graphite-fiber spinning rod during tackle tests off Key West, Fla.

28 Dynamics of Modern Tackle

A few people may feel that applying science to fishing takes all the delight and mystery out of the sport. This may be true for those who still consider success at fishing to be nothing more than a happy combination of hopefulness and luck. The person who seeks true understanding of the behavior of fishes, and how tackle works, finds that this knowledge does not make fruitful days less enjoyable, and it certainly makes the barren days easier to endure.

Modern fishing tackle is the result of considerable engineering research. Engineers devote many hours to the drawing board and the calculator before they finally come up with a rod designed to fulfill certain casting or fish-fighting functions. Then, before production can be started, the new equipment must be field-tested and compared with existing equipment of known quality.

Recently I was fortunate enough to take part in a tackle-testing session of Berkley and Company, under the direction of the chief development engineer, Paul Johnson. Johnson is a quiet, scholarly man whose specialty has been the study of polymers, the synthetic resins and plastics that are used to bind fiberglass and, in a different form, are extruded into nylon and other synthetic fibers.

We met at Key West and spent five days trying to break rods, line, and reels on the bonefish, tarpon, permit, snappers, and other game fish of the lower Keys. Our guide was Captain Bob Marvin, an independent charter skipper who also acts as one of Berkley's numerous field-testing agents.

The result of the session was that certain rod models were earmarked to go back to the development department for further refinement. They measured and tested well by static test standards, but the consensus of those who handled them was that they just didn't have the casting feel that equally good older models had. A rod may be technically perfect, but if it doesn't feel right to an experienced angler's hand, it won't sell well enough to justify tooling up for a big production run. This, as Johnson explained, is where "human engineering" comes in.

One rod that had wonderful feel snapped just above the reelseat the first time it was overloaded with a lure of twice the rod's rated casting capacity. Something was wrong with the combination of resin and graphite fibers in the new model, so back it went to the development shop.

THE ROD AS A PROJECTILE LAUNCHER

Any casting rod is essentially a projectile launcher. It works by absorbing muscle power from the angler, storing this power momentarily in the flexed rod shaft, then releasing the stored power by imparting kinetic energy (the energy of motion) to the lure.

How fast do casting lures move when they are released by the cast? Four forces, three of them variable, act upon a lure when it is cast by the rod. These are: the initial kinetic energy transferred to the lure by the rod, the force of gravity, air resistance acting on the lure, and drag resistance of the line attached to the lure. Of these, only gravity is a mathematical constant, so it is extremely difficult to predict how fast or how far a given lure will move when cast. But if air resistance and line drag were to be discounted, and only the force of gravity were considered to be working on a cast lure, arithmetic indicates that a standard lure cast to a distance of 200 feet, with a maximum flight-path altitude of 50 feet above the earth's surface, would have to have an average speed of about 40 miles an hour.

The same lure cast to a distance of 400 feet and a maximum flight-path height of 50 feet would have to have an average speed of about 80 miles an hour. If a tournament caster were to uncork a cast of 600 feet and stay within the 50-foot flight-path height, his lure would have to travel at an average speed of 120 miles an hour.

Now, if allowances were injected into the casting for air resistance and line pull, the average projectile speed in each case would remain the same, while the initial speed would be much faster and the terminal speed considerably slower. And because air resistance and line pull increase as the square of velocity, the initial speed would have to be even faster.

It seems reasonably safe to estimate that the initial speed in each case would be at least twice the average speed. This suggests the following initial speeds for the three casting distances just mentioned:

 200 feet = 80 mph
 400 feet = 160 mph
 600 feet = 240 mph

A casting rod is a mechanical transformer for converting slow, powerful muscle energy into the swift motion of a cast lure, as demonstrated by lure manufacturer Bob Pond on an Atlantic beach.

What is the rate of acceleration of the lure when cast to an initial speed of 240 miles an hour? The lure starts with an initial velocity of zero miles an hour, and it is released at 240 miles an hour. Its rate of acceleration, therefore, is dependent on how much time it takes to achieve escape velocity. Suppose we were to allow a fairly reasonable .2 second for the actual power stroke of the cast, and consider the power as being applied in a constant flow. Then we can determine the rate of acceleration of the lure by using the simple physics formula:

$$a = \frac{vt - vo}{t}$$

In which:
a = acceleration
vt = terminal velocity
 (240 mph = 352 ft./sec.)
vo = original velocity = 0
t = time = .2 sec.
Thus:

$$a = \frac{352 \text{ ft./sec.} - 0}{.2 \text{ sec.}} = 1760 \text{ ft./sec./sec.}$$

How can an acceleration of 1760 ft./sec./sec. be expressed in terms of "G's," or normal gravity? We know that the acceleration of gravity at the earth's surface is 32 ft./sec./sec. Therefore, if we divide the acceleration of gravity into the calculated acceleration of the lure, we can determine the "G's" of acceleration applied to the lure in this cast.

$$\text{Thus: } G = \frac{1760 \text{ ft./sec./sec.}}{32 \text{ ft./sec./sec.}} = 55$$

In terms made popular by space-age science, the lure undergoes 55 "G's" of acceleration during the cast. How can we use this to determine the average strain on the line during the cast? First, we must select a reasonable weight (w) for the lure. Let this be four ounces or .25 pound. Line strain(s) can then be calculated by using the simple formula:

$$s = G \times w = 55 \times .25 = 13.75 \text{ lbs.}$$

From this we can see that a 15-pound-test line would probably be stressed to its upper limits of strength in such a cast with a four-ounce lure, but a 30-pound-test line would be working at a safe 46 percent of its breaking strain. It is important to remember, however, that this assumes average velocities and strains, and constant application of forces.

Any experienced caster knows that the application of force during a cast is not linear; it progresses quickly from zero force to a peak that is almost impossible to calculate, and then back down again quickly to zero. This may introduce momentary line and rod stresses that far exceed the figures arrived at here. But, fortunately, the built-in flexibility of modern rods and lines provides a safety factor that largely counteracts these peak forces.

THE ROD AS A LEVER SYSTEM

Now let's consider what happens to a fisherman when he hooks a very large, powerful fish like a 600-pound tuna. If you were to tie a length of 130-pound-test line to something solid, put a baited hook on the other end, and then hook the tuna, the fish most probably could break the line on a dead pull. The tails of large game fishes are oscillating propellers fully as efficient as any man-made rotating propellers.

But if you give the fisherman a balanced 12/0 big-game rod and reel loaded with 130-pound-test line, plus a comfortable harness that enables him to use the tackle to the full extent of its power by taking the strain in his lower back rather than through his arms and

With a 1:4 leverage ratio, Don Leek's 50-lb.-line class, straight-butt marlin outfit will put about 4 lbs. of pull into the harness straps for every opposite pound of line pull.

shoulders, then the fisherman stands an excellent chance of landing the fish, after he has encouraged it to exhaust its reserves of muscular energy by working against the friction of the reel drag and the friction of the line passing through the water.

During a fight with a large fish like this, what forces actually are applied to the angler? First, we must consider the rod and reel combination. Big-game rods with straight butts average about 88 inches long, with the harness rings of the reel placed about 22 inches or one-fourth of the way up from the lever fulcrum, which is the gimbal fitting at the lower end of the rod.

This means that four times as much tension will be placed upon the harness straps as may be placed on the fishing line when the vectors of pull of line and straps are parallel. A 100-pound pull on the line will translate to a 400-pound pull on the harness straps. Very few men can stand this much body pressure for very long, if the harness is of the shoulder type that puts the pull of the straps high on the angler's body.

The same amount of harness-strap pull applied to the middle of the angler's back via a kidney harness may reduce to half the actual amount of muscle work

By contrast, the curved-butt 12/0 rig used by Arthur Klorfein to capture this 600-lb. bluefin tuna has a 2:7 leverage ratio and puts 7 lbs. of direct pull into the harness straps for each 2 lbs. of opposite line pull.

With a straight-butt big-game outfit in the 130-lb.-line class having a 1:4 leverage ratio, 100 lbs. of line pull could put as much as 400 lbs. of pull across the shoulders of an angler wearing a shoulder harness.

required to keep the body erect against the harness pull. And if the same amount of harness pull is applied to a seat type of harness, with the line of pull acting at the top of the angler's pelvic bones, he probably can sit there all day with 100 pounds of pull on the line, provided his lower extremities don't go to sleep from a restricted blood supply.

Fortunately for the success of big-game fishermen—and light-tackle specialists also, for that matter—the entire strategy of modern game fishing is built around the concept of causing the fish to work itself into a state of exhaustion while keeping the work effort of the angler within tolerable limits by requiring him to fight the fish with equipment of definitely limited power.

The only time an angler has to apply power to the lever system of the rod to the full extent of the line's strength is when he has to stop or turn a running fish that threatens to strip his reel, or when he has to lift a heavy dead or dying fish in deep water. For this work, a rod with a curved butt has three advantages over a rod with a straight butt.

First, the curved butt gives the angler a larger share of the overall rod lever to work with in applying pull to the line. Second, it adds needed butt length without placing the reel prohibitively far from the angler's body. Third, the lower working angle of the rod tip is a great advantage when it comes to lifting a heavy fish on an up-and-down dead pull. Because the curved butt is essentially a power-applying tool for heavy tackle, it is seldom seen on tackle lighter than

Curved-butt big-game outfit used by Elwood Harry on Bahamian bluefin tuna gives him the advantage of a lower rod-tip angle and a better leverage ratio while keeping the reel within proper operating distance of his body. His kidney harness is worn low to place the pull of the harness straps just above the pelvic girdle, the strongest part of the body.

80-pound-line class. Its use is sanctioned by the International Game Fish Association.

In stand-up light-tackle fishing, the use of a shoulder harness vastly increases the comfort and endurance of the angler. In this instance, the lever proportions are different from those that apply to using a harness in a fighting chair. The chair gimbal becomes a cup or small gimbal worn by the angler on a belt-supported metal or plastic shield, which covers the pubic region during use. This places the rod butt at an advantageous fulcrum position between the thighs at the base of the body.

The rod butt is shorter than that used with a chair, averaging about 16 inches from butt end to reel, or about 20 percent of the rod's average overall length of 80 inches. This puts the angler's lever ratio at one-fifth of the total rod length. This means that if you are fishing with, say, 30-pound-line-class tackle, a pull of 20 pounds on the line, parallel to the pull angle of the harness straps, results in a pull of 100 pounds on your shoulders. This is a lot of pull for any angler to support standing up. Fortunately, the harness translates the pull to the angler's strong body, leaving his arms free of line pull.

If the harness is eliminated and the

Above: *Surf spinning rod used by Charles R. Meyer has a 1:5 leverage ratio. Ten lbs. of pull on the line could build up to 50 lbs. of pull on the angler's hands and arms.* **Below:** *Champion angler Stu Apte demonstrates one of the limitations of the fly rod for saltwater fishing. With a 1:7 leverage ratio, 7 lbs. of pull on the line could build up to almost 50 lbs. of downward pull on his left hand.*

angler holds the rod by the foregrip with his left hand, a third set of lever proportions comes into play. Take, for example, a typical 30-pound-line-class boat rod suitable for trolling or bottom fishing. Its total length is 80 inches. The reel is placed 17 inches above the butt end, but the center of the cork foregrip is 24 inches above the lower end. The angler, holding the foregrip in his left hand, is working with 24/80, or 30 percent of the total lever above the fulcrum.

This means that a 15-pound pull on his line at right angles to the rod tip translates into 15/.3, or 50 pounds of pull on his left hand and arm. How long could you hold a 50-pound weight stomach-high in front of you with your left arm unsupported? Most anglers faced with this situation use the right hand and arm to relieve some of the strain on the left, but the great advantages of fishing with a comfortable gimbal belt and harness quickly become apparent.

FISHING LINES AND FISH POWER

The sheer power of some fish is amazing. Swordfish, when harpooned, often tow the line keg completely under. It takes a downward pull of 85 pounds to submerge a 10-gallon keg. How much horsepower do large game fish actually generate? How fast can they swim? Answers to these questions can help the angler in his struggle to catch a large game fish with line and tackle capable of supporting only a small fraction of the fish's weight.

A number of years ago Bob Edge, the outdoor writer, reported in *Sportfishing* magazine that while working with Captain Earl Thompson of Liverpool, Nova Scotia, on fish speed experiments, he had clocked a 60-pound bluefin tuna at 44 mph after it had taken out more than 200 yards of 36-thread linen line against a light reel drag. The clocking device was a motorcycle speedometer mounted on the rod and reel with the line running over a suitable drive pulley.

Harlan Major, in his authoritative book *Salt Water Fishing Tackle*, first published in the 1930s, told of experiments he had conducted on the friction of linen lines being towed through the water. Interpolation of a line friction graph published in his book indicates that the static pull of 200 yards of 36-thread linen line being towed at 44 mph equals 78 pounds.

An interesting question immediately arises: "How much power would be expended by a fish doing this much work at that speed?" The answer is not hard to find if we record one simple definition of speed and a power formula developed at the University of Rhode Island by Robert E. Taber for calculating the power expended by fishing trawlers in towing nets with cables.

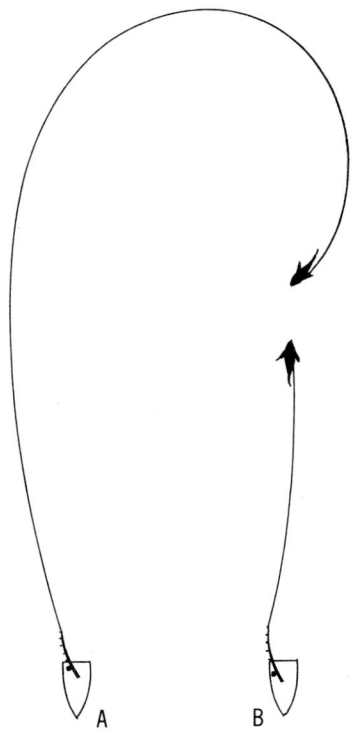

Fish with a long line (A) can easily break the line by swimming rapidly back toward the boat, putting tremendous tension on the line through side-cutting water friction. In (B), the angler keeps line water friction down to linear friction by fighting the fish close with a short line.

Definition: 44 mph = $\frac{3872 \text{ ft.}}{1 \text{ min.}}$

Power formula: hp = $\frac{TV}{33,000}$

In which: T = line tension (78 lbs.)
V = velocity (3872 ft./min.)

Thus: hp = $\frac{78 \times 3872}{33,000}$ = 9.152

This appears to indicate that a fish exerting a pull of 78 pounds on a line while swimming at 44 mph develops 9.152 horsepower in excess of the power needed to push the fish's body through the water at that speed. How does this compare with reliable estimates of the actual power output of swimming aquatic animals?

Dr. Leonard Harrison Matthews, former director of the Zoological Society of London, stated in the book *The Whales* that the calculated power of aquatic mammals (whales and porpoises) is close to that of a trained human athlete, or .01 to .02 horsepower per pound of muscle weight.

Tunas are not mammals, but they are geared for a high rate of metabolism and high power output. In *Scientific American* magazine, Dr. Francis G. Carey, of Woods Hole Oceanographic Institution, stated that telemeter tests he had conducted with live bluefins in cold Nova Scotian waters proved that these remarkable fish are actually warm blooded to a high degree and are capable of sustaining internal body temperatures in excess of 15°C. (27°F.) above the temperature of the surrounding water. This helps to explain their ability to generate great power in cold water, and it encourages the viewpoint that their muscle-power-per-weight-unit may be close to that of some mammals.

Bluefin tunas certainly are among the most beautifully streamlined and efficient swimmers in the sea. Their tails are oscillating propellers fully as efficient as any man-made rotating propeller of equal service characteristics. If we were to split the difference between the high and low muscle-power ratings quoted earlier for marine mammals, and assign a power rating of .015 horsepower per pound of muscle weight to bluefin tunas, we would have a workable if not orthodox means for estimating the swimming power of these fish. The formula is simple:

hp = muscle weight × .015

Using Bob Edge's 60-pounder, and allowing 50 percent of body weight for muscles, the formula works this way:

hp = 60 × .5 × .015 = .45 hp

Can it be that the rating of .45 horsepower actually is the swimming power of this 60-pound tuna at 44 mph? It hardly seems logical. Unfortunately, we have no direct means for measuring the swimming power of fish, but it can be demonstrated that both fish and marine mammals expend only a fraction of the power that would be required to drive exact mechanical models of their bodies at the same speed.

Dr. Matthews, in his discourse on cetaceans, stated that engineers have estimated it would take 14 horsepower to drive a mechanical copy of a six-foot, 300-pound porpoise at the porpoise's top sustained speed of 25 knots. Like whales, porpoises have an average of about 40 percent of body weight as muscle. So the power formula used on the tuna would look like this, giving the porpoise the top rating of .02 horsepower per pound of muscle:

hp = 300 × .4 × .02 = 2.4

Here we have a direct relationship between the 14 horsepower estimated to be required to drive the mechanical porpoise at 25 knots, and the 2.4 horsepower calculated to be expended by the living porpoise in achieving the same speed. Why the great difference?

The answer is that porpoises, whales, and the fast fishes have flexible rather than rigid body surfaces and even special muscles under the skin that automatically cause the skin to conform to slight exterior changes of water pressure. This preserves laminar flow of water around the swimmer's body. Turbulent flow is known to be a great thief of power in vessels or bodies moving through the water. With natural laminar flow around its body, a marine mammal or tuna can sustain high swimming speeds and still have reserve energy on tap for sudden extreme emergencies.

In the summer of 1975, I was assisted by John J. Burke of New York City and Montauk, New York, in testing tournament-quality monofilament and Micron lines for water friction. Our results consistently averaged about 60 percent of the friction values obtained by Harlan Major with linen lines of roughly equal breaking strain. This agrees with his published estimates that monofilament and braided nylon lines register 50 and 62 1/2 percent of the water friction of equivalent linen lines.

Our results also agreed with the law of physics that states that power expended increases as the square of the increase of speed. Following is a table of our friction values for monofilament and Micron lines of 130-pound test.

Speed	Friction
5 kn.	5 to 6 oz. per 100 yds.
10 kn.	22 to 24 oz. per 100 yds.
15 kn.	35 to 38 oz. per 100 yds.
20 kn.	88 to 96 oz. per 100 yds.

How does all this power talk relate to an angler who has just hooked a 600-pound tuna? From the table above, we can estimate that 130-pound-test synthetic line has an average straight line friction drag of 92 ounces, or 5.75 pounds per 100 yards at 20 knots. A 600-pound tuna striking and then running at 40 knots would generate 5.75 x 4 = 23 pounds of line friction per 100 yards at that speed. To this must be added reel drag friction, which we can peg at 45 pounds. At the 300-yard mark of a hot first run, the line strain situation could add up this way:

Line friction = 23 lbs. × 3 = 69 lbs.
Drag friction = 45 lbs.
Total line strain = 114 lbs.

This is dangerously close to the line's 130-pound breaking strain, and at 40 knots the fish has precipitated this line-breaking situation in just 13.5 seconds. As far as the fish is concerned, the power factors add up this way:

$$\text{Line hp} = \frac{114 \text{ lbs.} \times 4000 \text{ ft./min.}}{33,000} = 13.8 \text{ hp}$$

Swim hp = 600 lbs. × .5 × .015 = 4.5 hp
Total hp = 18.3 hp

The fish is expending four times its normal 40-knot swimming power, a situation the angler fervently hopes will exhaust the fish before the line breaks.

It is important to understand how lines break under tension. The factor of stretch cannot be separated from that of breakage. Stretch in a flexible line acts as a sort of built-in shock absorber. Dacron lines, for example, average about 10 percent elongation before breaking, but monofilament lines may stretch as much as 30 percent. This does not mean

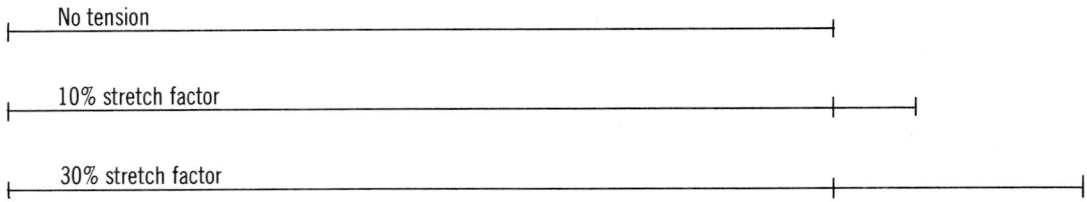

A = Unit of line without tension
B = Dacron line with 10% stretch factor, stretched to the breaking point
C = Monofilament line with 30% stretch factor, stretched to the breaking point

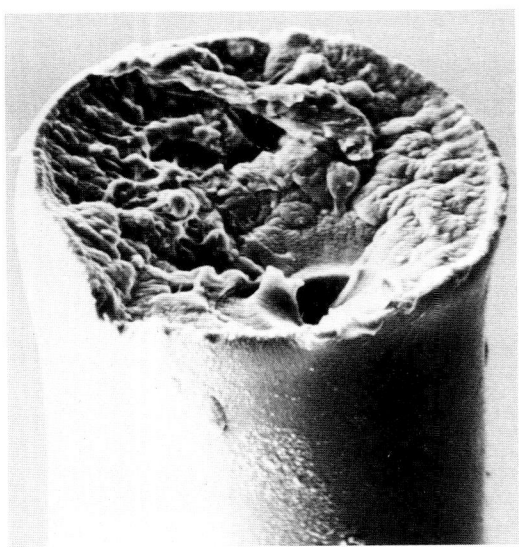

Above: Du Pont electron scanning microphotograph of a break in water-saturated nylon monofilament. **Below:** Breaking 130-lb.-test line with a 13-lb. weight.

A A 13-lb. weight is tied to 16 ft. of 130-lb. Dacron line (10% stretch factor) and hoisted to the point of attachment of the line.

B One second after release, the weight has fallen 16 ft. and is starting to stretch the line.

C After falling an additional 1.6 ft. (stretch factor length), the weight has been slowed to almost zero velocity, but its 10 'G's" of deceleration, plus its own weight of 13 lbs., are enough to break the line.

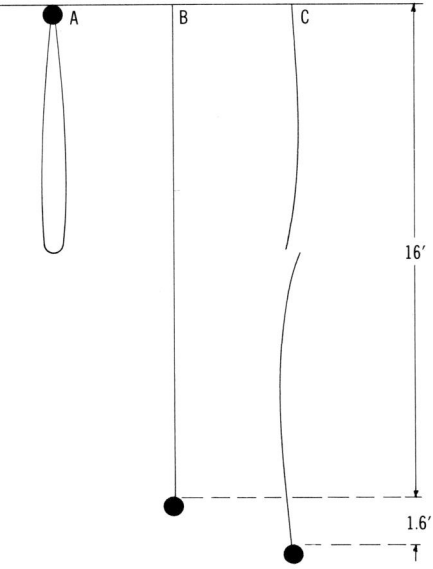

that monofilament line is "stronger" than Dacron of equal breaking strain. It just means that if a sudden shock is applied to the more stretchy line, the impact of the suddenly added weight is stretched out in time as well as in distance, bringing the shock effect down to a lower value without inducing "G" forces high enough to break the line.

As an example, we could break a piece of 130-pound-test Dacron line with a 13-pound weight falling from a height of only 16 feet. Here's how the experiment works:

A 16-foot length of line to be tested is tied to a firm support about 20 feet above the ground, and the 13-pound weight is tied to the other end. The weight is then raised to the height of the upper tie-point and released in a free fall. The Dacron line has a stretch factor of 10 percent. This means that it will stretch 1.6 feet before breaking.

The acceleration of gravity on any free-falling object at the surface of the earth is 32 ft./sec./sec. This means that, starting from zero velocity, the weight will have reached an instantaneous velocity of 32 ft./sec. at the end of the first second of fall. But because its *average* speed for the first second is only half of its final speed, it will have fallen only 16 feet.

The 10-percent stretch factor of the line acts on the falling weight like a stiff spring, slowing its velocity to zero at 10 times the acceleration of gravity. This translates into 13 lbs. x 10 = 130 lbs. of deceleration on the line, enough to break it at the extreme end of the deceleration-stretch period, provided the line is not underrated in actual breaking test by the manufacturer, as sometimes happens.

With stretchy line like some varieties of monofilament that have up to 30-percent stretch, the experiment just outlined probably would not work. This is not because the stretchy line is "stronger," but because its greater stretch decelerates the falling weight at a slower rate, resulting in less than 130 pounds of deceleration tension on the 130-pound line.

Understanding the stretch values of various kinds of lines is very useful to practical fishermen. For example, if you plan to fish for soft-mouthed species like sea trout or weakfish, you'll have fewer hook pull-outs if you use soft, stretchy line that puts lower "G" forces of tension on the fish's jaw when you set the hook.

On the other hand, if you cast long distances to hard-mouthed fish, or troll for billfish, a line with low stretch may save you many otherwise-missed strikes. For example, if you attempt to hook a fish on a long line with a 30-percent stretch factor, you will have to pull the rod tip back three times as far to accomplish the same amount of hook-setting tension as you would have to pull back with 10-percent-stretch line. This might be six feet with some monofilaments, versus two feet with Dacron line.

These remarks do not imply that Dacron is "better" than monofilament, but rather that for certain fishing situations, each has advantages and disadvantages.

The first shock of a sudden strike is like the effect of the falling weight in the experiment described earlier. Three factors in modern tackle help to keep the "G" forces of the strike within reasonable limits. They are: the stretch factor of the line, the spring action of the rod, and the slip action of the reel drag. The angler cannot alter either of the first two factors, but he does have complete control over the third.

Good fishing practice calls for setting the initial or striking drag of the reel at between 20 and 35 percent of the line's rated breaking strain. The following table gives minimum (20 percent) and maximum (35 percent) striking-drag values for the seven IGFA line classes.

IGFA line class	20% drag	35% drag
6 lb.	1.2 lb.	2.1 lb.
12 lb.	2.4 lb.	4.2 lb.
20 lb.	4.0 lb.	7.0 lb.
30 lb.	6.0 lb.	10.5 lb.
50 lb.	10.0 lb.	17.5 lb.
80 lb.	16.0 lb.	28.0 lb.
130 lb.	26.0 lb.	45.5 lb.

Above: *The first shock of a sudden strike puts great strain on the tackle. Line stretch, rod flexibility, and striking-drag setting combine to keep line tension within tolerable limits.* **Below:** *The striking drag is set by pulling on the line with a spring balance while the angler adjusts the drag to start slipping at exactly the desired amount of line tension.*

The striking drag is set by hooking a spring balance to the end of the fishing line and pulling on the spring balance while adjusting the drag to slip at the desired value of pounds in line tension. Calibrating lever- and star-drag reels for striking drag is described in detail in Chapter 5.

What happens to the relationship between the original striking-drag setting and the line tension when a hooked fish starts taking out line? Suppose we were to start tuna fishing with a reel full of line, with the diameter of the bulk of line on the spool measuring five inches. A tuna strikes and takes out line until the diameter of the line on the spool is reduced to 2 1/2 inches. How much line tension is now required to pull out line against the drag?

If the initial drag setting were 20 pounds, it would take 20 pounds of line pull to start the drag slipping with the reel full to five-inch diameter. But when this diameter is reduced to half, 2 1/2 inches, it takes 40 pounds of line tension to start the drag slipping. We haven't touched the star-drag adjustment; we have only let the fish pull against a lever half as long as before.

Mathematically, the new line tension is calculated by the formula:

$$X = \frac{A}{B} \times W$$

X = the new line tension, A = original spool diameter, B = new spool diameter, and W = original drag setting in pounds.

Thus: $X = \frac{5}{2.5} \times 20 = 40$ pounds.

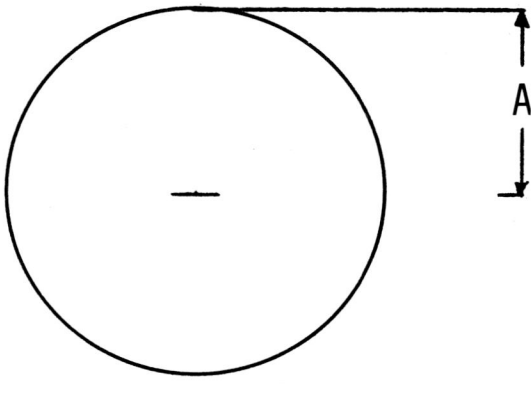

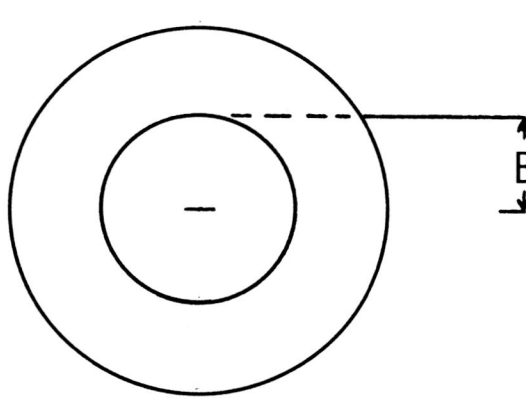

How line tension increases as line-spool diameter is reduced.

A *In a reel full of line, line tension to start the drag slipping remains constant as long as the radius of leverage remains the same. This radius is the distance from the spool axle center to the outside of the line on the spool.*

B *When the radius (or spool diameter) has been reduced to one-half the full value, the line is pulling on a radius of leverage only half as long as it had when the spool was full. Therefore it takes twice as much line tension to start the reel drag slipping.*

The important rule to remember is: *as the spool diameter decreases while a fish takes out line, slack off drag tension to reduce the danger of breaking the line.*

Suppose you were to form the habit, as many anglers do, of setting your striking drag at 25 percent of the line's rated breaking strain. At what reduced spool diameter would tension on the line cause increased drag slip to equal the breaking test of the line? Let us take 80-pound-test line as an example, although the formula works equally well on all classes of lines.

Use the formula: $Y = \frac{C}{D}$

In which: Y = percentage of original spool diameter,
C = striking drag in pounds, and
D = line test in pounds.

Thus: $Y = \frac{20}{80} = 25$ percent

This means that with any class of line, if you set the striking drag at 25 percent of the line's breaking test, line tension will cause the drag to slip at the breaking point of the line itself when the diameter of the line on the spool is reduced to 25 percent of the full value.

By the same token, if you set the striking drag to slip at 40 percent of the line's breaking test, drag friction will be enough to break the line when line diameter on the spool is reduced to 40 percent of the original diameter. Following are three examples of this phenomenon, all taken from everyday fishing life.

(1) An 80-pound-test line with drag set to slip at 20 percent of line test, or 16 pounds, will break if the reel spool diameter is reduced to 20 percent of the original diameter.

(2) A 30-pound-test line with drag set to slip at 30 percent of line test, or nine pounds, will break if the reel spool diameter is reduced to 30 percent of the original diameter.

(3) A 12-pound-test line with drag set to slip at 50 percent of line test, or six pounds, will break if the reel spool diameter is reduced to 50 percent of the original diameter.

29 Line Capacity of Pre-World War II Reels

Early saltwater game-fishing reels were rated in linen-line capacity. Some of these older reels are still around, giving good service. Their original linen-line capacity ratings have been converted to equivalent monofilament and Dacron line capacities, with an estimated accuracy of about ± 10 percent. Most of these reels had star drags.

Name/Model	Rated size	Line class	Capacity
J. A. COXE REELS			
C	2/0	20 lb.	400 mono, 425 Dacron
		30 lb.	275 mono, 300 Dacron
		50 lb.	160 mono, 170 Dacron
C	3/0	20 lb.	480 mono, 510 Dacron
		30 lb.	320 mono, 340 Dacron
		50 lb.	190 mono, 200 Dacron
C	4/0	20 lb.	800 mono, 850 Dacron
		30 lb.	535 mono, 570 Dacron
		50 lb.	320 mono, 340 Dacron
CW	4/0	20 lb.	965 mono, 1030 Dacron
		30 lb.	640 mono, 680 Dacron
		50 lb.	430 mono, 460 Dacron
CLT	4/0	20 lb.	800 mono, 850 Dacron
		30 lb.	535 mono, 570 Dacron
		50 lb.	320 mono, 340 Dacron
C	6/0	20 lb.	855 mono, 1010 Dacron
		30 lb.	640 mono, 680 Dacron
		50 lb.	430 mono, 460 Dacron
		80 lb.	280 mono, 300 Dacron
		130 lb.	170 mono, 180 Dacron
C	6/0	30 lb.	855 mono, 1010 Dacron
		50 lb.	515 mono, 550 Dacron
		80 lb.	320 mono, 320 Dacron
		130 lb.	200 mono, 215 Dacron
CR	9/0	30 lb.	1415 mono, 1490 Dacron
		50 lb.	855 mono, 1010 Dacron
		80 lb.	535 mono, 570 Dacron
		130 lb.	320 mono, 340 Dacron

Name/Model	Rated size	Line class	Capacity
CW	9/0	30 lb.	1845 mono, 1965 Dacron
		50 lb.	1115 mono, 1190 Dacron
		80 lb.	695 mono, 745 Dacron
		130 lb.	430 mono, 460 Dacron
CN	12/0	50 lb.	1390 mono, 1490 Dacron
		80 lb.	865 mono, 925 Dacron
		130 lb.	535 mono, 570 Dacron
CR	12/0	80 lb.	1000 mono, 1650 Dacron
		130 lb.	640 mono, 680 Dacron
CW	12/0	80 lb.	1215 mono, 1300 Dacron
		130 lb.	750 mono, 800 Dacron
C	14/0	130 lb.	1070 mono, 1145 Dacron
C	16/0	130 lb.	1600 mono, 1700 Dacron

EDWARD VOM HOFE REELS

Name/Model	Rated size	Line class	Capacity
800	2	20 lb.	300 mono, 320 Dacron
		30 lb.	215 mono, 230 Dacron
570	1	20 lb.	450 mono, 480 Dacron
		30 lb.	320 mono, 340 Dacron
650	1	20 lb.	450 mono, 480 Dacron
		30 lb.	320 mono, 340 Dacron
560	2	20 lb.	300 mono, 320 Dacron
		30 lb.	215 mono, 230 Dacron
560	1	20 lb.	320 mono, 340 Dacron
		30 lb.	215 mono, 230 Dacron
550	1/0	20 lb.	450 mono, 480 Dacron
		30 lb.	320 mono, 340 Dacron
550	2/0	20 lb.	450 mono, 480 Dacron
		30 lb.	320 mono, 340 Dacron
		50 lb.	160 mono, 170 Dacron
550	3/0	20 lb.	500 mono, 535 Dacron
		30 lb.	300 mono, 320 Dacron
		50 lb.	150 mono, 165 Dacron
621	1/0	20 lb.	320 mono, 340 Dacron
		30 lb.	215 mono, 230 Dacron
621	2/0	20 lb.	450 mono, 480 Dacron
		30 lb.	320 mono, 340 Dacron
		50 lb.	160 mono, 170 Dacron
621	3/0	20 lb.	500 mono, 535 Dacron
		30 lb.	350 mono, 370 Dacron
		50 lb.	215 mono, 230 Dacron
621	4/0	20 lb.	730 mono, 775 Dacron
		30 lb.	520 mono, 555 Dacron
		50 lb.	320 mono, 340 Dacron
621	6/0	30 lb.	550 mono, 590 Dacron
		50 lb.	345 mono, 370 Dacron
		80 lb.	215 mono, 230 Dacron
621	9/0	50 lb.	850 mono, 910 Dacron
		80 lb.	535 mono, 575 Dacron
		130 lb.	335 mono, 360 Dacron

Name/Model	Rated size	Line class	Capacity
722	10/0	80 lb.	640 mono, 680 Dacron
		130 lb.	430 mono, 455 Dacron
722	12/0	80 lb.	1070 mono, 1140 Dacron
		130 lb.	640 mono, 680 Dacron
732	14/0	130 lb.	1070 mono, 1140 Dacron
732	16/0	130 lb.	1540 mono, 1650 Dacron
742	12/0	130 lb.	750 mono, 800 Dacron
742	14/0	130 lb.	1260 mono, 1450 Dacron
742	16/0	130 lb.	1540 mono, 1650 Dacron

OCEAN CITY REELS (before World War II)

Name/Model	Rated size	Line class	Capacity
Ike Walton 100	250	20 lb.	400 mono, 430 Dacron
		30 lb.	275 mono, 300 Dacron
Ike Walton 105	300	20 lb.	475 mono, 500 Dacron
Ocean City 210	150	20 lb.	260 mono, 270 Dacron
		30 lb.	185 mono, 200 Dacron
Ocean City 104	200	20 lb.	320 mono, 340 Dacron
		30 lb.	235 mono, 245 Dacron
Ocean City 101	250	20 lb.	400 mono, 425 Dacron
		30 lb.	275 mono, 290 Dacron
Ocean City 102	300	20 lb.	475 mono, 500 Dacron
		30 lb.	340 mono, 375 Dacron
Ocean City 114	4/0	20 lb.	680 mono, 720 Dacron
		30 lb.	425 mono, 450 Dacron
		50 lb.	260 mono, 275 Dacron
Zephyr 130	150	20 lb.	275 mono, 290 Dacron
		30 lb.	190 mono, 210 Dacron
Zephyr 131	250	20 lb.	400 mono, 425 Dacron
		30 lb.	275 mono, 290 Dacron
Zephyr 132	300	20 lb.	475 mono, 500 Dacron
		30 lb.	340 mono, 375 Dacron
Fantum 133	150	20 lb.	275 mono, 290 Dacron
		30 lb.	190 mono, 210 Dacron
Fantum 134	250	20 lb.	400 mono, 425 Dacron
		30 lb.	275 mono, 290 Dacron
Fantum 135	300	20 lb.	475 mono, 500 Dacron
		30 lb.	340 mono, 375 Dacron
Ocean City 104W Far Kast	200	20 lb.	320 mono, 340 Dacron
		30 lb.	235 mono, 245 Dacron
Harbor City 106W Far Kast	200	20 lb.	320 mono, 340 Dacron
		30 lb.	235 mono, 245 Dacron
Bay City 201W Far Kast	150	20 lb.	260 mono, 270 Dacron
		30 lb.	185 mono, 200 Dacron
Bay City 112W Far Kast	250	20 lb.	400 mono, 425 Dacron
		30 lb.	275 mono, 290 Dacron
Bay City 113W Far Kast	300	20 lb.	475 mono, 500 Dacron
		30 lb.	340 mono, 375 Dacron
Chelsea 205W Far Kast	150	20 lb.	260 mono, 270 Dacron
		30 lb.	185 mono, 200 Dacron

Name/Model	Rated size	Line class	Capacity
Chelsea 108W Far Kast	250	20 lb.	400 mono, 425 Dacron
		30 lb.	275 mono, 290 Dacron
Chelsea 116W Far Kast	300	20 lb.	475 mono, 500 Dacron
		30 lb.	340 mono, 375 Dacron
Bay City 202	100	20 lb.	215 mono, 230 Dacron
Bay City 201	150	20 lb.	260 mono, 290 Dacron
		30 lb.	185 mono, 200 Dacron
Bay City 221	200	20 lb.	320 mono, 340 Dacron
		30 lb.	235 mono, 245 Dacron
Bay City 112	250	20 lb.	400 mono, 425 Dacron
		30 lb.	275 mono, 290 Dacron
Bay City 113	300	20 lb.	475 mono, 500 Dacron
		30 lb.	340 mono, 375 Dacron
Bay City 165	4/0	20 lb.	680 mono, 720 Dacron
		30 lb.	425 mono, 450 Dacron
Chelsea 206	100	20 lb.	215 mono, 230 Dacron
Chelsea 205	150	20 lb.	260 mono, 270 Dacron
		30 lb.	185 mono, 200 Dacron
Chelsea 222	200	20 lb.	320 mono, 340 Dacron
		30 lb.	235 mono, 245 Dacron
Chelsea 108	250	20 lb.	400 mono, 425 Dacron
		30 lb.	275 mono, 290 Dacron
Chelsea 116	300	20 lb.	475 mono, 500 Dacron
		30 lb.	340 mono, 375 Dacron
Jersey City 211	150	20 lb.	260 mono, 270 Dacron
		30 lb.	185 mono, 200 Dacron
Jersey City 122	300	20 lb.	475 mono, 500 Dacron
		30 lb.	340 mono, 375 Dacron
Brigantine 212	150	20 lb.	260 mono, 270 Dacron
		30 lb.	185 mono, 200 Dacron
Brigantine 111	250	20 lb.	400 mono, 425 Dacron
		30 lb.	275 mono, 290 Dacron
Brigantine 109	300	20 lb.	475 mono, 500 Dacron
		30 lb.	340 mono, 375 Dacron
Fortesque 103	250	20 lb.	400 mono, 425 Dacron
		30 lb.	275 mono, 290 Dacron
Lake City 215	150	20 lb.	260 mono, 270 Dacron
		30 lb.	185 mono, 200 Dacron
Lake City 123	250	20 lb.	400 mono, 425 Dacron
		30 lb.	275 mono, 290 Dacron
Catalina 145	250	20 lb.	400 mono, 425 Dacron
		30 lb.	275 mono, 290 Dacron
Catalina 146	300	20 lb.	475 mono, 500 Dacron
		30 lb.	340 mono, 375 Dacron
St. Lucie 241	150	20 lb.	260 mono, 270 Dacron
		30 lb.	185 mono, 200 Dacron
St. Lucie 143	250	20 lb.	400 mono, 425 Dacron
		30 lb.	275 mono, 290 Dacron
St. Lucie 144	300	20 lb.	475 mono, 500 Dacron
		30 lb.	340 mono, 375 Dacron

Line Capacity of Pre-World War II Reels

Name/Model	Rated size	Line class	Capacity
Seal Beach 240	150	20 lb.	260 mono, 270 Dacron
		30 lb.	185 mono, 200 Dacron
Seal Beach 136	250	20 lb.	400 mono, 425 Dacron
		30 lb.	275 mono, 290 Dacron
Seal Beach 137	300	20 lb.	475 mono, 500 Dacron
		30 lb.	340 mono, 375 Dacron
Olympic 151	250	20 lb.	400 mono, 425 Dacron
		30 lb.	275 mono, 290 Dacron
Olympic 152	300	20 lb.	475 mono, 500 Dacron
		30 lb.	340 mono, 375 Dacron
Jones Beach 150	250	20 lb.	400 mono, 425 Dacron
Long Key 110	4½/0	20 lb.	1350 mono, 1450 Dacron
		30 lb.	850 mono, 910 Dacron
		50 lb.	535 mono, 570 Dacron
Long Key 115	5/0	30 lb.	1080 mono, 1150 Dacron
		50 lb.	675 mono, 710 Dacron
		80 lb.	350 mono, 375 Dacron
Long Key 140	6/0	30 lb.	1500 mono, 1700 Dacron
		50 lb.	950 mono, 1000 Dacron
		80 lb.	535 mono, 570 Dacron
Panama 141	10/0	80 lb.	855 mono, 910 Dacron
		130 lb.	500 mono, 535 Dacron
Panama 142	12/0	80 lb.	1000 mono, 1070 Dacron
		130 lb.	600 mono, 640 Dacron
Panama 153	14/0	130 lb.	700 mono, 750 Dacron
Balboa 120	10/0	80 lb.	855 mono, 910 Dacron
		130 lb.	500 mono, 535 Dacron
Balboa 121	12/0	80 lb.	1000 mono, 1070 Dacron
		130 lb.	600 mono, 640 Dacron
Balboa 162	14/0	130 lb.	700 mono, 750 Dacron
PFLUEGER REELS (before World War II)			
Pontiac		20 lb.	500 mono, 535 Dacron
		30 lb.	325 mono, 350 Dacron
Norka 1335		20 lb.	400 mono, 430 Dacron
		30 lb.	250 mono, 275 Dacron
Templar 1419¾	4/0	20 lb.	1100 mono, 1200 Dacron
		30 lb.	700 mono, 750 Dacron
		50 lb.	400 mono, 430 Dacron
Templar 1420½	5/0	30 lb.	1200 mono, 1300 Dacron
		50 lb.	750 mono, 800 Dacron
		80 lb.	260 mono, 275 Dacron
Saltrout 1555		20 lb.	350 mono, 370 Dacron
		30 lb.	220 mono, 230 Dacron
Saltrout 1558		20 lb.	750 mono, 800 Dacron
		30 lb.	470 mono, 500 Dacron
		50 lb.	220 mono, 235 Dacron
Atlapac 1640	4/0	20 lb.	950 mono, 1000 Dacron
		30 lb.	600 mono, 640 Dacron
		50 lb.	350 mono, 375 Dacron

MODERN SALTWATER FISHING TACKLE

Name/Model	Rated size	Line class	Capacity
Atlapac 1660	6/0	30 lb.	900 mono, 965 Dacron
		50 lb.	550 mono, 590 Dacron
		80 lb.	325 mono, 350 Dacron
Atlapac 1690	9/0	50 lb.	950 mono, 1000 Dacron
		80 lb.	620 mono, 660 Dacron
Golden West 1878		20 lb.	525 mono, 550 Dacron
		30 lb.	325 mono, 340 Dacron
Interocean 1885		20 lb.	400 mono, 430 Dacron
		30 lb.	240 mono, 255 Dacron
Interocean 1888		20 lb.	525 mono, 550 Dacron
		30 lb.	325 mono, 340 Dacron
Interocean 1889		30 lb.	425 mono, 450 Dacron
		50 lb.	240 mono, 255 Dacron
Freespeed		20 lb.	225 mono, 240 Dacron
Ohio 1975		20 lb.	400 mono, 430 Dacron
		30 lb.	250 mono, 265 Dacron
Ohio 1978		20 lb.	525 mono, 550 Dacron
		30 lb.	325 mono, 340 Dacron
Ohio 1979		30 lb.	400 mono, 430 Dacron
		50 lb.	250 mono, 265 Dacron
Capitol 1985		20 lb.	400 mono, 430 Dacron
		30 lb.	250 mono, 265 Dacron
Capitol 1988		30 lb.	325 mono, 350 Dacron
		50 lb.	200 mono, 215 Dacron
Capitol 1898		30 lb.	425 mono, 450 Dacron
		50 lb.	250 mono, 265 Dacron
Sumco 2257		20 lb.	525 mono, 550 Dacron
		30 lb.	325 mono, 350 Dacron
Sumco 2258		30 lb.	375 mono, 400 Dacron
		50 lb.	225 mono, 240 Dacron
Autopla 2475		20 lb.	400 mono, 430 Dacron
		30 lb.	250 mono, 265 Dacron
Autopla 2479		30 lb.	425 mono, 450 Dacron
		50 lb.	250 mono, 265 Dacron
Alpine 2655		20 lb.	400 mono, 430 Dacron
		30 lb.	250 mono, 265 Dacron
Alpine 2657		30 lb.	325 mono, 350 Dacron
		50 lb.	200 mono, 215 Dacron
Alpine 2659		30 lb.	475 mono, 510 Dacron
		50 lb.	275 mono, 300 Dacron
Alpine 2669		30 lb.	475 mono, 510 Dacron
		50 lb.	275 mono, 300 Dacron
Alpine 2675		40 lb.	400 mono, 430 Dacron
		30 lb.	250 mono, 265 Dacron
Taxie 2838		30 lb.	475 mono, 510 Dacron
		50 lb.	275 mono, 300 Dacron
Oceanic 2857		20 lb.	415 mono, 450 Dacron
		30 lb.	275 mono, 300 Dacron
Oceanic 2858		20 lb.	520 mono, 550 Dacron
		30 lb.	325 mono, 350 Dacron

Name/Model	Rated size	Line class	Capacity
Oceanic 2859		30 lb.	400 mono, 430 Dacron
		50 lb.	250 mono, 265 Dacron
Bond 2955		20 lb.	400 mono, 430 Dacron
		30 lb.	250 mono, 265 Dacron
Taxie 3128		30 lb.	470 mono, 500 Dacron
		50 lb.	225 mono, 250 Dacron
Captain 4128		30 lb.	470 mono, 500 Dacron
		50 lb.	225 mono, 250 Dacron
SHAKESPEARE REELS (before World War II)			
Miller Autocrat 2260	6/0	30 lb.	650 mono, 700 Dacron
		50 lb.	425 mono, 450 Dacron
Miller Dictator 2240	4/0	20 lb.	700 mono, 750 Dacron
		30 lb.	525 mono, 550 Dacron
		50 lb.	325 mono, 340 Dacron
Ocean Prince 2225 and 2226		20 lb.	500 mono, 535 Dacron
		30 lb.	375 mono, 400 Dacron
Atlantis 2224		20 lb.	470 mono, 500 Dacron
		30 lb.	325 mono, 350 Dacron
Samson 2202		20 lb.	425 mono, 450 Dacron
		30 lb.	260 mono, 275 Dacron
Bald Eagle 2205		20 lb.	425 mono, 450 Dacron
		30 lb.	260 mono, 275 Dacron
Champion 1967½ and 1967		20 lb.	375 mono, 400 Dacron
		30 lb.	225 mono, 250 Dacron
Hercules 1966½ and 1966		20 lb.	375 mono, 400 Dacron
		30 lb.	225 mono, 250 Dacron
Service 1944 1944		20 lb.	225 mono, 250 Dacron
Ocean Queen 2215		20 lb.	425 mono, 450 Dacron
		30 lb.	260 mono, 275 Dacron
Ocean Queen 2216		20 lb.	500 mono, 535 Dacron
		30 lb.	375 mono, 400 Dacron
		50 lb.	200 mono, 215 Dacron
Ocean Prince 2222 and 2223		20 lb.	425 mono, 450 Dacron
		30 lb.	260 mono, 275 Dacron
ABERCROMBIE & FITCH REELS (before World War II)			
A&F Squidder	250	20 lb.	415 mono, 450 Dacron
		30 lb.	275 mono, 300 Dacron
A&F Weakfish	150	20 lb.	150 mono, 160 Dacron
WILLIAM MILLS REELS			
Intrinsic Surf	2/0	20 lb.	500 mono, 535 Dacron
		30 lb.	375 mono, 400 Dacron
		50 lb.	225 mono, 250 Dacron
Intrinsic Bonefish	1	12 lb.	500 mono, 535 Dacron
		20 lb.	320 mono, 340 Dacron
		30 lb.	200 mono, 215 Dacron

30 Manufacturers' Index

Saltwater fishing tackle, accessories, and components

Sources:
American Fishing Tackle Manufacturers Association, Chicago, Illinois.
SPORTFISHING Magazine, Yachting Publishing Corporation, New York, New York.

ABERCROMBIE & FITCH, Outfitters, Madison Ave. at 45th St., New York, NY 10017. Retail and mail-order sales of all types of rods, reels, lines, lures and baits, accessories, foul-weather gear; travel service; repairs. Catalog.

TONY ACCETTA & SON, 932 Avenue E, Riviera Beach, FL 33404. Trolling spoons, casting and trolling lures. Catalog.

ACME TACKLE COMPANY INC., 69 Bucklin St., Providence, RI 02907. Trolling and casting lures and baits. Catalog.

ACTION SPORTING SPECIALTIES, Wausau, WI 54401. Boots, waders, allied accessories. Catalog.

AL'S GOLDFISH LURE COMPANY, 516 Main St., Indian Orchard, MA 01501. Trolling and casting lures. Catalog.

ALADDIN LABORATORIES INC., 620 S. 8th St., Minneapolis, MN 55404. Rods and/or reels, accessories. Catalog.

ALEXANDRIA FISHING LURES, 1925 Lee St., Alexandria, LA 71301. Trolling and casting lures and baits. Catalog.

ALLAN MANUFACTURING CO., 325 Duffy Ave., Hicksville, NY 11801. Full line of rods, reels, lures and baits, accessories. Catalog.

CHARLES ALTENKIRCH & SON, Hampton Bays, NY 11946. Custom tackle builders, repairs, accessories.

ALLIANCE MANUFACTURING CO., 3125 N. Milwaukee Ave., Chicago, IL 60618. Full line of fishing accessories. Catalog.

ALVEY REPRESENTATIVES, 2308 Grant Ave., Redondo Beach, CA 90278. U. S. agents for Alvey reels. Catalog.

ANDE, INC., 1325 Broadway, Riviera Beach, FL 33404. U.S. agents for Ande tournament monofilament line. Catalog.

ANGLER PRODUCTS INC., Box 1682, 210 Spring St., Butler, PA 16001. Rods and rod components. Catalog.

ANGLER ROD CO., 1426 Oakland Ave., St. Clair, MI 48079. Rods and rod components. Catalog.

ANGLERS' MANUFACTURING CORP., 7729 N. Eastlake Terrace, Chicago, IL 60626. Fishing accessories. Catalog.

ANGLERS' SPECIALTIES INC., 676 W. 17th St., Costa Mesa, CA 92676. Complete line of deep-sea outriggers, rod holders, chairs, gaffs, related ocean fishing accessories. Catalog.

APPLE MFG. INC., 1307 Roosevelt Ave., Havertown, PA 19083. Rods and rod components, accessories. Catalog.

AQUAMAID DIV., SKYLINE PRODUCTS INC., 370 Grand Blvd., Deer Park, NY 11729. Monel and stainless-steel fish-tank liners.

AQUA-TROLL INC., 16920 Talbot Rd., Edmonds, WA 98020. Lures and prepared baits for salmon trolling. Catalog.

FRED ARBOGAST INC., 313 West North St., Akron, OH 44303. Artificial trolling and casting baits, accessories. Catalog.

ART WIRE & STAMPING CO., 227 High St., Newark, NJ 07102. Complete line of swivels, leader components, sinkers, planers, terminal tackle. Catalog.

ATLANTIC LURES INC., Box 6666, Providence, RI 02904. Complete line of trolling and casting lures. Catalog.

ATOM MANUFACTURING CO., 800 Washington St., Box 45, S. Attleboro, MA 02703. Complete line of Atom casting and trolling plugs and lures. Catalog.

AUTO-GAFF INC., 4 Reynolds St., East Providence, RI 02914. Gaffs, fishing accessories. Catalog.

AXELSON FISHING TACKLE MFG. CO. 1559 Placentia Ave., Newport Beach, CA 92660. Complete line of Aftco rod guides, roller tip-tops, rod hardware. Catalog.

JIM BAGLEY BAIT CO., Box 110, Recker at Spirit Lake Road, Winter Haven, FL 33880. Complete line of prepared artificial and natural trolling and casting baits. Catalog.

BAKER MFG. CO., Columbia, PA 17512. Hook-Out hook remover.

EDDIE BAUER, Outfitters, 417 E. Pine, Seattle, WA 98122. Retail and mail-order sales of all types of fishing accessories, rods, reels, baits and lures, foul-weather gear, boots, clothing, camping equipment. Catalog.

BEAD CHAIN MFG. CO., 110 Mountain Grove St., Bridgeport, CN 06605. Complete line of Bead Chain swivels, connectors, sinkers, leaders, terminal-tackle accessories. Catalog.

L. L. BEAN, Outfitters, Freeport, ME 04032. Retail and mail-order sales of all types of fishing accessories, rods, reels, baits and lures, foul-weather gear, boots, clothing, camping equipment. Catalog.

BERKLEY & COMPANY INC., Spirit Lake, IO 51360. Complete line of light-tackle rods, reels, lines, baits and lures. Catalog.

BEST TACKLE MFG. CO., Box 305, Northport, MI 49670. Complete line of light-tackle rods, reels, lures, accessories. Catalog.

BEVIN-WILCOX LINE CO., Main St., Moodus, CN 06469. Stranded and monofilament fishing lines. Catalog.

BIG JON INC., 14393 Peninsula Drive, Traverse City, MI 49684. Downriggers, deep-trolling accessories. Catalog.

BISCAYNE ROD MFG. CO., 3321 N. W. 7th Ave., Miami, FL 33137. Stock and custom-built saltwater rods. Catalog.

BOMBER BAIT CO., 326 Lindsay St. Gainesville, TX 76240. Casting and trolling baits and lures. Catalog.

BOONE BAIT CO. INC., Box 571, Forsythe Rd., Winter Park, FL 32789. Complete line of casting and trolling baits and lures. Catalog.

BREMER MFG. CO., Box 548, Elkhart Lake, WI 53020. Downrigger release clips and components. Catalog.

BROGDEN-LAMINATING CORP., 295 W. 23rd St., Hialeah, FL 33010. Rods and rod components, casting and trolling lures and baits. Catalog.

BROWNING MFG. CO., Mt. Green Plant, Rt. #1, Morgan, UT 84050. Silaflex rods, reels, accessories. Catalog.

BUCK KNIVES, 6588 Federal Blvd., San Diego, CA 92114. Buck-brand hunting and fishing knives. Catalog.

BURKE FISHING LURES, 1969 S. Airport Rd., Traverse City, MI 49684. Complete line of trolling and casting baits and lures, fishing accessories. Catalog.

CALIFORNIA TACKLE CO. INC., 430 W. Redondo Beach Blvd., Gardena, CA 90248. Rods and rod components, reels, full line of accessories. Catalog.

CANOR PLAREX, 4200 23rd Ave. W., Seattle, WA 98199; 6 Westchester Plaza, Elmsford, NY 10523; 41 Alexander St., Vancouver, B. C., Canada. Nautical clothing, boots, foul-weather gear, boating accessories. Catalog.

CAPE COD LINE CO., Easthampton, CN 06424. Monofilament line.

CARRY-LITE INC., 3000 W. Clarke St., Milwaukee, WI 53245. Fishing accessories. Catalog.

LEW CHILDRE & SONS INC., Box 535, Foley, AL 36535. Low-friction rod guides, rod components and hardware. Catalog.

THE COLEMAN COMPANY INC., 250 N. St. Francis Ave., Wichita, KS 67201. Full line of camping equipment, insulated food containers, portable lights, etc. Catalog.

COLUMBIA COMPANY, P. O. Drawer G, Columbia, AL 36319. Lures and baits, fishing accessories. Catalog.

COMPOSITE DEVELOPMENT CORP., 7569 Convoy Court, San Diego, CA 92111. Rods and rod components. Catalog.

CONTINENTAL MARINE PRODUCTS, 691 Broadway, Westwood, NJ 07675. Full line of marine and fishing accessories. Catalog.

CONVERSE RUBBER COMPANY, 55 Fordham Road, Wilmington, MA 01887. Boots, waders, waterproof nautical clothing. Catalog.

THE H. C. COOK CO., 28 Beaver St., Ansonia, CN 06401. Fishing accessories. Catalog.

CORDELL TACKLE INC., Box 2020, Hot Springs, AR 71901. Full line of artificial trolling and casting baits and lures, fishing accessories. Catalog.

CORTLAND LINE CO., 67 E. Court St., Cortland, NY 13045. Complete line of Dacron and monofilament lines, rods and reels, fishing accessories. Catalog.

COSSACK CAVIAR INC., 101 South Dakota St., Seattle, WA 98134. Prepared salmon eggs and salmon bait. Catalog.

CREEK CHUB BAIT COMPANY, 113 E. Keyser St., Garrett, IN 46738. Complete line of artificial trolling and casting baits and lures, accessories. Catalog.

CREME LURE CO., Box 87, Tyler, TX 75701. Trolling and casting lures and baits. Catalog.

J. LEE CUDDY ASSOCIATES INC., 450 N. E. 79th St., Miami, FL 33138. Trolling and casting baits and lures. Catalog.

DAISY MANUFACTURING CO., Box 220, Rogers, AR 73756. Lures and baits for trolling and casting, rods and reels, fishing accessories. Catalog.

DAIWA CORP., 14011 S. Normandie, Gardena, CA 90247. Complete line of rods and reels, fishing lines, accessories. Catalog.

DALLAS CAP AND EMBLEM MFG. INC., 2924 Main St., Dallas, TX 75226. Sport clothing, caps, sport trophies, emblems. Catalog.

DANFORTH DIV., THE EASTERN COMPANY, 501 Riverside Industrial Parkway, Portland, ME 04103. Full line of anchors, marine hardware and accessories, electronic sounders. Catalog.

LES DAVIS FISHING TACKLE CO., 1565 Center St., Tacoma, WA 98409. Lures and baits for trolling and casting, lines, fishing accessories. Catalog.

DE LONG LURES INC., 85 Compark Rd., Centerville, OH 45459. Baits and lures for trolling and casting. Catalog.

DEPEW MFG. CO., 359 Duffy Ave., Hicksville, NY 11802. Rods and rod components, reels, fishing accessories. Catalog.

DOLPHIN INDUSTRIES INC., Box 7295, Ft. Lauderdale, FL 33304. Fish, deck, and dock storage boxes and lockers. Catalog.

E. I. du PONT de NEMOURS & CO. INC., 1007 Market St., Wilmington, DE 19810. Stren nylon monofilament lines, monofilament in bulk orders. Catalog.

DYNAFLEX MFG. CO., Route #14, Box 370, 601 Aenon Church Road, Tallahassee, FL 32304. Rods, rod components. Catalog.

E-Z ACTION PRODUCTS CO., 1053 Riverside Dr., Battle Creek, MI 49916. Casting and trolling baits and lures. Catalog.

ELECTRIC FISHING REEL SYSTEMS INC., 1700 Sullivan St., Greensboro, NC 27405. Electric fishing reels, components, and accessories. Catalog.

DOUG ENGLISH LURE CO. INC., 619 S. Port St., Corpus Christi, TX 78405. Casting and trolling baits and lures.

LOU J. EPPINGER MFG. CO., 6340 Schaefer Highway, Dearborn, MI 48126. Dardevle casting and trolling lures, baits, bait and lure accessories. Catalog.

FENWICK, Box 729, Westminster, CA 92683. Complete line of rods, reels, lines, accessories, Knucklehead and Konahead lures. Catalog.

FEURER BROS. INC., 77 Lafayette Ave , No. White Plains, NY 10603. Rods, rod components, light-tackle reels. Catalog.

FIRE ISLAND DROP-BACK, 1375 E. 53rd St., Brooklyn, NY 11234. Stainless-steel rod or outrigger drop-back clip.

FISH IT, DIV OF IT INC., Box 1033, Torrington, CN 06790. Baits and lures, accessories. Catalog.

FISH WELLS UNLIMITED, 3100 State Rd. 84, Ft. Lauderdale, FL 33312. On-deck and under-deck fish wells, insulated fish boxes. Catalog.

FOSTER GRANT CO. INC., 280 N. Main St., Leominster, MA 01453. Various types of sunglasses. Catalog.

ISAAC FRANKLIN CO., 630 N. Pulaski St., Baltimore, MD 21217. Fishing accessories. Catalog.

FRIGIBAR INDUSTRIES INC., 6210 N. E. 4th Court, Miami, FL 33138. Portable, built-in, and kit refrigeration units for sport-fishing boats. Catalog.

THE GARCIA CORPORATION, 329 Alfred Ave., Teaneck, NJ 07666. Complete line of light-to-heavy spinning, star-drag, and lever-drag reels, saltwater fly tackle, lines, lures, accessories. Catalog.

GARELICK MFG. CO., 644 2nd St., St. Paul Park, MN 55071. Wooden, aluminum, and fiberglass fishing chairs. Catalog.

GLADDING-SOUTH BEND TACKLE CO., South Otselic, NY 13155. Complete line of rods, light and medium reels, line, baits and lures, accessories. Catalog.

GUDEBROD BROS. SILK CO. INC., 12 S. 12th St., Philadelphia, PA 19107. Dacron fishing lines, baits and lures, fishing accessories. Catalog.

H & H LURE CO., 10874 N. Dual St., Baton Rouge, LA 70814. Lures and baits for casting and trolling. Catalog.

HARPER-WILLIS BAIT CO., Rt. #5, Box 53, Abilene, TX 79605. Baits for casting and trolling. Catalog.

HARRINGTON & RICHARDSON INC., Industrial Row, Gardner, MA 01440. Light-tackle rods and reels, line, accessories. Catalog.

HARRISON-HOGE INDUSTRIES INC., 104 Arlington Ave., St. James, NY 11780. Rods, reels, lines, accessories. Catalog.

JAMES HEDDON'S SONS, 414 West St., Dowagiac, MI 49047. Baits and lures for casting and trolling, plugs, rods and reels, accessories. Catalog.

FRED HEIDE, 5112 Broadway, W. Palm Beach, FL 33407. Custom-built saltwater fishing rods. Catalog.

HELIN TACKLE COMPANY, 4099 Beaufait, Detroit, MI 48230. Complete line of casting and trolling baits and lures. Catalog.

Manufacturers' Index

HOPKINS LURES COMPANY, 1130 Boissevain Ave., Norfolk, VA 23507. Hammered-finish stainless-steel casting and trolling lures, jigs, spoons. Catalog.

L. B. HUNTINGTON CO., Luce Creek Drive, Annapolis, MD 21400. Drone spoons, casting and trolling lures. Catalog.

IDEAL FISHING FLOAT CO. INC., 2001 E. Franklin St., Richmond, VA 23203. Fishing floats, terminal-tackle components, accessories. Catalog.

IGLOO CORP., Box 19322, Houston, TX 77024. Full line of insulated food, beverage, and ice boxes. Catalog.

INVENTORS PRODUCTS CO., 331 Lake Hazeltine Drive, Chaska, MN 55318. Fish-holding cleaning board, accessories. Catalog.

RAY JARRY ASSOCIATES INC., 81 Winter Lane, Hicksville, NY 11801. Rods, rod components, lures and baits, accessories. Catalog.

LUHR JENSEN & SONS INC., Box 297, Hood River, OR 97031. Lures and baits for salmon trolling and casting, accessories, rods and rod components. Catalog.

LOUIS JOHNSON COMPANY, 1547 Old Deerfield Road, Highland Park, IL 60035. Rods, rod components, reels, baits and lures for casting and trolling. Catalog.

JOHNSON REELS COMPANY, 1531 Madison Ave., Mankato, MN 56001. Light-tackle casting and trolling reels. Catalog.

KEYSTONE FISHING CORP., 1344 W. 37th St., Chicago, IL 60609. Rods, rod components, reels, lures and baits, accessories. Catalog.

KNOTMASTER INDUSTRIES INC., Box 23201, San Diego, CA 92123. Knotmaster knot-tyer, accessories. Catalog.

LAMIGLAS INC., 237 Davidson, Woodland, WA 98674. Rods and rod components. Catalog.

LAND-O-TACKLE INC., 4650 N. Ronald St., Harwood Heights, IL 60656. Full line of accessories. Catalog.

LAZY IKE CORP., Box 1177, Ft. Dodge, IO 50501. Complete line of trolling and casting lures and baits, accessories. Catalog.

LEE'S TACKLE INC., 524 N. E. 13th St., Miami, FL 33132. Fishing and fighting chairs, outriggers, rod holders, gaffs, cockpit accessories for big-game fishing. Catalog.

LEISURELINE PRODUCTS, 4 Allwood Ave., Central Islip, NY 11722. Fishing accessories. Catalog.

LEISURE LURES, Box 353, Sta. #1, N. Hollywood, CA 91605. Plastic trolling lures. Catalog.

LENJO INDUSTRIES INC., 208 Market St., Philadelphia, PA 19106. Rods, rod components. Catalog.

H. L. LEONARD ROD CO., 25 Cottage St., Midland Park, NJ 07432. Quality fly rods, reels, accessories. Catalog.

LOOP-A-LINE INC., 1896 Coolidge Ave., Melbourne, FL 32935. Lures and baits, accessories. Catalog.

LUBRIPLATE DIV., FISK BROS. REFINING CO., Newark, NJ 07105, and Toledo, OH 43605. Reel lubricants.

M. V. TACKLE CO., Highway 35, Brielle, NJ 08730. Builders of custom fishing rods, accessories. Catalog.

MAC-JAC MANUFACTURING CO. INC., 1590 Creston St., P. O. Box 821, Muskegon, MI 49443. Downriggers, deep-trolling gear. Catalog.

MAGNUFLEX ROD CO., 1771 W. Flagler, Miami, FL 33135. Rods, rod components. Custom building.

MAJOR ROD MFG. CO. (U. S.) LTD., Demars Blvd., Tupper Lake, NY 12986. Rods, rod components. Catalog.

MARAILCO DIV., ALLIED PRODUCTS CORP., 3000 Grandy Bridge Rd., St. Petersburg, FL 33702. Flying-bridge and deck railings, bridge ladders, towers. Catalog.

MARATHON RUBBER PRODUCTS, 510 Sherman St., Wausau, WI 54401. Boots, waders, fishing clothing. Catalog.

MARINE METAL PRODUCTS, 1222 Range Ave., Clearwater, FL 33515. Fishing accessories. Catalog.

MARLIN FIBERGLAS CO., 2429 Birch St., Santa Ana, CA 92707. Fiberglass fishing chairs. Catalog.

MARLIN PRODUCTS INC., 1695 W. 32nd Pl., Hialeah, FL 33012. Gulfstream fighting chairs, fishing chairs. Catalog.

MARTIN REEL CO. INC., 30 E. Main St., Mohawk, NY 13407. Rods, reels, lines, accessories. Catalog.

RUDY MASSON PRODUCTS, 3607 W. Magnolia Blvd., Burbank, CA 91505. Fishing accessories. Catalog.

MASTER FISHING TACKLE CORP., 1005 E. Artesia Blvd., Carson, CA 90746. Rods, rod components. Catalog.

MAXWELL MANUFACTURING CO., 801 W. 8th St., Vancouver, WA 98660. Grizzly Brand rods, reels, and accessories, baits and lures for casting and trolling. Catalog.

MILDRUM MANUFACTURING CO., 230 Berlin St., E. Berlin, CN 06023. Rod guides, roller tip-tops, rod hardware. Catalog.

MINNOE LURE CO., 23 Overton Ave., Milford, CN 06460. Lures and baits for casting and trolling. Catalog.

MR. TWISTER INC., 200 Commerce St., Minden, LA 71055. Baits and lures for casting and trolling. Catalog.

MUMFORD TACKLE, 214 Talbot St., Ocean City, MD 21842. Custom rod building, game fishing accessories.

O. MUSTAD & SONS (USA) INC., 185 Clark St., Auburn, NY 13021. Complete line of fishhooks. Catalog.

MY FAIR LADY PRODUCTS, 2031 Yosemite Blvd., Modesto, CA 95351. Baits and lures for casting and trolling. Catalog.

NATIONAL FIBER GLASS PRODUCTS INC., 979 Saw Mill River Rd., Yonkers, NY 10701. Rods, rod components, accessories. Catalog.

NATIONWIDE LURE MFG. CO. INC., Box 53, Beaver Dam, KY 42320. Lures and baits for casting and trolling. Catalog.

NATURE FAKER LURES INC., 108 Benton St., Windsor, MO 65360. Baits and lures for casting and trolling, accessories. Catalog.

NEWPORT SUPPLY CO., 1630 Superior Ave., Costa Mesa, CA 92627. Bait Saver live-bait tank.

NICKELURE LINE INC., 1526 S. Dixie Ave., Vero Beach, FL 32960. Casting and trolling lures and baits. Catalog.

NORMAN MFG. CO., 2910 Jenny Lind Rd., Ft. Smith, AR 72901. Complete line of lures, baits, accessories. Catalog.

NORMARK CORP., 1710 E. 78th St., Minneapolis, MN 55423. Rapala lures and plugs, accessories. Catalog.

O. L. M. INTERNATIONAL CORP., 145 Sylvester Rd., S. San Francisco, CA 94080. Rods, rod components, accessories, baits and lures. Catalog.

ORVIS TACKLE CO., Manchester, VT 05254. Retail and mail-order sales of quality fly- and light-tackle rods, reels, big-game equipment, camping gear, accessories. Catalog.

PADRE ISLAND CO. INC., 2617 N. Zarzamora, P. O. Box 5310, San Antonio, TX 78201. Baits and lures. Catalog.

PENN DART LURE & EQUIPMENT CO INC., RD #6, Box 1, Carlisle, PA 17013. Lures and baits. Catalog.

PENN FISHING TACKLE MFG. CO., 3028 W. Hunting Park Ave., Philadelphia, PA 19132. Complete line of star-drag, lever-drag (Senator and International) reels, spinning and level-wind reels. Catalog.

J. F. PEPPER COMPANY, 604 Kent St., Rome, NY 13440. Fishing accessories. Catalog.

PEQUEA FISHING TACKLE INC., 19 Miller St., Strasburg, PA 17579. Hooks, jigs, terminal-tackle components. Catalog.

PERFECTION TIP COMPANY, 3020 E. 43rd Ave., Denver, CO 80216. Fishing accessories. Catalog.

PERKINS MARINE LAMP & HARDWARE CO., 16490 N. W. 13th Ave., Miami, FL 33164. Perko Brand marine and fishing hardware, rod holders, cockpit equipment. Catalog.

PFLUEGER SPORTING GOODS DIV., 301 Ansin Blvd., Hallandale, FL 33009. Rods, reels, accessories, taxidermy service. Catalog.

PIPE WELDERS INC., 234 W. 32nd St., Ft. Lauderdale, FL 33315. Custom-built tuna towers, railing, bridge ladders.

PLANO MOLDING CO., 113 S. Center Ave., Plano, IL 60543. Plano molded bait and tackle boxes. Catalog.

PLASTIC RESEARCH & DEVELOPMENT CORP., 3601 Jenny Lind Rd., Ft. Smith, AR 72901. Lures, plugs, and baits for casting and trolling. Catalog.

R. C. PLATH CO., 1637 S. E. Union Ave., Portland, OR 97214. Outriggers, live-bait wells. Catalog.

POMPANETTE INC., 190 Bryan Rd., Dania, FL 33004. Full line of outriggers, ginpoles, fishing and fighting chairs, gaffs, cockpit fishing accessories. Catalog.

EDDIE POPE & CO. INC., 25572 Stanford Ave., Valencia, CA 91355. Lures and baits for casting and trolling, accessories for fishing. Catalog.

POWERSCOPIC CORP., Box 278, Westwood, NJ 07675. Telescopic fishing rods. Catalog.

POWERWINCH CORP., 88 Garden St., Bridgeport, CN 06605. Electric winches for mobile recreational vehicles and boats. Catalog.

QUICK CORPORATION OF AMERICA, 620 Terminal Way, P. O. Box 938, Costa Mesa, CA 92627. Complete line of light-tackle star-drag and spinning reels and rods, components, accessories, lures and baits. Catalog.

RECREATIONAL INDUSTRIES, 6100 Nicholas Dr., Mableton, GA 30059. Lures and baits, accessories. Catalog.

REEL POWER EQUIPMENT INC., 811 42nd St. S., St. Petersburg, FL 33713. Electric reels and accessories. Catalog.

J. T. REESE, TAXIDERMY, 1918 S. Andrews, Ft. Lauderdale, FL 33316. Marine taxidermy.

RILSAN CORP., 139 Harristown Rd., Glen Rock, NJ 07452. Fishing lines. Catalog.

RIVIERA MANUFACTURING INC., 3859 Roger Chaffee Blvd. SE, Grand Rapids, MI 49508. Downriggers, weights, accessories, lines, rod holders, lures and baits. Catalog.

ROCK-A-WAY SPORT FISHING EQUIPMENT, Yale & Myrtle Aves., Morton, PA 19070. Fishing and fighting chairs, outriggers, rod holders, cockpit accessories. Catalog.

ROD CADDY CORP., 920 W. Cullerton St., Chicago, IL 60680. Tubes and caddies for carrying rods. Catalog.

JOHN RYBOVICH & SONS BOAT WORKS, 4200 Poinsettia Blvd., W. Palm Beach, FL 33407. Fighting chairs, outriggers.

ST. CROIX/COMPAC CORP., 9909 South Shore Dr., Minneapolis, MN 55441. Rods, reels, baits and lures, accessories. Catalog.

SAMPO INC., North Street, Barneveld, NY 13304. Tackle boxes, baits and lures, accessories. Catalog.

SEA-KEEPER INC., 4228 N. E. 6th Ave., Ft. Lauderdale, FL 33308. Insulated fish and ice tanks, wells. Catalog.

SEA-LAWN PRODUCTS CO., Box 719, Long Beach, NY 11561. Aluminum and fiberglass outriggers. Catalog.

SCIENTIFIC ANGLERS/#M, Box 2001, Midland, MI 48640. Full line of light-tackle and saltwater fly-casting equipment, rods, lines, reels, accessories. Catalog.

SENECA TACKLE CO., Box 2841, Elmwood Station, Providence, RI 02907. Lures and baits. Catalog.

SHAKESPEARE COMPANY, 1801 N. Main St., Columbia, SC 29202. Complete line of rods, reels, lines, accessories, electric trolling motors, baits and lures. Catalog.

SIBERIAN SALMON EGG CO., 4660 E. Marginal Way South, Seattle, WA 98134. Prepared salmon-egg baits. Catalog.

SKYLINE INDUSTRIES INC., Box 821, Ft. Worth, TX 76101. Rods, rod components, reels. Catalog.

SPERRY TOPSIDER, Box 338, Naugatuck, CN 06770. Nonskid deck and boating shoes and boots. Catalog.

SPORTS LIQUIDATORS, Box 1338-7, Burbank, CA 91905. Complete line of rods, reels, lines, lures, accessories. Catalog.

SPORTSMEN'S INDUSTRIES INC., 7878 N. W. 103rd St., Hialeah, FL 33012. Fighting and fishing chairs, outriggers, rod holders, cockpit accessories. Catalog.

SPORTSMEN ACCESSORIES INC., 434 Grand St., Bridgeport, CN 06604. Rods, rod components, accessories. Catalog.

STEFFEY MANUFACTURING CO., 10842 Martin Dr., N. Huntington, PA 15642. Lures and baits, accessories. Catalog.

STEMBRIDGE PRODUCTS INC., 2941 Central Ave., East Point, GA 30344. Baits and lures, accessories. Catalog.

STORM MANUFACTURING CO., Box 265, Norman, OK 73069. Baits and lures for trolling and casting. Catalog.

STRADER TACKLE INC., Box 4029, Tallahassee, FL 32303. Rods, rod components, reels, baits and lures. Catalog.

STRATTON & TERSTEGGE CO., 1520 Rowan St., Louisville, KY 40201. My Buddy tackle boxes. Catalog.

STRIKE KING LURE CO., 2805 Sanderwood, Memphis, TN 38118. Lures and baits for casting and trolling. Catalog.

STRIKE MASTER INC., 411 N. Washington Ave., Minneapolis, MN 55401. Lures and baits, accessories. Catalog.

SUBRIA CORP., Box 113, Montclair, NJ 07042. Accessories for fishing, baits and lures. Catalog.

SUNSET LINE AND TWINE CO., Jefferson & Erwin Sts., Petaluma, CA 94952. Fishing lines. Catalog.

SUPER SPORT, Box 696, Bishop, CA 93514. Fishing accessories, baits and lures for casting and trolling. Catalog.

SUPERWINCH, Pomfret, CN 06258. Power winches for boats and recreational vehicles. Catalog.

TACK-L-TYERS, 939 Chicago Ave., Evanston, IL 60202. Rods, components, reels, lines, accessories. Catalog.

TAPERFLEX OF AMERICA, 558 Library St., San Fernando, CA 91341. Rods, rod components, reels, accessories. Catalog.

TEMPO PRODUCTS CO., 6200 Cochran Rd., Cleveland, OH 44139. Rod holders, cockpit hardware for fishing boats. Catalog.

NORM THOMPSON, Outfitters, 1805 N. W. Thurman, Portland, OR 97209. Retail and mail-order sales of fishing accessories, tackle, camping equipment. Catalog.

3M COMPANY, LEISURE TIME PRODUCTS DIV., 3M Center, St. Paul, MN 55101. Rods and reels, lines, fishing accessories. Catalog.

TOURNAMENT MARINE PRODUCTS, 7 Commerce Dr., Cranford, NJ 07016. Full line of outriggers, fighting chairs, hardware, rod holders. Catalog.

TRIP-EZE COMPANY, Box 902, Pt. Orange, FL 32019. Trip-EZE spring-loaded outrigger line-release clips.

TROPHY PRODUCTS, 9712 Old Katy Rd., Houston, TX 77055. Fishing accessories. Catalog.

TRUE TEMPER CORP., TACKLE/FIBERGLASS DIV., 1623 Euclid Ave., Cleveland, OH 44115. Rods, rod components, fiberglass components, fishing accessories. Catalog.

TYCOON/FIN-NOR CORP., 7447 N. W. 12th St., Miami, FL 33126. Tycoon game fishing rods, Fin-Nor lever-drag reels, line, special accessories. Catalog.

U. S. LINE COMPANY, 22 Main St., Westfield, MA 01085. Fishing lines, accessories. Catalog.

UMCO CORP., Highway 25, Box 608, Watertown, MN 55388. Tackle boxes, fishing accessories. Catalog.

UNCLE JOSH BAIT COMPANY, 524 Clarence St., Ft. Atkinson, WI 53538. Uncle Josh pork rind products, baits and lures for casting and trolling, accessories. Catalog.

UNION MFG. INC., 54 Church St., LeRoy, NY 14482. Tackle and bait boxes. Catalog.

UNIVERSAL TELESCOPIC, 480 Princeton St., San Francisco, CA 96136. Telescopic rods, fishing accessories. Catalog.

USLAND ROD CO., 18679 W. Dixie Hwy., Miami, FL 33160. Stock and custom-built fishing rods. Catalog.

VARMAC MANUFACTURING INC., 4201 Redwood Ave., Los Angeles, CA 90066. Rod guides, rod components and accessories. Catalog.

VLCHEK PLASTICS CO., Box 97, Valplast Rd., Middlefield, OH 44062. Tackle and bait boxes. Catalog.

WEBER TACKLE CO., Box 47-R, Stevens Point, WI 54481. Hoochie Troll lures, baits, accessories. Catalog.

WESTERN CUTLERY CO., 5311 Western Ave., Boulder, CO 80302. Bait and fishing knives. Catalog.

WEST PRODUCTS CORP., 161 Prescott St., E. Boston, MA 02128. Mail-order sales of foul-weather gear, books, fishing and camping clothing, camping equipment. Catalog.

WHALE ENTERPRISES INC., 204 Dailey St., Piedmont, AL 36272. Fishing accessories. Catalog.

WHOPPER STOPPER INC., Hwy. 56 West, Box 1111, Sherman, TX 75090. Whopper Stopper lures and baits. Catalog.

WOODSTOCK LINE CO., 83 Canal St., Putnam, CN 06260. Fishing lines. Catalog.

WOODSTREAM CORP., Box 327, Lititz, PA 17543. Old Pal tackle boxes, rods, reels, baits and lures, accessories. Catalog.

THE WORTH COMPANY, Box 88, Stevens Point, WI 54481. Lures and baits, fishing accessories. Catalog.

WRIGHT & MCGILL COMPANY, 4245 E. 46th Ave., Denver, CO 80216. Rods, reels, lines, accessories, Eagle Claw brand hooks and tackle. Catalog.

YAKIMA BAIT CO., Box 310, Granger, WA 98932. Lures and prepared baits for salmon, lines, accessories. Catalog.

ZEBCO, DIV. BRUNSWICK CORP., 6101 E. Apache St., Tulsa, OK 74115. Complete line of rods, reels, lines, baits and lures, accessories. Catalog.

CARL ZEISS INC., 444 Fifth Ave., New York, NY 10018. Binoculars and optical products. Catalog.

Marine electronics for fishing

Source:
Yachting Publishing Corporation, New York, New York.

AIRMARC CORP., 13240 Northrup Way, Bellevue, WA 98005. VHF/FM.

ALLIED SPORTS COMPANY, 1 Humminbird Lane, Eufaula, AL 36027. Electronic sounders. Catalog.

ALTEC/CALMEC, 5825 District Blvd., Los Angeles, CA 90022. Autopilot systems for boats. Catalog.

AMERICAN MARINE ELECTRONICS, 3095 Red Hill, Costa Mesa, CA 92627. VHF/FM. Catalog.

THE ANTENNA SPECIALISTS CO., 12435 Euclid Ave., Cleveland, OH 44106. Antennas for CB, VHF/FM, SSB, etc. Catalog.

APELCO, 676 Island Rd., Manchester NH 03103. Complete line of electronics; VHF/FM, SSB, loran, radar, sounders. Catalog.

BENMAR, 3000 W. Warner, Santa Ana, CA 92704. Complete line of electronics; VHF/FM, SSB, loran, radar, sounders. Catalog.

BONZER INC., 90th & Cody, Overland Park, KS 66214. Radar. Catalog.

BRISTOL ELECTRONICS INC., 651 Orchard St., New Bedford, MA 02744. Digital depth sounders. Catalog.

BROCKS ELECTRONICS CORP., Edwards Court, Burlingame, CA 94010; 15752 Industrial Parkway, Cleveland, OH 44135. Full line of electronics; VHF/FM, SSB, navigation equipment. Catalog.

COLUMBIAN HYDROSONICS, 216 N. Main St., Freeport, NY 11520. Sounders, VHF/FM, detection instruments. Catalog.

COMMUNICATIONS CO., Box 520, Coral Gables, FL 33135. VHF/FM, RDF, SSB and AM CB gear. Catalog.

COURIER COMMUNICATIONS, 175 E. William St., Hopelawn, Perth Amboy, NJ 08861. AM and SSB CB gear. Catalog.

DATAMARINE INTERNATIONAL INC., 4 Commerce Park Rd., Pocasset, MA 02559. Sounders. Catalog.

R. L. DRAKE CO., 540 Richard St., Miamisburg, OH 45342. VHF/FM, SSB. Catalog.

GEMTRONICS MARINE ELECTRONICS, 356 South Blvd., Lake City, SC 29560. Sounders, loran, SSB, VHF/FM, antennas. Catalog.

GENERAL AVIATION ELECTRONICS INC., 4141 Kingman Dr., Indianapolis, IN 46226. VHF/FM. Catalog.

HEATH CO., Benton Harbor, MI 49022. Kits and factory-wired CB, VHF/FM, RDF and sounding gear. Catalog.

HY-GAIN ELECTRONICS INC., RR3, Lincoln, NE 68505. VHF/FM, antennas for CB, VHF/FM, SSB. Catalog.

INTECH INC., 1220 Coleman Ave., Santa Clara, CA 95050. VHF/FM and antennas. Catalog.

ITT—DECCA, 386 Park Ave. S., New York, NY 10016. Decca radar, autopilots, navigation equipment. Catalog.

E. F. JOHNSON CO., 299 10th Ave., Waseca, MN 56093. CB, SSB, VHF/FM radio units. Catalog.

KONEL CORP., 271 Harbor Way, S. San Francisco, CA 94080. Full line of SSB, VHF/FM, RDF, ADF, sounders, loran, radar. Catalog.

LINEAR SYSTEMS INC., 220 Airport Blvd., Watsonville, CA 95076. AM and SSB CB base and mobile stations. Catalog.

LOWRANCE ELECTRONICS INC., 12000 E. Skelly Drive, Tulsa, OK 74128. Sounders, detection instruments. Catalog.

MICRO INSTRUMENT CO., Box 1565, Escondido, CA 92025. Omega navigation units. Catalog.

MIECO INC., 1928 Green Spring Dr., Timonium, MD 21093. Loran and Omega navigation units. Catalog.

MORROW ELECTRONICS INC., Box 7064, Salem, OR 97304. VHF/FM, sounders, radar, loran, radio equipment. Catalog.

NARCO ANDREWS, Commerce Drive, Ft. Washington, PA 19034. Sounders. Catalog.

NAUTICAL ELECTRONICS INC., 7095 Milford Industrial Rd., Baltimore, MD 21208. Loran-A-C units. Catalog.

NORTHERN RADIO CO., 4027 21st Ave., W. Seattle, WA 98199. SSB. Catalog.

Manufacturers' Index

PACE COMMUNICATIONS, 24049 S. Frampton, Harbor City, CA 90710. CB, VHF/FM. Catalog.

PEARCE-SIMPSON DIV., GLADDING CORP., Box 800, Biscayne Annex, Miami, FL 44152. CB, VHF/FM, RDF, sounders. Catalog.

PHELPS DODGE COMMUNICATIONS CO., Rt. 79, Marlboro, NJ 07746. VHF/FM. Catalog.

RAY JEFFERSON INC., Main & Cotton Sts., Philadelphia, PA 19134. Full line of electronics, sounders, VHF/FM, RDF, ADF, radar, loran, SSB, detection instruments. Catalog.

RAYTHEON CORP., 141 Spring St., Lexington, MA 02173. Complete line of electronics, VHF/FM, radar, loran, RDF, ADF, VHF/FM, SSB, Omega navigation units. Catalog.

RF COMMUNICATIONS INC., 1680 University Ave., Rochester, NY 14610. CB, VHF/FM, SSB. Catalog.

RIDGE ELECTRONICS CORP., 604 Henry Ave., Charlottesville, VA 22901. Radar, full line of electronics. Catalog.

ROSS LABORATORIES INC., 3138 Fairview Ave., E. Seattle, WA 98102. Specializing in sounders. Catalog.

SEAGOING ELECTRONICS CORP., 1544 N. Federal Hwy., Pompano Beach, FL 33062. VHF/FM. Catalog.

SEA TEMP INSTRUMENT CO., 19250 E. Colima Rd., La Punte, CA 91745. Sea-temperature instruments. Catalog.

SHAKESPEARE CO., Box 246, Columbia, SC 29202. CB, VHF/FM, antennas. Catalog.

SIMPSON ELECTRONICS INC., 2275 N. W. 14th St., Miami, FL 33125. VHF/FM. Catalog.

SIMRAD, 1 Labriola Court, Armonk, NY 10535. Loran, sounders, sonar. Catalog.

SMITH INDUSTRIES INC., KELVIN HUGHES DIV., 4 Gill St., Woburn, MA 01801. Sounders, radar, RDF. Catalog.

SONAR RADIO CORP., 73 Wirtman Ave., Brooklyn, NY 11207. VHF/FM, CB, SSB, sounders, instruments. Catalog.

SOUTHCOM INTERNATIONAL INC., 2210 Meyers Ave., Escondido, CA 92025. SSB. Catalog.

STANDARD COMMUNICATIONS CORP., 639 Marine Ave., Wilmington, CA 90744. VHF/FM. Catalog.

SWAN ELECTRONICS INC., 305 Airport Rd., Oceanside, CA 92054. AM and SSB CB units. Catalog.

UNIMETRICS, 23 West Mall, Plainview, NJ 11803. VHF/FM, sounders. Catalog.

VEC-TRAK R&D CORP., 186 E. Main St., Elmsford, NY 10523. Portable RDF units. Catalog.

VEXILAR INC., 9345 Penn Ave., Minneapolis, MN 55431. Sounders, temperature gauges. Catalog.

WESTERN MARINE ELECTRONICS, 509 Fairview Ave. N., Seattle, WA 98109. Scanning sonar. Catalog.

Glossary

ADF. Abbreviation for "automatic direction finder."
Air bladder. Gas-filled bladder in fish's body used to maintain depth stability.
Algae. Primitive chlorophyll-bearing water plants.
Anadromous. Referring to fish that live most of their lives in salt water, but ascend freshwater rivers to breed.
Anal fin. Single fin on lower body surface between anus and tail.
Anoxia. Condition of being starved of oxygen.
Anterior. Forward part of any object.

Backlash. Tangle of line on reel spool caused by overrun of the spool in casting.
Bait. (a) Any natural substance that is used on a hook to entice fish to bite; (b) The act of presenting a lure or prepared bait to a fish; (c) Any of a large group of small fishes on which larger fish regularly feed.
Bait-casting. The act of casting a prepared bait or lure by means of a specialized revolving-spool reel and light rod, usually known as a "bait-casting rig." Primarily a freshwater technique, but sometimes used on salt water.
Ballyhoo. Balao; a small, thin bait fish widely used as a skipping bait for billfish.
Bearing. The direction by compass of any object as viewed from the observer's position.
Bill. Sword, spike, or spear of a billfish.
Billfish. Any Istiophorid game fish, such as marlin, sailfish, spearfish, and broadbill swordfish, considered as separate from all other fishes by virtue of their bills.
Biological clock. Innate reactive behavior of some fish that appears to be regulated by an inner time-sensitive mechanism.
Bottom fishing. Fishing while anchored or drifting, using heavy sinkers to carry the hooks to the bottom.
Bulldogging. Rapid swinging of the head by a hooked fish that sends repeated heavy shocks up the fishing line.
Butt. Lower extremity of a fishing rod below the reel.

Calibration. The act of determining the exact degree of work, stress, or tension applied to an adjustable instrument such as a fishing reel drag.
Cast. The act of throwing out a bait or lure by using the rod as a lever to give motion to the bait or lure.
Caudal fin. Tail fin.
Caudal peduncle. Narrow portion of tail just ahead of the caudal fin.
CB. Abbreviation for Citizens Band, certain radio frequencies in the high range reserved for broad public use.
Charter boat. Fishing boat that carries passengers for hire by charging a fixed overall fee per day.
Chum. Ground or finely chopped bait that is doled overboard for the purpose of attracting fish.
Cockpit. The open, sunken after deck of a sport-fishing boat.
Continental shelf. The plain that extends out under the surface of the sea to a depth of about 600 feet and is part of the true continental land mass.
Countdown. The act of mentally counting off the time it takes for something to happen, such as the time it takes for a lure of a given weight to sink to a given depth.

Deboner. A hollow tube about one-half inch in diameter and a number of inches long, with saw teeth cut into the working end; used to core out the backbone of bait fish like mullet.

Demersal. Pertaining to fish that habitually live on or near the bottom of the sea, rather than near the surface.

Dorsal fin. The prominent fore-and-aft fin on most fish down the centerline of the back.

Double-line. That portion of the fishing line that is doubled back on itself at the working end, according to specific tackle rules, to gain greater strength.

Downrigger. Underwater outrigger of adjustable depth, utilizing a heavy weight and a line-release clip.

Drag control. The clutch or brake system of a reel, by means of which the line may be allowed to be drawn out under variable tension.

Drail. A specialized trolling sinker shaped somewhat like a torpedo, but with an offset towing neck.

Drop-back. The act of dropping a trolled bait or lure back to a fish that has missed its strike to give the fish a better chance to try again.

Drop-off. Precipitous underwater cliff or bank, as at the edge of a sunken river channel or edge of the continental shelf.

Ecology. Study of the relationship of living species and their habitats.

Estuary. Bay, sound, or large river mouth forming a meeting place for salt and fresh water.

Fathom. Nautical measure equaling six feet.

Fathometer. Registered trademark for an electronic sounding machine produced by the Raytheon Corporation.

Feather lure. Lure dressed with or made from feathers.

Ferrule. A male or female metal part that forms a rod joint.

Fighting chair. Large, heavy, swiveling seat or chair equipped with a footrest, used for fighting large fish.

Finning fish. Fish swimming with dorsal and/or tail fin visible above surface of the water.

Fish box. Fixed or portable box kept in boat's cockpit to receive the catch. Usually insulated and equipped with drains.

Fish-finder. Colloquial word for electronic sounder.

Fishing belt. Adjustable belt supporting a leather or metal cup into which angler may thrust butt end of rod while fishing standing up.

Fishing chair. Lighter version of fighting chair, but without footrest, and sometimes nonswiveling. Has a rod butt gimbal, as does the fighting chair.

Fish well. Fish box built under the boat's deck.

Flatfish. Any flounder, fluke, or halibut.

Flat-line. Trolling line fished without benefit of outrigger.

Flying bridge. Open, elevated control station, usually atop the deckhouse.

Flying gaff. Very large gaff with detachable head to which is spliced a stout rope or wire cable.

Fly rod. Light casting rod that operates on the principle of casting the line rather than a weighted lure.

Footrest. Portion of fighting chair on which the feet are placed so as to oppose legs to the pull of rod and line while fighting large fish. Adjustable.

Foul-hook. Act of hooking a fish elsewhere than in the mouth.

Gaff. A strong metal hook mounted on a wooden or metal handle, used to snag fish up from the water so they will not have to be lifted by the leader.

Game fish. Any species of fish that is considered valuable primarily because of its characteristics when caught by hook and line.

Gimbal. Pivoted metal cup equipped with a cross-pin, into which a rod butt may be thrust. Usually mounted on fishing chair or fighting chair at edge of seat, between the angler's knees.

Gin pole. Tall, vertical wooden or metal pole equipped with a rope fall for hoisting large fish.

Guide. (a) Person who takes anglers out fishing for hire; (b) Metal ring or roller on rod shaft through which the line is led.

Halyard. Light rope or line, usually used to hoist flag or outrigger release clip.

Harness. Cloth, leather, or composition vest or belt that is worn around angler's back or shoulders for purpose of taking the weight of the rod via adjustable straps, leaving hands free.

Ichthyologist. One who makes a scientific study of fish.

I/O. Abbreviation for "inboard/outboard," a propulsion system with the motor inside the stern and the drive shaft extending through the stern to a turnable propeller assembly that provides steering and power thrust simultaneously.

Jig. Any small metal lure, heavy for casting or trolling, either plain or dressed with feathers or fibers.

Jigging. (a) The act of fishing with jigs; (b) Imparting a short, quick, back-and-forth rod action to a lure as it is trolled or retrieved.

kHz. Abbreviation for kilohertz, meaning thousands of cycles per second.

Kite. Special fishing kite used to carry out baits.

Knock-down. The act of an outrigger fishing line being pulled clear of the release clip by fish or angler.

Knot. Nautical unit of speed, one nautical mile per hour, or about 1 1/8 statute miles per hour.

Lateral line. Thin, horizontal, wavy line, visible on sides of many fish, that is a sensitive sound and vibration detector.

Leader. Section of wire or synthetic material placed between the hook or lure and the fishing line.

Littoral. A shore or coastal region.

Long-line. Type of commercial fishing gear featuring a very long line equipped with hundreds or thousands of hooks on shorter branch lines.

Loran. A type of electronic navigation system featuring lines of position obtained from comparing the times of receipt of radio signals from paired "master" and "slave" stations.

Mandrel. Thin, tapered metal rod around which a fiberglass rod shaft is molded.

MHz. Abbreviation for megaHertz, meaning millions of cycles per second.

Modulus. Relative degree of measurement of a quality, such as the "modulus of elasticity" of an elastic substance compared with an elastic standard.

Monofilament. Line made of a single continuous synthetic fiber, usually nylon.

Omega. A type of electronic radio navigation.

Outrigger. Long pole or shaft fastened to side of boat for purpose of giving lift and separation to trolling lines, usually arranged in matched pairs, port and starboard.

Panfish. Any small, edible, food fish.

Party boat. Boat that carries passengers for hire for fishing, charging so much per person as a fee.

Pectoral fins. Paired fins closest to the gills on underside of fish's body.

Pelagic. Pertaining to fish that spend most of their time in the upper levels of the ocean.

Pelvic fins. Paired fins located on belly behind pectorals.

Pick-up. The act of a fish picking up a bait or lure.

Planer. A device to take fishing lines down deep that depends on motion and angle-of-attack rather than on weight to achieve depth.

Plankton. Tiny plant or animal life floating freely.

Plug. Lure shaped like a fish, or simulating a fish in action, designed to be cast or trolled, usually made of wood or light plastic.

Polymer. A natural or synthetic chemical compound in which two or more small molecules combine to form larger molecules containing repeated structural units with their axes aligned to the axis of the overall structure. Nylon is an example.

Radar. Coined word meaning "radio detecting and ranging."

Range. Imaginary line through two visible objects on shore, extended out over the water to the observer's position.

RDF. Abbreviation for "radio direction finder."

Reel. Any mechanical device for storing fishing line on a fixed or revolving spool.

Reelseat. Metal sleeve attached to rod shaft, equipped to receive and lock onto the foot of the reel.

Retrieve ratio. Gear ratio of a reel; a 3:1 retrieve ratio causes the spool of the reel to turn three times for each full turn of the reel handle.

Rocket launcher. Special type of multiple rod holder often used in tournament fishing.

Rod. Any flexible, tapered shaft arranged to carry a reel and fishing line, and used in manipulating the bait or lure to the fish, and in handling the line after hooking the fish.

Rod holder. Metal or plastic tube arranged to receive and hold the butt end of a fishing rod while the rod is being used for trolling, or when it is in the standby condition.

Salinity. Percentage of salt in water.

Scoop. Unit of live bait measure on West Coast, about two-thirds of a bushel.

Seine. Form of vertically hung commercial fishing net.

Shoal. Broad shallow area.

Shooting head. Special weighted headline

for flycasting.

Single Sideband (SSB). A type of radio propagation in which the original carrier wave is suppressed and only one of the two original audio-modulated sidebands is amplified and transmitted.

Skimmer. The surf or bait clam.

Slick. Thin layer of oil on water surface.

Sound. The act of measuring the depth of water.

Sounder. Any device for measuring water depth.

Species. Scientific term for a group of identical fishes to which the same scientific name is applied. The species is indicated by the second part of the scientific name.

Spinner. Lure containing a revolving or spinning metal leaf.

Spinning. The fishing method that employs a reel with a fixed spool, the line being laid onto the spool by means of a revolving metal arm or bail.

Splice. Method of joining two pieces of rope, rope-laid line, or wire by means of interweaving without using knots.

Spool. The portion of a reel on which line is stored.

Spoon. Thin metal lure shaped like a spoon, equipped with one or more hooks.

Star drag. Reel drag operated by a star wheel.

Stern door. Opening in boat's stern for hauling in fish.

Strike. (a) The act of a fish attacking or biting at a bait or lure; (b) The act of an angler pulling back with the rod and line to hook the fish.

Striking drag. The amount of tension to which a reel's drag is preset in anticipation of striking a given species of fish.

Strip bait. Bait made from strip of fish, pork rind, or similar thin material.

Stylus. Rotating or reciprocating arm, carrying a marking device, that creates depth marks on the paper graph of an electronic depth sounder.

Swivel. Metal device placed between leader and line to form connection and reduce line-twist.

Tag. Small metal or plastic device fastened to a fish to identify it for scientific purposes for future recapture.

Tailing fish. A fish such as a marlin or bonefish that frequently exposes its tail in a characteristic manner.

Teaser. An artificial lurelike device designed to entice fish through attractive action.

Terminal tackle. Any part of fishing tackle placed or used at the lower end of the fishing lines, such as sinkers, hooks, leaders, etc.

Thermocline. The transition layer of swift temperature change between warm water near the surface and cold water below.

Tide rip. Visible surflike condition or clash of water caused by: (a) swift current flowing over a reef; (b) two opposing currents meeting.

Tip. Upper flexible portion of rod above the reel.

Tippet. The lightest part of a fishing leader used in fly casting, usually the section closest to the fly.

Tournament. Any fishing contest operated according to accepted rules of proper fishing behavior.

Tournament tackle. A grade of tackle considered to be superior by virtue of being built to conform to special tournament requirements.

Tower. Elevated structure for fishing lookout, usually mounted amidships on sportfishing boats.

Toxic. Poisonous.

Transducer. Device that changes electric pulses into sound pulses, and vice versa.

Trawler. Commercial fishing boat that fishes by dragging a net over the bottom of the ocean.

Trolling. The act of fishing by pulling baits or lures through the water behind a moving boat.

Ventral. Pertaining to the underside of a fish.

VHF/FM. Abbreviation of the term "Very High Frequency, Frequency Modulation," used to designate a particular form of radio communication.

Weed line. A line of floating sea weeds on the water surface.

Wetland. Coastal intertidal area that is wet at high tide, dry at low tide.

Wire line. Any metallic fishing line.

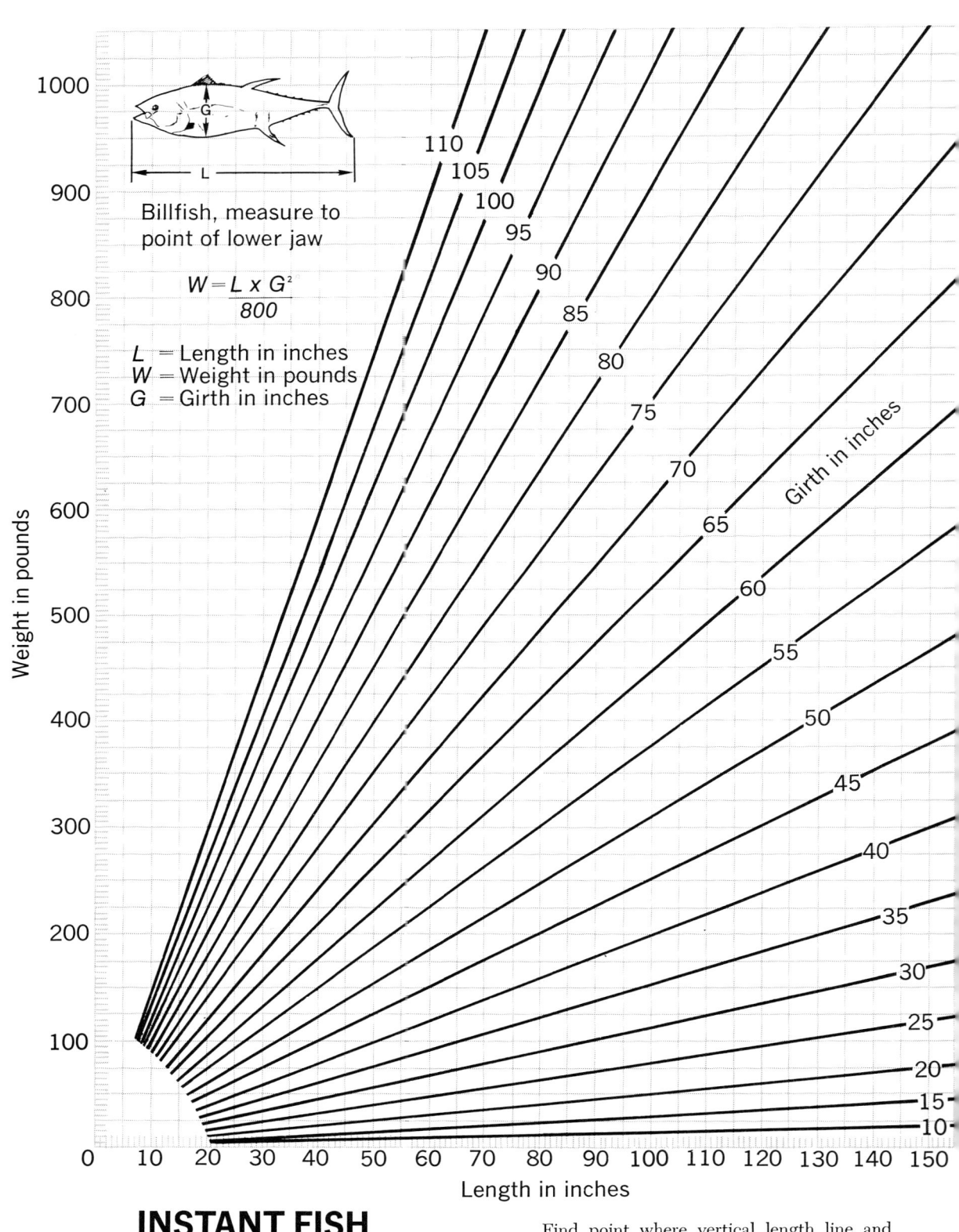

Picture Credits

Jacket photo by Stanley Rosenfeld

Abbas: 36
Tony Accetta & Son: 246
Aftco Corp.: 29
Allan Tackle Mfg. Co. Inc.: 30
Allied Sports Inc.: 217
Aluma-Craft: 252
Alvey Reels: 139
Bernice Apte: 143
Aquasport: 255
Ashaway Line & Twine Co.: 4
Avon Products Inc.: 253
Bahamas News Bureau: 64, 122, 279
Foster Bam: 14
Bill Barnes: 106, 140
Bead Chain Corp.: 166
Nelson Benedict: 9, 111, 117, 127, 184, 197, 210, 224, 225
Berkley & Co. Inc.: 24, 75, 147
Bermuda News Service: 109, 145
Bertram Yachts: 250
Big Jon Inc.: 119, 185
Victoria Blanchard: 98
Bluefin Marine: 255
Harry Bonner: 112, 113, 124, 244
Frank M. Borth: 215, 227
Breuil Boat Co.: 259
Burke Tackle Co. Inc.: 238
Chrysler Marine Corp.: 254
Ralph Clock: 124
Coast Tackle Corp.: 163-165
Cordell Tackle Co.: 267
Cortland Line Co.: 97
Les Davis Tackle Co.: 187
DeLaney & Beers: 11
Bob Duffy: 130
DuPont Corp.: 77, 284
Captain Angelo Durante: 184
Dave Edwardes: 137
Everol Reels: 47-49
Jack Fallon: 177
Florida State News Bureau: 110, 119, 209
Frigibar Industries: 197, 198
Garcia Corp.: 30, 41, 47, 65
Al Goldberg — OPL: 109
Dennis Good: 193
Gudebrod Line & Silk Co.: 269-273
Hawaiian International Billfish Tournament: 128
Dr. Howard Jaffee: 285
Luhr Jensen: 185
Johnson Reels: 70
Bernard (Lefty) Kreh: 67
Frank Kurchirchuk: 146, 280
Mako Marine: 180, 192, 254
Red Marston: 116
Jim Martenhoff: 62, 135, 144, 145, 184
Martin Reel Co.: 66
Captain Bob Marvin: 209
Pete McLain: 108, 142
McLear & Harris Inc.: 214
Charles R. Meyer: Frontispiece, 5, 13, 26, 83, 107, 134, 138, 207, 216, 229, 276, 280

Modar Electronics Inc.: 219
Frank T. Moss: 2, 18-21, 23, 25, 28, 34, 35, 39, 40, 68, 75, 76, 79, 82, 84-88, 91-93, 96, 100-103, 113, 114, 121, 124, 129, 169, 173, 182, 183, 186, 192-195, 199, 202, 204, 208, 210, 220, 226, 227, 236, 238, 239, 244, 246, 262, 274, 278, 281, 283-286
O. Mustad Corp.: 148, 150-156, 160, 161
New Zealand Publicity Studio: 71
Northern Radio Co.: 219
Nova Scotia Information Bureau: 42, 72, 201, 207
Karl Osborne: 132
Penn Fishing Tackle Mfg. Co. Inc.: 38, 46, 52, 194
C. Boyd Pfeiffer: 265
Norman Phillips: 228
Phillipson-3M Corp.: 31
Photo-Art Commercial Studio: 259
Plano Molding Co.: 206
Willard Porter: 232
Powerscopic Corp.: 147
Pro-Line Corp.: 255
Quick Tackle Co.: 63
Sam R. Quincey: 32
Rapala Lures: 234
Ray Jefferson Inc.: 217
Raytheon Mfg. Co. Inc.: 216
George Reiger Collection: 7
Riviera Corp.: 186
Robalo Marine: 183
Rockaway Marine: 191
Claude Rogers: 226
June Rosko: 136
Milt Rosko: 107, 112, 116, 125, 172, 200, 208
Sampo Tackle Corp.: 264
Seamaster Reels: 67
Ellis Shires: 231
Simrad Corp.: 218
Mark Sosin: 10, 173, 232
Sportfishing: 99
Robert D. Stearns: 16, 178, 226
Striker Aluminum Yachts: 257
Swanby Industries Inc.: 185
Tournament Marine Corp.: 191
Trip-Eze Corp.: 182
Trojan Yachts: 257
Tycoon/Fin-Nor Tackle Corp.: 46
Umco Corp.: 206
Unknown: 8, 50, 90
Steven vander Woert: 17, 71, 94, 137, 142, 249
Vineyard Yachts Inc.: 258
Waller Corp.: 222
Willard Boat Works: 258
Bill Wisner: 44, 71
Alain Wood-Prince: 139
Woodstream Corp.: 146
Frank Woolner: 4, 195
Worth Tackle Co.: 260
Hamilton Wright: 129, 144
Wright & McGill Corp.: 157, 158
Yachting: 200, 257
Yachting (Rosenfeld): 190, 277

Index

Aelianus, Claudius, 1
Aftco Corp., 29
Akron, OH, 3
Albacore *(Thunnus alalunga)*, 110, 230, 237, 242
Amberjack *(Seriola dumerili)*, 110, 120, 121, 143, 144, 230, 237, 242
American Fishing Tackle Manufacturer's Association (AFTMA), 95
American Optical Company, 211
American True Temper Co. Inc., 6
Anchovy *(Engraulis sp.)*, 196, 225, 223
Anna Lee, 220
Annapolis River, N.S., 207
Apte, Capt. Stu, 13, 68, 106, 143, 280
Art of Angling, 7
Ashaway Line & Twine Co., 4
Ashaway, RI, 4
Ashaway River, 4
Astracus River, 1
Atlantic Ocean, 110, 111
Australia, 139
Automatic direction finder (ADF), 221

Bahamas, 64, 116, 139, 191, 279
Baja California, 110
Balao *(Hemiramphus balao)*, 10, 225, 228-231, 236, 237
Ballyhoo. *See* Balao
Bam, Foster, 14
Barker, Thomas, 7
Barracuda *(Sphyraena barracuda)*, 117, 134, 135, 143, 227, 237, 241, 242
Bass, black sea *(Centropristis striata)*, 105, 110, 168, 227
Bass, channel *(Sciaenops ocellata)*, 62, 110, 115, 120, 121, 132-134, 142, 176, 226, 231, 237, 245
Bass, freshwater, 61, 235, 237
Bass, giant sea *(Stereolepis gigas)*, 110, 123, 125, 128
Bass, kelp *(Paralabrax clathratus)*, 110, 115, 230, 247
Bass, striped *(Morone saxatilis)*, 8, 17, 49, 61, 67, 114, 115, 119, 120, 121, 133, 134, 137, 142, 173, 176, 207-209, 217, 227, 230, 237, 241, 242, 245, 247, 248, 251
Bass, white sea *(Cynoscion nobilis)*, 230
Bead Chain Tackle Co., 162, 166
Beliveau, Jean, 72
Bergall *(Tautogolabrus adspersus)*, 105
Bergman, Gunnard, 26
Berkley & Company, 22, 24, 75, 147, 209, 275
Bermuda, 109, 145
Berners, Dame Juliana, 4
Billfish (general), 6, 67, 123, 127, 129, 174, 175, 192, 224, 227, 230, 285
Bimini, Bahamas, 125
Bimini top (shelter on a boat), 255
Binoculars, 211
Bizzigotti, Ray, 208
Blowfish *(Sphoeroides maculatus)*, 105
Bluefish *(Pomatomus saltatrix)*, 8, 17, 49, 61, 106, 111, 115, 120, 121, 133, 134, 142, 149, 175, 217, 230, 237, 241, 242, 245, 247, 248
Bo Ann, 214
Boca Grande, FL, 116
Bonefish *(Albula vulpes)*, 17, 49, 61-63, 106, 135, 141, 142, 176, 209, 211, 230, 231, 237, 245, 251, 253, 275
Bonito, Atlantic *(Sarda sarda)*, 1, 7, 110, 117, 136, 142, 143, 226, 227, 229, 230, 231, 242, 245, 248
Bonner, Harry, 112
Book of St. Albans, 4
Boschen, William, 8, 37
Brantner, Capt. Johnny, 5
Bricole (predecessor of hook), 2
Brooks, Joseph, 66, 178
Buell, Julio T., 10
Burke, John J., 283

California, 10, 94, 112, 137, 142, 210, 258
Canada, 72
Cape Breton Island, N.S., 36
Cape Cod, MA, 177
Cape Hatteras, NC, 108, 132
Carey, Dr. Francis G., 282
Casey, Jack, 223

Castro (Fidel), Frontispiece
Catalina Island, CA, 8
Catalina Tuna Club, 8
Clam (general), 168, 225, 227
Cleaning gear, 208
Clemenz, Capt. Harry, Sr., 114, 121
Clothing for fishing, 212
Cobia *(Rachycentron canadum)*, 110, 117, 134, 176
Cochran, Capt. Cal, 178
Cockpit equipment, 206
Cod *(Gadus morhua)*, 8, 10, 168, 207, 217, 227, 230, 247
COMMUNICATIONS, 218
    amplitude modulation (AM), 218
    Citizens Band radio (CB), 218
    double sideband radio (DSB), 218
    Federal Communications Commission (FCC), 218
    Modar Triton VHF/FM, 219
    Northern Radio Co. SSB, 219
    single sideband radio (SSB), 218
    VHF/FM radio, 218
The Compleat Angler, 7
CONNECTORS, 162
    Bead Chain connectors, 166
    Coastlock connectors, 163
Coos Bay, OR, 67
Cordell Tackle Co., 267
Cortland Line Co., 97
Coxe, Joseph A., 8, 37
Cox, George, 142
Cozumel, Mexico, 28, 44
Crabs (general), 168, 225
Crandall, Capt. Lester, 4
Croaker (general), 110

Deboner, 227
De-Liar fish weighing scale, 167
DeMott, Jay, 83
De Natura Animalium, 1
Denver, CO, 3
Depthfinder, 213. *See also* Sounders
Dolphin *(Coryphaena hippurus)*, 115, 117, 135, 136, 143, 230, 237, 241, 242, 245
Dominy, Jerry, 107
Dowagiac Creek, MI, 10
DOWNRIGGERS, 185
    downriggers defined, 12, 119, 185
    installing and using, 186
    Big Jon downrigger, 185
    Luhr Jensen downrigger, 185
    Riviera downrigger, 186
    drail as a downrigger, 185
    sash weight as a downrigger, 185
Drails, 167, 170, 185
Drum, black *(Pogonias cromis)*, 115, 133, 134, 138, 226, 248
Dunaway, Vic, 62
DuPont Corp., 74, 77, 81, 104, 284
Durante, Capt. Angelo, 184

East Coast, 10
Edge, Bob, 281
Eel (general), 10, 177, 225, 227, 228, 230, 231, 236, 237
Eel, electric *(Electrophorus electricus)*, 235
Egypt, 1, 3, 6
Enterprise Manufacturing Co., 3
Europe, 172
Everglades National Park, FL, 67

Fallon, Jack, 177
Farnsworth, Capt. George, 2, 8
Feeding behavior, artificial lures, 235
Feeding behavior, stimulation of, 9, 10
Fenwick (tackle company), 26, 67
FIGHTING AND FISHING CHAIRS, 189
    fighting chair, conversion of, 192
    fighting chair, purpose of, 12
    fighting chair, Pompanette, 192, 193
    fighting chair, Rockaway, 191, 193
    fighting chair, Tournament Marine, 191
Fin-Nor tackle, 67, 128, 129, 147
First aid equipment, 211
FISH-BOATING EQUIPMENT, 199
    fish hoist, Rockaway, 200
    fish hoisting davit, 199
    gin pole, 199
    stern door, 179
FISH BOXES (ON-DECK), 196
    Frigibar fish boxes, 197, 198
Fish finders, 213. *See also* Sounders
FISHING LINES AND FISH POWER, 281
Fish poisoning, first aid for, 212
FISH WELLS (UNDERDECK), 196
Flamingo, FL, 67
Flatfish (general), 110
Florida, 110, 134, 142, 144, 184, 195
Florida Keys, 13, 67, 106, 141, 208, 209, 251, 253
Flounder (general), 105, 107, 149, 168, 230
Fluke *(Paralichthys dentatus)*, 105, 149, 230, 245
Fly fishing technique, described, 95
Flying fish *(Cypselurus californicus)*, 236

Ford Motor Company, 37
FORMULAS (mathematical)
    acceleration of a cast lure, 277
    acceleration of gravity, 284
    length of a gin pole fall rope, 200
    for determining "G's" of gravity, 277
    for determining line strain, 277
    mammalian muscle power, 282
    towing power consumed, 282
    for determining total line strain, 283
    for determining total swimming power, 283
    line tension vs. spool diameter, 286
    relative striking drag, 286

GAFFS, 206-208
Garcia Tackle Corp., 41
Gibson, Glen, 36
Gifford, Capt. Tom, 2, 11, 259
Good, Dennis, 193
Gorge (predecessor of hook), 1, 2
Gowdy, Curt, 4
Grand Banks, 10
Great Lakes, 185, 254
Green, Larry, 94, 137, 142
Green, Mary, 94
Grey, Zane, 7
Grouper (general), 106, 110, 217, 227, 247, 248
Grunt (general), 110, 225, 226
Gudebrod Bros. Line & Silk Co. Inc., 76, 83, 268
Gulf of Mexico, 110
Gutwein, Dick, 108

Halibut, Atlantic *(Hippoglossus hippoglossus)*, 1
Handline casting, 8
Hardie, Jim, 130
Harness, kidney, 279
Harness, seat, 204, 210
Harness, shoulder, 12, 113, 278, 280
Harry, Elwood K., 112, 279
Harvey, Fred, 184
Hatch, Capt. Bill, 2
Hawaii, 128, 183
Haywire twist for wire leaders, 173
Heddon, James, 10
Hemingway, Ernest, Frontispiece
Henze, Otto, 37
Herculaneum (ancient Italy), 1
Herodotus, 2
Herring *(Clupea harengus)*, 10, 229, 236
Hodgins, Aka, 194

Holder, Charles Frederick, 8
HOOKS, history of, 2
    Eagle Claw hooks, 3, 149, 160, 168, 226
    Mustad Beak hook pattern, 149
    O'Shaughnessy hook pattern, 149
    Pacific salmon hook, 149
    Siwash hook, 149
    Virginia hook pattern, 149
    Chestertown hook pattern, 155
    Mustad Viking hook, 159
    hook eye, defined, 160
    hook manufacture, antique, 3
    hook point, defined, 149, 160
    hook shank, defined, 159
    hook sizes, defined, 162
    hook wire size, defined, 159

International Game Fish Association (IGFA), 4, 5, 18, 33, 42, 43, 73, 74, 78, 117, 123, 126, 127, 128, 176, 188, 208, 228, 280, 285
International Women's Fishing Association (IWFA), 127

Jacks (general), 117, 134, 227, 237, 241, 245
Jansik, Arthur, 67
Jewfish *(Epinephelus itajara)*, 67
Jig, cod, antique Norse, 5
Jig, diamond, 10
Jig, double-hooked bone, 10
Jigit nylon eel, 244
Jig, Japanese feather, 10
Jig, Upperman bucktail, 244
Jigs, Canadian Indian-Eskimo, 1
Jigs, casting, 244
Johnson, Paul, 22, 24, 209, 274, 275
Jomar III, 193

Key West, FL, 117, 143, 274, 275
Kirby, Charles, 149
KITE FISHING, origins, 1, 2
    kite, described, 144, 184
    kite fishing techniques, 12, 145, 181
    kite fishing, East Coast, 2
    kite fishing, Florida, 2
    kite fishing, tackle for, 141, 143, 145
Klorfein, Arthur, 278
Knife, X-acto, 272
KNOTS AND BENDS
    Becket Bend, 91
    Bimini Twist, 100-101
    Blood Knot, 177

Blood Knot, Improved, 177
Double Clinch Knot, 179
Clinch Knot, Improved, 179
Stu Apte Knot, 177
Surgeon's Knot, 91
Kona Coast, Hawaii, 194
Kreh, Lefty, 179

Lacustrine fishermen (Swiss), 2
Lake Bomoseen, VT, 10
Lake Michigan, 186, 251
Laminar flow of plastics, 283
LEADER MATERIALS, history of, 5
    gut, silkworm, 5
    monofilament, nylon, 6
    wire, cable-laid, 171
    wire, Monel, 6
    wire, piano, 6
    wire, stainless steel, 6
LEADERS FOR GAME FISH TROLLING, 174
LEADERS FOR SURF AND BOAT CASTING, 176
LEADERS FOR SALTWATER FLY CASTING, 178
Leek, Don, 191, 277
Lewis, Capt. Bob, 184
Li, K. C., 220
LINES FOR FISHING, history of, 3, 4, 73
    Air-Cel line, 67
    Cuttyhunk line, 4
    braided nylon line, 80
    breakage under shock, 283
    "commercial rating" of lines, 126
    Dacron line, defined, 81
    Dacron line, splicing, 81
    Dacron line, stretch factor, 83
    DuPont monofilament, 55
    elastic compressibility of nylon, 80
    elongation under tension, 76
    fly lines, described, 96-97
    linen line compared with synthetic line, 73
    manufacturers' test ratings, 77, 78
    monofilament knot strength, 77
    monofilament manufacture process, 74
    monofilament diameter variations, 80
    nylon monofilament, defined, 74, 78
    nylon, molecular arrangement, 76
    nylon, tensile strength, 74
    nylon, water absorption, 76
    Stren fishing line, 104
    synthetic lines, comparative stretch factor, 76-77
    "tournament rated" line, defined, 126
    unlimited class, big game line, 126
    wire line, defined, 89
    wire line, lead core, 89
    wire line, length-depth ratio, 89
    wire line, metal fatigue, 90
    wire line, solid Monel, 89
    wire line, splicing, marking, 90-93
    wire line, stretch factor, 90
Line Snatcher line release, 185
Ling (general), 110
LIVE BAIT WELLS AND BOXES, 196
Liverpool, N.S., 281
Loggerhead Key, FL, 68
London, England, 149
Long Island Beach Buggy Association, 83
Lures, history of, 9
LURES, LEADHEAD, AND CASTING JIGS, 244
LURES, SPECIAL TYPES
    AutoCast lures, 246
    Hopkins lures, 246
    Konahead lures, 183, 194
    lures, floating, invention of, 10
    plastic lures, 236, 239
    Vi-Ke lures, 246

Macedonia, 1, 9
Mackerel, Boston (*Scomber scombrus*), 105, 115, 121, 134, 149, 224, 225, 229, 230, 231, 242
Mackerel, king (*Scomberomorus cavalla*), 1, 44, 49, 123, 125, 127, 128, 130, 191, 194, 200, 224, 229, 230, 237, 242
Mackerel, Spanish (*Scomberomorus maculatus*), 248
Major, Harlan, 4, 8, 11, 281
Malay native fishermen, 1
Marathon, FL, 5
Marlin (general), 7, 17, 143, 174, 175, 193, 202, 208, 211
Marlin, black (*Makaira indica*), 123, 125, 127, 128, 130, 229, 230, 237
Marlin, blue (*Makaira nigricans*), 1, 44, 49, 123, 125, 127, 128, 130, 191, 194, 200, 224, 229, 230, 237, 242
Marlin, striped (*Tetrapturus audax*), 8, 50, 123, 125, 127, 128, 229, 230, 237, 242
Marlin, white (*Tetrapturus albidus*), 11, 35, 49, 109, 123, 127, 173, 175, 227, 228, 229, 230, 237, 242

Marvin, Capt. Bob, 274, 275
Matthews, Dr. Leonard Harrison, 282
McCarthy, Mrs. Daniel J. W., 127
McCarthy, Don, 64
Mediterranean Sea, 1
Melanesian native fishermen, 1
Menhaden *(Brevoortia tyrannus)*, 225
Meyer, Charles R., 280
Miami, FL, 184
Migdalski, Edward C., 42
Minnow (general), 61, 198
Mitchell II, 200
Montauk, NY, 6, 86, 114, 129, 185, 192, 204, 223, 251, 283
Morris, Robert, 109
Mount Vesuvius, Italy, 1
Mullet *(Mugil sp.)*, 10, 208, 225, 227, 229, 230, 231, 232, 236, 237
Muskellunge *(Esox masquinongy)*, 61
Mussel (general), 168
My Genna, 124

Naples, Bay of, 1
NAVIGATION, 220
    Loran-A system, 220, 221
    Loran-C system, 220, 221
    Omega system, 220, 221
Nebraska Shoal, RI, 119
Needles, bait rigging, 227
Nets, 206, 208
Newell, Carl, 113
New England, U.S.A., 195, 258
New Orleans, LA, 193
New York, NY, 109, 283
New Zealand, 71
Nile River, 1
Noank, CT, 213
Nova Scotia, Canada, 42, 130, 201, 207

The Old Man and The Sea, Frontispiece
O. Mustad Co., 3
Oregon, 259
Orvis Tackle Co., 146, 147
Osborne, Karl, 132
Oslo, Norway, 3
OUTRIGGERS, 2, 12, 181-182
Oxygen pills (aeration of bait), 198

Pacific Coast, 137
Pacific Northwest, 251
The Peak, Australia, 124
Penn Fishing Tackle Mfg. Co., 8, 41
Permit *(Trachinotus falcatus)*, 17, 142, 176, 211, 226, 230, 253, 275
PERSONAL EQUIPMENT, 210

Pfeiffer, C. Boyd, 265
Pflueger, Al, taxidermist, 117
Philadelphia, PA, 8, 37, 76
Phillips, Ethel, 50
Pike (freshwater), 10, 61
Pilar, Frontispiece
Pinfish *(Lagodon rhomboides)*, 225
Planer, defined, 186
Planer, Les Davis, 187
Plano Molding Company, 206
PLASTIC IMITATOR BAITS, 236
    plastic balao, 237
    plastic eel, 237, 244
    plastic mullet, 237
    plastic shrimp, 237
    plastic squid, 237
PLUGS, CASTING AND TROLLING, 239
    bait-carrier plug, 239
    color and finish of plugs, 240
    countdown plug, 239
    darter plug, 239
    diving plug, 239
    popping plug, 239
    popping plug, Gibbs, 239
    Rapala plug, 235
    Salty Bogie plug, 239
    sonic attractiveness of plugs, 240
    swimming plug, 239
Pollock *(Pollachius virens)*, 42, 111, 115, 120, 121, 133, 168, 230, 237, 241, 242, 245, 247, 248
Polynesian fishermen, 1, 3
Pompano, African *(Alectis crinitus)*, 116
Pompano *(Trachinotus goodei)*, 139, 145
Pompeii, Italy, 1
Pond, Bob, 276
Porgy (scup) *(Stenotomus chrysops)*, 35, 105, 110, 168, 217, 226, 227, 247
Pork rind, 225, 232
Porpoise (general), 282
Prohaska, Ray, 137
Puerto Rico, 259

Radio direction finder (RDF), 221
Rathbun, Capt. Benjamin Franklin, 213, 215
Ray (general), 71, 123, 125
Recorders, 217. See also Sounders
    Ray Jefferson, 217
    Raytheon, 216
Redditch, England, 3
Red Hackle fly (ancient use), 1
REELS, history of, 7
    Alvey reels, 70, 71, 139
    bait-casting reels, 42, 61, 63

Bronson reels, 37
capacity, conversion of line classes, 43
Daiwa reels, 37
drag, clutch type, 8
drag, lever type, 45, 48, 49
drag, star type, 30, 38, 40, 41
drag, star and lever types compared, 48
drag, thumb pad, 7
drag washers, Teflon, 41
Eagle Claw reels, 37
Everol reels, 37, 45, 47, 48, 72
fly reels, saltwater, 66-70
Fin-Nor reels, 30, 37, 38, 45, 46, 50, 116, 125
Garcia reels, 37, 47, 65, 113
Heddon reels, 37
Johnson reels, 70
Kovalovsky reels, 37
Luxor spinning reel, 64
Martin reels, 66
Ocean City reels, 37, 38
Penn reels (general), 8, 28, 36, 37, 40, 41, 42, 44, 45, 46, 48, 82, 113, 114, 119, 124, 130, 137, 138, 139, 211
Pflueger Bond reel, 37, 113, 147
Quick reels, 63
Reel-King reels, 37
Scarborough reels, 70, 71, 139
Seamaster reels, 67
Shakespeare reels, 37
spin-casting reels, defined, 9, 70
spinning reels, defined, 63-66
St. Croix reels, 37
True Temper reels, 38
REFRIGERATION, 198
REPAIRING PLUGS AND LURES, 266
REPAIRING REELS, 267
Rice, Sally, 194
ROD AS A LEVER SYSTEM, 15, 28, 33, 277
ROD AS AN ENERGY TRANSFORMER, 17, 22
ROD AS A PROJECTILE LAUNCHER, 275
RODS, history of, 6
    rod action, defined, 32, 33
    bait-casting rods, 30
    rod belt, 113, 210
    butt end, defined, 32
    classes of rods, 15, 27
    curvature, result of stress, 20
    curvature, parabolic, 33, 34
    curved butt, 32, 129, 130, 194, 278
    design technology, 22, 33
    exterior protective finishes, 32
    "fencing foil" rod, 6
    ferrules, 30, 31
    FIBERGLASS RODS, 19-22
    fly rods, Battenkill, 146
    fly rods, purpose and analysis, 16
    foregrip, defined, 29, 30
    Garcia Conlon rods, 30
    guides, Carboloy, 28, 29, 121
    guides, CerAllan, 30
    guides, ceramic, 28, 29
    guides, chrome-plated brass, 29
    guides, friction damage of, 28, 29
    guides, roller, 29
    GUIDES, HOW TO WIND, 268
    holders, 193, 195
    materials, 6, 7, 19, 20, 27
    overload factor of rods, 34
    Phillipson-3M "Bass Tamer" rod, 31
    Powerscopic rod, 147
    rod power, defined, 32
    rod power rating, IGFA line class system, 33
    rod power rating, thread-count system, 33
    ROD REPAIRS, EMERGENCY, 261
    rod storage, 208
    surf casting rods, 30
    testing machine, 24
    tip, defined, 27
    tip-top fittings, 27, 29
    trolling rods, 18, 33, 34
    winding machine, 262
Rope fall, preparation of, 200
Rosko, Bobby, 107
Rosko, June, 107, 125, 200
Rosko, Milt, 116, 129, 136, 208
Rounick, Jack, 204
Runner (general), 225, 229
Running line, defined, 7

Sailfish *(Istiophorus platypterus)*, 2, 17, 49, 123, 125, 127, 142, 143, 144, 173, 175, 184, 195, 227, 228, 229, 230, 237, 251
Salmon (general), 1, 6, 10, 17, 115, 117, 120, 121, 149, 185, 186, 217, 223, 230, 242, 248, 251
Salt Water Fishing Tackle, 281
Salt Water Fly Rodders of America, 18, 143
Sandeel *(Ammodytes marinus)*, 8
Sardine (general), 225, 228
Sawfish (general), 123, 125
Scad *(Trachurus trachurus)*, 110
Scientific American, 282

Seaman, Capt. George, 200
Seatrout *(Cynoscion nebulosa)*, 120, 126, 231, 237, 241, 245, 285
Shad *(Alosa sapidissima)*, 227
Shakespeare Company Inc., 7, 146, 147
Shark, blacktip *(Carcharhinus limbatus)*, 274
Shark (general), 67, 71, 123, 125, 128, 130, 134, 135, 143, 144, 173, 174, 175, 181, 202, 211, 223, 229, 230, 237
Shark, hammerhead *(Sphyrna sp.)*, 128
Shark, mako *(Isurus oxyrinchus)*, 49
Shiner (general), 10, 227
Shrimp (general), 10, 16, 62, 196, 198, 225, 231, 237
Sigler, Ted, 86
SINKERS, 167
Skimmer clam (bait), 227
Snapper (general), 105, 217, 237, 245, 275
Snapper, red *(Lutjanus campechanus)*, 10, 230
Snook *(Centropomus undecimalis)*, 61, 63, 71, 134, 231, 237, 242
Somme River, France, 1
Sopwell Nunnery, England, 4
Sosin, Mark, 112, 142
SOUNDERS, 213
    digital-readout sounders, 215, 218
    flashers, 213
    flasher-recorders, 217
    how sounders work, 215
    Humminbird sounder, 217
    Lowrance sounder, 216
    meter-readout sounder, 215, 218
    recorders, 215
    Simrad sounders, 218
South Africa, 71
South Pass, MS, 193
Spalding, Rufus, 128
Spearfish (general), 123, 127, 175
Spirit Lake, IA, 22
SPLICES FOR DACRON AND WIRE LINES, 84
    basket weave splice (wire), 92-93
    Becket Bend splice (wire), 91
    Dacron line splice, 84-85
    Dacron loop splice, 86-87
SPOONS, 246
    invention of spoons, 10
    Tony Accetta Pet spoon, 246
Sportfishing, 281
SPORT FISHING BOAT TYPES, 252
    Aquasport center console, 255
    Avon Inflatable, 253
    Aluma-Craft skiff, 252
    Bertram Convertible 46', 250
    Bluefin 26', 255
    Boston Whaler, 195
    Cape Island boats, 201
    Cape Kawanda dory, 259
    cartop portable boats, 252
    center and side console boats, 255
    Chrysler outboard skiff, 254
    Hatteras Tournament 42', 124
    Huckins 85' super-fisherman, 257
    inflatable portable boats, 253
    Mako center console, 192, 254
    Pacemaker, 191
    Pacific Clipper, 255
    Pro-Line center console, 255
    Striker Canyon Runner, 257
    super-cruiser fishing boats, 256
    tournament fishing models, 256
    trailable skiffs, small, 253
    trailable skiffs, large, 254
    Trojan 44' sport fisherman, 257
    vest-pocket offshore models, 255
    Wasque 32' fisherman, 258
Spot (general), 110
Squid (general), 10, 168, 225, 228, 229, 230, 236, 237
Stearns, Bob, 178
Striking drag, calibration of, 49, 50, 51
Sunglasses, 211
Surf casting equipment, 146
SWIVELS, 162
swordfish, first rod and reel capture, 8
swordfish *(Xiphias gladius)*, 6, 8, 49, 51, 123, 125, 127, 128, 129, 130, 174, 202, 204, 208, 211, 224, 229, 230, 237, 281
Sydney, Australia, 124

Taber, Robert E., 281
TACKLE (GENERAL)
    balanced tackle, definition of, 10, 12
    big game tackle, defined, 123
    tackle boxes, 108, 109, 146
TACKLE FOR BEGINNERS, 105
    party boat outfit, 105
    trolling, casting, bottom fishing, 107
    shore and surf casting outfit, 108
    beginner's basic tackle box, 108
    how much to spend, 109
TACKLE FOR BOTTOM FISHING, 110
    Atlantic inshore party boat fishing, 110
    Atlantic offshore wreck fishing, 111
    Atlantic inshore bay and inlet fishing, 111

Gulf of Mexico deep reef fishing, 111
Southern inshore boat-bridge fishing, 112
Southern offshore deep reef jigging, 112
Pacific kelp-bed party boat fishing, 113
Pacific big game bottom fishing, 113
Pacific live-bait fishing, 113
TACKLE FOR SMALL GAME SURFACE TROLLING, 115
    bluefish, school stripers, pollock, 115
    trophy stripers, red and black drum, 115
    mackerel, weakfish, redfish, seatrout, 115
    king mackerel, large salmon, 117
    bonito, barracuda, large jacks, 117
    tarpon, cobia, wahoo, big dolphin, 117
    spinning tackle substitutions, 117
    warning on line substitutions, 118
TACKLE FOR DEEP TROLLING, 118
    deep trolling with soft lines, 118-120
    deep trolling with wire lines, 121
TACKLE FOR BIG GAME, 123
    light tackle, 30-lb. class, 123
    medium-light, 50-lb. class, 125
    medium-heavy, 80-lb. class, 125
    heavy tackle, 130-lb. class, 125
    unlimited class, 126
TACKLE FOR THE RECORD HUNTER, 126
    IGFA classes 6, 12, 20, 30: 127
    IGFA class 50: 128
    IGFA classes 80, 130: 130
TACKLE FOR BOAT CASTING, 133
    northern 'longshore boat casting, 133
    southern 'longshore boat casting, 134
    Florida-Bahamas flats fishing, 135
    offshore game fish casting, 135
    northern-style spinning tackle, 136
    southern-style spinning tackle, 136
    West Coast tackle preferences, 136
TACKLE FOR SHORE AND SURF CASTING, 137
    Hatteras Heaver spinning tackle, 137
    Hatteras Heaver conventional tackle, 137
    medium-duty surf spinning tackle, 138
    medium-duty conventional surf tackle, 138
    light-duty surf spinning tackle, 138
    light-duty conventional surf tackle, 139
    ultra-light surf spinning tackle, 139
    bait-casting tackle for the surf, 139
    western long-line surf tackle, 139
    tackle travel kit, 141
TACKLE FOR SALTWATER FLY FISHING, 141
    light saltwater fly tackle, 142
    medium saltwater fly tackle, 142
    heavy saltwater fly tackle, 143
TACKLE FOR KITE FISHING, 143
TACKLE FOR THE TRAVELING MAN, 145
    dual-purpose casting-trolling outfit, 146
    dual-purpose spinning-fly casting gear, 147
    all-purpose spinning-fly casting gear, 147
Tahiti, 7
Tailor *(Pomatomus saltatrix)*, 71
Tail rope, 201
Tarpon *(Megalops atlanticus)*, 5, 9, 12, 17, 49, 61, 63, 67, 68, 115, 116, 117, 135, 142, 143, 175, 211, 226, 230, 237, 242, 245, 251, 253, 275
Tautog (blackfish) *(Tautoga onitis)*, 34, 110, 149, 168, 217, 247
Temperature sounder, how to make, 222
Teti, Joseph, 193
Thermocline, 221
The Whales, 282
Thompson, Capt. Earl, 281
Throw net, 209
Tippet test, defined, 18-19
Toms River, NJ, 108
Torpedo ray *(Torpedo nobiliana)*, 235
Trace, defined, 5
Transducer, defined, 213
Tripani, Sicily, 1
Trip-Eze outrigger release, 182
TROLLING BAITS, NATURAL, USING, 230
Trout (general, freshwater), 1, 3, 4, 6, 61, 149, 185, 186
Tuamotu Pearl antique fishing lure, 1
Tuna (general), 1, 6, 8, 10, 40, 49, 51, 67, 110, 117, 120, 121, 123, 125, 142, 143, 173, 176, 201, 211, 231, 237, 283
Tuna, bigeye *(Thunnus obesus)*, 128, 230
Tuna, blackfin *(Thunnus atlanticus)*, 117, 230, 242
Tuna, bluefin *(Thunnus thynnus)*, 36, 72, 128, 129, 130, 175, 192, 201, 202, 208, 229, 230, 242, 278, 279, 281, 282
Tuna, little *(Euthynnus alletteratus)*, 136
Tuna, skipjack *(Euthynnus pelamis)*, 226, 230

TUNA TOWERS, 202
Tuna, yellowfin *(Thunnus albacares)*, 113, 128, 135, 183, 210, 230, 242, 247
Tungsten carbide, 28

Umco Tackle Co., 206
University of Rhode Island, 281
U.S. Atlantic Tuna Tournament, 199
U.S. Coast Guard, 212, 220

vom Hofe, Edward, 37
vom Hofe, Julius, 8, 37

Wahoo *(Acanthocybium solanderi)*, 117, 121, 135, 136, 144, 237, 242, 248
Walker's Cay, Bahamas, 112
Walton, Izaak, 4, 7
Warm-blooded fishes, discussion of, 282
Water analyzer, Fish Hawk, 222
WATER TEMPERATURE, 221
Watters, Gene, 124
Weakfish *(Cynoscion regalis)*, 8, 34, 105, 108, 110, 115, 120, 121, 134, 142, 149, 208, 231, 237, 241, 242, 245, 248, 285
Whales (general), 282
Whiting (general), 110, 229
Wicopesset Passage, Fishers Island Sound, 213
Willard Boat Works, 258
Williams, Ted, 9
Woeber, Clyde, 28, 44
Wood-Prince, Alain, 139
Woods Hole Oceanographic Institution, 282
Woolner, Frank, 4, 195
Worms (general), 168, 225, 236
Worth Tackle Co., 260
Wright & McGill Co., 3
Wu, Emperor of China, 4

Yale University, 42
Yellowtail *(Seriola dorsalis)*, 110, 113, 120, 121, 136, 176, 230, 241, 247
Yucatan Channel, Mexico, 28

Zwirz, Bob, 178